Land and labour

Manchester University Press

Land and labour

The Potters' Emigration Society, 1844–51

Martin Crawford

MANCHESTER UNIVERSITY PRESS

Copyright © Martin Crawford 2024

The right of Martin Crawford to be identified as the author of this work has been asserted in accordance with the Copyright, Designs and Patents Act 1988.

Published by Manchester University Press
Oxford Road, Manchester M13 9PL

www.manchesteruniversitypress.co.uk

British Library Cataloguing-in-Publication Data
A catalogue record for this book is available from the British Library

ISBN 978 1 5261 7135 1 hardback
ISBN 978 1 5261 9491 6 paperback

First published 2024
Paperback published 2026

The publisher has no responsibility for the persistence or accuracy of URLs for any external or third-party internet websites referred to in this book, and does not guarantee that any content on such websites is, or will remain, accurate or appropriate.

EU authorised representative for GPSR:
Easy Access System Europe – Mustamäe tee 50,
10621 Tallinn, Estonia
gpsr.requests@easproject.com

Typeset by Newgen Publishing UK

Contents

List of figures	*page* vii
Acknowledgements	viii
Maps	x
Introduction	1
1 Industrial origins	17
2 1844: An emigration plan	46
3 1845–6: Finding land	77
4 1847–8: Settling the land	111
5 1849: Expansion and scrutiny	144
6 1850–1: Crisis and decline	177
Conclusion	218
Select bibliography	238
Index	247

It had been said that Land and Labour were the source of all wealth; this was true.

> William Evans, potters' delegate to the National Conference of Trades, in the *Northern Star*, 29 March 1845

Figures

1.1 Rev. Isaac Smith and his wife Sarah, pioneer Potters' Emigration Society settlers. Permission from Marquette County Historical Society. Originally printed in Fran Sprain, *Places and Faces in Marquette County, Wis.* Volume 1 (Westfield, WI: Isabella Press, 1991).   *page* 18
1.2 William Evans (1816–87). Permission from Stoke-on-Trent City Archives.   35
5.1 Blue Swallowtail Line transatlantic packet *Patrick Henry*, which suffered a cholera outbreak in 1849 (oil painting by Philip John Ouless, c.1859). Wikimedia Commons.   160
6.1 Potters' Emigration Society dollar note. Permission from Stoke-on-Trent City Archives.   183
C.1 Potters' Emigration Society marker, Columbia County, Wisconsin. Permission from Historical Marker Database. Photograph by Keith L. of Wisconsin Rapids.   232

Acknowledgements

The origins of *Land and labour* derive from conversations with the much-missed David Adams, founder and long-time head of the American Studies programme at Keele University. He also founded the David Bruce Centre which in the early 1970s commissioned work on North Staffordshire emigration to the United States. David prompted me to pick up a thread from this work, and I was happy to do so when retirement beckoned. I thank him for this, and for much else. Many others have contributed to the project's completion, including American descendants of Society emigrants who contacted me. Librarians and archivists on both sides of the Atlantic were invariably helpful. I am particularly grateful to Helen Burton, Keele's Special Collections administrator, for her continuing assistance. Another Keelite, the historian Richard Blackett of Vanderbilt University, has been a steadfast ally. He read every word written, never letting me forget the essentials of good research and writing, or the essentials of friendship. Thanks, Dick. Two individuals, neither of whom I had previously met, made exceptional contributions to the study's progress. Born in the Potteries, Roger Bentley emigrated to Quebec in 1964 and, learning of the Potters' Emigration Society, determined in retirement to discover more. After completing a fine article, Roger gifted me his research findings gathered during trips to Wisconsin, including some hard-to-find local items. I cannot thank him enough for his generosity. Sadly, Roger died on 27 August 2023 at the age of 93. I was equally fortunate to make the acquaintance of Mike Beckensall, William Evans's great-great-great grandson. Unlike Roger, it turned out that he lived just along the road from me. Mike's research into his ancestor's life and career has proved of inestimable value, and I am indebted to him for his willingness to share it with me. He too read the entire manuscript, saving me from numerous errors and in the process generally helping improve it. Thanks also to Meredith Carroll, Humairaa Dudhwala and colleagues at Manchester University Press for taking a chance with the book and for their editorial shepherding and design and cartographic efforts; to staff at

Newgen for seeing it through production; and to Dan Shutt for exemplary copy-editing. It has greatly benefited from their professionalism and care. And thanks to the Press's anonymous readers for their helpful suggestions. My best friend Christine Turner encouraged me from the outset. She surely did not anticipate how long this would take. When I slammed the study door, pledging not to look at the darned thing again, she knew exactly what to do. Her love and support, in this and our life together, have made all the difference.

I am grateful to Liverpool University Press for permission to use material previously published in *Labour History Review* 76:2 (2011), 81–103.

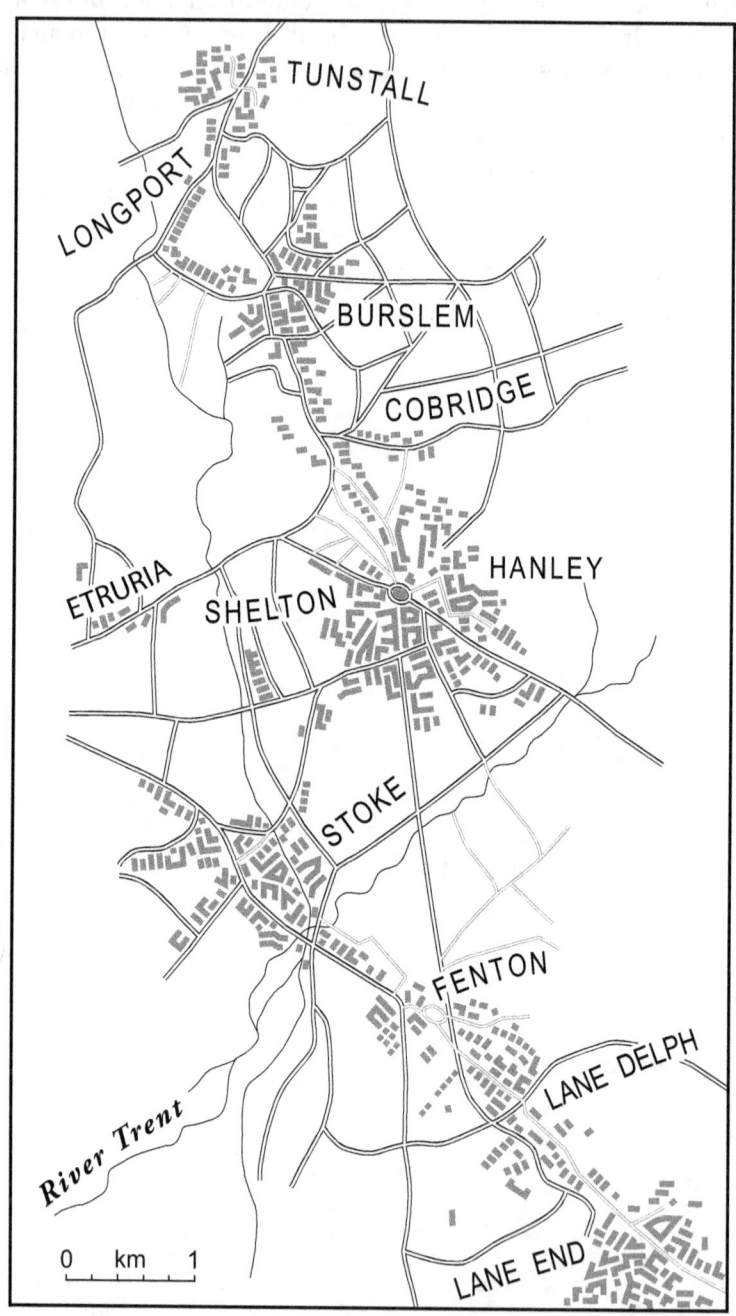

Map 1 Map of the Potteries' 'manufacturing districts' from an illustrated article in *The Art-Union*, 1 November 1846. The names Lane End and Longton were often used interchangeably. The two were originally separate towns, and incorporated as the unified borough of Longton in 1865. Lane End was the location of the Longton area's main pottery manufactories.

Map 2 Map of southern Wisconsin indicating the sites of the Potters' Emigration Society settlements in Columbia County. Pottersville, the original settlement, was located in the township of Scott, named in November 1849 after the Mexican War commander, General Winfield Scott.

Introduction

Thousands of British working men crossed to republican America in the middle decades of the nineteenth century, part of a broader transatlantic and global movement. Travelling singly or with their families – the proportion of single men rose as the century advanced – they came from diverse backgrounds that included agriculture, mining, the professions and, not least, a multitude of craft and industrial trades. Questions remain about the complexion of this migratory stream; the emigrants' chosen destinations are less in doubt. The 1850 Federal Census was the first to record a person's country of origin, and it reveals concentrations of British-born in the industrialising states of the Northeast, notably New York and Pennsylvania, and increasingly across the states of the Old Northwest, a region experiencing explosive demographic growth in the half-century before the Civil War.[1] 'If I were a young man I would sever myself from the old world and plant myself in the western region of the United States', wrote Richard Cobden in 1859.[2] Clearly, many had heeded the advice.

Among those seeking a fresh start were workers from North Staffordshire's pottery industry. Skilled potters had first gone to America before the Revolution, attracted by reports of rich Carolina and Florida clay deposits, and in 1783 no less a luminary than Josiah Wedgwood was prompted to issue a public address on the hazards awaiting those considering a move there.[3] As it turned out, Wedgwood's fears about an exodus of skilled workers were unfounded, or at least premature. In the years after American Independence, it was the export of earthenware and not the transfer of labour that cemented Staffordshire's close ties to the western republic. By 1812 nearly a third of all wares produced in the Potteries were destined for the United States, a figure set to rise as its fledging pottery industry proved unable to meet its burgeoning consumption needs.[4]

The quickening pace of American development after 1815 saw acceleration in the movement of people across the Atlantic. By the second quarter of the nineteenth century increased numbers of Staffordshire men could be found at scattered locations throughout the United States. Among the early venturers west was John Hancock, who had been apprenticed to Wedgwood at Etruria. Hancock crossed to America in 1828 and built his first pottery at South Amboy, New Jersey, producing stoneware and yellow ware. In 1840 he moved to Louisville, Kentucky, and shortly thereafter to East Liverpool, Ohio, where he died two years later. His son Frederick was equally peripatetic; after learning the stoneware trade from a renowned upstate New York potter, Israel Seymour, in 1839 he went to work for the United States Pottery Company in Bennington, Vermont. Accompanying his father to Louisville, he returned to Bennington the following year, later relocating to Worcester, Massachusetts.[5] Other early migrants included the celebrated modeller Daniel Greatbach, who joined the American Pottery Company in Jersey City in 1839 before moving to South Amboy and then to Bennington,[6] and the master potter James Clews, whose Cobridge factory John Hancock had once managed. In 1834, following the bankruptcy of the firm he ran with his brother Ralph, Clews sailed for America, where he hoped to capitalise on the popularity of his family's blue printed earthenware, with its well-known 'Clews Warranted Staffordshire' mark.[7] Like another master potter, William Ridgway of Hanley, Clews failed to revive his business fortunes in America and by 1849 had returned with his family to the Potteries. As Frank Thistlethwaite noted in a pioneering article, established Staffordshire firms had little incentive to risk moving to America in this period. Ultimately, journeymen potters, not their employers, were responsible for the transatlantic migration of the pottery industry in the nineteenth century.[8]

Without assisted passage and the promise of work, a move to the United States was still a distant prospect for most operatives. In 1830 John Hancock brought over three Staffordshire men, two turners and a thrower, to help set up his new manufactory at South Amboy.[9] Six years later James Clews imported thirty-six men to work at the newly established Indiana Pottery Company, located seventy miles down the Ohio River from Louisville at Troy. (The Louisville entrepreneurs who recruited Clews seemed unaware of his business failures in Britain.) A major strike that closed sixty-four Staffordshire firms in November 1836 was almost certainly behind the potters' decision to join Clews in America, but what happened to the men and their families afterwards is unclear. After Clews's departure from Troy in 1838, management of the company passed to another Staffordshire-born potter, Jabez Vodrey, who had been plying his craft in Louisville since 1829 and before that in Pittsburgh, where he had arrived two years earlier. Some of the Troy men may have stayed on to work under Vodrey; most probably returned to the Potteries in the wake of the strike's settlement in 1837. Vodrey himself managed the company until shortages of capital and skilled labour forced him to abandon production in 1846. The next year he and his family moved to East Liverpool, Ohio, soon to emerge as the leading centre of earthenware production in the United States.[10]

East Liverpool's growth owed much to Staffordshire skill and sweat. By 1850 over 70 per cent of the town's workforce was English-born, with the majority originating in the Potteries. Among the earliest arrivals was Bernard Howson from Burslem, formerly of Minton's in Stoke. Howson's nomadic career typified that of many journeymen potters who went to America during the 'wildcatting phase'[11] of the industry's migration. One of the men contracted by John Hancock to work at his New Jersey pottery, Howson moved a few years later to Maysville, Kentucky before gravitating to East Liverpool, where his skills found ready employment. In a letter home to his elder brother John in September 1843, he highlighted the opportunities available in a town where specialist craftsmen were in short supply. 'I am getting 87 cents *per* score from throwing and 7 cents for turning; so now you can judge in regard to price, and whether a thrower be wanted or not', he wrote.[12] Bernard was keen that John and another brother Thomas, then employed as a presser and handler in Louisville, join him in Ohio. John Howson landed in America at the beginning of August 1844, initially working at a small pottery in Utica, New York. After nine months he moved to Zanesville, Ohio, ninety miles from East Liverpool, where Bernard joined him. The two brothers set up in business, producing yellow and Rockingham wares, but the partnership did not last. By the end of the decade Bernard, together with his four children and new wife Rebecca, had left Zanesville and migrated the short distance south to Waterloo in Athens County. There they settled, combining potting with farming, until Bernard's death in 1871.[13]

Chains of circumstance pulled journeymen potters such as the Howson brothers across the Atlantic. Disaffected at home – 'nothing before you but Slavery and Starvation', Bernard told John – they were drawn to America by the prospect of higher wages, an improved working environment and, not least, freedom from the restraints and indignities of employment practices in the pottery industry. 'I have sworn my life against England', wrote Benjamin Brunt from West Sterling, Massachusetts in 1849. 'I bless God that I was born so haughty, that is what Mr Challenor, of Tunstall, discharged me for.'[14] Emigration promised a journeyman greater control over his own labour and, for the more able and enterprising, the chance of rising to the ranks of master potter, a difficult ascent in England, where modern production methods led to increased specialisation and consequent loss of craft independence. An added incentive was the widespread availability in the United States of cheap land. Land ownership offered an alternative path to economic and social independence, one rooted in family self-sufficiency. Yet none of this came without risk. In the 1840s, as the trade cycle exacted a heavy toll on employment security and conditions in the pottery industry, it was uncertain how many were prepared to take it.

Mesmeric performance was all the rage in early Victorian Britain. In May 1844 'Dr Owens of Wolverhampton', a sometime associate of the nationally renowned London mesmerist W. J. Vernon, visited North Staffordshire, giving half-a-dozen lectures at Newcastle-under-Lyme and at the Potteries Mechanics' Institute in Hanley. Owens promoted himself as a 'phreno-mesmerist', a recent development that fused mesmerism – or animal magnetism, as it was often known – with another popular scientific phenomenon, phrenology. Among his onstage volunteers was a 'tall, robust' pottery worker from Burslem, James Broadhurst, whom a newspaper described as being about thirty years old. Although Owens claimed not to have met him previously, Broadhurst soon emerged as his star attraction, appearing at both towns and arousing considerable comment from those who witnessed the performances.[15] Phreno-mesmeric demonstration involved the physical agitation or 'excitement' of the brain, the aim being to stimulate different sentiments depending upon the area being addressed. After placing him in a trance, Owens duly applied his hands to Broadhurst's skull, with entertaining results. He ended the performance by manipulating that part of the brain responsible for 'locality and language'. At this point the Burslem man revealed his intention 'to leave his country and emigrate to America immediately'. He 'wouldner stey here ony longer', he announced before being demesmerised.[16]

Whether James Broadhurst was a genuine subject or an accomplice of the enterprising Owens is difficult to say, but he seems to have persuaded most who witnessed the spectacle of his authenticity.[17] Irrespective of its design, Broadhurst's reverie would have struck a chord among Staffordshire audiences in 1844, especially with pottery workers and their families. 'Emigration seems to be the all-absorbing subject with potters at the present time', wrote one observer in July.[18] The immediate source of this interest is evident. In April, only a few weeks before Dr Owens's visit, an Act of Parliament established the Potters' Joint-Stock Emigration Society and Savings Fund, initiating a project that would affect working-class activity and organisation in the area for years to come. Its aim was bold: the transformation of employment conditions in the Staffordshire Potteries through the removal of surplus labour to the American West; its architect was a young, charismatic, Swansea-born editor and trade union leader called William Evans.

This study will investigate the history of the Potters' Emigration Society from its origins and founding in 1844 to its demise at the beginning of the following decade. The potters' was not the only trade union-assisted emigration scheme in the mid-nineteenth century – between 1840 and 1880 fifty to sixty unions provided or considered providing emigration benefits to their members[19] – but the 'unusually wide contemporary notice' it attracted,[20] and the scale and nature of its ambition, makes it the most significant. Evans's associational project was distinguished by its agrarianism; emigrant potters would set aside their industrial skills, trading the wheel and the kiln for the ox, the plough and the axe, the factory for the farm. The ideological and emotional intensity the Welshman brought to its advocacy also marked it out. Evans presented emigration as both a practical solution to the problem of underemployment and a fundamental rejection of a factory system whose inequities he relentlessly catalogued. In the final reckoning, he manifestly failed to deliver on his promise of transforming the lives of North Staffordshire's pottery community. Faced with a shortfall in support, in May 1848 the Society opened its doors to other regions and trades, resulting in an inevitable loss of focus on the potters' condition. Two-and-a-half years later, after expanding at one point to over 100 branches, it dissolved in clouds of debt and recrimination, leaving settlers in Wisconsin struggling to retain their land. Several hundred emigrants participated in the scheme, although the exact number is impossible to determine. Also unclear is the number who returned home, their dreams of independence and prosperity in the New World dashed. On the other hand, many of the emigrants prospered, successfully assimilating into American society and in a number of cases making demonstrable progress up the socio-economic ladder.

The Potters' Emigration Society proved controversial in its time and has remained so. Labour historians, generally resistant to emigration as an outlet for working-class despair, poured scorn on Evans's agrarian prescription, finding it intellectually flawed, culturally regressive and ill-suited to the needs of those whose lives it was designed to ameliorate. In their seminal study of trade union history, first published in 1894, Sidney and Beatrice Webb briefly noted the appearance of emigration funds in many large societies by the mid-1840s, including the potters', but dismissed them as having produced 'no visible effect' in reducing surplus labour, the avowed objective.[21] While the couple made no specific judgement on the potters' project in their published history, it is plainly visible in Sidney Webb's handwritten notes, where he characterised Evans's plan as 'foolhardy'. For many years, Webb recorded, 'the whole of the activity & energy of the best men in the trade was absorbed in this scheme to the neglect of all their trade interests & the ultimate collapse & ruin of the Union'. The main source for these judgements were personal reminiscences of 'old men' confided to William Owen, a prominent North Staffordshire union leader, to whom Webb had spoken.[22] In 1901 Owen's son Harold produced the first detailed account of the Society in his book *The Staffordshire Potter*. Unsurprisingly, Owen matched the Webbs' criticisms of Evans's venture, condemning it for its lack of realism and for sacrificing the potters' union to the chimera of emigrationism. The scheme 'was perfection itself' in theory, but it failed to command the universal support of the 'essentially indigenous' potters who recoiled from the idea of severing ties of family and home. 'It was too plausible to be trusted – too extensive to be possible', he wrote.[23]

Subsequent labour histories were equally judgemental. W. H. Warburton's study of trade unionism in the North Staffordshire pottery industry, published in 1931, lacked Owen's ardency but shared his doubts about Evans's grand project. Warburton was particularly critical of the potters' failure to grasp the opportunities offered by general unionism, and attacked Evans personally for 'his inability to appreciate or to have sympathetic understanding of the ideas' of the National Association for the Protection of Labour, whose conference the Welshman had harangued on his pet topic of emigration in June 1846.[24] By the 1970s, as trade union membership and influence reached its peak in Britain, condemnation of Evans's scheme had become second nature for labour scholars. In his history of the Staffordshire potteries, published in 1971, John Thomas, the son of a South Wales miner, dismissed the emigration initiative for having done nothing but 'provide a sweepstake for a few innocents to make a trip to the New World'. He especially ridiculed Evans's exploitation of workers' fears of mechanisation, claiming that he 'out-Morrised William Morris in his contempt for machinery'.[25] Frank Burchill and Richard Ross were similarly scathing six years later in their officially commissioned history of potters' unionism. Pouring water on the scheme's ideological pretensions, they claimed it was 'hard to believe' that the economic arguments for relocating surplus labour to the New World 'required complex intellectual origins'. As for Evans, his 'dynamic, if eccentric' leadership was a 'disaster' for trade unionism in North Staffordshire, bringing the potters 'to national disrepute' and contributing to their 'ultimately insular and isolated posture' in the second half of the nineteenth century.[26]

Historians of emigration shared many of these criticisms. In the first comprehensive survey of the transatlantic movement, published in 1913, Stanley C. Johnson noted that trade union funds were 'an important source of assistance' to emigration but saw little need to investigate them closely. Endorsing the Webbs' belief in the ultimately futile nature of such projects, Johnson failed to render any specific judgement on the potters' scheme, whose emergence he briefly described.[27] Less inhibited was the American historian Wilbur S. Shepperson. Writing in 1957, Shepperson roundly castigated union advocates of surplus labour emigration for their belief in 'the unique and somewhat perverted philosophy of strength through scarcity'. Evans was again judged to have led pottery workers astray. More and more 'an apostle and prisoner of his own ideas', the potters' leader 'blindly assumed that emigration could right all the wrongs of English society', Shepperson wrote.[28] American historians were not uniformly critical or indifferent. Americans traditionally celebrated British immigration for its essential contribution to national enlargement, and the potters' scheme, notwithstanding its origins, was otherwise unexceptional. Local historians, in particular, weighed the potters' move to Wisconsin for its pioneering value. In the compendious *The History of Columbia County, Wisconsin*, first published in 1880, Evans failed to garner a mention; the attention was naturally on the migrants themselves, their journey west and their struggle to survive in the unfamiliar frontier environment. While the volume properly recorded the history of the Society's origins, travails and demise, this was by no means a chronicle of failure. 'A few of the emigrants returned to England', the writer concluded, 'but the greater part remained, some of whom entered land for themselves elsewhere in this and adjoining counties, and in due course of time became substantial citizens'.[29]

A half-century later, a leading historian of the American West, Grant Foreman, picked up this redemptive thread in an essay on the potters' settlement in Wisconsin. Although Foreman had little to say about ideology and was uninterested in trade unionism, he was highly critical of the scheme (and of some of its less-than-industrious participants), noting the 'fatal infirmities' inherent in an enterprise that depended upon the 'often fatuous hopes of [immigrants] changing over night from factory workers to successful farmers, capable of making a living and more, from twenty acres of land'.[30] But was the scheme such an outright failure? Echoing the early histories, Foreman argued that despite the 'disappointments and hardships' the emigration project had proved beneficial to its participants, most of whom 'preferred to remain in their new home rather than return to England'. The essay ends with a list of names, extracted from the 1860 Census and designed to indicate how successfully the incomers had established themselves in Columbia and adjacent Marquette Counties.[31] Foreman's emphasis on settler persistence and accomplishment was subsequently endorsed by William Van Vugt in his major study of mid-nineteenth-century British emigration to the United States, which appeared in 1999. Van Vugt noted the 'unrealistic hopes' and mismanagement that caused the scheme's collapse, yet concluded that once in America most emigrants 'were able to dig themselves out of poverty and become prosperous farmers'.[32]

Equally critical as their labour history colleagues of the Society's deficiencies, emigration scholars have become more receptive to the scheme's broader social outcomes. A third approach has concentrated on its political and intellectual roots, about which labour historians were traditionally dismissive. In 1969 J. F. C. Harrison laid down the gauntlet by characterising Evans's initiative as a 'special' byproduct of Owenite socialism, a movement whose influence on Potteries trade unionism dated from at least 1833, when Robert Owen made two visits there. Harrison discovered Owenite footprints throughout the letters and editorials of Evans's newspaper, *The Potters' Examiner*, but argued that the solution proposed – 'individualist farming in Wisconsin' – was significantly at odds with Owen's cooperative vision. In Harrison's view, Evans and his followers simply borrowed what they wanted from Owenism, unconcerned, or most likely unaware of, inconsistencies in their social thought.[33] Evans's Owenite credentials were strongly pressed five years later by Ray Boston in an unpublished but widely circulated essay. Tracking Evans back to his birth in South Wales and early life in Worcester, Boston portrayed him as a dynamic, evangelical personality whose views were strongly shaped by his environment. Historians had underrated the union leader's 'considerable achievements', and he took issue with those who regarded the emigration project as inevitably flawed. It '*was* a visionary plan but it was not necessarily an impracticable one', he insisted.[34]

An intriguing aspect of Boston's essay was the attempt to link the potters' leader to two prominent transatlantic figures, the brothers Frederick William and George Henry Evans. Although Boston's research failed to uncover a familial relationship with the brothers (which did not prevent him referring to Frederick as William's 'distant relative'),[35] he did usefully identify intellectual connections between them, particularly with George Henry, the co-founder in 1844 of the National Reform Association and principal architect of American land reform.[36] A quarter-of-a-century later American historian Jamie L. Bronstein reinvestigated the relationship between George Henry and William Evans as part of a wider inquiry into working-class land reform in Britain and the United States. For the first time the potters' scheme was appraised in the context of a transatlantic reform movement which, notwithstanding its personal and intellectual schisms, was united in its aim of delivering working families from the thraldom of industrial labour through the acquisition and utilisation of land. Plainly, the Potters' Emigration Society failed to accomplish its aims; it 'fizzled in a sea of transatlantic acrimony' and 'suffocated for want of cash'. But ultimate outcomes were not what concerned Bronstein and she made scant mention of the fact that many settlers remained in America, and even thrived. After the Society collapsed, she wrote, Evans returned to Wales, 'leaving the Wisconsin emigrants to shift for themselves, which, ostensibly, they did'. In her view, the Society's principal achievements, like those of the National Reform Association and the Chartist Land Company, were not to be found in concrete results, which were meagre at best, but in the attempt to put agrarian ideas into practice and in the 'worker-based culture' created in the process of mobilising beneath the banner of land reform.[37]

Despite shared goals and strategies, the Potters' Emigration Society had little direct association with American land reform. Its links to Chartism, by contrast, were intimate, complex and finally adversarial. Completed in the same year as Bronstein's study, Robert Fyson's thesis on Chartism in North Staffordshire offered a striking counterpoint to her internationalist history by returning the emigration scheme to its industrial home in the Potteries. Fyson's contribution included information on Evans's career in the Potteries following his relocation in 1839 from Worcester, where he had worked as a china painter and gilder and served as secretary of the local Owenite branch. By 1842 Evans was an active Chartist, and he remained committed to the cause at least until March 1845, when he represented his union at the Chartist national trades conference in London. His views changed thereafter; determined that emigration was the potters' panacea, he became trapped in a maze of locally competing strategies and allegiances from which there was no obvious exit.[38] Opposition to his emigration project was fuelled in May 1845 by the arrival in the Potteries of Feargus O'Connor's Land Plan and from the challenge posed by the Chartist-backed National Association of United Trades for the Protection of Labour, which began recruiting heavily in the area. In Fyson's view, the effect of this tribal rivalry was to 'weaken and divide Potteries trade unionism' while at its most vulnerable during the depressed second half of the 1840s.[39]

Modern scholarship has thus served to temper the blanket condemnation of the Society by paying greater heed to its intellectual and grassroots credentials and to the values and aspirations of pottery workers themselves, ironically neglected in early labour history, with its strong institutional focus. A 1993 essay by a German specialist in labour migration, Horst Rössler, revealed the weaknesses in the old orthodoxy. Rössler investigated the extent to which pottery workers, by reading emigrant letters printed in the *Examiner*, became convinced that a move to America provided the best hope of achieving 'independence', a concept he invested with broad meaning. The images conveyed of a free, bounteous and healthy America were powerfully persuasive (and contrasted with more critical commentaries from radical and Chartist papers), but were given added authority by Evans's fervid editorial prompting. In America, journeymen potters would realise the independence being denied to them at home in a trade which had seen rising employment insecurity, loss of status and shattered hopes of upward mobility. Cheap land also gave migrating workers the choice as to whether to continue as pottery makers, branch out into agriculture or combine both pursuits. Rössler described the potters' dreams of enhanced independence as broadly realistic, and concluded that it was the heightened expectations aroused by the emigrant letters and by Evans's 'overtly positive and uncritical articles' in the *Examiner* that were mainly responsible for the project's failure.[40]

Rössler's emphasis on the journeymen's search for independence chimed well with the work of other late-twentieth-century scholars who explored the motives underpinning transatlantic migration in the early industrial era. As Charlotte Erickson argued, the widespread availability of cheap land in America offered a powerful incentive for English workers, many of whom underestimated the hardships facing them and the true costs involved in its acquisition and use. Yet the question of how far the 'agrarian myth' of cheap land and subsistence farming seduced potters and other trades is difficult to answer. Also moot is the extent to which these migrants were, as Erickson put it, 'unwilling to make the social and psychological adaptations' that pervasive changes in the British economy demanded.[41] For some commentators, any deviation from the prevailing logic of modernity was difficult to concede. Writing in 1969, the economic historian Peter Mathias derided those who expended 'misguided energy and enthusiasm' on back-to-the-land resistance to emergent industrialisation.[42] Although Mathias's target was O'Connor's Land Plan, his strictures could have applied equally to Evans's scheme. In contrast, Malcolm Chase's researches into the vitality of popular agrarianism yielded strong evidence of the close spatial and psychological ties connecting industrial labour to the land in the first half of the nineteenth century. From time immemorial, 'the vast majority of the common people had been rural workers', Chase noted, and it was understandable 'that even those deviating from this pattern should have retained so much that was involved with the values and habits of the countryside'.[43] Viewed through this lens, the choice of farming in the American West over continuing toil in the harsh, often poisonous air of the Staffordshire potbank seems anything but regressive, notwithstanding the unrealistic expectations held by many seeking a new start across the Atlantic.[44]

Every historical investigation poses a different empirical challenge. As John Tosh has written, while emigration was 'an inescapable social fact' in nineteenth-century Britain, it 'left only a small cultural residue'.[45] In the potters' case, a specific difficulty compounds the general one: a gap in the topic's key source, *The Potters' Examiner and Workman's Advocate*. The paper began publication in December 1843; a continuous run survives to the beginning of July 1847, shortly after the receipt of the first letters from the Society's Estate Committee, which had departed for America in April. Three further issues from September–October permit us to trace the Committee's passage to Wisconsin. There followed a critical period which saw the end of the potters' union and the emigration scheme's expansion. By the time the paper, under its altered title, *The Potters' Examiner and Emigrants' Advocate*, again becomes available in the summer of 1849, the Society was transformed into a national organisation with branches the length of breadth of Britain (issues from mid-October to mid-December 1850 are also missing). The hiatus is particularly unfortunate, a gap in the narrative that deprives us of detailed evidence about the Society's organisation and financing as well as information on emigrant identities and departures. Also missing from this period are the reports and correspondence from the settlements in Wisconsin. Although papers such as *The Staffordshire Advertiser* and *Staffordshire Mercury* (the latter ceased publication in May 1848) printed occasional news of the Society's activities, they hardly compensate for the loss of the *Examiner*, a journal run by and for workers. Finally, there is the loss of Evans's own voice. While numerous accounts of his speeches survive, there can be no substitute for the passionate commentaries on the potters' condition that headlined virtually every issue of his paper.

Extant testimony from the emigrants themselves is even more elusive. The problem is especially acute in trying to establish the motives behind the decision to leave Britain. Letters home are an obvious port of call, although, as Charlotte Erickson warned, we should be careful not to infer too much about original intent from statements born of the subsequent experience of settlement, nor should we ignore, as David A. Gerber discussed, the issues arising from using such epistolary material as authentic representations of immigrant consciousness.[46] Correspondence from Potters' Emigration Society members is in short supply. Surviving letters contain vivid accounts of the journey west and reports of conditions in Wisconsin but betray little about pre-migration circumstances. How did potters and other workers arrive at the decision to emigrate? And what consideration was given to the views of family members, especially wives and children? Did women have a different image of 'America' to men?[47] The sources rarely reveal. Nor do they shed much light on the motives of those who returned home to Britain or of those – the overwhelming majority – who did not emigrate. If, as Evans claimed, the day-to-day lives of pottery workers were fast becoming intolerable, why did relatively few choose to take advantage of the offer of a new start across the Atlantic?

The situation is brighter regarding emigration outcomes, although definitive conclusions on numbers, destinations and economic and social trajectories are unlikely to be forthcoming. The digitisation of passenger lists and census data has greatly facilitated the tracking of individual migrants, while the explosion of interest in family history over recent decades has produced much valuable material. The main problem concerns bias; the footprints left by those who settled permanently and contributed to their communities are naturally more detectable than those who did not. Early county histories are especially helpful in charting the progress of the more successful, adding flesh to the bare bones of information retrieved from the census. Often, the achievements of offspring provide the means of uncovering an emigrant's history. A good example is George Skinner, a young pottery worker from

Burslem, who went to America in 1848. Skinner's unremarkable life as a farmer in Marquette County, Wisconsin, which ended with his death from pneumonia at the age of 52, is rendered more visible by his son Thomas's election as the county superintendent of schools in 1889, just in time for the family's inclusion in a local history published the following year.[48] For the less successful, the trail often peters out quickly. Premature death, family dispersal and economic misfortune all contributed to an individual's disappearance from view (females, who invariably changed surname on marriage, are particularly hard to track). Tantalising glimpses in the census and other sources point to the difficulties experienced by many newcomers in putting down roots in America. A final challenge is to identify those who abandoned the struggle and returned home to Britain. Scholars are now taking this return movement seriously, recognising it as an essential component of emigration history. The barriers to further progress are formidable; for the 1840s and 1850s, census data provides the only realistic means of tracking return migrants, as inward passenger lists to the United Kingdom have mainly not survived and personal testimony is almost nonexistent.[49]

Such issues notwithstanding, enough evidence exists for a fresh look at the Potters' Emigration Society, a self-help initiative that promised much but seemingly delivered little. The emigrants themselves, men and women unable or unwilling to accommodate industrial society's sharper edges, deserve a reappraisal, as does William Evans, who remains a controversial, elusive figure. The Society's founder worked tirelessly to advance the potters' welfare, and his emigration project, if ultimately ill-executed, was by no means a fanciful response to the anxieties and displacements wrought by industrialisation, not the least of which was the perceived threat to livelihoods posed by new machinery. As Eric Richards has written, the Industrial Revolution 'was highly equivocal in its results for many decades', and while its benefits remained 'ambiguous or even negative, emigration was bound to be a serious alternative'.[50] As it turned out, too few potters responded to Evans's call to sustain the scheme, which nonetheless aroused enthusiastic interest in North Staffordshire, as the canal-side crowds who cheered the departing Estate Committee and other groups testified. It subsequently found approval in other labouring communities, from London in the Southeast to Nottingham, Birmingham, the Lancashire textile districts and Kirkcaldy and Dundee in the Scotland lowlands. Weavers, bleachers, hatters, tailors, carpenters, stonemasons, gun makers and iron moulders joined pottery turners, pressers and handlers in signing up to Evans's vision. To these men and their families, homesteading in America was not a pipedream but a once-in-a-lifetime opportunity for social renewal, and for potters particularly an escape from a regime that depressed and alienated them.

'You say it is about hiring time with you in the Potteries', wrote the former Hanley ovenman Isaac Smith to his brother-in-law from Wisconsin in 1871; 'that never troubles me, George, in this country, like it did in England. Every man is his own boss here. We are all *equals*. Some, it is true, are better off than others, but there is no bowing and moving our hats here.'[51]

Notes

1 James Belich, in *Replenishing the Earth: The Settler Revolution and the Rise of the Anglo-World, 1783–1939* (Oxford: Oxford University Press, 2009), p. 229, calls it 'perhaps the highest rate of growth in human history'.
2 Quoted in Eric Richards, *Britannia's Children: Emigration from England, Scotland, Wales and Ireland since 1600* (London: Hambledon, 2004), p. 162.
3 Brian Dolan, *Josiah Wedgwood: Entrepreneur to the Enlightenment* (London: Harper Collins, 2004), pp. 345–6.
4 Neil Ewins, '"Supplying the Present Wants of our Yankee Cousins …": Staffordshire Ceramics and the American Market 1775–1880', *Journal of Ceramic History* 15 (1997), 8.
5 Edwin Atlee Barber, *The Pottery and Porcelain of the United States* (New York: G. P. Putnam's Sons, 1893), pp. 156–7.
6 John Spargo, *The Potters and Potteries of Bennington* (Boston, MA: Houghton Mifflin Co., 1926), 221–34.
7 John Spargo, *Early American Pottery and China* (Garden City, NY: Garden City Publishing Co., 1926), p. 208. On Clews, see Frank Stefano, Jr., 'James and Ralph Clews, Nineteenth Century Potters, Part I: The English Experience', and 'James and Ralph Clews, Nineteenth Century Potters, Part II: The American Experience', in Paul Atterbury (ed.), *English Pottery and Porcelain: An Historical Survey* (London: Peter Owen, 1980), pp. 202–9.
8 Frank Thistlethwaite, 'The Atlantic Migration of the Pottery Industry', *Economic History Review* 11:2 (1958), 268.
9 Barber, *Pottery and Porcelain*, p. 156.
10 Ibid., p. 161. See also Diana Stradling and J. Garrison Stradling, 'American Queensware: The Louisville Experience, 1829–1837', *Ceramics in America 2001*, ed. Robert Hunter, https://chipstone.org/issue.php/2/Ceramics-in-America-2001 (last accessed 19 November 2022). On East Liverpool's emergence, see William C. Gates, Jr., *The City of Hills and Kilns: Life and Work in East Liverpool, Ohio* (East Liverpool, OH: East Liverpool Historical Society, 1984), pp. 1–73; and William E. Van Vugt, *British Buckeyes: The English, Scots, and Welsh in Ohio, 1700–1900* (Kent, OH: Kent State University Press, 2006), pp. 135–8.
11 Thistlethwaite, 'Atlantic Migration', 272.
12 *The Potters' Examiner and Workman's Advocate* (hereafter *PEWA*), 16 March 1844.

13 John Howson remained in business at Zanesville until his death in 1863. Miranda Goodby, '"Our Home in the West": Staffordshire Potters and Their Emigration to America in the 1840s', *Ceramics in America 2003*, ed. Robert Hunter, www.chipstone.org/article.php/75/Ceramics–in–America–2003 (last accessed 19 November 2022); and J. F. Everhart (comp.), *History of Muskingum County, Ohio, with Illustrations and Biographical Sketches of Prominent Men and Pioneers* (Columbus, OH: A. A. Graham, 1882), p. 89.

14 *The People*, vol. 1, no. 42, p. 333.

15 *The Staffordshire Advertiser*, 18 and 25 May 1844. On W. J. Vernon, see Terry M. Parsinnen, 'Mesmeric Performers', *Victorian Studies* 21:1 (1977), 94–5. On phreno-mesmerism, see Alison Winter, *Mesmerized: Powers of Mind in Victorian Britain* (Chicago, IL: University of Chicago Press, 1998), pp. 117–19.

16 *The Staffordshire Advertiser*, 25 May 1844.

17 For audience reactions, see *ibid.*; and *North Staffordshire Mercury*, 25 May 1844.

18 *PEWA*, 27 July 1844.

19 R. V. Clements, 'Trade Unions and Emigration, 1840–80', *Population Studies* 9:2 (1955), 172. See also M. D. Wainwright, 'Agencies for the Promotion or Facilitation of Emigration from England to the United States of America, 1815–1861' (MA dissertation, University of London, 1951), pp. 125–68.

20 Wilbur S. Shepperson, *British Emigration to North America: Projects and Opinions in the Early Victorian Period* (Minneapolis: University of Minnesota Press, 1957), p. 95.

21 Sidney Webb and Beatrice Webb, *The History of Trade Unionism* (London: Longman, Green and Co., 1902), pp. 183–4.

22 'Historical Notes' on 'The North Staffordshire Potteries', A44, Webb Trade Union Collection, London School of Economics and Political Science Archives.

23 Harold Owen, *The Staffordshire Potter* (London: G. Richards, 1901), pp. 72, 75.

24 W. H. Warburton, *The History of the Trade Union Organisation in the North Staffordshire Potteries* (London: George Allen & Unwin, 1931), pp. 129–31.

25 John Thomas, *The Rise of the Staffordshire Potteries* (Bath: Adams and Dart, 1971), pp. 200–6 (quotations pp. 205, 200).

26 Frank Burchill and Richard Ross, *A History of the Potter's Union* (Hanley: Ceramic and Allied Trades Union, 1977), pp. 83–98 (quotation p. 98).

27 Stanley C. Johnson, *A History of Emigration from the United Kingdom to North America, 1763–1912* (London: Routledge & Kegan Paul, 1913), pp. 80–1.

28 Shepperson, *British Emigration to North America*, p. 95.

29 *The History of Columbia County, Wisconsin, Containing an Account of Its Settlement, Growth, Development and Resources …* (Chicago, IL: Western Historical Company, 1880), pp. 465–7, 854 (quotation p. 467). See also J. E. Jones (ed.), *A History of Columbia County Wisconsin: A Narrative Account of Its Historical Progress, Its People, and Its Principal Interests*, 2 vols (Chicago and New York: Lewis Publishing Company, 1914), p. 87; and Andrew Jackson Turner, *The Family Tree of Columbia County, Wisconsin* (Portage: Press of the Wisconsin State Register, 1904), pp. 70–1, which reiterate

the point. Turner's son Frederick Jackson Turner, born in Portage in 1861, was the renowned historian of the 'frontier' origins of American exceptionalism.
30 Grant Foreman, 'Settlement of English Potters in Wisconsin', *Wisconsin Magazine of History* 21:4 (1938), 375–96.
31 Ibid., pp. 386, 392, 394, 396.
32 William E. Van Vugt, *Britain to America: Mid-Nineteenth Century Immigrants to the United States* (Urbana: University of Illinois Press, 1999), pp. 75–6. Also using Foreman's work was Rowland Berthoff, *British Immigrants in Industrial America, 1790–1850* (Cambridge, MA: Harvard University Press, 1953), p. 75. After the scheme's collapse, he notes, 'some emigrant potters did become farmers, and other started kilns in Illinois'.
33 J. F. C. Harrison, *Robert Owen and the Owenites in Britain and America: The Quest for a New Moral World* (London: Routledge and Kegan Paul, 1969), pp. 228–9.
34 Ray Boston, 'William Evans and the Potters' Emigration Society', Keele University Library, 1974, 4, 47. Boston's was not the first scholarly essay on the potters' leader. See W. A. G. Armytage, 'William Evans: A Proponent of Emigration', *Dalhousie Review* 34:2 (1954), 167–72, which is generally positive about the project. Armytage used much of the same material in *Heavens Below: Utopian Experiments in England, 1560–1960* (London: Routledge and Kegan Paul, 1961), pp. 254–8.
35 Boston, 'William Evans and the Potters' Emigration Society', p. 12.
36 Ibid., p. 6.
37 Jamie L. Bronstein, *Land Reform and Working-Class Experience in Britain and the United States, 1800–1862* (Stanford, CA: Stanford University Press, 1999), pp. 21, 23–51, 231, 250.
38 Robert Fyson, 'Chartism in North Staffordshire' (PhD dissertation, University of Lancaster, 1998), pp. 295–304.
39 Ibid., pp. 300–4; Warburton, *The History of the Trade Union Organisation*, p. 130.
40 Horst Rössler, 'The Dream of Independence: The "America" of England's North Staffordshire Potters', in Dirk Hoerder and Rössler (eds), *Distant Magnets: Expectations and Realities in the Immigrant Experience, 1840–1930* (New York: Holmes & Meier, 1993), pp. 138–59 (quotation p. 148). Historians are traditionally sceptical about the role of private letters and emigrant guidebooks as catalysts of emigration, although accepting they provided useful information for those already determined to migrate. See Maldwyn A. Jones, 'The Background to Emigration from Great Britain in the Nineteenth Century', *Perspectives in American History* 7 (1973), 18–20.
41 Charlotte Erickson, *Leaving England: Essays on British Emigration in the Nineteenth Century* (Ithaca, NY: Cornell University Press, 1994), pp. 34–59 (quotation p. 59).
42 Peter Mathias, *The First Industrial Nation: An Economic History of Britain, 1700–1914* (London: Methuen & Co., 1969), p. 363. See also Clements, 'Trade Unions and Emigration', p. 174, which describes the potters' scheme 'as a means of flight … to a rural utopia'.

43 Malcolm Chase, *'The People's Farm': English Radical Agrarianism, 1775–1840* (Oxford: Clarendon Press, 1988), p. 15. See also Malcolm Chase, 'Out of Radicalism: the Mid-Victorian Freehold Land Movement', *English Historical Review* 106:419 (1991), 319–45. Marguerite W. Dupree, *Family Structure in the Staffordshire Potteries, 1840–1880* (Oxford: Clarendon Press, 1995), p. 78 notes that even from 'the most densely populated town [in the Potteries], it was less than half a mile to open countryside'.
44 The most recent account of the potters' scheme is Roger Bentley, 'The Road to "Desolation Ferry": The Story of the Potters' Emigration Society', *Wisconsin Magazine of History* 94:1 (2010), 2–13. It is particularly useful in describing the Society's final months and the efforts of settlers to secure their property.
45 John Tosh, *Manliness and Masculinities in Nineteenth-Century Britain: Essays on Gender, Family and Empire* (Harlow: Pearson, Longman, 2005), pp. 186–7.
46 Charlotte Erickson, *Invisible Immigrants: The Adaptation of English and Scottish Immigrants in Nineteenth-Century America* (Ithaca, NY: Cornell University Press, 1972), p. 22; David A. Gerber, *Authors of Their Lives: The Personal Correspondence of British Immigrants to North America in the Nineteenth Century* (New York: New York University Press, 2006), esp. pp. 45–56. See also Bruce S. Elliott, David A. Gerber and Suzanne M. Sinke (eds), *Letters across Borders: The Epistolary Practices of International Migrants* (New York and Basingstoke: Palgrave Macmillan, 2006); and Eric Richards, *The Genesis of International Mass Migration: The British Case, 1750–1900* (Manchester: Manchester University Press, 2018), pp. 58–61.
47 Dirk Hoerder, 'Labour Migrants' Views of "America"', *Renaissance and Modern Studies* 35:1 (1992), 8.
48 *Portrait and Biographical Album of Green Lake, Marquette and Waushara Counties, Wisconsin* (Chicago, IL: Acme Publishing Co., 1890), pp. 774–5.
49 Wilbur S. Shepperson, *Emigration and Disenchantment: Portraits of Englishmen Repatriated from the United States* (Norman: University of Oklahoma Press, 1965) is useful but limited. For more recent work, see Marjory Harper (ed.), *Emigrant Homecomings: The Return Movement of Emigrants, 1600–2000* (Manchester: Manchester University Press, 2005); and John Killick, 'Transatlantic Steerage Fares, British and Irish Migration, and Return Migration, 1815–1860', *Economic History Review* 67:1 (2014), 170–91.
50 Richards, *Britannia's Children*, p. 149.
51 *Reynolds's Newspaper*, 12 November 1871.

1

Industrial origins

For those who participated in it, the emigration scheme's origins were simply explained. 'In the spring of 1847', recalled Isaac Smith (see Figure 1.1) over three decades later,

> I came with others from England to Wisconsin. The Potters' Emigration Society in England formed a part of the Potters' Union there. We had just expended six thousand pounds in one strike for wages there, and all to no purpose. We found that we were battling with effects and not with causes. Seeing that our efforts failed in this respect, we decided to remove the surplus labor out of the market.[1]

William Evans, the scheme's architect, was equally clear. Addressing former colleagues in 1854, Evans maintained that he had:

> a sincere object to serve in starting the Potters' Emigration Society. He had witnessed, with feelings of regret, the immense amount of surplus labour which was being gradually incorporated into the trade; and his object was to remove that redundant labour, and thereby to confer a great blessing on the trade. They all knew that, as labour was removed, wages must rise.[2]

The removal of surplus labour was the Society's siren call. How far pottery workers absorbed classical economic ideas about emigration's ability to improve labour's condition is hard to say; Evans himself had no doubts on the matter, constantly invoking it as other factors, including mechanisation, waxed and waned in his discourse.[3] At the root of potters' anxieties was the insecurity experienced by all craft and industrial workers in the late 1830s and 1840s. The trade cycle was a capricious master, sometimes benevolent but periodically instilling fear and misery in the communities that served it. Sharp downturns in 1837, 1841–2 and again in 1847–8 saw conditions deteriorate throughout the manufacturing economy. The depression of 1841–2 was particularly harsh, 'the deepest and most widespread ... of the period, affecting almost all industries in all parts of the country', according to one authority.[4] Black spots in early 1842 included Dundee, where half the mechanics and shipbuilders were unemployed, and Bolton

Figure 1.1 Rev. Isaac Smith and his wife Sarah, pioneer Potters' Emigration Society settlers.

in Lancashire, where fewer than one in five men in the carpentry and bricklaying trades had full-time work. Five years later another severe downturn provoked similar distress, with Lancashire cotton towns again hard-hit. In November 1847 only 46 per cent of Manchester's 19,000 textile workers were in full employment.[5]

While it is unlikely that unemployment in North Staffordshire reached these devastating levels, the pottery industry was not immune from the economic storms engulfing British manufacturing communities in this period. Writing a century later in the shadow of another major depression, W. H. Warburton described the years from the end of 1837 until 1842 as 'the most hopeless' in the potters' history, when 'trade was almost consistently bad, hosts of potters during that time were out of work, and almost all were thrown on short time'.[6] Unemployment and short-time work were facts of life in the Potteries as elsewhere, and their consequences were as keenly felt. Although pottery manufacturers were often reluctant to lay off skilled staff, preferring to lower piece rates or move to three or four-day working, the less skilled and casual workers had little protection when orders dried up.[7] Ann Smith was a transferrer who spent thirty years at the potbank and in the winter of 1840–1 was employed at Minton and Boyle's in Stoke. Interviewed by Dr Samuel Scriven during his investigation into child labour in the industry, she acknowledged that masters could not always provide work and that at the present there were 'a great many' unemployed in the parish. 'I don't know how they live', she admitted.[8] Winters were especially hard. Charles Shaw, who started work in 1839 at the age of 7 as a mould runner in Enoch Wood's Burslem factory, remembered the chronic destitution of his growing years, adding that, 'when winter came with its stoppage of work, this destitution became acute'.[9]

No single thread connects the emigration of Staffordshire pottery workers, or those from other trades who joined Evans's scheme, to the economic crises of the late 1830s and 1840s. Numbers crossing the Atlantic fluctuated considerably from year to year – the unreliability of available statistics before 1847 clouds the issue – and historians have struggled to identify the precise relationship at any given time between migration and economic performance and the relative role of 'push' and 'pull' factors, that is, changing conditions in Britain against those in the United States.[10] In 1838 a slump in American business activity was the most likely cause of the sharp decline in emigrant numbers; a similar decline a few years later requires more explanation. In 1841–2, when the depression was at its severest, numbers leaving again rose before falling back in 1843, when just over 28,000 British- and Irish-born immigrants were recorded entering the United States, a drop of nearly 62 per cent over the previous year. In this instance, improving economic conditions at home appear to have played the greater role in the downturn, although, as Raymond Cohn admits, nothing is certain.[11] After 1845 the volume of transatlantic emigration swelled to record levels. While some of this increase, especially that emanating from Ireland, is attributable to the effects of the potato famine, it coincided with a significant improvement in British industrial output when, as William Van Vugt writes, 'opportunities for many workers were expanding'.[12] Summing up the evidence, Eric Richards concludes that, Ireland apart, there was 'no unambiguous correlation between economic decline and emigration' in this period.[13]

Weighing and balancing the separate elements that encouraged emigration to the United States in this period is thus a daunting task. After 1830 the numbers leaving Britain rose markedly, driven by economic, demographic and other factors. But perhaps the most remarkable aspect of the emigration phenomenon, as Richards notes, was 'its sheer spontaneity: it happened outside government control and beyond contemporary understanding'.[14] Shrinking costs of oceanic travel, the liberalisation of official attitudes – laws restricting the emigration of artisans were finally repealed in 1824 – and rapidly expanding knowledge of transatlantic society created an unprecedented opportunity for working men and their families to reinvent themselves in the New World. At the same time, as James Belich argues, it is important to recognise that spontaneity – what he calls 'the ease of transfer' – only takes us so far.[15] We need to understand the circumstances and ideas and, where evident, the anger and unhappiness that prompted specific groups to risk everything on a new life abroad. Analysis of emigrant correspondence and other sources shows that the majority of those crossing to America in this period did so for 'essentially positive reasons'.[16] In the potters' case, belief in the western republic as a land of opportunity and independence went hand-in-hand with a profound sense of grievance that traditional means of resolution had failed to assuage.

The origins of the Potters' Emigration Society lie embedded in the unique workplace environment of the Staffordshire potbank. Abundant local resources of clay, coal and water ensured the vitality of pottery making in North Staffordshire from earliest times, but not until the final quarter of the seventeenth century did the area begin to acquire its distinctive reputation for earthenware production. Growth thereafter was rapid; by 1710–15 Burslem had seven potworks engaged in the profitable manufacture of stoneware; by 1750 factories in the neighbouring towns of Hanley, Shelton, Stoke and Tunstall were turning out an impressive range of specialised goods. Augmenting the rising domestic demand was a healthy export trade, with the American market an important driver of growth. By the turn of the nineteenth century the radical developments in materials, techniques, organisation and marketing pioneered by Josiah Wedgwood and his contemporaries had further accelerated the industry's expansion. Although the export trade suffered badly from the disruptions of the Napoleonic wars, in the years after 1822 pottery manufacturing experienced tentative but sustained recovery, with transatlantic consumers again playing a valuable role. By the 1840s there were over 120 established potteries in North Staffordshire. Employing between 20,000 and 25,000 men, women and children, they represented a remarkable concentration in an area whose total population was barely three times that figure.[17]

Few industries matched pottery making for the intricacy of its organisation and social relations; few were so dependent on customary practice and behaviour. By the nineteenth century the production of pottery – transforming clay, stone, flint and other raw materials into finished earthenware and porcelain – involved dozens of specialised occupational groups. Every stage of manufacture, from the preparation of the clay through the various shaping, glazing, firing and decorating processes, required high levels of expertise, with the most skilled workers such as hollow- and flat-ware pressers, throwers and turners determined to protect their independence and traditional status. Tradition was further upheld in the age-old hierarchy of master, journeyman and apprentice and the complex system of subcontracting that sustained it, in the continued employment of children and in clearly observed gender roles that saw the majority of female labour confined to finishing tasks such as painting, transferring, paper cutting and scouring. Women and girls made up between a third and a half of the workforce in the 1840s and their sizeable albeit subordinated presence reinforced the unusually close connection between work and home that characterised the pottery community in North Staffordshire.[18]

Such a complex division of labour made concerted resistance difficult. As economic conditions hardened, potters struggled to oppose the actions of employers who sought to lower wages and cut costs. It was in the mid-1820s, as legal barriers to 'combination' were lifted, that pottery workers first formed recognisable trade unions, although ad hoc association had been evident as early as 1772, when Wedgwood's employees made abortive demands for higher pay. Two separate unions were established in 1824 representing clay potters and printers, while other branches, including slip makers, ovenmen and painters, remained unorganised. In 1825 a strike by clay potters produced agreement on the abolition of truck and the standardisation of ware sizes. But employers were reluctant to concede claims for higher piece rates, prompting further industrial action. The strike in the end fell victim to lack of unity and to bad timing; a sharp downturn in trade left workers defenceless against masters prepared to keep factories closed rather than return rates to 1815 levels, as the union demanded. The failure of the clay workers' action led to victimisation and a halt to trade union organisation in the industry, but the experience had not been without value. Among the strike's noteworthy aspects were a brief foray into cooperative manufacturing and the establishment of a newspaper, the *Potters' Friend*. Although its life was short, an organ run by and for trade unionists set a useful precedent; its successor, *The Potters' Examiner*, would play a pivotal role in the revived unionism of the 1840s and the emigration project that grew from it.[19]

The legal recognition achieved by trade unions following the repeal of the Combination Acts left much to judicial discretion. Unions had gained the right to exist for the purposes of bargaining over wages and working hours. But workers were still subject to the common law of conspiracy, and in 1825 saw penalties for intimidation and violence extended to 'molesting' and 'obstructing' behaviour, ill-defined offences at best and at worst a green light for action against individual and group dissent. Although employers were now required to acknowledge trade unions, most did so grudgingly, firmly believing that they 'could be dispensed with should opportunity arise'.[20] To assist them, Parliament in 1823 passed a new Master and Servant Act, injecting fresh blood into a centuries-old sanction against breach of contract. The Act retained the maximum penalty, imposed in 1766, of three months' hard labour for workers who abandoned their employment or were temporarily absent or otherwise negligent; it also extended the law's remit to oral contracts. Its most coercive feature lay in its summary justice. Following a master's sworn complaint, a magistrate was required to issue a warrant for the arrest of the accused employee with no provision made, as with earlier laws, for proceeding by summons. The threat of immediate imprisonment and prosecution was a powerful disincentive for workers considering leaving work or taking strike action.[21]

Employers' resort to the criminal law to enforce industrial discipline would fuel labour's growing assertiveness in the years after the repeal of the Combination Acts. By the early 1830s pressure for change had intensified across large swaths of British society. Trade unions were part of this reform landscape, but it did not define them; their chief concern remained the defence of wages and working conditions rather than political or social transformation. Workers were not deaf to the clamour for change, however. In a period of intense ferment over parliamentary reform, poor relief and many other issues, they proved receptive to voices demanding greater value for their labour and, more ambitiously, greater control over the production process. In 1830 widespread distress in the pottery community helped fuel familiar grievances, including the continuing use of truck payments by smaller manufacturers. The anti-truck campaign drew support from various elements of respectable society. At an anti-truck rally in Hanley in October 1830, a delegate from the Lancashire-based National Association for the

Protection of Labour (NAPL) threw down a challenge to cross-class collaboration by insisting that low wages as much as truck payments were responsible for the workers' condition. A few weeks later the NAPL leader John Doherty and other 'Manchester men' addressed an open-air meeting in Wolstanton, which resolved to establish a general union of pottery workers. The immediate outcome was more modest: the setting-up of a local China and Turners' Earthenware Society, with affiliation to the NAPL delayed until February. Potters had opted to proceed cautiously, scrutinising the fine print of the NAPL's rules and regulations before committing themselves to labour's wider embrace.[22]

The NAPL's campaign in North Staffordshire was intense but brief, and after October 1831 it was no longer a presence in the area. Yet its impact on the development of trade unionism in the pottery industry should not be underestimated. The early 1830s saw widespread unrest across many industrial areas, and the immediate purpose of the campaign was to drum up support for striking Ashton-under-Lyne spinners. Abetted by local activists including the Hanley shoemaker and future Chartist John Richards, Doherty and his fellow missionaries sought to convince pottery workers that the fight against wage reductions was part of a wider resistance to the exploitation wrought by capitalist competition. They stressed the need above all for strong organisation and trade unity. These lessons, at least, were well learned; by the end of 1831 a general union of potters was already in the making. Although the NAPL itself soon collapsed under the pressure of financial and other issues, by giving pottery workers practical and ideological confidence, its intervention proved decisive.[23] This bore fruit with the formation of the National Union of Operative Potters (NUOP). Much noticed by historians, including the Webbs,[24] its size and contemporary reputation marked it out as a leading union of its day. The NUOP was the industry's first national labour organisation, representing workers in Staffordshire and the out-potteries, including Bristol, Worcester, Derbyshire, Yorkshire and Newcastle-on-Tyne. Comprising nine branches covering nine separate trades overseen by a Board of Management, also known as the Grand Lodge, the secrecy that surrounded its proceedings offered an easy target for conspiracy-minded masters. In October 1833, after a successful second annual meeting in Hanley, reported membership was 8,000, three-quarters of which was from Staffordshire. While the figures are impossible to verify, support was undoubtedly widespread, and at a level probably not repeated until the modern era.[25]

'In 1833, Mr. Owen, of New Lanark, visited the Potteries, and encouraged the spirit of union among the workmen. He took every means of advancing his principles, and some of the most active agents of the Union were considered to be his followers.' So wrote the Stoke manufacturer John Boyle in a paper delivered to the Statistical Society of London in April 1838.[26] Robert Owen's name invariably attaches itself to that of the National Union of Operative Potters, even though, Boyle's assertions notwithstanding, his role and influence are difficult to assess. The union was up and running when Owen, then in his sixties, came to North Staffordshire in the autumn of 1833; it was actually its successful establishment that drew him there. Owen's cooperative ideas and plans for a labour exchange generated considerable enthusiasm in the Potteries, but working-class interest in cooperation was already evident before his appearance. Nonetheless, his coming energised potters' leaders. In November 1833 they formed a Cooperative Society and in the spring embarked on a short-lived scheme of cooperative production. Owenism was not universally accepted, however, and operation of the scheme was kept separate from the union's affairs. In an area of strong Methodist attachment, the NUOP could suffer serious harm by identifying too closely with a man whose views on religion proved distasteful to many working people.[27]

Potters also responded to another Owenite project: general unionism. In early 1834 an appeal for support from locked-out Derby silk and other workers led to the establishment of the Grand Nation Consolidated Trades Union (GNCTU). Like its predecessor the NAPL, this ambitious attempt at national labour coordination was short-lived, but, as Malcolm Chase notes, the brevity of its history is almost beside the point. Despite the new organisation's practical failings, the enthusiasm for general unionism signified labour's growing awareness of its own potential and was an important step in workers' adjustment to accelerating economic change.[28] Fears of a loss of independence predictably shaped the potters' response to the GNCTU. Although the NUOP declined to affiliate, potters showed their maturing sense of working-class solidarity, contributing to the support of the Derby strikers and, most conspicuously, demonstrating against the conviction and transportation of the Dorchester labourers.[29]

Confirmation of the union's emerging confidence came in the shape of resistance from manufacturers and their political allies. The NUOP's activities were not confined to the workplace, and from early 1834 it participated in a range of local campaigns, including opposition to the church rates, poor relief and, most dear to manufacturers, the incorporation of the Potteries towns as a municipal borough.[30] Although not all manufacturers opposed the union's activism, the flexing of industrial muscle in defence of pay and conditions bred resentment and inevitably conflict. Employers' patience finally ran out in the autumn of 1834, following the demise of the GNCTU. By refusing to abide by the sale price and piece rate agreement negotiated the previous year, manufacturers in Tunstall and Burslem directly challenged the NUOP's authority over wages and other workplace issues where, they insisted, the union had overstepped its mark. Resurgent anti-unionism was not unique to North Staffordshire. Across Britain, trade unionists faced repression by employers buoyed up by the calculated indifference of the post-1832 government to further political and social reform.

In November 1834 Burslem and Tunstall pottery workers responded in large numbers to the manufacturers' refusal to pay agreed rates. The strike, which dragged on until March, was something of a triumph for union members, who successfully resisted attempts to dilute their original demands. But the factories' reopening proved more of an armed truce than a victory. In the wake of their capitulation, employers were more determined than ever to curb union intervention in the workplace. W. H. Warburton wrote that in the space of a little over two years, employers' relations with the potters' union changed 'from genuine respect, and friendship, real or assumed, to undisguised hostility'.[31] A low-level guerrilla war had broken out between capital and labour in the Staffordshire pottery industry. The keys to success on both sides would be unity and organisation. The manufacturers had one obvious advantage: a political and judicial system strongly weighted in their favour. In August 1835 action against striking potters and their leaders culminated in a mass trial in Leek. Against a backdrop of demonstrations and the growing nervousness of local authorities, which saw the deployment of troops to North Staffordshire, twenty-six men were sentenced to three months' hard labour for refusing to return to work; another four received varying prison terms for the offence of intimidation. Although there was no evidence of verbal or physical coercion, in the judgement of the magistrate, Rev. John Sneyd, 'intention' alone was sufficient to convict.[32]

Such tactics failed to deflect pottery workers. With economic conditions in labour's favour, they renewed their campaign for improved contracts. In response, manufacturers in March 1836 set aside their differences and formed the Potteries' Chamber of Commerce. Designed to protect the interests of the trade, its target was the NUOP, which, it claimed, 'had destroyed the legitimate control of the masters over their business, and exposed them to constant and increasing annoyance'.[33] In 1834–5 remuneration rates had been the main grievance prompting industrial action. The union now turned its attention to two practices woven into the fabric of employment at the potbank: annual hiring and good-from-oven payment.

The manufacturer John Boyle defended these 'established usages of the trade' in his contemporaneous account of the 1834 and 1836 strikes. The annual hiring of potters, he wrote, was essential given the trade's varied nature; with so many hands immediately dependent on each other, 'great inconvenience' would ensue 'if masters and workmen were allowed to separate at short notice'.[34] Operatives saw matters in a different light. Bound to masters for twelve months, they were subject to harsh punishment from an unsympathetic magistracy if leaving employment before the end of their contract. The employers for their part saw little obligation to provide work when demand slackened. With piece rate prices fixed for the duration of the contract, workers had few means of redress other than strike action when serious disagreements occurred. Good-from-oven payment, the second target of union protest, required more detailed validation. The principle was simple: operatives – flat-ware and hollow-ware pressers were mainly affected – were paid only for work that emerged from first firing in perfect condition, irrespective of who was responsible for any defects. Boyle admitted that the system was liable to abuse, but claimed that masters had eliminated its most objectionable aspects and that good-from-oven afforded 'the only feasible check upon the unskillfulness of their workmen'.[35] To the potters directly affected, it was a practice, like annual hiring, in which the scales of advantage tipped excessively towards the employer.

The stage was set in 1836 for a major confrontation between labour and capital, as workers' ambitions for greater security and better conditions collided with the masters' determination to resist further union encroachment. Buoyed by its success the previous year, the NUOP proposed the replacement of good-from-oven with good-from-hand payment, a system already operating in some branches. It also demanded that annual contracts should include the provision for one month's notice on either side. In July the union scored a significant victory when the established firm of William Adams of Tunstall agreed to accept the new terms. However, the majority of employers, represented by the Chamber of Commerce, were not about to concede. In September, with the new contract season approaching, they not only rejected the proposal for a month's notice, but also required all new agreements to contain a clause permitting a general suspension of manufacturing without breach of contract. Despite the employers' assertion that the clause – drawn up, they claimed, on the advice of the highest legal authorities – would benefit both masters and workers, there could be no disguising its true intent, the granting of virtually unlimited power to suspend an employee, or its true aim, the NUOP, whose representative authority they consistently refused to acknowledge.

The manufacturers' insistence on the suspension clause met with defiance from the union, which immediately called out 3,500 workers at fourteen pottery firms in Burslem and Tunstall. But the action failed to deter an increasingly emboldened Chamber of Commerce, which rebuffed conciliation talks and pledged to recompense its members for any losses incurred in the weeks running up to 11 November, Martinmas, when the new contracts would begin. The arrival of that date saw the closure of sixty-four Staffordshire factories; nearly four-fifths of the pottery workforce was now idle. In the ensuing battle of wills, it was perhaps inevitable that the employers, with their newly found unity and superior resources, would prevail. On 30 December a conference at Betley brought together manufacturers, trade unionists and non-union labour affected by the lock-out. The results of the meeting confirmed that the balance of power had swung irrevocably away from the NUOP. A modified annual agreement guaranteed sixteen days' work per month and made some concessions on good-from-oven deductions, but fell far short of the union's demands. Support for continued action was rapidly eroding within the pottery community, which was experiencing serious privations because of the dispute. On 27 January 1837 there was a general return to work. The strike had lasted in total five months; its effects on workers and their families and on trade unionism in the Potteries would be considerably longer.[36]

After the resumption of work, the potters' union 'collapsed like a house of cards'.[37] The speed of its demise was remarkable. The NUOP had been a 'well organised and well financed' body, which at its peak recruited an impressive proportion of the work force, including large numbers of women.[38] Despite the fears aroused among authorities by the union's mass appeal – which again saw the mobilisation of troops in North Staffordshire – its self-discipline during the dispute drew the admiration of critics such as John Boyle who noted that not a single act of violence had been committed against person or property.[39] The strike brought widespread respect from trade unionists across Britain. Prominent among them were members of the London trades, led by the shipwright John Gast. For Gast, the Staffordshire lock-out was a symbolically important episode in the contest between labour and capital, further proof that the working classes would only achieve 'complete emancipation' through concerted action and the revival of general unionism.[40] It also generated considerable financial support in the shape of gifts and loans. The loans would prove a mixed blessing, however, and over the next decade would hang heavily around potters' necks as they struggled to recover from a costly and demoralising defeat.

The strike's failure, and the NUOP's inability to survive it, points to the fragile and contingent nature of trade unionism in this era. Potters' leaders faced challenges aplenty in their conduct of the 1836–7 dispute and they undoubtedly made errors. From the outset, the strike lacked universal appeal. Good-from-oven payment affected only a portion of the skilled workforce (and was unknown in china making),[41] yet pottery workers as a whole, with their myriad fault lines, were enjoined to support the walkout. Historians attempting to explain the union's collapse also point to the decision to prolong industrial action after the gaining of concessions. Potters had begun returning to work well before the Betley conference, with the majority of those who returned employed by Chamber of Commerce-affiliated firms. Sharply dwindling domestic resources had brought many families to the brink of destitution and the pressure to resume work was intense.[42] The erosion of support for the strike had predictable consequences; by the first week in December the NUOP had lost over half of its membership. Six weeks later, when resistance ended, the union's fate was sealed.

In the following months inquests into the strike's failure took second place to the matter of economic survival. Compounding individual and family hardship was the problem of collective debt. By the conclusion of the strike the NUOP had received in excess of £5,500 in loans and other financial assurances, over half of which came from sources outside the Potteries. While there were efforts to organise local collections, repayment fell victim to the worsening trade conditions and the residual mistrust arising from the union's collapse. The Sheffield debt proved the most intractable. In December 1839, nearly three years after the strike's end, Sheffield trade unionists despatched a delegation to North Staffordshire in a vain attempt to achieve a settlement. Only £300 of the outstanding debt of £2,000 had been repaid.[43] Matters failed to improve over the next few months and in May 1840, with only £450 collected, potters suspended repayment. For the organising committee, the affair was a matter of 'honour and honesty', qualities that only 'a very small sprinkling' of pottery workers had displayed, it concluded with regret.[44]

Potters had equally little appetite for a revival of industry-wide trade unionism. Branch organisations in some form continued to exist after 1837, their activities largely obscured from the historian, and in March 1841 there were reports of an attempt to establish a new union.[45] But the strike had shaken workers' confidence in their ability to exert significant control over production. Employers for their part now seized the opportunity to press home the advantage. They were helped by the economic cycle, which from the end of 1837 until 1842 saw pottery manufacturing, like many other trades, in regular recession. When demand for ware slackened, labour market conditions greatly benefited those masters who regarded even modest concessions on good-from-oven payment and annual hiring as steps too far. Matching the revival of old practices was the appearance of new. Particularly egregious was the spread of the 'allowance system', whereby employers deducted a sum – initially two pence in every shilling – from journeymen's wages, effectively reducing them to the level of those traditionally paid to apprentices. More a set of individual arrangements than a system, allowances permitted masters to lower wages without affecting collectively agreed piece rates. Although opposition to it would ultimately help bring about the establishment of a new union, in the short term potters were powerless to resist a practice which, as W. H. Warburton wrote, was unlikely to 'have survived a period of good trade' and whose dubious legality was never tested in the courts.[46]

The collapse of the union left operatives unshielded against masters resolved to assert their authority in the workplace, and many suffered victimisation for their involvement in the strike. The winter following the strike's ending was particularly severe, bringing widespread hardship. Although trade conditions improved in the summer of 1838, there could have been little cause for optimism. Despite the absence of a union, workers continued to protest about the injustices of good-from-oven payment, the allowance system and, not least, the enforcement of annual contracts, in which after 1839 masters had the assistance of a new stipendiary magistrate, Thomas Bailey Rose, a zealous defender of property rights. Charles Shaw told the story of his father, who worked as a painter and gilder at Davenport's factory in Longport. Following a walkout in 1841 over new working arrangements, Enoch Shaw was dismissed by the firm's owner, William Davenport, whose lack of sympathy for his employees' welfare matched his lack of interest in pottery making itself.[47] Enoch's dismissal should have come as no surprise. Charles recalled seeing a letter from his father's brother-in-law, a manager at the works, pointing out that if Enoch did not abandon his support for the strike, Davenport 'would ruin him, and force him and his family into the workhouse', a 'bitter prophecy', observed the son, that 'became bitterly true'.[48]

The Wolstanton and Burslem workhouse at Chell, where the Shaws found themselves, was the potential destination for anyone unlucky enough to fall foul of the harsh economic and managerial imperatives of the 1840s. Despite his brief stay there, the 'Bastille's' rigid segregation (which limited contact with his mother to Sunday afternoons), humiliating and often brutal discipline and 'offensively poor' food made an indelible impression on the 10-year-old potter. Salvation came after a few weeks, when Enoch, having been refused employment at other firms, found work with a friend, a toy manufacturer.[49] Safety nets were few and far between for all victims of the economic downturn. During the mid-1830s poor relief had provoked fierce political argument in North Staffordshire, with the NUOP's leaders campaigning fruitlessly for a greater working-class voice on the bodies that administered it, notably the Boards of Guardians set up under the 1834 Poor Law Amendment Act.[50] Workers impelled into strike action received no public relief, but anyone seeking assistance faced a parsimonious parochial system that conceded nothing to sentiment. In March 1840 severe distress prompted an open meeting at the Burslem Town Hall. A fund set up at the time of the queen's marriage in February but now exhausted had given notice of the 'alarming extent' of local suffering. The meeting resolved to press the Board of Guardians to distribute food under section 53 of the 1834 Act, which permitted 'occasional relief' in 'cases of urgent necessity'. The following day the guardians convened at the Chell workhouse and rejected the call. The 'interests of ratepayers' must be protected, they avowed; relief should come from private subscription, not public money.[51]

The NUOP's defeat in early 1837 left working-class activism in the Potteries in abeyance. Filling the vacuum was a new programme designed to transform economic and social relations through radical reform of the nation's governance. Rather than a narrow reaction to working-class hardship, Chartism drew upon entrenched resentments that transcended the vicissitudes of the trade cycle. Loss of workplace authority and identity, rampant job insecurity, the widening gap between rich and poor and the degraded conditions of urban and industrial living were among the ingredients in a stew of class antipathy which was exacerbated by the failure of the Whig governments, and the middle classes who sustained them, to promote further reform.[52] Popular radicalism had been gaining strength throughout the decade. Campaigns in support of the ten-hour day and against the New Poor Law fed the radical appetite, with the latter especially effective in mobilising discontent. Also instrumental in politicising class attitudes was the continued hostility exhibited towards trade unions. The prosecution and transportation of the Dorchester labourers in 1834 and the similar treatment meted out to the Glasgow cotton spinners four years later elicited widespread protests, intensifying the sense of injustice felt by working-class communities everywhere.

The older view that saw minimal connection between Chartism and organised labour is no longer tenable. As Malcolm Chase notes, the prolonged depression between 1836 and 1842 'accentuated the relevance of Chartism to trade unionists', who struggled to defend workers' interests in the face of sustained legal and political attack.[53] In North Staffordshire the Chartist appeal found a receptive audience among working men and women, with potters conspicuous from the outset. Robert Fyson describes the trade union contribution to the early Chartism movement in the Potteries as 'considerable', and finds a 'substantial continuity of leadership' with potters' unionism and the general unionism of the 1830s.[54] Of the relationship between rank-and-file potters and Chartism, we know much less. From the first public meetings held in August 1838 at the Sea Lion inn in Hanley, crowds gathered in their thousands to hear Chartist orators urge political reform. Potters made up a large proportion of those present, yet the depth of enthusiasm for the Charter, and for the strategy of seeking social and economic transformation through political means, is difficult to gauge. Although local Chartism built upon existing radical foundations, including trade unionism, its trajectory closely followed that of the national movement. In the twelve months after its launch in 1838–9, when crowd numbers were at their peak, trade and employment conditions actually improved in the Potteries. However, by the spring of 1840 the depression had returned with a vengeance. As the suffering intensified over the next two years, Chartists consolidated and expanded their organisational activities, with potters again to the fore.[55]

The working-class unity proclaimed by the People's Charter concealed a marked diversity in local response.[56] An impressive 10,000 people from North Staffordshire signed the 1842 petition to Parliament calling for greater political and other rights, but support for the movement was far from uniform across the six towns. The main centre of Chartist activity was Hanley; there, at a mass demonstration on 14 November 1838 during the potters' holiday week, Feargus O'Connor, Chartism's acknowledged national leader, made his first public appearance in the area. By 1842 the town boasted two well-supported branches of the National Charter Association. Chartism also found strong support in Longton, to the southeast. In contrast, Burslem, 'the mother town' to the north, proved more resistant, a fact celebrated by the solicitor John Ward, who wrote that few of his town's operatives had succumbed to the 'revolutionary doctrines which, under the name of *Chartism*, are at present so widely and fearfully inculcated by reckless and unprincipled men'.[57] Why Burslem, a populous industrial community and a stronghold of trade unionism, lagged behind in its enthusiasm for political reform is difficult to determine. Fyson suggests a number of factors, including the attitude of the town's ruling elite and the competition from neighbouring Hanley, which had established itself as the focus of radical activity.[58] At the base of these loyalties lay the strength of community identity in the six towns, whose predominantly working-class populations remained resiliently independent of one another.

Chartist beliefs were not the only ones vying for popular approval in the Potteries. After January 1839 large crowds turned out to hear campaigners press for repeal of the Corn Laws. Anti-Corn Law League meetings attracted working-class as well as middle-class audiences, and repeal petitions included many working men and women among the signatories.[59] However, for Chartists and their supporters, the League's momentum proved problematic. Although working-class radicals were traditionally sympathetic to free trade, fears that cheaper bread meant lower wages left many workers unpersuaded by repeal's merits. In North Staffordshire troubled relations between the two movements culminated in a mass confrontation in Hanley in May 1841. Yet Chartists could not ignore the benefits of cross-class collaboration. In August's general election they actively supported the Liberal free-trader J. L. Ricardo, and later in the year helped Liberal manufacturers in Stoke defeat the laying of a church rate.[60]

Owenite socialists also returned to the fray. Owenism in North Staffordshire was 'entirely a working-class movement', untainted by wealthy philanthropic or middle-class commercial influence,[61] and its supporters included prominent Chartists such as the potters George Mart and William Ellis. Even more than in 1833–4, religious rather than class antagonism posed the greatest difficulty for Owenite campaigners. Local debates with Christian speakers in 1838 and 1839 drew audiences in their hundreds, but Owenism's organisational revival was now spreading alarm among the Anglican establishment, headed by the Bishop of Exeter, Henry Phillpotts, which vilified the movement and its founder as synonymous with infidelity.[62] Matters came to a head in the Potteries on 22 June 1840, when Owen himself fell victim to a well-orchestrated ambush, involving dissenters as well as Anglicans. Rioters physically prevented him lecturing at the Social Institution in Burslem, ironically forcing him to take refuge a quarter of a mile away at the home of an opponent, the master potter Enoch Wood. Among those defending Owenite beliefs was a 24-year-old Welsh-born pottery worker, William Evans, who had relocated to North Staffordshire from Worcester the previous year. Evans's anger blazed brightly at Owen's manhandling in Burslem, and he was in no doubt as to who was responsible. A short time earlier John Brindley, Owen's most dogged critic, had given a series of lectures in Stoke and Hanley in which he sought to expose the 'infidelity and atheism' of socialism. Evans roundly condemned Brindley's incitement of the 'lawless mob'; he was equally disparaging of his impact upon the local industrial community at a time of severe hardship. 'Many at the present moment in this district, and elsewhere, are in want of employment; and, perhaps, in want of bread, through the influence and calumnies of this star of modern intolerance', he wrote.[63]

Owenite activity diminished in the Potteries after 1840, but the deepening depression proved fertile ground for Chartists. By 1842 support for the movement in Hanley, Longton and other towns had reached impressive levels. In April Parliament again rejected the Chartist petition, increasing popular frustration at the political classes' insensitivity to democratic reform. The summer of 1842 brought unprecedented tension and ultimately violence to many communities across industrial England, including the Potteries. Such tensions were not new to the area; in May 1839, as Chartists delivered their first petition to Parliament, an outbreak of violence in Longton resulted in a riotous confrontation involving police and yeomanry, leaving two people dead and others injured and arrested. Three years later, with economic conditions even more critical, the level of violence – and the level of reprisal – was far greater, as class resentments boiled over into two days of sustained destruction.

Such an explosion could not have occurred without a deep-rooted alienation from the prevailing order.[64] The Potteries outbreak of 15–16 August had its immediate origins in a strike by Longton colliers over wage reductions. As the action spread, pottery manufacturers suspended production due to the lack of fuel, exacerbating the general distress and, as Charles Shaw remembered it, the 'disaffection'.[65] Chartists were actively involved from an early stage. Their confidence was high; in July William Ellis led a raiding party on a meeting at the Shire Hall, Stafford, forcing the county's rulers into an ignominious exit. Less symbolically, Chartists intensified their campaign against the New Poor Law. Applications for relief had swelled, outstripping the capacity of workhouses to accommodate them. On the last day of July large numbers of paupers marched through the Potteries protesting their plight. Nine days later thousands gathered on the Crown Bank to hear Chartist orators demand action against a system that in the words of the veteran John Richards – whose long life would end in 1856 in the Stoke workhouse[66] – threatened 'to overwhelm us in universal poverty'.[67]

A further Chartist intervention helped precipitate the dissolve into violence. On 14 August, a Sunday, the Leicester poet and lecturer Thomas Cooper spoke in Fenton and Longton before addressing a massed evening crowd in Hanley. Perched on a chair in front of the Crown Inn, he condemned the 'human suffering' of those whom unjust laws and inadequate wages had reduced to penury and starvation. After learning that a Manchester trades' conference had issued a call for a general strike in support of the Charter, he returned the next morning to Hanley, where he urged the assembled throng to join the turnout, insisting that 'no government on earth could resist their demand' and that, if peaceably done, 'no law could touch them'.[68] Mass action was already underway in the textile towns of Stalybridge, Ashton-under-Lyne and Oldham, where manufacturers had made deep cuts to wage levels; this action now intensified as striking workers pulled the plugs from boilers, disabling the machinery that operated the mills. As the unrest spread into West Yorkshire and beyond, there were violent confrontations with the police and military.

In the Potteries Chartist pleas for an orderly turnout were quickly set aside as a crowd of men and boys descended on Shelton colliery, where they drained boilers and pumping engines. Shortly afterwards a mob invaded the Hanley police office, releasing prisoners and seizing weapons. The two days of mayhem that followed saw widespread destruction and intimidation. Some of the violence was random and opportunistic; elsewhere, crowds sought revenge against those deemed responsible for the current misery. Buildings targeted included the Court of Requests (a small debtors' court with the power to impose prison terms), the Stoke workhouse and the office of the Poor Law Board secretary. Among private houses to suffer were those of the poor rates' collector, and master potter, C. J. Mason. In Penkhull invaders gutted the home of the stipendiary magistrate Thomas Bailey Rose; the contents lost included his valuable law library. Albion House in Shelton, home of the county magistrate William Parker, was also reduced to ruins, while in Longton a mob looted and set fire to the Rectory, ransacking the wine cellar with predictable results. Although a local newspaper judged the attack 'inexplicable',[69] the rector, Rev. Benjamin Vale, was a member of the Stoke Board of Guardians and had earlier made ill-chosen comments on the plight of the poor. A similar fate befell the Hanley parsonage, whose occupant was also a Board member and widely regarded as indifferent to those in need.

A dispute over miners' wages had mutated into a large-scale uprising, the course of which no one, least of all local Chartist leaders, could anticipate or control. The authorities were initially wrong-footed by the outbreak, but the renewal of violence on the second day galvanised them into action. In Burslem troops opened fire on a stone-throwing crowd, killing a young shoemaker from Leek. Order was largely restored the following morning, 17 August, and shortly afterwards the mines and pottery factories reopened. The August turnout was not the end of industrial action in North Staffordshire; colliers struck again in Longton a few months later and again the following year. But there was to be no repeat of the events that for two days turned the Potteries upside-down. The aftermath was no less dramatic. In September and October 276 individuals accused of participation in the violence came before the courts in special sessions in Stafford. They included many pottery workers, among them William Ellis, convicted and transported – almost certainly on the basis of perjured evidence – for his alleged role in the sacking of the Hanley parsonage.[70] Potters had not planned or led the outbreak of 15–16 August, but were drawn into it as the violence gathered momentum. Of the 56 North Staffordshire men transported, and of the 116 men and women imprisoned for up to two years in the wake of the upheaval, the largest number, 21 and 67 respectively, were potters.[71]

In the immediate wake of the uprising, the *North Staffordshire Mercury* expressed the hope that a 'few weeks of good trade would bring a perfect restoration to tranquillity'.[72] But the depression proved stubborn and not until the following summer did conditions start to ease, helped by a recovery in the transatlantic market. Finally, in September 1843 the *Mercury* could report that trade in the Potteries was 'gradually improving', with 'regular work' at most manufactories.[73] How would pottery workers respond to the upturn? The events of the past decade had left them scarred and vulnerable. With no industry-wide organisation, operatives had few safeguards against masters' attempts to lower wage costs and retain control in the workplace. The allowance system was especially irksome. While not all employers engaged in it, the practice was an affront, a daily reminder of individual and collective impotence. The approach of the new contract season also brought rumours of a reduction in wages, concentrating workers' minds. On 6 September 1843 a new union, the United Branches of Operative Potters (UBOP), was established. Its prime objective was the elimination of the allowance system and the curbing of other trade abuses, including good-from-oven payment. Three months later, on 2 December, the union's newspaper, *The Potters' Examiner and Workman's Advocate*, made its first appearance. Its editor was the young Owenite activist William Evans (see Figure 1.2).

Evans was born to a potter's family in Swansea on 23 January 1816. David, his father, was a highly regarded floral and fruit artist; William described him as 'the finest wild-flower painter in the trade'.[74] In 1823 the family left South Wales and moved to Coalport and then, about 1827, to Worcester, where David took employment at the Grainger, Lee factory at St Martin's Gate and William and his elder brother Alexander began seven-year apprenticeships as painters and gilders. Although we do not know when William first became involved in defending workers' rights, the 1836–7 strike seems to have been a turning point in his life, and he constantly returned to the topic in his public utterances. Responding in the following decade to criticism of his record as a labour activist, Evans

Figure 1.2 William Evans (1816–87).

insisted that he had done everything possible as a member of the 'Worcester Miscellaneous Lodge of United Potters' to help the Staffordshire workers who were suffering 'the full persecuting powers of the employers'. Apart from raising funds and soliciting support from other trades, he also claimed to have written the first account of the strike to appear in the London newspapers.[75] Such activities came at a price and led to him, according to his own testimony, being refused employment in the trade in which he had 'served a legitimate apprenticeship'. Years later Evans remarked that he could not believe 'that his efforts to promote the interests of labour would have led to his proscription'.[76]

If Evans's employment history sometimes proves elusive, we can be surer of his involvement in the Owenite movement, in which he served as first secretary of the Worcester branch in 1837–8.[77] Forty years later he described how he became acquainted with Owen, 'the great philanthropist', in Worcester through a mutual friend, the furniture dealer and poet Vincent Cooke.[78] We also know that on the last day of April 1838 he married a local woman, Susan Miller. Their union would endure for nearly half a century, ending in William's death in 1887. In 1839 the Evans family moved to the Potteries, where William found work at Samuel Alcock's Hill Pottery in Burslem, where his father was already employed. It was at Alcock's, he recalled near the end of his life, that 'I perfected my training in the art of pottery'.[79] The birth in February 1840 of a daughter, Julia,[80] increased his domestic responsibilities but brought no lessening of his commitment to popular radicalism. Like William Ellis, Evans had no difficulty in reconciling Owenite values with the fight for political reform, and by 1842, if not much earlier, he had become an active Chartist, rising quickly through the ranks. On 21 May, on the Crown Bank, Hanley, he chaired a large public meeting to welcome Feargus O'Connor to the Potteries; later that evening the crowd reassembled at nearby premises, where Evans, described in a newspaper report as 'an operative from Burslem', again took the chair.[81]

Evans's growing presence was confirmed at a Chartist meeting at the Sea Lion inn on 5 July. After seconding the motion calling for a unified stance among the middle and labouring classes, he urged the adoption of the Charter 'as the cure for all monopolies'.[82] On 9 August, a week before the outbreak, he was back on the Crown Bank, where he was among those who addressed the huge crowd, including hundreds of paupers, at the rally chaired by William Ellis. After John Richards had spoken for an hour and twenty minutes, it was Evans's turn. Seconding the resolution that called for immediate action to stem the tide of suffering, he lashed out at the class of capitalists – the Arkwrights, the Peels and the Cobdens among them – whose very existence, he argued, derived from the introduction of machinery. This new breed had raised the 'anti-population cry' and designated the real producers of wealth, whom the machines had displaced, as a 'surplus population'. To rid the country of its surplus, they proposed emigration, but finding public opinion against them, they turned to 'that brilliant specimen of Whig christian legislation, the infernal New Poor Law'. In Evans's view, only one plan could relieve existing poverty, and that was to bring together 'the uncultivated land and the unemployed labour of the country'. There was more than adequate land – 14 million acres – to supply the hungry population with food, clothing and shelter, 'and it was the height of cruelty for a Government to see the people starve, whilst such abundant means existed for making them happy'. It had after all voted immense sums for war in India and the benefit of the East India Company; it also freed the 'black slaves', again at huge cost, but 'the white slave was not an object of their compassion'.[83]

Still only in his twenties, Evans was already a seasoned performer on the radical stage by the time of the union's founding in September 1843. The United Branches of Operative Potters differed from its predecessor, the NUOP, in the more limited power vested in its central committee and in the extent of its support – membership levels never reached above 2,000. A federation rather than an amalgamation of branch unions, its constitution left each branch free to conduct its own business, make its own decisions, including that of whether to take strike action, and levy its own subscriptions. Evidence of the condition of individual branches after the NUOP's collapse is hard to find; according to W. H. Warburton, there is no 'definite proof of their existence between the end of 1837 and February 1842'.[84] But branches had clearly survived in some, albeit attenuated, form. With the labour market improving, they now sought to regain the initiative in the struggle to defend potters' wages and conditions.

Historians have applauded the early achievements of the new union. Lacking the 'high incentive of its predecessor', noted Harold Owen, it compensated for it by 'the quiet resolve of its methods, and the definite, unheroic character of its aims'.[85] Warburton, writing a generation later, agreed. Relatively weak in numbers, the union was 'virile and active' in its opposition to allowances and in its 'strenuous efforts' to raise wages, in both of which endeavours it achieved success.[86] Historians have also acknowledged that UBOP took seriously the question of historic debt. In December 1843 Sheffield unionists were again in the area, petitioning 'to get back a portion of that money which we so generously lent when the Potters were in the greatest distress imaginable'.[87] In response, the UBOP committee put in place plans to repay that and other, smaller obligations arising from the 1836–7 strike. Unfortunately, bringing such a long-standing matter to a satisfactory resolution proved easier said than done. Collections produced only a fraction of the sums owed, and nearly three years after the union's establishment, William Evans could lament the 'few paltry hundreds' that had been remitted.[88]

Evans would have a decisive role in shaping the future of the union he had helped found. His main instrument was *The Potters' Examiner*, the weekly newspaper that he edited, published and printed on UBOP's behalf. It is hard to overstate the extent of the paper's importance to the new body. From the outset, Evans used it to help weld together the industry's separate trades, to give a greater representation to the out-potteries, which had expanded over the past decade, and above all to give a voice to working potters. Evans dedicated the paper to his 'fellow labourers', the real producers of wealth, 'the very foundation of all social existence'. If its editorial tone was often moralistic and its language florid, its intent was practical, even conservative. 'We ask not for wealth, – we care not for title, – we seek, only, to defend, in the purest feelings of justice and equity, the interests of labour, without infringing on the rights of capital', the opening issue declared. Evans eschewed political affiliation, turning away from Chartism even as he continued to subscribe to its broad tenets. The *Examiner*, he wrote, 'is the organ of a Trade's Society and as that Society is composed of individuals of every grade of political opinion, it would be the height of folly, under these circumstances, to mix up politics with the advocacy of the rights of labour'.[89] Yet he was not averse to dispensing political advice, for example, recommending in March 1844 that manufacturers made unsuitable candidates for election to the Poor Law Guardians Board.[90]

Evans consistently opposed the use of strike action, a position he claimed in a speech to the National Conference of Trades in March 1845 that reflected the views of his 'constituents'.[91] The events of the previous decade loomed large in his memory. Writing in 1846, he argued that the 'disastrous turnout of 1836–37 should stand as a warning to all future combinations of working potters'. During it, 'every possible suffering was endured by the determined operatives' before they were compelled to bend to 'the more potent power' of the employers. In particular, he noted the strike's ruinous affect upon the family economy. 'The savings of years were scattered in the space of twenty weeks; and no after exertion could replace the little hoarded means, thus irreparably lost', he wrote.[92] Asked two decades later by the chair of a parliamentary committee as to whether the strike had brought any change to good-from-oven and other practices that prompted the potters' walkout, he replied that no, it had not brought a permanent change, adding: 'it led to a great amount of distress among the workmen; 20 weeks of distress and an expenditure of 50,000*l*. of money; and the sacrifice of their household goods, and then the men had to return to work thoroughly beaten and impoverished'.[93]

Evans's rejection of strikes meant no dilution of his resistance to the abuses that continued to bedevil industrial relations at the potbank. In December 1843, under his *nom de plume* of 'Mentor', he pressed Burslem's chief constable to take action against manufacturers who evaded the 1831 Truck Act.[94] He was equally forthright in advising C. J. Mason to settle a long-running dispute at his Fenton works. 'It is a well known fact, that, throughout the length and breadth of the Potteries, there is not a single manufacturer, be his price never so bad, that pays such an extremely low price for labour as you do', the editor told him.[95] Above all, Evans resented the underlying unfairness of the industry's contractual arrangements, which he likened to enslavement, a standard comparison in radical discourse by this period. The annual agreement is 'nothing less than the sale of human flesh and blood – the transfer of one human being to the care of another, to be used, or abused, as the purchaser pleases, for the space of one year'.[96] Erring employers aside, the focus of his anger was Thomas Bailey Rose. The magistrate's unabashed enforcement of the master's prerogative cost him dearly in the 1842 outbreak, but failed to curb his hostility to organised labour. In December 1843, in the wake of a strike at William Hackwood's Hanley factory, he threatened union members who contravened the 1823 Master and Servant Act with three months' hard labour. Responding, Evans derided Rose's version of justice: 'There is a thoughtless defiance in your words, that borders on a total disregard of all law, and a supreme contempt for all judicial investigation.'[97]

Although Evans would continue to campaign against employers and their defenders who trampled on the rights of labour, in early 1844 his ambition to free working potters from the shackles of industrial slavery took a new turn. We cannot be certain exactly when he converted to emigrationism; in August 1842, as already noted, wearing his Chartist clothes, he criticised capitalists' promotion of emigration as a means of reducing Britain's population surplus. On 6 January the editor advertised for sale at his Shelton office a list of eighty-two books and pamphlets. First and second on the list were two well-known primers for those considering a transatlantic move: George Flower's *The Errors of Emigrants* and *America and England Contrasted, or, the Emigrants' Handbook and Guide to the United States*.[98] The following week the *Examiner* began publishing a series of letters from Staffordshire residents who had settled in America. Evans's purpose, on the face of it, was transparent: as 'the spirit of Emigration seems to increase, daily', it behoved him to provide those wishing to leave their homeland 'for the more liberal institutions and broad lands of the far west' with as much reliable information as possible.[99] And what better source was there than the first-hand testimony of friends and neighbours who had already taken the momentous step? The following month another, grander motive surfaced, as he outlined a visionary plan for ridding the pottery industry forever of the curse of underemployment.

The tribulations pottery workers experienced during the 1830s and early 1840s did not lead inevitably to emigration; however, without that experience, it is unlikely that the Potters' Emigration Society would have come into being. Pottery workers were deeply resentful of their treatment, as the testimony of pioneer settlers will show. Comparatively well recompensed for their labour, their resentment embodied a broader disenchantment with industrial culture and a surprising degree of disaffection with the country of their birth and upbringing. Seven years had elapsed since the settlement of the great strike, but the frequency and intensity of its recollection suggests a lasting impact on potters' attitudes, while for those who needed it, the Sheffield debt provided a continuing reminder. Yet these factors counted for little without William Evans. A youthful veteran of Owenite, Chartist and workplace battles, he urged potters to learn the correct lessons from the events of 1836–7 and 1842. Strikes had proved ineffective, leaving unionism in disarray and workers defenceless against newly empowered masters and the march of mechanisation. Only by removing surplus labour to the virgin lands of the American West, he believed, could potters guarantee their trade's survival.

Notes

1 Isaac Smith, 'Early Days in Columbia County: Potters' Emigration Society', *Wisconsin State Register*, 12 June 1880.
2 *Staffordshire Sentinel*, 22 April 1854.
3 On the broader canvas, see Clements, 'Trade Unions and Emigration, 1840–80', pp. 167–80; and Marjory Harper, 'Obstacles and Opportunities: Labour Emigration to the "British World" in the Nineteenth Century', *Continuity and Change* 34:1 (2019), 43–62.
4 John Burnett, *Idle Hands: The Experience of Unemployment, 1790–1990* (London: Routledge, 1994), p. 92.
5 *Ibid.*, p. 93.
6 Warburton, *The History of the Trade Union Organisation*, p. 104.
7 Francis William Botham, 'Working-Class Living Standards in North Staffordshire, 1750–1914' (PhD dissertation, London School of Economics, 1982), pp. 169–70, 176–7.
8 *Parliamentary Papers: Children's Employment Commission. Second Report of the Commissioners. Trades and Manufactures. Part 1. Reports and Evidence from the Sub-Commissioners* (London, 1842), p. c2.
9 [Charles Shaw,] 'An Old Potter', *When I Was a Child* (London: Methuen, 1903), p. 42.

10 Pioneering work on emigration and the economic cycle includes Brinley Thomas, *Migration and Economic Growth: A Study of Great Britain and the Atlantic Economy* (Cambridge: Cambridge University Press, 1954; 2nd edn, 1973); and Dudley Baines, *Migration in a Mature Economy: Emigration and Internal Migration in England and Wales, 1861–1900* (Cambridge: Cambridge University Press, 1985). On incomplete data, see Raymond L. Cohn, *Mass Migration Under Sail: European Immigration to the Antebellum United States* (Cambridge: Cambridge University Press, 2009), pp. 25–8.

11 Cohn, *Mass Migration Under Sail*, pp. 79, 83–5, 88.

12 Van Vugt, *Britain to America*, p. 10.

13 Richards, *The Genesis of International Mass Migration*, pp. 129–30.

14 Richards, *Britannia's Children*, p. 149.

15 Belich, *Replenishing the Earth*, pp. 106ff.

16 William E. Van Vugt, *Portrait of an English Migration: North Yorkshire People in North America* (Montreal and Kingston: McGill-Queen's University Press, 2021), p. 8.

17 M. W. Greenslade and J. G. Jenkins, *The Victoria History of the County of Stafford* (London: Institute of Historical Research, 1967), vol. 2, pp. 1–27; M. I. Nixon, 'The Emergence of the Factory System in the Staffordshire Pottery Industry' (PhD dissertation, University of Aston, 1976), pp. 1–40; Frank Burchill and Richard Ross, *A History of the Potters' Union* (Hanley: Ceramic and Allied Trades Union, 1977), p. 27; Dupree, *Family Structure in the Staffordshire Potteries*, pp. 52–3.

18 Richard Whipp, *Patterns of Labour: Work and Social Change in the Pottery Industry* (London: Routledge, 1990) is invaluable on the workplace environment. On status divisions, see also [Shaw,] *When I Was a Child*, pp. 193–4.

19 For the 1825 dispute, see Warburton, *The History of the Trade Union Organisation*, pp. 29–33; Burchill and Ross, *A History of the Potters' Union*, pp. 57–8; and Thomas, *The Rise of the Staffordshire Potteries*, pp. 187–90.

20 Michael Haynes, 'Employers and Trade Unions, 1825–1850', in John Rule (ed.), *British Trade Unionism, 1750–1850: The Formative Years* (London: Longman, 1988), p. 249.

21 For the 1823 Act, see John V. Orth, *Combination and Conspiracy: A Legal History of Trade Unionism, 1721–1906* (Oxford: Clarendon Press, 1991), pp. 109–11; Malcolm Chase, *Early Trade Unionism: Fraternity, Skill, and the Politics of Labour* (Aldershot: Ashgate, 2000), pp. 110–12; Robert J. Steinfeld, *Coercion, Contract, and Free Labor in the Nineteenth Century* (Cambridge: Cambridge University Press, 2001), pp. 47–9; and John Saville, *The Consolidation of the Capitalist State, 1800–1850* (London: Pluto Press, 1994), 21–3.

22 Warburton, *The History of the Trade Union Organisation*, pp. 52–4; Thomas, *The Rise of the Staffordshire Potteries*, pp. 190–1; and Robert Fyson, 'Unionism, Class and Community in the 1830s: Aspects of the National Union of Operative Potters', in Rule (ed.), *British Trade Unionism*, pp. 201–3.

23 For the NAPL, see Chase, *Early Trade Unionism*, pp. 140–5; and Robert Sykes, 'Trade Unionism and Class Consciousness: The "Revolutionary" Period of General Unionism', in Rule (ed.), *British Trade Unionism*, pp. 180–6.
24 Webb and Webb, *The History of Trade Unionism*, p. 118.
25 Warburton, *The History of the Trade Union Organisation*, pp. 66–7.
26 John Boyle, 'An Account of Strikes in the Potteries, in the Years 1834 and 1836', *Journal of the Statistical Society of London* 1:1 (May 1838), 38.
27 W. Hamish Fraser, 'Robert Owen and the Workers', in John Butt (ed.), *Robert Owen: Prince of Cotton Spinners* (Newton Abbot: David & Charles, 1971), pp. 94–5; Warburton, *The History of the Trade Union Organisation*, pp. 72–7.
28 Chase, *Early Trade Unionism*, pp. 138–9, 148–52.
29 Fyson, 'Unionism, Class and Community in the 1830s', pp. 206–8.
30 *Ibid.*, pp. 209–12.
31 Warburton, *The History of the Trade Union Organisation*, p. 81.
32 Burchill and Ross, *A History of the Potters' Union*, p. 64; Warburton, *The History of the Trade Union Organisation*, pp. 87–8.
33 Owen, *The Staffordshire Potter*, p. 28.
34 Boyle, 'An Account of Strikes in the Potteries', p. 38.
35 *Ibid.*, p. 42.
36 This account of the strike has been compiled from Warburton, *The History of the Trade Union Organisation*, pp. 88–101; Burchill and Ross, *A History of the Potters' Union*, pp. 65–74; Owen, *The Staffordshire Potter*, pp. 27–46; Fyson, 'Chartism in North Staffordshire', pp. 69–71; Fyson, 'Unionism, Class and Community in the 1830s', pp. 213–14; and Boyle, 'An Account of Strikes in the Potteries', pp. 41–3.
37 Owen, *The Staffordshire Potter*, p. 44.
38 Burchill and Ross, *A History of the Potters' Union*, p. 74.
39 Boyle, 'An Account of Strikes in the Potteries', p. 44.
40 Iorwerth Prothero, *Artisans and Politics in Early Nineteenth-Century London: John Gast and His Times* (London: Methuen, 1979), pp. 316–17.
41 Good-from-oven's absence may explain the strike's more limited affect in the Lane End area of the Potteries, where china making was centred. See Botham, 'Working-Class Living Standards in North Staffordshire, 1750–1914', pp. 175–6.
42 Warburton, *The History of the Trade Union Organisation*, p. 103.
43 *The Times*, 17 December 1839, quoting the *Staffordshire Examiner*.
44 *North Staffordshire Mercury*, 9 May 1840.
45 Fyson, 'Chartism in North Staffordshire', p. 291.
46 Warburton, *The History of the Trade Union Organisation*, pp. 106–11 (quotation p. 111); Owen, *The Staffordshire Potter*, pp. 56–60.
47 T. A. Lockett, *Davenport Pottery and Porcelain, 1794–1887* (Newton Abbot: David & Charles, 1972), pp. 20–5.
48 [Shaw,] *When I Was a Child*, pp. 90–1.
49 *Ibid.*, pp. 96–118 (quotation p. 101).
50 Fyson, 'Chartism in North Staffordshire', pp. 65–7.
51 *North Staffordshire Mercury*, 7 and 14 March 1840.

52 Malcolm Chase, *Chartism: A New History* (Manchester: Manchester University Press, 2007), pp. 20–2.
53 Chase, *Early Trade Unionism*, p. 186. See also Robert Sykes, 'Early Chartism and Trade Unionism in South-East Lancashire', in James Epstein and Dorothy Thompson (eds), *The Chartist Experience: Studies in Working-Class Radicalism and Culture, 1830–1860* (London: Macmillan, 1982), pp. 152–93.
54 Fyson, 'Chartism in North Staffordshire', pp. 93–5.
55 Fyson, 'Chartism in North Staffordshire', pp. 117–32.
56 Asa Briggs (ed.), *Chartist Studies* (London: Macmillan, 1960), p. 26.
57 John Ward, *The Borough of Stoke-upon-Trent* (London: W. Lewis and Son, 1843), p. 239.
58 Fyson, 'Chartism in North Staffordshire', p. 127.
59 See, for example, *North Staffordshire Mercury*, 19 February 1842.
60 Fyson, 'Chartism in North Staffordshire', pp. 142–6.
61 Harrison, *Robert Owen and the Owenites in Britain and America*, p. 228.
62 *Ibid.*, pp. 216–18.
63 *Sun* (London), 2 July 1840. See also *New Moral World*, 4 July 1840.
64 Robert Fyson, 'The Crisis of 1842: Chartism, the Colliers' Strike and the Outbreak in the Potteries', in Epstein and Thompson (eds), *The Chartist Experience*, pp. 194–220 is the most authoritative discussion of the 1842 disturbances in North Staffordshire. Robert Anderson, *The Potteries Martyrs* (Stoke-on-Trent: Heritage Books, 1993) is a lively account. For the wider setting, see Chase, *Chartism*, pp. 193–229.
65 [Shaw,] *When I Was a Child*, p. 158.
66 Robert Fyson, 'Homage to John Richards', in Owen Ashton, Robert Fyson and Stephen Roberts (eds), *The Duty of Discontent: Essays for Dorothy Thompson* (London: Mansell, 1995), p. 89.
67 *Northern Star and Leeds General Advertiser*, 20 August 1842.
68 *The Life of Thomas Cooper*, with an introduction by John Saville (Leicester: Leicester University Press, 1971), pp. 187–91. Mick Jenkins, *The General Strike of 1842* (London: Lawrence and Wishart, 1980), pp. 142–59, describes the events surrounding the strike call. On Chartists' conflicted attitude to the outbreaks, see E. H. Hunt, *British Labour History, 1815–1914* (London: Weidenfeld & Nicolson, 1981), p. 225.
69 *North Staffordshire Mercury*, 20 September 1842. The *Mercury*'s report provides the most detailed contemporary account of the rioting. See also [Shaw,] *When I Was a Child*, pp. 155–71.
70 See Robert Fyson, 'The Transported Chartist: The Case of William Ellis', in Owen Ashton, Robert Fyson and Stephen Roberts (eds), *The Chartist Legacy* (Woodbridge: Merlin Press, 1999), pp. 80–101. Sentenced to twenty-one years' transportation in Van Diemen's Land, Ellis would never return to England or see his wife and children again.
71 Fyson, 'The Crisis of 1842', p. 211. See also George Rudé, *The Crowd in History: A Study of Popular Disturbances in France and England, 1730–1848* (New York: John Wiley, 1964), pp. 187–91.

72 *North Staffordshire Mercury*, 17 September 1842.
73 *North Staffordshire Mercury*, 2 September 1843.
74 Henry and John Sandon, *Grainger's Worcester Porcelain* (London: Barry & Jenkins, 1989), pp. 20, 34. See also William Turner, *The Ceramics of Swansea and Nantgarw: A History of the Factories* (London and Derby: Bemrise & Sons, 1897), pp. 219–20.
75 *PEWA*, 11 April 1846.
76 *Staffordshire Sentinel*, 22 April 1854.
77 Fyson, 'Chartism in North Staffordshire', pp. 295–6.
78 *Co-operative News*, 11 May 1878.
79 *Pottery Gazette*, 1 October 1886. Evans was involved in the painters' and gilders' walkout at Davenport's factory in 1841, although it is unclear if he was employed there. *Northern Star and Leeds General Advertiser*, 18 September 1841.
80 The couple's first child, also named Julia, had been born the previous January but survived only four months. In total, Susan Evans gave birth to eleven children, five of whom died before the age of two. I am indebted to Mike Beckensall for information on the Evans family.
81 *The Staffordshire Advertiser*, 28 May 1842. See also *North Staffordshire Mercury*, 28 May 1842.
82 *North Staffordshire Mercury*, 9 July 1842.
83 *Northern Star and Leeds General Advertiser*, 20 August 1842.
84 Warburton, *The History of the Trade Union Organisation*, p. 112.
85 Owen, *The Staffordshire Potter*, p. 49.
86 Warburton, *The History of the Trade Union Organisation*, pp. 112–13. See also Burchill and Ross, *A History of the Potters' Union*, p. 95. On unions and wage rises, see Botham, 'Working-Class Living Standards in North Staffordshire, 1750–1914', pp. 182–3.
87 *PEWA*, 16 December 1843.
88 William Evans, *Art and History of the Potting Business* (Shelton: privately printed, 1846), p. x.
89 *PEWA*, 2 December 1843.
90 *PEWA*, 9 March 1844.
91 *Northern Star and National Trades' Journal*, 29 March 1845. The paper changed its subtitle in November 1844 following its move to London.
92 Evans, *Art and History of the Potting Business*, p. ix.
93 *Parliamentary Papers: Report from the Select Committee on Master and Servant*, 1866, p. 60.
94 *PEWA*, 23 December 1843.
95 *PEWA*, 20 January 1844.
96 *PEWA*, 16 December 1843; Marcus Cunliffe, *Chattel Slavery and Wage Slavery: The Anglo-American Context, 1830–1860* (Athens: University of Georgia Press, 1979), p. 11.

97 *PEWA*, 30 March 1844; Christopher Frank, ' "Let But One of Them Come before Me, and I'll Commit Him": Trade Unions, Magistrates, and the Law in Mid-Nineteenth-Century Staffordshire', *Journal of British Studies* 44:1 (2005), 71–6. Also valuable is Marc W. Steinberg, 'Capitalist Development, the Labor Process, and the Law', *American Journal of Sociology* 109:2 (2003), 445–95. For a memoir of Rose's deterrent justice, see T. Hawley, *Sketches of Pottery Life and Character in the Forties and Fifties* (Longton: Hughes & Harber, n.d.), p. 27.
98 *PEWA*, 6 January 1844.
99 *PEWA*, 13 January 1844.

2

1844: An emigration plan

Emigration proved a thorny issue for politicians and policy-makers in early-nineteenth-century Britain. Although the numbers leaving England, Scotland, Wales and Ireland began to rise after 1815 following decades-long interruptions of revolution and war, the mercantilist belief that a nation's strength and prosperity equated principally with the size of its population was hard to dislodge. Resistance to emigration was strong. In 1803, without a single dissenting vote, Parliament passed the Passenger Vessels Act. Described by Eric Richards as 'a piece of class legislation', its humanitarian intent cloaked a desire to reduce emigrant numbers by placing the costs of oceanic travel beyond plebeian reach.[1] The law proved unenforceable. 'Too complex, burdensome and repressive', in the words of one historian, its implementation would have effectively prevented the emergence of the passenger trade in the first half of the nineteenth century.[2]

Westminster lawmakers returned to the trade on a regular basis in the decades after the 1803 Act, and with each parliamentary engagement it was evident how much attitudes to emigration were changing. The change occurred through the perception that the major threat to national prosperity was not a declining but a rapidly rising population. Between the 1811 and 1821 censuses England experienced its highest recorded decennial growth rate, while across the United Kingdom as a whole during the first half of the century population numbers swelled from 16 to over 27 million.[3] Thomas Malthus's warnings about the dire consequences of overpopulation, first aired in 1798 in his 'An Essay on the Principle of Population', helped dissolve opposition to emigration. Malthus himself remained unpersuaded of its long-term value, although acknowledging it could provide temporary relief in meeting the demographic challenge.[4] Others, though, were persuaded, prompted by anxieties over the deteriorating fabric of British life. The return of peace in 1815 brought widespread unemployment and social misery. In the years to follow there was much soul-searching about what a parliamentary committee in 1826, employing a widely used phrase, called the 'redundancy of population' that existed in Britain and especially Ireland, where the impoverishment was deemed most acute.[5] The answer for many lay in Britain's overseas and crucially underpopulated colonies. State-aided emigration to the Cape of Good Hope and the Canadas – there were six such initiatives between 1815 and 1826 – failed to make any dent in Britain's pauper numbers, however.[6] Parish-assisted emigration also failed to have a substantial impact. Although 27,000 people would ultimately benefit from parochial funding under the provisions of the 1834 Poor Law Amendment Act, the annual numbers affected were low, with just over 1,000 leaving England in 1841.[7]

As the pace of industrialisation quickened and Britain experienced intensified social, economic and political turbulence, emigration was increasingly seen as an inevitable and even desirable consequence of the demographic shift. Leading the ideological charge was Edward Gibbon Wakefield, whose theory of systematic colonisation – honed during a three-year residency in Newgate prison – furnished the blueprint for government-aided emigration after 1830. Wakefield's ideas were most fully realised in Australia and New Zealand; they had little direct impact in North America, to where the vast majority of British emigrants journeyed without government assistance, although not without government protection. As opinion changed, successive Acts of Parliament effected a gradual improvement in passenger conditions, in food, space, medicines and other vital matters. If enforcement was lax and the sanctions against ship owners and masters who disobeyed or circumvented the law inadequate, the legislation established an important principle. In 1833 pressure from authorities in Liverpool led to the appointment of the first emigration officer; other ports including Cork, Bristol and Glasgow followed suit. Recruited from the half-pay naval list, emigration officers oversaw enforcement of the Passenger Acts and dispensed sorely needed advice and assistance to those about to embark. They were less effective in monitoring the conditions of on-board travel, as the personal testimonies in Lord Durham's 1838 report vividly confirmed. Two years later, partly in response to Durham, the Whig government established a new body, the Colonial Land and Emigration Commissioners, bringing overdue authority and energy to emigrant protection.[8]

Tighter regulation of the passenger trade mirrored the rise in voluntary emigration and was prompted by the historically low costs of oceanic travel in the early 1830s.[9] Accurate judgements on the volume and destination of transatlantic emigration are notoriously difficult, as available data almost certainly underestimates the number of people leaving Britain for the western continent. During the early 1830s recorded annual arrivals at Britain's North American ports ranged from 30,000 to 66,000, outstripping those received by their republican neighbours to the south; but by the end of the decade the United States had nudged ahead, establishing a lead it would extend after 1847. Muddying the statistical waters was cross-border migration. Lord Durham's assertion that 60 per cent of those landing on Canadian soil subsequently moved to the United States cannot be verified, but the numbers were undoubtedly considerable.[10] By the 1840s the United States had become the principal magnet for British emigrants seeking a new life in the West. Yet this was still a long way from being a mass movement, as least so far as non-Irish emigration was concerned. Of the nearly half a million British men, women and children identified as entering the United States between 1830 and early 1844, when the Potters' Emigration Society was established, by far the largest percentage came from Ireland, where, even before the Great Famine, 'the profound structural and psychological effects of commercialization' helped create the conditions for a large exodus.[11]

If not a mass movement, emigration from England, Scotland and Wales nonetheless recruited from a broad spectrum of society. Flaws and question marks over the data have prevented a definitive judgement on the occupational make-up of emigration to the United States in the 1830s and 1840s. Before 1830, the relatively high costs of travel ensured that the more highly skilled and thus better-paid were overrepresented in emigrant ranks. As travel became more affordable, increased numbers of unskilled workers left for America, although the very poorest, rural and urban, were still largely excluded. In Maldwyn Jones's words, emigration was not a movement of people 'who had already been engulfed by poverty but of those who feared a loss of status if they stayed where they were'.[12] Identifying the changing participation of craft and industrial labour in the transatlantic movement is particularly problematic. As a result it is difficult from passenger and census records to arrive at firm conclusions on how the Industrial Revolution shaped emigration decisions across the occupational terrain. What seems likely is that, Ireland apart, Malthusian fears were largely unrealised. Despite the suffering caused by periodic slumps and by the bad harvests that often accompanied them, Britain's economy, although registering an overall labour surplus after 1830, proved adept at absorbing the nation's rising population, drawing the rural underemployed and displaced into cities and factories rather than impelling them en masse to pursue new lives overseas.[13]

Still, large numbers did leave Britain, and the majority – six out of ten by 1844 – headed for the United States. Why did so many choose the republic as their preferred destination? For a small number of individuals, America offered political or religious sanctuary, but for the remainder emigration was predominantly an economic decision. To conclude that is not to deny a broader impulse; for one thing, economic prospects were rarely defined in narrow wage or cost-of-living terms. What pioneer America promised was the unique opportunity to improve one's condition – material, social and even physical – without the restraining hand of birth, class or status.

Would-be emigrants, whether farmers, labourers, artisans or industrial or white-collar workers, saw emigration to the United States as a path to personal and familial independence. And for so many in the 1830s and 1840s the focus of that ambition was land, a commodity overwhelmingly denied to them at home but widely and inexpensively available in America. To what extent most British emigrants anticipated a swift ascent into the ranks of independent freeholders is a moot point; as James Belich has argued, a move across the Atlantic was as much about freeing people from reliance upon others as it was about economic self-sufficiency. Emigrants sought 'independence from masters, not markets', he concludes.[14] Yet the yeoman ideal was never far away, and in their letters home recent arrivals in the West invariably linked the acquisition of property to the material and emotional contentment enjoyed in what the Penkhull potter William Brunt, writing from Ohio in 1843, termed 'this glorious land of liberty'.[15]

Thirty-eight-year-old William Brunt had arrived in the United States the previous year. Travelling with him from Staffordshire were his wife Eliza, their two sons and William's cousin Job Rigby and his wife, also Eliza. Disembarking at New Orleans, the party boarded the Mississippi steamboat for the journey into the interior. It was already mid-November, and winter. About eighty miles south of St Louis, near Chester, Illinois, frozen conditions brought a premature halt to their progress upriver. A fortuitous encounter with a local farmer directed William to the community of Six-Mile Prairie about thirty miles to the northwest; there, unable to find anyone willing to sell him a farm, he purchased a quarter section, 160 acres, of 'partly wooded and partly Prairie' government land for $200, 'or about £41 5s in English money'. Returning to the Mississippi, William conducted his family in three hired wagons to their new home. Six months later the Brunt farmstead was well established, with a log cabin and barn, twenty acres 'cultivated in Indian corn, wheat, oats, and potatoes' and an impressive collection of livestock and domestic animals. All of them, 'together with our family', were 'in good health', Brunt told his relatives in England.[16]

Brunt's letter from Six-Mile Prairie appeared in *The Potters' Examiner* on 13 January 1844. It was the first in the series published by the paper. Like its successors, Brunt's letter combined information with exhortation. Proud at having put down roots in American soil, his happiness in great measure derived from the hospitable and tolerant society to which his family now found themselves joined. 'The neighbours here are chiefly Americans, and very kindly disposed. They are all *true lovers of liberty*!' he wrote. His cousin Job Rigby, a shoemaker from Burslem, shared his satisfaction. Lacking Brunt's capital resources, Job struggled to make a living at his trade, but through the generosity of a local family, who let them stay rent-free and furnished a two-acre plot for planting, he and his wife took tentative steps to fulfilling their dream of independence. In a letter home, the second in the *Examiner* series, Job enthused about their new-found life on the frontier, indicating they had no desire to return to England. He especially wanted to point up the contrast between old- and new-world society; here they judged a man by his actions, not his external appearance, 'and if he be an honest man he is respected'. Included were instructions on how his parents might reach Illinois, and which items to bring with them. The list included 'prints to make some bonnets; some leather hemp, and thread' as well as a variety of pots ('cups, twifflers, dishes, & c.') which could be exchanged for food or livestock but not for money, which was in short supply everywhere. He ended on the subject of land; for £40 he and Eliza could acquire a forty-acre farm, '*all fenced*', he maintained.[17]

The testimonies of Brunt, Rigby and other recent emigrants were essential to William Evans's purpose. Letters home were the most effective source of information for those considering a move across the Atlantic. By publishing them, Evans hoped to shape an image of the United States as a country of boundless potential, a place where opportunity and freedom were taken for granted rather than being constantly and fruitlessly pursued, as at home. Most of the material in the correspondence was of a practical bent, 'valuable, homely intelligence', as the editor put it. In his second contribution, printed on 10 February, William Brunt responded to questions from a Moses Simpson on topics that included the minimum acreage of government land that could be purchased, whether farming in the West required both horse and oxen, the price of leather, flower cultivation and the costs of erecting a log house.[18] One theme predominated: although a man should take every opportunity to employ the skills of his trade, labour conditions in America were far from settled and it was land that offered the surest route to prosperity and independence. From Scott County, Illinois, William Thompson reported that while he could just about make enough as a carpenter, America was a country best suited to the farmer, with thousands of acres of available land '*without a tree or a stone on; and as level as a Bowling-Green*'.[19] The Hanley-born potter Thomas Filcher, a convert to Mormonism, agreed. Almost anyone could farm in this country, he wrote from Nauvoo, Illinois, 'and when you have gotten 20 acres of land of your own, fenced in and cultivated, you will be as independent as any of the great ones in England'.[20]

On 3 February 1844, three weeks after the publication of Brunt's first letter, the *Examiner*'s editor, writing as 'Mentor', presented his plan ('I give it merely as a suggestion') for solving the problem of underemployment in the pottery industry. The article was ostensibly prompted by a letter the previous week from Peter Watkin, a Burslem potter who would go on to play a leading role in the Society's settlement. But this was no spontaneous rejoinder and Evans had clearly invested considerable thought in his proposal. Watkin had advocated putting the unemployed to work, '*not* in a manufactory, but in a field'.[21] Responding, Evans praised the principle underpinning the idea, but differed on the means of achieving the desired outcome. Instead of the potters' union '*renting* land in England', he argued, 'they should purchase it in America; which, in my opinion, might be more easily and efficiently done, including the expenses of migration'. Warming to his theme, he compared the costs of acquiring land on the two sides of the Atlantic, with predictable results: 'In England, the average price of the most inferior land would be from £30 to £60 per acre; in the Western States of America, the most superior may be purchased at sixty pence per acre! and all freehold!!'

To buttress his argument about the superiority of American land, Evans called upon a 'highly interesting and valuable work', George Flower's *The Errors of Emigrants*, published in 1841, which we have previously noticed him advertising for sale from his Shelton office. Historians of the Potters' Emigration Society have largely ignored Flower's slim volume, but its influence on the project's evolution was considerable. Evans described its author as 'a man of sterling character' with twenty years' experience in the western states. Flower, he wrote,

> established the flourishing town of New Albion, raised the first building! who have risen with hundreds of others, who accompanied him from Old England, from a state of indigence to that of affluence and perfect independence; and who is now living, and enjoying the fruit of his labour, in a free country.

It was in fact over twenty-five years since Flower and fellow dissenter Morris Birkbeck founded the 'English Prairie' settlements in Illinois. Conceived as a response to the dire economic conditions suffered by English farmers and labourers in the aftermath of the Napoleonic wars, the Illinois experiment generated widespread interest and no little controversy in Britain, but its progress was marred by a personal rift between the two men that resulted in the setting-up of separate communities. By the 1840s Birkbeck was long dead (drowned in the Fox River clutching that most English of accoutrements, an umbrella) and his Wanborough community abandoned. Flower's Albion settlement, two miles to the west, did survive, but its founder struggled to make ends meet. In 1849 the family would be forced to sell their farm and relocate to Mount Vernon, Indiana, where George found work as an innkeeper. He and his wife died on the same day in January 1862 while visiting their daughter in Illinois.[22]

In the spring of 1844 Flower's decline into dependency was still some way distant. In *The Errors of Emigrants* he offered a practical guide to transatlantic settlement which sought to demonstrate how to negotiate the pitfalls and idiosyncrasies of American life. At the core of the book was a simple premise. Addressing his brother Edward in England in the opening chapter, he wrote: 'You live in a country where people want land. I live in a country where land wants people.'[23] For Evans, Flower's volume was a valuable amalgam of advocacy and advice, and in his 3 February article he included four extracts designed to give a flavour of the work as a whole. In the first Flower sang the praises of the 'beautiful prairies of Illinois'; but it was the fourth, taken from a chapter on German emigration, to which the editor directed attention. In it the author reported a conversation with a Professor Jaeger of Princeton College, who had expressed the opinion that 'one or more capitalists' might combine to purchase 'a township of land' (or 36 sections of 640 acres) from which each immigrant family would be allocated sixty acres for settlement. As the resulting community prospered, the unallocated land would rise in value, enabling repayment to investors.[24]

Acknowledging his debt to Jaeger, Evans revealed his own plan for reducing surplus labour through emigration to America's West. According to his estimation, out of a total of 7,000 operatives employed in the Staffordshire pottery industry, no more than 600 were out of work; his plan would cut that number in half, while those that remained 'would be in a better position *to demand* a reasonable price for their labour'. Evans calculated the cost of relocating 100 families to America to be £5,000; to fund the scheme he proposed setting up a joint-stock emigration company with 5,000 shares at £1 a share to be paid by weekly instalments of 1s. The principal expenditure would be for the land itself, a half-township, or roughly 12,000 acres, to be acquired at the prevailing government price of $1.25 per acre at a total cost of £3,000. For passage money and other travel expenses across the Atlantic he allocated a further £1,500; the remaining £500 would be spent on livestock which the Company would present to the first settlers in order 'to give them a start in the New World!' Each of the 100 families, typically consisting of three adults and two underage children, would be granted 20 acres of land, making 2,000 in total. The remaining 10,000 acres would, according to the Jaeger model, increase in value as the new township developed.

Evans's other purpose was to imbue pottery workers with the spirit and necessity of transatlantic emigration. He had no patience with understatement. After comparing and dismissing the relative costs of enacting a similar scheme on home soil, he launched into an indictment of British industrial society, whose 'dreary prospect' had already prompted thousands into leaving. So long as the 'manufacturing portion of this nation', he wrote, have to work twelve, fourteen or sixteen hours a day 'in a heated and confined atmosphere, amid whirling dust and rattling engines', so long as they feel themselves wasting away 'from excessive toil and poisonous workshops', they will 'fly to the beautiful prairies of the Far West; — to the freedom of nature, and the most liberal institutions of present man; — to the untaxed plains, rivers, and lakes of a *free* country', where they will pursue 'an unfettered life of ease, health, happiness and content amidst the varied scenes of nature, and the handiworks of God!' Summing up, he insisted again on the plan's practicability. To drive home the message, he returned to George Flower and the 'flourishing' town of 'several thousands of inhabitants, all enjoying the fruits of their labour in plenty and peace' at New Albion. If one man and a few families could accomplish all this, what might be reasonably expected from 7,000 men and hundreds of families?[25]

In the months following his 3 February article Evans reiterated the arguments he hoped would convince pottery workers of the merits of emigration. To justify his plan to place potters 'beyond the fear of want – beyond the influence of those corroding causes which now harass every step of our own existence through life',[26] he drew extensively from a well of artisan ideas that, in Richard Price's words, envisaged 'a productive sphere free from the distortions of unrestrained market competition'.[27] In the editor's view, man's creation, the English factory system, threatened to reduce workers to the status of slaves. Echoing the tone of his Chartist speeches two years earlier, he lashed out at capitalist greed, demanding now not political reform but a modification of the antagonistic social system that proved so detrimental to working-class lives. Evans cast his radical net wide in search of inspiration. In April he commended a proposal for a 'Practical Christian Union' to fight for the establishment of a harmonious society in which wealth would be fairly shared between capital, skill and labour, 'the three great elements' of production'.[28] But while receptive to any solution that brought amelioration to the poor and degraded, nothing in the end would deflect him from his chosen path. Only through renewal in America, he urged, could working-class enslavement be averted: 'American land! – the soil of the free!! – the great refuge for the oppressed labour class of this and all other countries of the known world!!!'[29]

Although Evans invariably linked the potters' plight to wider class resistance, he also reminded them of their advantages over other victims of the factory system. 'We are a concentrated body of men, with every facility for combined and powerful operations', he told them at the beginning of March.[30] Two weeks later Evans conceded that potters 'had not yet arrived at that depressed state' experienced in other industries and were 'better paid for their labour' than the majority of workers elsewhere. However, he warned that this 'superiority of position' was rapidly worsening, and that 'every succeeding day is bringing us nearer to a level with the starving operatives of other trades'. To halt the decline, surplus labour must be reduced, with emigration the surest way to achieve it, although he was also aware that many factors contributed to the oversupply. He especially urged action to restrict the number of apprentices, 'shoals' of whom had been entering the Glasgow, Derby and Worcester out-potteries from other, depressed trades. Another, potentially more serious threat to livelihoods came from 'the great sea of mechanical invention', the tide of which had proved so damaging for textile workers. Although machinery had not yet been introduced into pottery production, prototypes were already available following the award in 1840 of a patent to the Hanley manufacturer John Ridgway and his colleague, the engineer George Wall.[31] The machine's appearance was only a matter of time, and Evans spared nothing in his prophetic outpourings on its likely impact: 'The tendency of all scientific improvements, or mechanical inventions, is to equalise the price of labour, not by raising the lowest ... but *vice versa* or, rather, by *lowering the lowest still lower, and by bringing the highest down to the same frightful level*'.[32]

If pottery workers did not yet feel the effects of mechanisation, the same could not be said for the toxic air of the potbank itself. Mortality rates in North Staffordshire were high in the mid-nineteenth century but significantly higher among those engaged in pottery manufacturing. This was especially the case among males, for whom pulmonary disease was a fact of life. As Marguerite Dupree has pointed out, the disparity reflected gender divisions in an industry where men were exposed to larger amounts of dust for longer periods than women, who were more often employed in finishing tasks.[33] Potting's unhealthy character was widely acknowledged throughout this period. In 1845 Friedrich Engels, drawing upon the Scrivens' investigation conducted four years earlier, was excoriating in his indictment of industry conditions. Children, he wrote, 'with scarcely a single exception, are lean, pale, feeble stunted; nearly all suffer from stomach troubles, nausea, want of appetite, and many of them die of consumption'.[34] In Evans's view, workplace conditions were simply unacceptable, and he charged the pottery industry with inflicting untold physical damage on its workers. What better remedy was there than removal from the factory's 'murderous compound of dust and death' to the pure air of the American prairie. Health and liberty were, for Evans, inextricably linked.[35]

It would be hard to overstate Evans's faith in the transatlantic republic's restorative powers, but establishing how he acquired his views of America, a country he never visited nor to which had any close connection, is difficult. In his Owenite, Chartist and trade union associations, Evans encountered a wide range of ideas in which the United States loomed large. As Gregory Claeys has written, to many radicals and liberals in the post-Revolution decades, America 'remained a beacon of republican virtue, democratic constitutionalism and private enterprise', proof of the compatibility of prosperity and popular rule.[36] However, by the late 1830s critical views had become more common. Many Owenites, in particular, were less impressed by the republic's political achievements than by its social inequalities, which they ascribed to the American worship of private property.[37] Failure to erase the stain of Black slavery also inhibited radical applause. In Evans's usage, the word 'slavery' usually connoted industrial servitude, but he was aware of the South's labour system and of the sectional and racial dynamics that by the mid-1840s threatened to derail the democratic experiment. Had he not been, George Flower, active in the campaign to prevent slavery's legalisation in Illinois, would have made him so. 'Although Britain originally planted the bitter root of slavery upon American soil', Flower wrote in *The Errors of Emigrants*, 'America has now adopted the institution as her own, and has cultivated and extended it, with assiduity and care'.[38]

The absence of personal correspondence limits our assessment of Evans's American vision. His focus on land was shared by many prospective emigrants to the United States in the second quarter of the nineteenth century; less clear are his views on the types of social and economic organisation required to extract maximum benefit from it. As a follower of Robert Owen, Evans knew of his efforts at community-building on both sides of the Atlantic; he was also familiar with the American Shaker and Rappite communities, accounts of which he reprinted in the *Examiner*. 'Will you see this PARADISE before you, and within your reach — and yet quietly and supinely dwell in abodes of poverty?', he typically asked.[39] But in praising these utopian experiments, he drew no specific lessons from them or endorsed the various socialist, cooperative and millenialist beliefs that inspired their founding. Like many working-class activists in this period, Evans did not necessarily share Owen's conception of community. Cooperation for them, according to Robin Thornes, 'meant the act of co-operating with one another for mutual benefit rather than a closely defined system' of the kind created by the Welsh reformer.[40] In March 1844, a month after Evans first outlined his plan, a writer to the *Examiner*, Daniel Alcock, tentatively suggested that it 'might be made to work more efficiently if the Emigrants would adopt the principle of Cooperative Associations'. Alcock detailed the advantages of cooperative agriculture, including economies in boundaries and machinery and protection against livestock disease and family illness. He also suggested that the planned community could engage in pottery manufacture alongside farming. Alcock's ideas failed to resonate with the *Examiner*'s editor, who made no reference to the letter even though he clearly shared its writer's Christian values and belief in a fairer distribution of wealth.[41] The closest Evans came to incorporating cooperative thinking into his emigration plan came in an article published on 4 May. Its theme was 'universal brotherhood' and it painted a picture of shared community endeavour, with migrating expenses paid for from 'a common fund'. To build a new settlement on the American prairie, Evans acknowledged the need for specialised labour, including expertise in agriculture. In another gesture to cooperativism, he also suggested that there 'must be a store opened, if necessary, in the Potteries, for the sake of their surplus produce; — and where is the potter who would not buy at that store?'[42]

Evans made no further mention of his store; nor did he pursue other cooperative ideas. Debating a few months later with the Chartist leader Feargus O'Connor, he adamantly rejected 'experiments' such as labour exchanges and cooperative stores as destructive of labour's hopes and security.[43] If a settlement model were needed, Flower's Albion would supply it. On 20 April Evans printed another extract from *The Errors of Emigrants*, in which the author credited the growth of the Illinois community to 'the fruits of constant industry and patient labour' rather than any overarching principle or theory. In passages (the paper would reprint some in August) immediately preceding the extract, Flower described the history of Harmony, Indiana, location of the Rappite and Owenite experiments nearly two decades earlier. The cautionary lessons he drew were obvious: every attempt of small communities 'to attain a high degree of perfection seems strongly to impress the mind with the possibility of its ultimate attainment and at the same time to place the period of fruition at a greater distance'. Those considering settlement in America, therefore, should eschew perfection for gradual perseverance. Practical application, not utopian dreams, was needed to tame the frontier soil and establish an enduring community in the West. 'What a field do the foregoing extracts open to the Potters' Union', agreed Evans. 'They show the high road to health and competency.'[44]

The efforts began with organisation and money-raising. The initial speed of mobilisation was impressive. On 24 February, three weeks after Evans first mentioned his plan, the *Examiner* published the laws of the revived union, the United Branches of Operative Potters, drawn up by its central committee. Rule ten pledged the union to:

> enter immediately, into practicable operation for the formation of a United, Joint Stock, Emigration Company, consisting of an unlimited number of Subscribers, in Shares of £1 each, to be paid by weekly instalments of not less than 1s., for the purpose of placing on the land, in easy and comfortable circumstances, numbers of our unfortunate fellow-operatives; and of giving to all a more favourable opportunity of accomplishing the great object we have in view; viz., a fair and just remuneration for labour.[45]

Shortly afterwards meetings were convened throughout the pottery districts to address the question of 'what shall be done with the unemployed' and to discuss the emigration proposal. By mid-March the central committee had endorsed Evans's plan.[46] On 20 March union members gathered at the Temperance Hall in Burslem to give their verdict. The meeting occasioned an extended report in the area's leading newspaper, the *North Staffordshire Mercury*; it was the first notice of the plan outside of union sources.

According to the *Mercury*, the Temperance Hall was 'crowded to excess', with perhaps 500 present to hear officials promote the plan. The opening speaker, Henry Heath, noted 'that all past unions had partially failed to accomplish their objects', but defended the union as the working man's capital, 'on which alone he could fall back in a time of need, as the rich man fell back on his estate, when other revenues were cut off'. On surplus labour, Heath concluded that 'a system of associative emigration' was 'the only and the best remedy at present offering itself'. Next to speak was William Coates, who reassured members that in repudiating strikes the union had not sought to sacrifice labour's rights but to support them by 'all lawful means'. Finally, it was Evans's turn. He began with a discussion of the Corn Laws, a topic of intense local interest following a rambunctious meeting two weeks earlier in Shelton addressed by Richard Cobden.[47] Evans described the laws as 'bad in principle' but, in a challenge to Malthusianism, argued that the country was fully capable of supporting itself with 'an improved system of cultivation'. Turning to the main business, he again invoked George Flower as an example of what could be achieved through emigration. The emigration proposal then was put to the meeting and 'carried without a dissentient'. In the discussion that followed, Evans confirmed that allowing other trades into the Society 'was not at present contemplated', although he offered assistance to any that wished to pursue its own project.[48]

The conclusion of the 20 March meeting saw the appointment of a provisional enrolment committee with instruction to accept no monies until legal registration was complete. By the end of the month the *Examiner* reported that committees had been appointed in Burslem, Tunstall and Stoke, 'for the purpose of receiving the names of all Potters who may feel disposed to take shares in the proposed Joint-Stock Emigration Society'.[49] Determined to attract as many subscribers as possible, the editor reassured workers that trade union support for emigration was nothing new, even though the principle underpinning his proposed scheme undoubtedly was. Although very small-scale, levies to provide grants for emigration had been a feature of many craft unions since the 1820s.[50] Early on Evans raised the case of the Glasgow cotton spinners whose mistake, he argued, was in paying 'the migrating expenses of their starving brethren without the purchase and gift of Land and Stock'.[51] A few weeks later he noted that emigration fever was rising across the land and that joint-stock companies were 'springing up in all parts of the empire', including London, Halifax, Huddersfield and Leeds. Although Evans was conscious of the risk in asking potters for contributions over and above their regular dues, he was adamant about what they could have achieved had an emigration plan been enacted earlier instead of resorting to 'hasty strikes' and other ill-fated remedies. What 'a vast saving of money might have been accomplished! — what numbers of happy homes might now have existed on the beautiful prairies of Western America', he urged.[52]

The first round of public meetings to discuss the plan for eradicating surplus labour was completed by early April, the last one being held in Fenton. 'The work goes bravely on!' Evans touted. 'Emigration is the great moving principle at the present time'. He also reported that the new society's laws had been 'arranged' and submitted for scrutiny to the revising barrister for friendly societies in London.[53] Speed was again of the essence. To expedite drafting, Evans had borrowed from the rules and regulations of the Liverpool-based British Temperance Emigration Society, established in December 1842, lengthy extracts from which he published on 18 May. With their 'display of practical knowledge and honesty of intention, highly calculated to give confidence to the shareholders', they were 'a most excellent code of laws for the governing of a Joint Stock Company, for the purpose of emigration', he advised.[54] The decision to register the Potters' Emigration Society under the Friendly Societies Act was significant. Friendly society membership strongly attested to self-help strivings; it was 'a statement of aspiration as much as an economic investment'. With their rituals of fellowship and conviviality, often centred on the public house, friendly societies were vital contributors to working-class life and identity, and also important conduits to radical politics.[55] More immediately for the Society's leaders, prompt registration served as a cheap and expeditious means of achieving legal protection, important in light of the scheme's trade union origins. During the late 1820s and 1830s there occurred a major shift away from friendly society supervision by the local magistracy.[56] As a result, the Potters' Emigration Society, unlike the rival Chartist Land Company, which was denied registration, would operate largely free from political oversight or intervention.

The Potters' Emigration Society and Savings' Fund, to give its fuller and more revealing name, was officially registered under the Friendly Societies Act on 15 May 1844. Evans's vision had become legal reality. The twenty-four rules and regulations – there was no rule thirteen – extended to twenty-seven printed pages and covered all aspects of the Society's business and conduct, including the procedures for its termination. The list of officers comprised a president, Charles Stanley, a vice-president, a secretary, two money stewards, three trustees, two treasurers and six committee members; the latter included Peter Watkin, whose January letter had prompted discussion of land colonisation, and Daniel Alcock, the proponent of cooperativism.

Identified as general agent – he is referred to as the 'Secretary' in the original handwritten submission – was William Evans, who also contributed a three-page preamble, a clear sign of his directing role. Among the striking aspects of the rules themselves was the object 'to make a savings' fund for those who may not wish to emigrate', pledging, in accordance with friendly society law, 'to allow more interest for their money than can be obtained in any similar investment'. The rules also confirmed that the minimum weekly payment for membership would be 6d rather than the original 1s. The other arresting feature is the evidence of changing minds on key matters of eligibility. Appended bylaws, which were subject to final ratification, included the provision that no member be permitted to hold more than one twenty-acre section, although multiple shares and thus multiple entry into the ballot were permitted; and that fully paid-up members could bypass the ballot, taking possession of twenty acres of Society land, and migrating and settling at their own expense.[57]

Reporting in the *Examiner* on a meeting on 20 May at the Talbot Inn in Hanley, Evans noted that with the certification of the Society's laws and enrolment under the Act of Parliament, it had taken its first 'great practical step'. The next step involved 'negotiation with the States' Government, relative to the purchase of land; namely twelve thousand acres'. In order that the funds raised could be used to send 'surplus hands' to America as quickly as possible, he stipulated that the land would be paid for 'by instalments, in the course of ten years', a commitment, it transpired, he would be unable to meet. Evans was keen throughout to impress upon potters the proper governance of the new Society and the personal honesty of those charged with running it.[58] A fortnight later another meeting at the Talbot Inn formally elected the Society's officers. It also confirmed that every shareholder would receive a printed copy of the laws.[59] To complete the organisational round, the committee agreed to meet every Monday evening at the Talbot Inn, with every fourth Monday a 'general' meeting.[60] At the second of these, on 17 June, the paper reported large numbers of new enrolments, the business being 'so great, that the secretary could attend to no other work'.[61]

On 22 June Evans set out to describe the Society's nature, object and laws. The article was an important and necessary one – it would be reprinted as the preamble to the published rules – and followed a meeting ten days earlier at Burslem's Temperance Hall, when members from all branches heard a deputation appointed by the union's central committee explain the emigration plan. The tone of Evans's article clearly reflected the questions raised at this and other meetings. He turned first to money and eligibility. Having emphasised the affordability of individual subscriptions, he was determined to convey to potters the financial situation in which the union found itself. For the past six months UBOP had been supporting unemployed members at a total outlay of between £60 and £70 per week. The emigration plan would dispense with this cost 'by the removal of its claimants to happy homes in the Western World'. However, in order not to be 'misunderstood', he made it clear that it was 'not requisite that the unemployed alone should migrate … All that is necessary is, that *the surplus be removed*'. He next reiterated the actions required for the plan to proceed. Once sufficient funds were raised to pay for the first instalment on the 12,000 acres and meet initial relocation and settlement costs, a lottery, called a 'ballot or allotment' in the rules, would take place to select a number of families from among the shareholders. Those fortunate to draw a prize would receive payment of their travel expenses to the Society's lands where they would take possession of a twenty-acre section, five acres of it cultivated. They would also find a building for shelter and other needs. Should any lottery winners decline to take up the prize, they could 'transfer the privilege to any *potting* family they please'. The draw would be repeated periodically 'until the objects of the company are obtained', or the 12,000 acres disposed of. If necessary, the Society would purchase another 12,000 to continue the work 'of making labour scarce'.

The selection of emigrants by lottery has come to define the Potters' Emigration Society in popular memory. But the scheme's success would ultimately depend upon attracting more than those willing to trust their future to mere fortune. From the outset there was an assumption that there were many families in the Potteries anxious to transform their circumstances, and incidentally contribute to the reduction in surplus labour, by relocating to the American West under their own resources. Any member, Evans now confirmed, 'having paid £1 into the society's funds, by paying his own migrating expenses, raising his own building, and cultivating his own land' may take possession of twenty acres, the same as any duly allotted shareholder. A more surprising turn in light of the declaration at the March meeting came with the provision allowing individuals from trades other than potting to purchase Society land. But Evans made it clear that outsiders would not be permitted entry in the land ballot, and such purchases would be limited to twenty acres, for which they would pay 'the *government* price' if made at the commencement of the Society's operations but more thereafter due to the anticipated increase in land values.

Evans focused in the final part of his article on the twenty-acre limit on allotments and the conditions of land tenure. The choice of twenty acres, which he defended as 'sufficient to supply a family with all the necessaries and comforts of life', stemmed from the desire to locate as many as possible on the land in accordance with the emigration plan's 'one great object': the removal of surplus labour from the pottery districts. It was also designed to prevent a few individuals acquiring large landholdings to the exclusion of fellow operatives. Supplementing the provision was a requirement forbidding the transfer of allotments before the end of the ten-year period when settlers would receive full title to the land for themselves and their heirs. The rule was important to Evans's vision of how the prairie community would develop and to the overall financial strategy. If title transfers were permitted on possession, individuals might choose to sell their land and leave the settlement. The Society would then lose the power 'to dispose of the unoccupied land at the increased price which it will inevitably fetch from an increase in population'. He also indicated that branches could take out shares independent of those individually purchased; these they would dispose of according to need and circumstance. 'If a member be persecuted for his adherence to the union', he wrote, 'it is only requisite to make his case known, and forthwith there is a home for him in the POTTER'S CITY OF REFUGE, in the Western World!'[62]

Outlining the Society's rules and procedures was important work, but attracting the support vital to the scheme's success required more than textual exegesis. Local interest in the scheme was high, at least as reported by its advocates. Committee member Aaron Wedgwood noted in mid-July that emigration had become 'the chief topic of conversation at inns, in the market, in the workshops, and in the chief places of concourse'.[63] Such interest meant little, however, if not accompanied by financial commitment. Through the columns of his newspaper, Evans relentlessly pressed the virtues of emigration, simultaneously warning of the consequences for the industry if his plan were not enacted. There is 'too much labour in the market; and so long as that evil exists, low prices and the Allowance System will follow as a natural consequence', he reminded potters.[64] Reinforcing these efforts was the testimony of those already in America. The editor trawled far and wide for suitable correspondence to help convince would-be emigrants and their supporters of the beneficence of transatlantic life. 'I do not wish to entice you away from smoky Stoke, but only make use of your reason', wrote the potter Samuel Walker from upstate New York, after praising the 'gloriously free country' to which he had moved in 1842.[65] Other printed letters were less recent and had little connection to the pottery community. John Kilham, a millwright who had left Yorkshire with his wife and five children in April 1829, wrote two years later that they were 'well satisfied' with their life in Morgan County, Illinois: 'I think it is the finest country in the world'.[66] To supplement the letters, the *Examiner* published extensive accounts of conditions in the Midwestern states. Heading the list was Illinois, still the likely choice for the Society's settlement; among the descriptions of life in the Prairie State was another extended extract from *The Errors of Emigrants*.[67]

The three letters from Samuel Walker deserve particular attention. Although land remained Evans's obsession, he was mindful that some workers might be averse to a life in agriculture, and would prefer instead to employ their skills as potters across the Atlantic. 'I think potting would suit you better than farming; working on the land is very hard work, for a person that has not been used to it', Walker advised the Hanley thrower George Garner, who was planning emigration.[68] Walker was the son-in-law of the celebrated ceramic painter William Billingsley, with whom Evans's father David had worked decades earlier. Arriving with his family in New York in April 1842, Samuel established a small business at West Troy near Utica which he named the Temperance Hill Pottery.[69] For Evans, his letters provided reassurance of the prospects available to skilled potters in America, a raw country where a man's abilities would not be stifled by deadly competition and overbearing masters. As Horst Rössler has argued, the *Examiner* presented 'a very rosy picture of work opportunities in the New World', notwithstanding the difficulties Walker and others faced in raising capital and finding labour and materials.[70] Walker was in no doubt of his progress:

> In respect of myself, my little place is not exactly a Spode's, nor a Minton's, having had to do all the work myself, or every description, and almost without money. Nevertheless, I have succeeded, and have earned a comfortable livelihood to boot! Could I have done this in the Potteries?[71]

The advice in emigrant letters about the prospects for skilled labour in America did not contradict Evans's idea of turning potters into western farmers. Workers continued to leave Staffordshire and other potting districts for the United States after the establishment of the Emigration Society in early 1844. Some, following Walker, set themselves up as master potters in locations from New York to the Mississippi River; others gravitated to industrial communities, including East Liverpool, Ohio, fast emerging as a centre of earthenware production. Any removal of surplus labour was welcome for the Society's founder, and he ridiculed the claim that emigration would lead to the ruination of Britain's pottery industry. Noting that Americans did not require any further knowledge about the manufacture of pottery, he argued that it mattered 'little to us, as working men to what quarter of the globe our trade may go, so that that quarter be healthy in climate, free in its institutions, and pays a good price for labour'.[72] He was equally prepared to publicise the victimisation suffered by potters in defence of their rights, for which assisted emigration would provide a remedy. The Hanley ovenman Enoch Bradshaw was a case in point. Bradshaw had been dismissed from his job on charges relating to his union activities, which led to the branch granting him a gift of £5 to help fund a move to America.[73] 'Already I feel that I am free from the trammels and tyrannies of English factory existence', he wrote in a farewell letter. 'Join! Join! make haste! make haste! and enrol your names for a home in the west!' he instructed fellow operatives.[74]

How many pottery workers were heeding Bradshaw's advice at this stage is difficult to assess. The *Examiner* reported intense recruitment efforts which extended well beyond Staffordshire's borders. In July it announced that a deputation had travelled to Yorkshire, receiving an 'enthusiastic' welcome and 'several' enrolments at Swinton before moving on to Hunslet and Leeds.[75] Other out-potteries visited included Glasgow, Greenock, Whitehaven, Newcastle-upon-Tyne and Middlesbrough.[76] Scotland appeared especially fertile; a union meeting at the Victoria Hall in Glasgow on 6 August prompted the setting-up of a local committee and thirty subscriptions.[77] Activity at home continued unabated in the meantime. On 20 July Evans claimed that 400 individual shares had been taken out in Hanley and Shelton alone.[78] Local union branches convened to discuss the plan, while all of the Potteries towns received at least one visitation from 'The Emigration Working Committee'.[79] A general meeting of crate makers and packers on 8 July in Hanley saw a particularly high level of enthusiasm, with an estimated 400 operatives in attendance.[80] But Evans had set potters a formidable challenge. By the end of August, six months after the revived union incorporated emigration into its laws, the target of 5,000 shares was far from being met, with insufficient numbers apparently willing to support the scheme through £1 subscription. In an open letter on 24 August, Evans proposed that committees record the name, branch and residence of every subscriber, and those who had not subscribed were to be 'waited on at their homes, and the necessity and duty of their taking out individual shares laid fully before them'. In Evans's view, these measures, reportedly acted upon a few days later, were vital to realising the goal of ending surplus labour.[81]

The sense often conveyed in the *Examiner* of near-universal levels of enthusiasm for the emigration scheme needs to be treated with caution, therefore. In its account of the July meetings, the *Mercury* offered a more nuanced judgement, one attuned to the patchwork trade and political loyalties of the Potteries. The meetings as a whole had been well attended, the paper found, 'except those at Fenton and Hanley'.[82] Worries about the numbers subscribing coincided with the emergence of voices critical of the Society. Signs of opposition were visible in Evans's article of 20 July in which he sought 'to combat a few of the prevailing objections which have been urged by some individuals' against the scheme; but it was the visit to the Potteries in August of the Chartist leader Feargus O'Connor that posed an immediate challenge to its long-term prospects. Chartists in North Staffordshire had struggled to recover from what O'Connor called the 'mad pranks' of 1842.[83] Tarred with the brush of 'violence, criminality and destruction',[84] and subject to police surveillance and the backlash of employers, much of their energies in the following year were expended on fundraising in support of detained colleagues. Activities increased in early 1844, and Chartists were a highly vocal presence at the Anti-Corn Law League meeting at the Bethesda Chapel, Shelton on 9 March. On 4 May the release of John Richards from Stafford Gaol gave local Chartists an opportunity to demonstrate their continued commitment to political reform, with large crowds turning out in Longton and Hanley to honour the veteran radical.[85]

O'Connor's visit on 19 August was his first to North Staffordshire in over two years. Chairing the meeting on Crown Bank, Hanley, where a crowd estimated at between 800 and 1,000 had assembled, was the former potters' union leader George Mart. Unfortunately, the event was blighted by wretched weather which forced O'Connor to cancel his planned address.[86] Retreating indoors, he made, in his own words, 'a short speech' and promised to repair the disappointment by visiting again.[87] After defending Chartism as a force for moral and political good, he offered a few further remarks during which he referred to the potters' scheme. According to the *Mercury*, O'Connor likened it 'to drawing the working bees from the hive, to enrich a distant country with British skill and industry'. *The Staffordshire Advertiser*, no friend to Chartism or organised labour, reported him saying that instead of an emigration society, a 'British colonization society' should be established in the Potteries, before adding, to cheers, that if the principles of the Charter were enacted, the English people would have 'a greater taste for home' and prefer 'laying their bones in their native country to going in search of labour in other climes'.[88] True to his promise, O'Connor returned to the area in November to open the new Working Men's Hall in Longton. There are no reports of him mentioning emigration during his three-hour address.[89]

Such brief remarks should have occasioned little notice; O'Connor himself made no reference to emigration in his report of his August visit in the *Northern Star*. Evans, however, could not ignore the intervention. Despite its diminishing momentum, there was still impressive support for Chartism in the Potteries, especially in the traditional strongholds of Longton and Hanley. He would also have assumed that the remarks were not made by accident. By the time of his visit O'Connor was well on the way to launching his own domestic land plan. At its 1843 convention the National Charter Association had adopted a new constitution which enshrined land reform as a core objective. The adoption signalled a major shift in strategy, an attempt to reconfigure Chartism's appeal in the wake of the previous year's setbacks.[90] But O'Connor's comments also posed an implicit challenge to potters' unionism. The preceding months had seen the union and emigration society grow ever closer, to the point where separate identities were becoming harder to discern. Writing to the *Examiner* in August, a 'Member of the Black Lion Lodge' admitted that he now looked upon 'the Emigration

Society as being substantially THE UNION, because it has been shown that we cannot permanently improve our present condition by any other plan which has, as yet, been propounded'.[91] Evans could not have put it better.

'Incidents thicken around us. Opposition comes from parties least expected', grumbled the editor at the end of August. Evans regarded O'Connor's swipe at his emigration project as unhelpful at least, and he again set about refuting the idea that a domestic land plan offered labour a better solution than a transatlantic one. His arguments were well-rehearsed, and he supplemented them by emphasising his scheme's contribution to the advance of universal democratic values: 'To emigrate to the United States Republic is to give strength to that form of government in which the natural equality and political independence of man is acknowledged, and which acknowledgement must ultimately sway the destinies of all other nations of the civilized world'. Although critical of O'Connor's presumption, Evans was keen to demonstrate his respect for him and the principles he espoused. 'He and his objects have had, and shall have my most strenuous advocacy. But, in giving this advocacy, I *will* think for myself', he wrote.[92] Replying two weeks later, the Chartist leader's tone was initially emollient but soon betrayed the gulf between them. He noted that the 'question of Emigration appears to have considerable interest for the working classes of the Potteries' and insisted that while not opposing the potters' scheme, he could not compare it to the advantages of home colonisation. Variously describing Evans's arguments as 'superfluous', 'curious' and 'truly absurd', he expressed puzzlement at the philosophy of 'sending a few drops of English republicanism' to strengthen democracy in America, and suggested it would be 'more prudent and politic to keep this large amount of independent "leaven" at home'. He also criticised the emigration scheme for its parochialism. 'This is a national malady which can only be met by one national remedy', he argued.[93]

Evans declined to prolong the matter. 'The working classes have sufficient to contend against without disputing amongst themselves', he wrote in a note appended to O'Connor's letter. The editor was in a difficult situation. As Robert Fyson has described, Chartists and potters' unionists still had much in common at this time. Evans himself remained publicly committed to the movement and as late as March 1845 served as his union's delegate to the Chartist national trades conference in London, where he spoke on machinery and emigration.[94] Moreover, although the exchange with O'Connor had revealed a sharp divide over the issue of foreign versus domestic colonisation, their views derived from a common tradition of popular agrarianism. Throughout the early nineteenth century land reform was a focus for those arguing for 'the restoration and maintenance of labour's independence'.[95] The 1820s and 1830s saw a proliferation of projects aimed at returning workers to the land through which, it was supposed, society would recover its natural productive vigour and incidentally relieve it of the problem of underemployment. These projects differed greatly in scope and design and had varying connections to Owenite beliefs, but all showed evidence of the land's grip upon working people desperate to reclaim their dignity, self-reliance and control over their own labour.[96]

The rivalry between the competing visions of emigration and home colonisation would lie mostly dormant until such time as the Chartists returned to the Potteries to promote their newly minted land plan. Evans pressed on in the meantime with mobilising support for his scheme. The end of August had brought a boost in the shape of a communication from Thomas H. Blake, the commissioner of the General Land Office in Washington. The letter was in reply to one of several sent out two months earlier, including one to Blake's employer, the president, John Tyler.[97] Accompanying the commissioner's letter was the Land Office's latest report, whose array of statistical material on surveying and settlement in the American interior Evans described as a 'valuable present'. Overall, he was pleased with Blake's response, which he published in the *Examiner* on 14 September, writing that it would give 'general satisfaction' to Society members.[98] There was much with which to be satisfied; in his letter Blake had confirmed that with 'upwards of one hundred millions of acres' available across the various states and territories, and more being surveyed all the time, there would be 'no difficulty' in obtaining government land of the desired quantity, quality and 'healthy situation'. There was also some unwelcome news. Although the land was plentiful, 'the credit system in disposing of the public domain has long since been abandoned'. It had in fact been abolished more than two decades earlier. The Land Act of 1820 had lowered the minimum price of government land to $1.25 per acre, but now required full payment in cash, a crucial stipulation of which Evans and his colleagues were unaware.[99]

If Evans was shaken by the realisation that the Society could not procure government land by instalment plan, he was not about to show it. Declining to mention the matter directly, he urged renewed efforts at fundraising, including proposing that additional monthly or fortnightly levies might be invested in branch shares. So 'noble' was the object, he believed, that 'few, if any, would object to the step suggested'.[100] He remained bullish, noting 'the spirited manner' of those attending the public meetings. Further encouragement came in the replies to the letters the Society had sent out in June. Whereas the head of America's Land Office had talked in generalities, the public auditor for the State of Illinois offered more specific advice – and assistance. William Lee D. Ewing was an experienced frontier politician, a former governor and US senator, and he sought to persuade the potters of the Prairie State's merits and of his unique ability to help them settle there. Ewing was no stranger to using public office for personal profit.[101] He told Evans that if granted power of attorney, he would secure land 'of the very best quality and on favourable terms'. While it would not be possible to get 12,000 acres of suitable government land *en bloc*, he could obtain the desired amount by private purchase 'for two dollars & a half to three dollars per acre' at an annual rate of 6 per cent. After giving details of expenses, building costs, productivity and stock prices, Ewing promised a full description and survey of every twenty-acre lot selected, pointing out Illinois's 'great abundance' of clay for the manufacture of porcelain and earthenware: 'Come to our country! Its government is mild and parental. It is boundless in extent, the fertility of its soil incomparable.'[102]

There is no record that Evans replied to Ewing's letter; regardless of doubts about its author, the potters were unlikely to be tempted by an offer that failed to deliver the scheme's core aim: the acquisition of a single tract of land at the lowest available price for the joint purposes of settlement and investment. The letter was still a helpful reminder of the costs and complexities of land acquisition and use in the democratic republic. Alongside its publication, Evans printed another extract from *The Errors of Emigrants* outlining the qualities of Illinois. The next week he published a response from the author himself. George Flower lauded the potters' ambition, but advised that twenty-acre farms were 'too small' and asked whether forty would not 'do better'. Describing the scheme as 'a land speculation and a business', he urged potters to combine farming with another branch of agriculture, wool growing, for example, in which he himself was engaged. They then had 'two legs to stand on, instead of one'. But Flower's overall tone was encouraging, and he reassured Evans that, if managed well, the scheme would afford a 'sure foundation for a continually increasing stream' of emigration. Concerned about the would-be emigrants' lack of experience, he recommended that the Society 'mix farmers with your potters' and advised it to 'send out two or three persons as a Committee' with whom he would 'digest, or rather correct, the details of the plan'. He could point out the districts suitable for settlement, 'and perhaps be of some service in saving much useless expenditure in the first outlay', before reminding Evans again 'that Government land is not purchased on credit'. Above all, they 'must not be in a hurry when they come; they must take time'.[103]

Flower's letter was well meant and likely well received; his recommendation that the potters dispatch an advance party to America was certainly acted upon. However, all the information and advice was worthless if the Society could not afford to cover land, emigration and settlement costs. The loss of the credit option brought new urgency to the tasks of fundraising. In September the Society's committee announced the establishment of a 'fund for the unemployed'. Subscriptions and donations were invited 'from the charitably disposed of all classes', with all the money raised to be invested in the emigration scheme for the benefit of those who 'from the want of employment, are incapacitated to take out shares for themselves'.[104] In a further appeal in October, the Society's vice-president, Daniel McAllister, addressed workers in the out-potteries who, he claimed, had not suffered the same burden of unemployment as their Staffordshire brethren.[105] Pleased with its early progress, William Evans suggested that the new fund would help bind the union together and be the committee's 'anchor'. Reporting at the same time on the Society's general receipts, he confidently expected that with the new hiring season the previous week's total of £20 would 'speedily' rise to £30; £25 pounds a week would still bring in £1,300 a year, which in three years would purchase 12,000 acres of land, leaving £600 'to spare'.[106]

Evans's optimism could not disguise the project's lengthening horizons or the potters' inability, whether through necessity or desire, to furnish the required financial backing. One obvious factor was the industry's own organisational limitations. The revived union, UBOP, recruited only a minority of operatives, its membership of between 1,500 and 2,000 being a fraction of that reportedly achieved at its peak by its predecessor. Branch autonomy remained strong; the new union was dominated by the hollow-ware and flat-ware pressers, who made up an estimated three-quarters of its membership, while a number of branches, including the ovenmen, throwers and painters, declined to affiliate.[107] Adding to the challenge of engaging across the various skilled communities was the fragmented nature of the Potteries. Although individual frustrations at the scheme's lack of progress rarely surfaced, one Tunstall flat-presser wondered what had become of his local emigration committee. Burslem was already up and running: 'Cannot the Tunstall Committee do the same?'[108] The improved state of the Potteries' economy may also have affected support for emigration. In mid-November *The Staffordshire Advertiser* reported that the 'trade of the district, which revived a few months ago after a long season of depression', now appeared 'healthy and satisfactory'. Condemning those who sought 'to prevent an amicable arrangement betwixt masters and men', the paper hoped that with 'full employment' workers would be satisfied with their remuneration, 'which, on the whole, is exceeded in very few trades throughout the kingdom'.[109] Although Evans himself scorned such counsel, he was attuned to the upturn's potential impact, and cautioned operatives not 'to let your present prosperity lull you into apathy'.[110]

It is ironic that when potters were better able to meet Evans's repeated calls for financial support, their incentive for doing so may have weakened.

In general, early trade union sponsorship of emigration was invariably subject to the paradox that need and motivation were greatest when funds were at their most scarce.[111] As domestic conditions improved, the panacea of emigration, of uprooting oneself and one's family for an uncertain life in the New World, seemed less appealing. Yet Evans had never relied upon narrow economic arguments in his efforts to persuade pottery workers to his view. Now, six months after the scheme's launch, the opportunity arose to regain the initiative by showing that, notwithstanding the upturn, the potters' long-term situation was still precarious.

In August the Hanley manufacturer John Ridgway had introduced at his Cauldon Place works a machine for the production of turned ware, specifically 'patch-' or 'paste-boxes'. Although the experiment was soon abandoned, it confirmed Evans's conviction of the dangers posed by mechanisation and led to unseemly exchanges between the two men and their supporters in the columns of the *Examiner* and *Mercury*. Evans had a personal regard for the liberal Ridgway, which tempered his criticism, but he could not ignore the potential effect of the action upon the pottery industry's 7,000 operatives. As 'a *private* gentleman, he has my deepest respect', he admitted, 'but as the *public* introducer, in manufacturing processes, of scientific appliances, which appliances I conceive calculated to produce a vast amount of misery to the class to which I belong, I am his honest opponent'.[112] He had no such respect for C. J. Mason, who in November installed a similar machine at his ironstone works in Fenton. Mason was an old adversary and heaven-sent to reignite Evans's assault on the evils of mechanisation. 'Working potters are placed on the verge of a precipice, which is fast crumbling beneath them. A year, a month, nay a day may topple them to the bottom; leaving them the crushed and hopeless victims of mechanical improvements', the editor wrote on 2 November.[113]

Historians have dealt harshly with Evans's campaign against Mason's flat-ware machine, judging it as an opportunistic attempt to intimidate potters into supporting emigration. Harold Owen went so far as to argue that the scheme 'would have languished to an early death but for the fortuitous circumstance of the introduction of machinery'.[114] While there can be no doubt that Evans sought full advantage from Mason's action, he sincerely believed in mechanisation's threat to workers' security and wellbeing. In one of his earliest contributions to the *Examiner*, he wrote that the 'inventions and discoveries introduced by Arkwright, Cartwright, and Watt, and improved upon by others, have raised an insuperable barrier between the working man and prosperity'.[115] Owenites were often ambivalent about mechanisation, seeing its potential to liberate as well as to displace; but there was still widespread hostility among radicals, who claimed it depreciated the value of labour, resulting in unemployment and impoverishment, as evidenced most clearly by the history of the handloom weavers.[116] Evans could not reconcile himself to the machine's place in earthenware production. Writing in 1846, he argued that it damaged not only the interests of the operatives, but also failed to advance those of the manufacturers; moreover, he doubted its effectiveness in a process where the ductility of the clay demanded 'human touch and skill'.[117]

Mason's 'jolley' proved a technical failure; hairline cracks appeared in the ware after firing, and he was soon forced to withdraw it.[118] (A quarter of a century later Evans admitted that Wall's model, which Mason had installed, might have been made to work with a minor adjustment in design.[119]) But in the brief period of its existence, it provoked an extraordinary response. Throughout November and early December the editor gave full throttle to his anti-machinery convictions, leaving potters in no doubt that this was a struggle they must not lose. While acknowledging that the machine's introduction had caused no perceptible injury, he issued apocalyptic warnings of the consequences of non-resistance to the 'mortal foe'.[120] Wretchedness, desperation, poverty, crime and starvation were his watchwords; the dreaded workhouse, the 'Bastille', the certain destination for those who failed to heed his message. 'The day has arrived when the question is one of life and death', he concluded on 23 November.[121] Public meetings and a poster campaign accompanied the editorial barrage, with the union's committee pointedly reminding pottery workers that their wives and families demanded the utmost 'exertions' if they were to avoid the fate of the 'starving' weavers.[122]

To confront the challenge posed by Mason's machine, the union now proposed yet another call on operatives' wages. After the machine's first appearance at the beginning of November, Evans had urged workers not to let their emigration subscriptions flag; but almost immediately the union issued a new appeal, one tailored to the new threat. The 'Five Thousand Pound Fund' was established with the aim of 'obstructing the introduction of Machinery into the Pottery Business'.[123] The fund would consist of eight levies of a half-crown each, and the money used to purchase 12,000 acres of land, 'on which it is intended to locate all those who may now, or hereafter be injured by machinery'. More dramatically, following the collection of the first levy, Mason's hands would be 'legally requested to leave their employment' and place themselves 'on the general funds of the Union', under whose care they would remain until the land was acquired. How many of Mason's workforce the union envisaged would actually relocate to America is unclear; the abandonment of the machine in mid-December left that question unanswered and indeed irrelevant. The land is 'a resource, on which you fall back, when any other great emergency may take place in your trade', Evans told potters.[124]

If the withdrawal of Mason's machine undercut the union's plan for a mass exodus of labour, it failed to moderate its anti-mechanisation stand. Across the industry the sound and fury of the machinery scare masked a complex set of responses that makes it difficult to judge the extent of workers' fears. Many potters were genuinely apprehensive of change. 'I am comparatively rich to what I shall be when machinery comes into operation!' admitted 'A Hanley Turner' in late November.[125] Others questioned whether the situation was as bad as represented. 'I wish to be charitable to my fellow-men, but I cannot help thinking that there is too much selfishness at the bottom of this outcry against machinery', wrote 'An Operative' in December.[126] Many manufacturers, especially those unable to bear the costs of innovation, were suspicious of mechanisation, while 'the gap between expectation and performance' proved an obstacle to its advance.[127] Not until the 1860s did the Staffordshire pottery industry make significant progress towards machinery's implementation. Recalling the episode years later, Charles Shaw noted that 'it scared not only the workpeople but the masters themselves', with even large employers fleeing from the machine's introduction 'as from a ghost'.[128] But experimentation was bound to continue. Within weeks of Mason's withdrawal, the union's committee was noting the improvement in a modified version of Wall's prototype.[129]

For William Evans, desperate for funds to sustain his emigration plans, the war against the machine had become a vital rhetorical weapon. 'Now is the day for redemption!' he warned operatives in February 1845 after reports of further trials at Swinton and Leeds. 'To-morrow may bring with it mechanical appliances, want, wretchedness and ruin; and the apple of prosperity may have passed, never to return. It is now, for you to decide whether working potters shall become possessed of TWELVE THOUSAND ACRES OF LAND, or not.'[130] Nearly a year had elapsed since Evans first floated his plan to rid the pottery industry of surplus labour. Having made every conceivable argument to persuade pottery workers of emigration's benefits, he now resorted to warning them of the dire consequences of their rejection. The strategy was risky; workers were not united in their attitudes to mechanisation, while the technology itself proved stubbornly resistant to successful application, potentially undermining the argument about imminent danger. Would repeated iteration of a far-from-clear threat prove counterproductive? Over the next twelve months the Society's officials strove tirelessly to sustain a plan whose success depended entirely on the financial support of workers and their families. If the dream of landed independence remained intact, acquiring the means of achieving it looked increasingly challenging.

Notes

1. Richards, *Britannia's Children*, p. 92.
2. Oliver MacDonagh, *A Pattern of Government Growth, 1800–60: The Passenger Acts and Their Enforcement* (London: MacGibben & Kee, 1961), pp. 61–3.
3. S. G. Checkland, *The Rise of Industrial Society in England, 1815–1885* (London: Longman, 1964), p. 27.
4. The Malthus literature is extensive. A valuable essay is Eric Richards, 'Malthus and the Uses of British Emigration', in Kent Fedorowich and Andrew S. Thompson (eds), *Empire, Migration and Identity in the British World* (Manchester: Manchester University Press, 2013), pp. 42–59.
5. 'Report from the Select Committee on Emigration from the United Kingdom … 26th May, 1826', in *Emigration in the Victorian Age: Debates on the Issue from 19th Century Critical Journals*, introduction by Oliver MacDonagh (Farnborough: Gregg International Publishers, 1973), p. 343.
6. See H. J. M. Johnston, *British Emigration Policy, 1815–1830: 'Shovelling out Paupers'* (Oxford: Clarendon Press, 1972).
7. Erickson, *Leaving England*, p. 173. On parish-assisted emigration, see Gary Howells, ' "For I Was Tired of England Sir": English Pauper Emigrant Strategies, 1834–60', *Social History* 23:2 (1998), 181–94.
8. MacDonagh, *A Pattern of Government Growth*, pp. 129–37.
9. Cohn, *Mass Migration Under Sail*, pp. 64–8.
10. Johnson, *A History of Emigration*, p. 179.
11. Kerby A. Miller, *Emigrants and Exiles: Ireland and the Irish Exodus to North America* (New York: Oxford University Press, 1985), p. 201.
12. Jones, 'The Background to Emigration from Great Britain in the Nineteenth Century', p. 40.
13. Cohn, *Mass Migration Under Sail*, pp. 115–16; Richards, *Britannia's Children*, pp. 145–9; Hunt, *British Labour History*, p. 172; Van Vugt, *Britain to America*, pp. 76–7.
14. Belich, *Replenishing the Earth*, p. 156.
15. *PEWA*, 23 March 1844.
16. *PEWA*, 13 and 20 January 1844.
17. *PEWA*, 20 January 1844. A twiffler was a small plate.
18. *PEWA*, 10 February 1844.
19. *PEWA*, 27 January 1844.
20. *PEWA*, 2 March 1844.
21. *PEWA*, 27 January 1844.
22. For the Illinois settlement and controversies, see Jane Rodman, 'The English Settlement in Southern Illinois, 1815–1825', *Indiana Magazine of History* 43:4 (1947), 329–62; 'The English Settlement in Southern Illinois as Viewed by English Travelers, 1815–1825', *Indiana Magazine of History* 44:1 (1948), 37–68; Charles Boewe, *Prairie Albion: An English Settlement in Pioneer Illinois* (Carbondale: Southern Illinois University Press, 1962); and Joseph Eaton, 'A New Albion in New America: British Periodicals and Morris

Birkbeck's English Prairie, 1818–1824', *American Nineteenth Century History* 9:1 (2008), 19–37.
23 George Flower, *The Errors of Emigrants* (New York: Arno Press, 1975 [reprint of 1841 edition]), p. 5.
24 *Ibid.*, p. 49. Dr Benedict Jaeger was born in Vienna in 1788 and moved to America in 1831. He was professor of natural history and modern languages at Princeton College from 1832–43. Letters from Flower to Jaeger are in the Benedict Jaeger Collection, Princeton University Library.
25 *PEWA*, 27 January 1844.
26 *PEWA*, 4 May 1844.
27 Richard Price, *Labour in British Society: An Interpretative History* (London: Routledge, 1990), p. 51.
28 *PEWA*, 27 April 1844.
29 *PEWA*, 2 March 1844.
30 *Ibid.*
31 *The Staffordshire Advertiser*, 6 March 1841; Andrew Lamb, 'Mechanization and the Application of Steam Power in the North Staffordshire Pottery Industry, 1793–1914', *North Staffordshire Journal of Field Studies* 17 (1977), 53.
32 *PEWA*, 16 March 1844.
33 Dupree, *Family Structure in the Staffordshire Potteries*, pp. 82–6.
34 Friedrich Engels, *The Condition of the Working Class in England* (London: Penguin, 1987), p. 217.
35 *PEWA*, 2 March 1844.
36 Gregory Claeys, 'The Example of America a Warning to England? The Transformation of America in British Radicalism and Socialism, 1790–1850', in Malcolm Chase and Ian Dyck (eds), *Living and Learning: Essays in Honour of J. F. C. Harrison* (Aldershot: Scolar Press, 1996), p. 67. Other useful studies include G. D. Lillibridge, *Beacon of Freedom: The Impact of American Democracy upon Great Britain, 1830–1870* (Philadelphia: University of Pennsylvania Press, 1955); Frank Thistlethwaite, *The Anglo-American Connection in the Early Nineteenth Century* (Philadelphia: University of Pennsylvania Press, 1959); and Michael J. Turner, *Liberty and Liberticide, The Role of America in Nineteenth-Century British Radicalism* (Lanham, MD: Rowman and Littlefield, 2013).
37 *Ibid.*, pp. 70–1.
38 Flower, *The Errors of Emigrants*, p. 16.
39 *PEWA*, 8 June 1844. On early American utopian communities, see Harrison, *Robert Owen and the Owenites in Britain and America*; Arthur Bestor, *Backwoods Utopias: The Sectarian Origins and the Owenite Phase of Communitarian Socialism in America, 1663–1828* (Philadelphia: University of Pennsylvania Press, second enlarged edition, 1970); and Donald E. Pitzer (ed.), *America's Communal Utopias* (Chapel Hill: University of North Carolina Press, 1997).
40 Robin Thornes, 'Change and Continuity in the Development of Co-operation, 1827–1844', in Stephen Yeo (ed.), *New Views of Co-operation* (London: Routledge, 1988), p. 30.
41 *PEWA*, 2 March 1844.

42 *PEWA*, 4 May 1844.
43 *PEWA*, 31 August 1844.
44 *PEWA*, 20 April, 24 August 1844; Flower, *The Errors of Emigrants*, pp. 54–7.
45 *PEWA*, 24 February 1844.
46 *PEWA*, 16 March 1844.
47 *PEWA*, 9 March 1844.
48 *North Staffordshire Mercury*, 23 March 1844.
49 *PEWA*, 30 March 1844.
50 Alastair J. Reid, *United We Stand: A History of Britain's Trade Unions* (London: Penguin Books, 2005), pp. 88–9; R. A. Leeson, *Travelling Brothers* (St Albans: Granada Books, 1975), pp. 183–4; A. E. Musson, *Trade Union and Social History* (London: Frank Cass, 1974), pp. 88–9.
51 *PEWA*, 10 February 1844.
52 *PEWA*, 16 March 1844.
53 *PEWA*, 13 April 1844.
54 *PEWA*, 18 May 1844.
55 Simon Cordery, *British Friendly Societies, 1750–1914* (London: Palgrave Macmillan, 2003), pp. 12–97 (quotation p. 74). See also Clive Bradbury, 'The Impact of Friendly Societies in North Staffordshire', *Staffordshire Studies* 13 (2001), 127–44.
56 P. H. J. H. Gosden, *The Friendly Societies in England, 1815–1875* (Manchester: Manchester University Press, 1961), pp. 178–80.
57 *Rules and Regulations of the Potters' Emigration and Savings' Fund, established April 18th, 1844* (Shelton: printed by Bate). National Archives, FS 1/657, which contains the original handwritten submission.
58 *PEWA*, 25 May 1844.
59 *PEWA*, 8 June 1844.
60 *PEWA*, 15 June 1844.
61 *PEWA*, 22 June 1844.
62 *Ibid.*
63 *PEWA*, 27 July 1844.
64 *PEWA*, 13 July 1844.
65 *PEWA*, 22 June 1844.
66 *PEWA*, 29 June 1844. For the family's emigration and settlement, see *Portrait and Biographical Album of Morgan and Scott Counties* (Chicago, IL: Chapman Brothers, 1889), pp. 211, 237; and James Stuart, *Three Years in North America* (Edinburgh: printed for R. Cadell, 1833), vol. 2, pp. 381–4.
67 *PEWA*, 28 September 1844. See also *PEWA*, 22 June, 6, 13, 20 July.
68 *PEWA*, 3 August 1844.
69 On Walker, see Warren F. Broderick, 'An English Porcelain Maker in West Troy', *The Hudson Valley Regional Review* 5:2 (1988), 23–40. Thanks to Mike Beckensall for information on the Evans–Billingsley connection.
70 Rössler, 'The Dream of Independence', pp. 139–42 (quotation p. 141).
71 *PEWA*, 22 June 1844. Walker's first letter was published on 17 February 1844.
72 *PEWA*, 20 July 1844.

73 *PEWA*, 5 October 1844.
74 *PEWA*, 15 June 1844.
75 *PEWA*, 13 July 1844.
76 *PEWA*, 27 July 1844.
77 *PEWA*, 17 August 1844.
78 *PEWA*, 20 July 1844.
79 *PEWA*, 27 July, 17 August 1844.
80 *PEWA*, 13 July 1844.
81 *PEWA*, 24, 31 August 1844.
82 *North Staffordshire Mercury*, 13 July 1844.
83 *Northern Star and Leeds General Advertiser*, 24 August 1844.
84 Fyson, 'Chartism in North Staffordshire', p. 180.
85 *Ibid.*, pp. 180–6.
86 *North Staffordshire Mercury*, 24 August 1844.
87 *Northern Star and Leeds General Advertiser*, 24 August 1844.
88 *The Staffordshire Advertiser*, 24 August 1844.
89 *The Staffordshire Advertiser*, 16 November 1844; *Northern Star and Leeds General Advertiser*, 23 November 1844; *The Staffordshire Advertiser*, 16 November 1844.
90 Chase, *Chartism: A New History*, pp. 247–9.
91 *PEWA*, 24 August 1844.
92 *PEWA*, 31 August 1844.
93 *PEWA*, 14 September 1844.
94 Fyson, 'Chartism in North Staffordshire', p. 298; *Northern Star and National Trades' Journal*, 29 March 1845.
95 Chase, *'The People's Farm'*, p. 67.
96 *Ibid.*, pp. 147ff. See also James Epstein, *The Lion of Freedom: Feargus O'Connor and the Chartist Movement, 1832–1842* (London: Croom Helm, 1982), pp. 249–57.
97 *PEWA*, 29 June 1844.
98 *PEWA*, 31 August, 14 September 1844.
99 The law followed a severe economic crisis and concerns over land speculation. See R. Carlyle Buley, *The Old Northwest: The Pioneer Period, 1815–1840* (Bloomington: Indiana University Press, 1950), vol. 1, pp. 123–36; Malcolm J. Rohrbough, *The Land Office Business: The Settlement and Administration of American Public Lands, 1789–1837* (New York: Oxford University Press, 1968), pp. 140–1; and Roy M. Robbins, *Our Landed Heritage: The Public Domain, 1776–1970* (Lincoln: University of Nebraska Press, 2nd edn, 1976), pp. 33–4.
100 *PEWA*, 21 September 1844.
101 Rohrbough, *The Land Office Business*, p. 198.
102 *PEWA*, 28 September 1844.
103 *PEWA*, 5 October 1844.
104 *PEWA*, 14 September 1844.
105 *PEWA*, 19 October 1844.

106 *PEWA*, 16 November 1844.
107 Thomas, *The Rise of the Staffordshire Potteries*, pp. 198, 202; Burchill and Ross, *A History of the Potters' Union*, p. 88.
108 *PEWA*, 2 November 1844.
109 *The Staffordshire Advertiser*, 16 November 1844.
110 *PEWA*, 2 November 1844.
111 See Jones, 'The Background to Emigration from Great Britain', p. 51; and Humphrey Southall, 'British Artisan Unions in the New World', *Journal of Historical Geography* 15:2 (1989), 167.
112 *PEWA*, 17 August 1844.
113 *PEWA*, 2 November 1844.
114 Owen, *The Staffordshire Potter*, pp. 76–7. Harshest of all is Thomas, *The Rise of the Staffordshire Potteries*, pp. 200–6.
115 *PEWA*, 9 December 1843.
116 Maxine Berg, *The Machinery Question and the Making of Political Economy, 1815–1848* (Cambridge: Cambridge University Press, 1980), pp. 269–90.
117 Evans, *Art and History of the Potting Business*, pp. vii–ix.
118 Lamb, 'Mechanization and the Application of Steam Power', p. 53.
119 'The Progress of Pottery Manufacture', *Pottery Gazette*, 1 April 1882, p. 343.
120 *PEWA*, 9 November 1844.
121 *PEWA*, 23 November 1844.
122 *Ibid*.
123 *PEWA*, 30 November 1844.
124 *PEWA*, 7 December 1844.
125 *PEWA*, 30 November 1844.
126 *North Staffordshire Mercury*, 14 December 1844.
127 Raphael Samuel, 'Mechanization and Hand Labour in Industrializing Britain', in Lenard R. Berlanstein (ed.), *The Industrial Revolution and Work in Nineteenth-Century Europe* (London: Routledge, 1992), pp. 36–7.
128 [Shaw,] *When I Was a Child*, pp. 186–7.
129 Andrew Lamb, 'The Press and Labour's Response to Pottery-Making Machinery in the North Staffordshire Pottery Industry', *Journal of Ceramic History* 9 (1977), 5.
130 *PEWA*, 1 February 1845.

3

1845–6: Finding land

In the spring of 1842 Hannah and Thomas Rhodes and their three sons, the youngest barely a year old, left the Yorkshire farming community of Exleyhead near Keighley and travelled to Liverpool, where on 2 April they boarded the New York-built sailing vessel *United States* for passage to America. Accompanying them were numerous relatives and neighbours, including Thomas's cousin Abraham and his family. The group altogether comprised about twenty individuals, a significant local exodus. Disembarking at New York after thirty-one days at sea, they made their way via Albany and the Erie Canal to Buffalo; here they began the 1,000-mile journey by steamboat to Southport (now Kenosha) on the southwestern edge of Lake Michigan in Wisconsin Territory. After securing accommodation, their first objective on arrival was to acquire property. Rejecting offers of 'second-hand land' near Southport, they probed west, and sixteen miles inland, on the Burlington road, the Rhodeses and their friend William Leache purchased adjacent eighty-acre government lots on which they developed thriving farmsteads. 'You may put in the plow the first thing, and every thing seems to grow plentiful', Hannah wrote to her parents, adding: 'I like the country well; the people are very kind and friendly, more so than in England.'[1]

In Exleyhead Thomas had worked as a stonemason and farmer; Hannah, when not engaged in domestic chores, had worked as a handloom weaver. Like that taken by many others of their class and circumstance, their decision to leave was prompted by the harsh economic and political conditions of the early 1840s – Thomas's father William was an active radical – and the belief that a move to the United States would dramatically improve the family's fortunes. The attractions of America as a land of opportunity and freedom were well-rooted in the popular imagination by this time; the choice of final destination, however, required specific information and advice about conditions across the Atlantic. The couple were not the first family members to venture a new life in America; Thomas's younger brother William had gone to Pennsylvania in 1829. But it was Abraham's eldest son

John who provided the key to the Rhodeses' migration course. A weaver by trade, he had moved to the United States in 1839, alighting in upstate New York, where he worked on the construction of the Welland Canal connecting Lakes Erie and Ontario. Through his brother-in-law, a surveyor, who had gone there in 1842, he learned about Wisconsin and in particular the Southport area. This knowledge he communicated to his relatives in Exleyhead in persuading them to join him in the New World.[2]

Hannah's letter home appeared in *The Potters' Examiner* on 21 December 1844, together with one from her husband outlining their plans to obtain more property. Settlers 'are coming in very fast and buying up the land', Thomas reported. The Rhodeses' letters were among numerous items that William Evans began publishing in December in an obvious bid to highlight Wisconsin's appeal. Remarking in the same issue on the 'excellent quality' of American land, John Bullard, another Southport settler, claimed that he had 'not seen any so good and rich looking as Wisconsin'. The 'accounts I have [of Wisconsin] are most flattering. Good soil, moderate climate; and very healthy!' wrote the potter William Maddock from New York to his mother in Burslem.[3] Aside from emigrant correspondence, Evans also printed American reports on the territory, including a statement from Governor Henry Dodge, who maintained that Wisconsin 'unites more advantages' than any other part of the United States.

> The fertility of the soil of the country, its abounding in lead, iron, and copper, the salubrity of the climate, added to advantages resulting from the navigation of the Mississippi, Wisconsin, and Rock rivers, present an extensive field for the capitalist, as well as to the enterprising and industrious who may emigrate to that country.[4]

By the beginning of 1845 Wisconsin threatened to supersede Illinois as Evans's favoured location for the potters' settlement. Driving the change was the inexorable logic of America's agricultural frontier. As population pressures intensified across the Old Northwest, newcomers were forced to play catch-up in the hunt for cheap land. The change also reflected the increased awareness in Britain of the opportunities available across the Upper Mississippi Valley. While letters played their part in disseminating knowledge, the early 1840s saw more active efforts to sell the region as an emigrant destination. In 1843 John B. Newhall, a Massachusetts-born merchandiser-turned-booster, toured English towns and cities promoting his adopted home in the West. An early settler in Iowa Territory, Newhall's pioneering credentials were impeccable, and his lectures were full of practical advice for those considering a move to the frontier. He brought with him an array of visual aids, including minerals and 'specimens of the prairie soils', together with samples of the Indian corn and wheat grown in them, all designed to highlight the region's 'inexhaustible treasures'.[5] Newhall had already published one account of the region; on returning home, he produced another, lengthy extracts from which Evans printed. The book's target readership was clear: *The British Emigrants' 'Hand Book' and Guide to the New States of America, Particularly Illinois, Iowa, and Wisconsin.* In it Newhall made a point of endorsing 'associative' emigration, commending the societies formed for that purpose. It is the 'true principle to work upon', he wrote, and 'will effectively strip emigration of the miseries and hardships that have so frequently attended the isolated wanderer'.[6]

Among the projects Newhall praised was that of the British Temperance Emigration Society. In August 1844 the Society published a forty-eight-page pamphlet, *The Emigrant's Instructor on Wisconsin and the Western States of America.* The pamphlet was the source for most of the Wisconsin material published in the *Examiner*, including the Rhodes, Bullard and Dodge letters, and was probably instrumental in prompting Evans to switch attention from Illinois to its territorial neighbours where government land was more widely available. The British Temperance Emigration Society and Savings Fund held its inaugural meeting in Liverpool on Boxing Day 1842. Its objectives and procedures closely resembled those of the potters' scheme, whose rules and regulations were modelled on it, including selection by lottery. Dues were levied at 1s a week. For the lucky subscribers, the reward was an eighty-acre lot in Wisconsin, five of which would be in cultivation, together with a log house and goods. Emigrants would in effect lease the land at an annual rent of £5 per share, gradually redeeming it over a period of up to fifteen years. Although the Society's promoters lacked the potters' craft identity, they shared their belief in the American West as a refuge from the deteriorating conditions of industrial society.[7] In his introduction to *The Emigrant's Instructor*, the Society's founder, Robert Gorst, noted that England's population was growing at a rate of 1,000 a day: 'The land gets no larger for us to live upon; there is a general depression of trade, and at the same time no prospect of improvement ... It is under these considerations that many thousands of our countrymen have migrated, to seek their bread on a foreign soil.'[8]

Evans must have been impressed with the speed of the Liverpool Society's progress as his own scheme struggled to gain momentum. In October 1843, only ten months after its first meeting, an advance party led by its agent, Charles Wilson, arrived in Milwaukie[9] to begin selecting the site for a new settlement. Weeks of exploration on horseback led them on Christmas Day to a sparsely populated area of Dane County on the Wisconsin River not far from the territorial capital, Madison. Braving the conditions, the three men and two women spent two weeks in a deserted tepee, during which 'the thermometer sunk lower than it had done all winter'.[10] On land purchased for $1.25 per acre from the federal land office forty miles away at Mineral Point, they set about constructing cabins for themselves and the other Society members due to arrive in the spring. The first party of eleven families reached the newly named Gorstville on 3 July. It is 'a very pretty place indeed, it having a creek of water running through the land, and bluffs or hills at the side, which gives it a very grand appearance', wrote 16-year-old Emma Reeve two weeks later. Three more families followed, and by the end of the summer the population had risen to eighty-four. Despite problems arising over the building of log houses, the Society's organisation and choice of location appear to have been vindicated. One of the emigrants, William Wrigglesworth, who had returned home to Sheffield at his wife's insistence, reported that the future looked bright for the new settlement, although he admitted there were many 'inconveniences and trials' to endure. 'The climate I found healthy, the land good, the water pure and plentiful, and the scenery surpassing anything I have seen even in Scotland', he wrote.[11]

In January the *Examiner* published the Society's quarterly report. It made striking reading. One year after its establishment subscription numbers had topped the 700-mark; in March seventy more members were scheduled to leave England for its estates in Dane County.[12] In publishing the report, Evans hoped to encourage potters into renewed support for their own scheme, whose headway, by comparison, looked meagre. Over the next few months he kept his readers informed of the Society's progress, reprinting correspondence from Charles Wilson defending Wisconsin as a settlement location[13] and a letter from the estate steward, Charles Reeve, disputing the reports of dissatisfaction that invariably accompanied such ventures. Put no confidence in the 'contrary statements from returned emigrants, who have no connexion to us', wrote the former Liverpool watchmaker.[14] The paper also reported on other projects, hoping they too might arouse potters to greater exertions. These included the Sheffield-based Cooperative Emigration Society, whose planned use of the 1841 Preemption Act Evans believed could be of 'great service' to the development of the potters' scheme,[15] and the ambitious Tropical Emigration Society, founded by the utopian socialist John Adolphus Etzler, which the editor 'heartily' wished a success and further praised in remarks to a trades' conference in March.[16] But the exotic landscapes of South America held no appeal for Evans. His gaze was firmly on the western territories, whose 'rapidity of growth in population' was 'unparalleled in the world'; there, on the North American frontier, the potters would establish their new town and realise their ambitions of prosperity, security and independence.[17]

In early 1845 their best hope of achieving that goal lay with the Five Thousand Pound Fund, set up in November to counter the onset of mechanisation. 'The foundation is now laid; and success is certain', wrote Evans in January as the second half-crown levy was collected.[18] Evans believed that subscribing to the Fund was not just a practical necessity but a test of fidelity and solidarity, 'a familiar standard, by which the character of every working potter will be judged'.[19] Despite machinery's limited incursion into the industry, he continued to press workers, in Staffordshire and the out-potteries, on the perils of non-resistance. Each victory was greeted as proof of the effectiveness of the union's strategy. After learning that Samuel Barker's Swinton factory had withdrawn its machine, Evans dared anyone to affirm that the potters' plans were not progressing. 'All your power lies in your funds. Get funds! – funds!!' he commanded.[20] Adroit at exploiting trade and local rivalries, he had no qualms about shaming those guilty of 'procrastination', for example, berating the Hanley and Shelton committee for failing to match the efforts of their colleagues in Burslem and Tunstall: 'If you will not do your duty without being tickled into it, by smooth words, you may keep every farthing of your grasped-up money, and may devote it to whatsoever unimportant object you please, for all that we care to the contrary.'[21]

Although the union's main focus was the anti-machinery fund, it was important to maintain the regular Society subscriptions. In January it reminded members that any shareholder neglecting to do so faced a fine and possible expulsion.[22] The financial pressure on operatives and their families was now intense. Harold Owen estimated that if a working potter 'had answered to all the calls made upon him, directly or indirectly, by his Union, he would have paid away fully one-tenth of his income'.[23] Adding to the burden on the union and its members was the unresolved matter of the Sheffield debt. In November a delegation from Yorkshire visited North Staffordshire in yet another attempt to gain repayment of the money loaned during the 1836–7 strike. Alert to the potters' fundraising efforts, the Sheffield officials pulled no punches in denouncing their 'base conduct' in failing to give priority to the historic debt. 'You may cross the "Atlantic", but curses loud and deep from all the trades in the kingdom will linger in the air you breathe', they told UBOP leaders.[24] The campaign was relentless. Lectures, paid newspaper advertisements and a stream of written communications demanded that potters adhere to the principles underwriting the original loan. 'Justice, gratitude, and *our necessity*, all require that you should reciprocate our feelings', the secretary of the Sheffield debt committee advised the union in January. He noted at the same time the 'improbability' of the debt ever being repaid if the current plans to raise £5,000 to support emigration stayed intact.[25]

Potters had long conceded the legitimacy of the Sheffield debt. Meeting in Hanley two days before Christmas, the union's debt committee expressed the hope that 'the present improved state of trade' afforded an opportunity for its 'speedy' liquidation. To this end, it agreed to establish district committees and to publish all relevant accounts in the *Mercury*.[26] Evans, too, had always considered repayment to be a matter of honour. But the Sheffield trades' apparent lack of sympathy for the potters' situation now prompted a change of view. In a lengthy response published twelve days later, the central committee explained why, despite the 'justice of your claims', it was unable to act. The committee sought to distinguish the 'old union', which had received the original loans, from the current one, whose 'peculiarity of organization' limited its power. Each branch in the potting business 'forms a union of itself', it maintained. Included in the response was a list of all gifts and loans received during the strike, information designed to remind the Sheffield trades that they were not the potters' only creditors and that those who made the security of the union 'a secondary consideration' were unlikely to be favoured. 'That all Union debts may be paid, is our heart-felt wish', the committee noted, '… but that we will make the debt question take the precedence of the question of machinery, or the safety of our society, is the farthest desire from our hearts'.[27]

The debt issue would rumble on, a nagging reminder of the potters' once elevated status within labour's ranks. Fundraising meanwhile continued unabated. March brought the collection of the fifth levy, April the sixth. 'Heed not the apathy of some and the opposition of others', the editor thundered, 'but let your motto continue to be, "TWELVE THOUSAND ACRES OF LAND, AND OBSTRUCTION TO MACHINERY!"'[28] In truth, that much-trumpeted target was a long way from being met. In January Evans estimated that collecting £50 per week over the next six months, when combined with the regular subscriptions, would bring the funds available for emigration to £3,000.[29] Even that amount fell well short of what was needed. On 19 April his fellow committee member Aaron Wedgwood, in a carefully reasoned letter, conceded that in the forty weeks since the scheme's inception the Society had failed to raise the anticipated sum. It would have, 'had potters come forward as expected; but they have not done so'. Calculating that the amount raised 'does not equal more than one-seventh part of the potters in Staffordshire, although there be two-sevenths of the potters in the union', Wedgwood offered various explanations for the shortfall, including the workers' belief that there was 'not sufficient personal security' for the money subscribed. But the chief reason was that potters had 'too many ends to attend to'. His solution was to condense the 'diversities of objects and matters', with potters paying a single sum of 1s per week for the 'protection of the trade'. Half of this sum would be allocated to supporting the unemployed and paying off the union's debts; the remaining half, an estimated £8,750 a year, would go towards emigration.[30]

Evans was unmoved. Having reassured potters in March that the Society had enough money to purchase 4,000 acres of American land, he now refocused their attention on the benefits of emigration. On April 12, under the heading 'Lesson No. 1', he published the first of several extracts from *The British Emigrants' 'Hand Book'*. Newhall's guide provided valuable advice on transatlantic conditions, but the extracts may also have been prompted by another intervention from Feargus O'Connor, who was in the final stages of refining his domestic land plan. Writing in the *Northern Star*, the Chartist leader called emigration 'a sickening, heartless depravity' and 'the worst description of economy' and claimed that it would not require half the amount to locate workers 'upon the land at home that it would require to transport them from their country'. Responding, Evans drew upon Newhall's evidence to again rebut the idea that home colonisation represented the better value.[31] But the editor must also have been aware that potters needed more concrete evidence of progress before committing themselves further to a project that, as its first anniversary approached, seemed barely to have got off the ground.

That evidence arrived the following week. On 19 April, in a momentous announcement, Evans revealed that the Society would begin selecting the three officers who would travel to America to acquire land for the potters' settlement. The main qualities needed for the positions of estate steward, deputy estate steward and conductor were 'honesty' and 'energy of character'; however, it was vital that among them was someone with 'a little *practical* knowledge of farming', including livestock, and of land surveying, at least 'in the ability to draw up a map of our estate on mathematical principle, – according to scale, and with some slight skill in drawing'. To strengthen identification with the Society, Evans recommended the holding of farewell dinners in each district, at which the land officers' friends could impress upon them 'the importance of the great duties which they will have to perform'.[32] Two days later the Society's monthly meeting endorsed the selection process. As a further inducement for potters to invest, the meeting also resolved that any paid-up member be allowed to buy land for 5s 6d per acre prior to the Society's own purchase. The land would be held in trust with all rights protected and would 'by peopling around it, increase vastly in value'.[33] In Evans's view, that increase 'was not of a visionary character, but of the greatest probability: – nay, even certainty', given the region's rapidly rising population. 'Who will be without land, where it can be had for such an extremely low price?', he demanded.[34]

Getting workers to part with their wages remained an uphill task. The publication of extracts from Newhall's *Handbook* – 'Lesson No. 2' was on the profitable nature of American farming – was designed as much to persuade reluctant potters of emigration's merits as to offer practical advice to those about to move. Articles promoting the territories continued to appear regularly, and Evans let no opportunity slip to divert potters' minds westwards (and from the spring of 1845 even began serialising James Fenimore Cooper's frontier romance *The Pioneers*). 'It will only cost you the labour of reading it', he told them of a question-and-answer piece about life on the prairie.[35] There was similarly no end to the flow of emigrant letters. 'I too, was a poor man when I first came to this country', wrote Gloucestershire-born Stephen Price Tucker from Racine, Wisconsin in the forty-second contribution to the paper's series. Reporting that his neighbours had valued his farm at $1,000, Tucker concluded: 'I am healthy, happy, and contented, and no pecuniary offer would induce me to return to England.'[36] The *Examiner* also printed another communication from Job Rigby at Six-Mile Prairie in which the former Burslem shoemaker lamented the conduct of his brother William, who had 'misrepresented our country very much' on his return to England from America. Dissatisfaction born of exaggerated hopes was a common feature of emigration discourse. 'People must not come here expecting to find palaces for them; they must make them for themselves', Job wrote.[37]

The Potters' Emigration Society convened its first annual meeting on 19 May 1845 at the Talbot Inn, Hanley. Much of the meeting was taken up with procedures for the land officers' election. Having confirmed that the Society's committee would decide which of the three successful candidates was best suited to the individual posts, it now agreed they should answer seven questions designed to establish their fitness for office. Drafted by Aaron Wedgwood, these addressed practical matters such as the ability to read and write and do accounts, but were mainly directed at the candidates' moral character and their willingness to act with 'pure and honest' intent for the members' good. Of note was the attempt to ensure that the wishes and interests of 'wife and family' were properly accommodated. Although it was assumed that families would accompany the land officers across the Atlantic, the committee was impelled to probe deeper into the domestic emotional sphere and ask whether it would 'cause any unpleasantness to take place between you and them' if elected.[38]

Three months would pass before the declaration of the election result and many more before the land officers departed. In the meantime battle was again joined with the advocates of home colonisation. At the end of May the Chartist lecturer Thomas Clark arrived in the Potteries as part of a campaign to promote the domestic land plan. Progress had been slow in gaining approval for the Chartist plan, which involved the purchase of land through the issuance of subscription shares and its subdivision into two-acre smallholdings, with individual plots being assigned by ballot; not until April

1845 did the National Charter Association, at a sparsely attended convention, ratify it in principle. A close ally of Feargus O'Connor, the Irish-born Clark was a member of the NCA's executive committee and a director of the recently launched Chartist Co-operative Land Society. According to his biographer, his enthusiasm for the land plan was 'second to none'.[39] Clark was aware that the plan faced competition in the Potteries from the emigration scheme. Writing in the *Northern Star* after his first lecture in Hanley, he anticipated 'opposition from a certain quarter' at his next appearance when he was due to speak about land.[40] He now proposed a debate on the respective merits of home and foreign colonisation. Inevitably, the Society chose William Evans to carry its standard. The first two debates were held on 12–13 June in Hanley, the centre of Chartist activity, and the third five days later in Burslem, which Clark described as a Society 'stronghold'. That view was endorsed when, according to the *Mercury*, the majority of those present in the town's packed Temperance Hall appeared to favour 'the Emigration advocate'.[41] All the debates were well attended and well conducted and, as Clark commented after the Burslem meeting, the two speakers emerged with the 'distinct understanding that we had *both* been victorious'.[42]

The debates with Clark, and the commentaries that accompanied them, were essentially a continuation of Evans's running battle with O'Connor, whose offensive description of emigration still rankled. Addressing a Chartist-organised national trades' conference in London in March, the potters' delegate had spoken in conciliatory terms about emigration and home colonisation.[43] After Clark's arrival he reiterated that he and his colleagues had 'never condemned the *principles* of the latter' – he had, it will be remembered, endorsed domestic land reform in his August 1842 speech in Hanley – but only argued that emigration offered the more practicable solution.[44] Time and again Evans returned to the issue of relative costs. Every domestic initiative of the past two decades, he claimed, from Orbiston in the 1820s to 'the present sinking, and almost irretrievably lost, experiment of the Socialists, in Hampshire',[45] had ended in failure, and the main cause was the excessive price of land. He pointed out that the country's population was doubling every forty years, and argued that the Chartist's 'crude' plan would do nothing to solve the problem of surplus labour. Clark tended to agree, retorting that neither, for that matter, would emigration. He was still convinced that 'cottage farms' at home were preferable to colonisation abroad.[46]

While the overall temper of the debates was respectful, the gloves of civility sometimes came off. In the quarrel over land and settlement costs, Evans had relied on evidence from John B. Newhall, whose probity he compared to that of O'Connor 'or any other public man breathing'.[47] Clark bristled at the comparison. He, it transpired, had lodged with Newhall in London. One day he 'had occasion to leave home, and when he returned, he found that this good Mr. Newhall had ran away with his, Mr. Clark's coat, and had taken it clear away to America'. If this 'gratuitous fling' annoyed Evans, he was even angrier at the Chartist's reference to letters from the potter John Sutherland, who had gone the previous year to Wisconsin with the Temperance Emigration Society. Clark accused Evans of blocking the publication of Sutherland's letters, in which he narrated his unhappy experiences in the United States, a charge the editor robustly disputed. For Evans, the issue was not the veracity of Sutherland's testimony; rather, it was his belief that home colonisation had become a vehicle for those intent on undermining the potters' project. Writing a week after Clark's appearance, he described a 'little knot of some thirty individuals' who had delayed joining the union until months after its formation and 'were now to be found sowing the seeds of dissention, whenever, and however, they can'.[48] In September the *Examiner* published the contentious correspondence. Is there anything in it, asked Evans, 'to warrant the opinion, that the Potters' plan of Emigration is an injudicious one? – is there anything in it, to warrant carping men in secretly circulating the false and foolish statements?'[49]

The tit-for-tat exchanges would continue as the Chartist land plan gathered momentum. For the potters' leaders, countering the challenge of home colonisation required above all a demonstration of their ability to deliver on the promises of emigration. On 16 August the Society announced that John Sawyer, Hamlet Copeland and James Hammond would fill the positions of estate steward, deputy estate steward and conductor respectively, and that 'about January next' they would leave England 'to select, and purchase land in one of the Western States of the North American Union, on which to locate, in agricultural homes, the surplus labourers of these districts'.[50] It was a significant step, one the Society's leaders believed must arouse potters to greater exertions on its behalf. Their language was again uncompromising. In an open address, the committee reviewed the history of the emigration scheme and insisted that for workers to remain inactive would be 'the height of criminality'. The issue at stake was not whether American land would be purchased, but only how much. As previously reported, the Society had raised sufficient funds for the acquisition of 4,000 acres; another penny a day for forty weeks would fulfil the project's aims and thereby confound 'the most heartless and reckless opposition ever yet experienced by a body of working men'.[51]

On 1 September, at the Rose and Crown, Longton, the Society held the first 'Farewell Dinner' for the newly appointed land officers, on whose pioneering skills the success of the emigration project now largely depended. The dinner was attended by 'upwards of eighty working potters', its ritual speeches, toasts and songs setting a pattern for the events at the Odd-Fellows Arms, Tunstall (6 October); the Angel, Fenton (2 November); the Red Lion,

Stoke (1 December); and the Talbot, Hanley (29 December). The celebratory round concluded on 25 January in Burslem, where crowds packed two large rooms at the Hill Chapel before adjourning to the town's Temperance Hall. A final party gathered at the Black Lion Inn two days later, the eve of the group's departure. Not surprisingly, these were all highly convivial events, but equally ones abounding in serious purpose, a point underlined by Aaron Wedgwood, who reminded those present at the Rose and Crown that they were not there 'to gratify the sensual appetites alone'. He also cautioned pottery workers against complacency induced by their relatively favourable situation compared to other trades. Then it was the land officers' turn. Unaccustomed to speech-making, they kept their comments short. At the opening dinner John Sawyer, from Burslem, urged 'Longton men' to match the spirit and contributions of their colleagues at 'the other end of the Potteries', where, he said, the union had achieved so much in the fight against the allowance system and in the raising of operatives' wages.[52]

Sawyer's defence of the union's record confirms how crucial emigration had become to UBOP's identity, indeed, to its survival. Reporting later that month on the take-up of branch shares, William Evans invoked a familiar metaphor.

> The Emigration Society is a part and parcel of the Potters' Union, called into existence by the Central Committee; nurtured by the Committee; and brought into its present perfect state by the exertions of working potters; it is the child of the Union and the parent ought to look to the prosperity and successful maturity of its own offspring.[53]

Many of the toasts and speeches at the farewell dinners focused on the union's fight for permanency. At the second dinner in Tunstall, following a turn by the Burslem Glee-Singers, a final toast proposed: 'The Emigration Society, the off-spring of the Potters' Union, and may it ultimately place its Parent beyond the fear of want.'[54] The previous week Evans made an identical plea in a review of the emigration scheme's progress. Restating his belief that the purchase of Society shares kept the 'four great Branches of our trade permanently together', he anticipated a time when the 'mushroom combinations of "six weeks before Martinmas until six weeks after Martinmas" should pass from amongst us; and that something, substantial, and lasting, should be raised in their stead'.[55] Similar refrains were heard at the Fenton dinner, chaired by the ovenman Isaac Smith. Smith reminded his audience of the scheme's core purpose, the removal of surplus labour, and stressed the interdependency of the union and its emigration progeny. Instead of a toast to the queen, he proposed 'The Potters' Union'; instead of Prince Albert, 'The Potters' Joint Stock Emigration Society'. Finally, he suggested replacing 'The Glorious Constitution in Church and State' with 'The

Glorious Connection of the Union and the Emigration Society; and may they remain united forever'.[56] At the fourth dinner in Stoke, Henry Heath described potters as the 'the princes of working men' when compared to the wretched conditions endured in other manufacturing districts, but, echoing Sawyer, argued that this was largely down to the union which during its first year destroyed the allowance system and obtained a rise in prices. In his brief comments Hamlet Copeland was unstinting in his praise for the union, without which, he maintained, 'he would have sunk very low indeed'.[57]

The union's survival could not be taken for granted. Over the coming year its leaders would face serious challenges in attempting to shore up an organisation that had failed to recruit the majority of the pottery workforce. Wider developments in trade unionism added to the strain on the United Branches. At the Easter trades' conference in London, plans were drawn up for a National Association of United Trades for the Protection of Labour (NAUT). William Evans was a prominent participant at the conference, and on his return home he campaigned for affiliation to the new body. He was equally conspicuous at the follow-up meeting in July, standing in for the radical MP Thomas Duncombe as conference chair during the latter's absences at Westminster.[58] More significantly, in an apparent change of heart, he now proposed separating the NAUT's employment aims from its function as the defender and promoter of workers' interests. The result was the setting-up of two distinct organisations, one for mutual assistance and protection, the other for the employment of surplus labour in agriculture and manufactures. Evans reassured union members on his return from the six-day meeting that he had followed their instructions 'to avoid identifying our society with any general movement for strikes and turnouts'. He especially emphasised his achievement in inserting a clause into the employment association's constitution affirming the principle of emigration, thereby laying to rest 'the passionate and foolish assertion' that it was, in O'Connor's phrase, a 'heartless, sickening depravity'.[59]

The decision to reject the NAUT and affiliate with its offshoot, the National Association of United Trades for the Employment of Labour, of which Evans became a provincial director, would have long-term consequences for the union and emigration scheme. Although potters were traditionally reluctant to embrace general unionism – W. H. Warburton wrote of their 'paralytic cautiousness'[60] – the decision showed how much emigration had come to shape the union's actions. Raising money for the land and preparing the mission of those charged with locating and purchasing it was now all-consuming. In December the union proposed the establishment of yet another fund, to be devoted to the persecuted and unemployed; like its predecessors, the money raised from the penny-a-week collection would be invested in Emigration Society shares. Far from an attempt to make up lost financial ground, the fund was promoted as a contribution to the general good, in this case one that afforded industrialisation's victims the chance of renewal through emigration and land ownership. As 1845 drew to a close, meetings were held throughout the Potteries to celebrate the future acquisition of American land – and the independence and freedom that must inevitably flow from it. Optimism was rife; emigration's enemies were in retreat. A more realistic end-of-year assessment came from the *Mercury*. Reporting on the meetings, its correspondent concluded that while the Potters' Emigration Society had not progressed at the 'railway speed' anticipated, 'moderate headway' had still been made.[61]

Writing in the *Examiner* a few days after Christmas, the editor emphasised the 'gigantic strides' that had been taken to improve navigation so that 'all horrors of a sea voyage are in a great measure dispelled'.[62] Evans had a point; but, as so often, he overstretched it. Despite the advances in ship design and construction, transatlantic travel in the mid-1840s remained a demanding and occasionally hazardous undertaking. Stricter regulation and enforcement – Parliament passed the latest measure in 1842 – had removed or mitigated the worst abuses of the passenger trade, but had brought little amelioration in on-board conditions, at least for the majority of emigrants confined in the cramped, ill-ventilated reaches of steerage.[63] Adding to the worries of those due to travel was the risk of maritime disaster. En route from Liverpool in late 1844, one North Staffordshire family suffered a harrowing ordeal when their ship, the *Atlantic*, struck a reef off the Florida coast during a hurricane. Rescued by a Key West wrecker, leaking and with damage to its masts and hull, the vessel limped to the mouth of the Mississippi, from where the passengers were delivered by steamer to their destination, New Orleans. Fortunately, such episodes were infrequent; and those considering emigration may have been consoled by the family's account of their safe arrival and settlement in Upper Alton, Illinois.[64]

We do not know with what apprehension the land officers and their families viewed their imminent departure for America, and their separation, most likely permanent, from the people and places they had known since birth. Although the men at least were reported in January to be in the 'best of spirits' and impatient to be on their way,[65] anxiety at the prospect of weeks on the high seas followed by an uncertain future on the western frontier was inevitable. Leading the party was its oldest member, a 40-year-old Burslem potter, Hamlet Copeland. Originally appointed as deputy estate steward, Copeland had by the time of the men's departure assumed the senior role. Travelling with him was his wife Ellen. His deputy was John Sawyer, also from Burslem and a hollow-ware presser; with him were his wife Elizabeth and their son Henry, born in 1840, and the only child in the party. Sawyer came from a large family; the second of ten children, his father Ralph had absconded to Sweden three years earlier after failing to curb his enthusiasm for horse racing. Left to fend for themselves, John's mother and eight of his siblings would cross to America before the end of the decade.[66] Completing the group was James Hammond, a flat-presser from Shelton, and his wife Martha. Like Elizabeth Sawyer, Martha had worked at the potbank; she was also the only member of the three families with close relatives in the United States, her elder brother Elijah Floyd having gone to Philadelphia in 1828. Hammond was the Society's conductor, responsible for meeting and shepherding the newly arriving emigrants. By a few months the youngest of the officers, he was in one way the best-qualified. As Evans wrote: 'Although a potter, he is also a practical farmer; and has had much experience in the land. The great portion of his life has been passed in agricultural pursuits; and nearly the whole of his family connections follow the occupation of the soil.'[67]

Preparations for the land officers' departure were all but complete by the middle of January. After eighteen months of deliberation in which Wisconsin had emerged as the preferred site for the potters' colony, the Society had surprisingly decided – probably under Newhall's influence – that it should begin its search in neighbouring Iowa Territory, where land acquired from the Sac and Fox tribe after the 1837 Black Hawk War was said to be 'exceedingly rich, fertile, and healthy'.[68] If the group discovered no suitable site, they were to explore other areas. More intriguing was the decision to send the men to Washington to call on Commissioner Thomas H. Blake at the General Land Office. Blake had furnished the Society with valuable statistical material and it now sought to repay the favour with the gift of a pedestalled urn, 'grounded in a beautiful morone colour' and adorned with 'beautiful lizard candlesticks'. Inscribed in gold as a 'tribute of respect', the object would, it was believed, demonstrate 'Old England's skill in the art of Porcelain manufacture'.[69] The Society also crafted an address to Commissioner Blake in which it hoped that 'political liberty, and social and domestic happiness may continue to be the leading characteristics of your progressive Republic'. We have gone back, it claimed, 'to the first principles of life, and have sought, by a combination of peace, and in conformity with the laws of our country, to unite Land and Labour, to the end, that the former may give employment to the latter'.[70]

Leaving day from the Potteries was Thursday, 28 January. 'Crowds of individuals were on the road to bid them a last adieu; and to wish them success', reported the *Examiner*. Members of the Black Lion Lodge and other supporters accompanied the party to the Madeley railway station, where the officers and their families boarded the Liverpool train. With them was William Evans. As the Society's general agent, Evans's job was to oversee the final departure, including arranging insurance and supervising the loading of a large shipment of earthenware and haberdashery which they proposed to sell in New York to cover expenses. He was also responsible for the contract drawn up by the Society's trustees. Signed by himself, Copeland, Sawyer and Hammond and witnessed by Robert Armstrong, the US Consul in Liverpool, it specified the men's duties and remuneration. The officers would each receive a weekly wage of 10s plus travelling expenses; once settled on the land, this would rise to £1 a week for one year, with a further agreed wage for the residue of a three-year period. In accordance with the Society's laws, the men and their families would be allocated twenty acres of land and a 'good substantial' log dwelling. As to their duties, the contract reiterated what was previously agreed; their mission was to select and purchase 4,000 acres of land for the Potters' Emigration Society settlement, with the search to begin in Iowa Territory.[71]

They were booked to sail on the 1,000-ton packet *New York*, built at Webb and Allen's Manhattan shipyard in 1839 and captained by a Virginian, Thomas B. Cropper.[72] In 1842 the British government had awarded Cropper a gold medal for his part in rescuing passengers and crew from a Dublin-bound vessel discovered floundering in the Atlantic.[73] The original arrangement was that the men and their families would travel in steerage, but in Liverpool Harnden's shipping office made them 'a liberal offer' of second-class berths which they gratefully accepted. Accompanying them on the crossing to New York was another Burslem potter, William Cartlidge, whose older brother Charles had gone there in 1832 as agent for the Hanley manufacturer William Ridgway.[74] Of the ship's remaining 200 passengers, three-quarters were Irish, a tiny slice of the thousands now fleeing famine and destitution for a new start in America. 'Poor injured Ireland seemed to be pouring forth its children to seek refuge in the west world', observed Evans from the dockside. They were 'jabbering away like a tribe of wild Indians'. James Hammond's language was even less charitable. A week into the crossing he wrote in the party's journal: 'There is on Board, individuals from many nations of the Earth ... but by far the greater number are Irish; who are as filthy and lousy as they are numerous'.[75] John Sawyer described the Irish passengers as 'some of the most filthy, ragged, and degraded looking' individuals he had ever seen.[76]

Wrong wind direction among other factors delayed the party's departure and not until Thursday, 5 February, after four days on-board, did the ship clear Liverpool's waters. As it did so, the city received news, probably avoided by the *New York*'s passengers, of the dreadful fate of another emigrant vessel. The Quebec-built *Cataraqui* had left the Mersey port in April 1845 bound for the southern hemisphere. Off King Island in the Bass Strait northwest of Tasmania, the ship struck rocks, quickly breaking up in the gale-driven seas. Only nine of the 409 passengers and crew survived.[77]

The *New York*'s voyage, by contrast, was unexceptional, although at one point the captain was forced to steer sixty miles off-course to free the ship from floating weed. The seasonal weather brought boisterous conditions and often extreme cold. All of the potters' party bar one suffered sickness; the exception was the oldest member, Hamlet Copeland, who assumed the role of doctor.[78] Physical discomfort aside, the most serious deprivation was the absence of news from home, with the loss of the *Examiner* particularly regrettable. Finally, on the morning of Friday, 13 March, after over five weeks at sea, the *New York* docked at its home port.

Unlike many British and Irish emigrants landing in New York in the mid-1840s, the potters could draw on local resources. Meeting them at the dockside was Charles Cartlidge, who had arranged accommodation at a Lower Manhattan boarding house. Also there to help was another émigré potter, William Maddock from Burslem, who had previously applauded the Emigration Society's associational plan.[79] The most pressing task was to secure the safe arrival of the pottery and haberdashery the men had brought with them for resale. As it turned out, the goods were more trouble than they were worth. The crates could not be retrieved until 29 March, more than two weeks after docking, and the sum raised from the sale was much less than anticipated. Cartlidge and Maddock questioned the potters' strategy, with the former describing it as 'bad speculation'; both suggested that carrying money rather than merchandise would have been the better option. Navigating through the Custom House proved laborious, especially in regard to the haberdashery, for which no bill of lading could be found, requiring the intercession of Captain Cropper. The pins, paper and thread also incurred duties of between 20 and 35 per cent. Pins, the officers ruefully reported, 'are manufactured here, and can be bought as cheap as in England'. The haberdashery was at least saleable, unlike much of the pottery, which, on opening the twenty-two crates, was found to be either 'very much broken' or short of expected quantities (Evans blamed the packing company). Mistakes were also made in the choice of items sent for sale, '*handled teas* instead of *unhandled*', for example. After much difficulty, the whole consignment was sold for $791, a sum Cartlidge told the men was more than he would have paid. Reflecting on the episode, John Sawyer wrote that it had caused them 'trouble and anxiety'. He admitted that they had been unprepared for the very different methods of doing business in America.[80]

The land officers' mission had begun unpromisingly. Forced to endure several weeks' costly delay, they did not leave New York until 10 April. Back in the Potteries, Evans was undaunted, dismissing the idea that sending the merchandise had been an error. He also rejected the criticism that the men had taken insufficient funds for the land purchase, describing it as 'a matter not of the greatest importance'. Once the estate is selected, payment can be forwarded through the American consul with 'but a trifling loss of time', he wrote.[81] As for the earthenware and haberdashery, Evans saw the consignment as not only providing for immediate expenses but as part of a wider strategy in which the sale of goods offered future investment for the Society's surplus funds. Never one to moderate his dreams of independence, he anticipated 'a system of traffic' developing between the two countries following the establishment of the Society's colony, 'the profits of which will be at the disposal of working potters'. Is it unrealistic, he asked, to imagine warehouses in America selling British-manufactured goods and shops in Britain reciprocating with transatlantic produce such as pork and corn? Noting the success of the union's printing establishment, he believed that the economic power generated by such free-trade activity could help relieve potters from their dependency upon traditional capital.[82]

There was another reason for the party's delayed departure west. It is unclear exactly what the Society hoped to gain by sending a delegation to Washington. There was certainly a symbolic aspect to Hamlet Copeland and John Sawyer's visit: working-class potters presenting their credentials at the seat of America's democratic government. The two men left New York on 1 April. Travelling by rail, they paused in Philadelphia to call on Martha Hammond's brother, who was working in 'a crockery store' there. Arriving in Washington the following day, they made their way to the Capitol, where Congress was debating the Oregon question.[83] A letter of introduction brought a meeting with the Whig senator from New Jersey, Jacob W. Miller, who confessed that 'he did not know much' about the West, but offered to inquire after Commissioner Blake, whom the potters were anxious to find. The next morning, on their own initiative, the men located the General Land Office in the Treasury Building at the other end of Pennsylvania Avenue. On entering, they found to their surprise that Blake had left his position the previous April and returned to Indiana. After explaining to officials the object of their mission, they were introduced to one of his brothers, who was employed in the Land Office. Unfortunately, he 'did not appear to have any knowledge of the circumstance' but thought that another brother, who worked in the adjoining Treasury Department, might. Soon fetched, he proved more helpful.[84] Dr John Blake told Copeland and Sawyer that they would need to go to Indiana to see the former commissioner and offered instead to send him the Society's Address, together with copies of the *Examiner* and the presentation urn. Later that day, at his house, he explained that such gifts were not permitted in the American system, and had his brother been in office he would most likely have refused it, upon which it would have been sold at auction and the money paid into the Treasury.

As a statement of purpose, designed to impress America's highest land official, the Society's delegation to Washington was unsuccessful; letters of introduction aside, nothing material came from the visit. It achieved more on a personal level. Dr Blake was an admirable substitute for his absent brother. After introducing the two potters to various officials in the Treasury Building, all of whom encouraged them in their project, he conducted them to the nearby President's House, where they briefly conversed with the vice-president, George M. Dallas, before shaking hands with President James K. Polk himself. A visit to the Patent Office was followed by an escorted tour of the Capitol which commanded a fine view of the city and its surroundings. A less comfortable sight were the enslaved African Americans they encountered in the city's houses, including that of their Virginia-born host. 'I do not much like the buying and selling of human beings; but, in other respects, they generally appear to be better fed, and better clothed, than a great many of your white slaves at home', wrote Hamlet Copeland, drawing the habitual comparison. Leaving Washington on the morning of 4 April, the potters endured further delay when a second visit to Martha Hammond's brother resulted in a narrowly missed connection. They did not reach New York until the following afternoon.[85]

Five days later the reunited party was on its way west. Journeying by rail and steamboat via Albany and Buffalo, they arrived in Milwaukie on 20 April, from where the officers sent back a detailed account of their adventures thus far. Also in communication from Milwaukie was Ellen Copeland. Writing to her brother, she attempted to persuade him to join her in Wisconsin, noting that James Hammond's brother John was due to come over in the following summer. 'Some of the towns are like paradises, compared to England', she told him. She praised the food, the wooden houses and the absence of children begging for bread and was especially gratified by the country's positive effect on her husband's wellbeing. In a comment that hinted at earlier difficulties, she wrote that 'he scarcely wants anything stronger than water, to drink', and that he is 'a better man without liquor'. Reprinting her account in the *Examiner*, the editor hoped that its 'hearty spirit of satisfaction at the social condition of the people of the New World' might convince reluctant families, female members especially, of emigration's restorative powers.[86]

For Hamlet Copeland and his two colleagues, the hard work had already begun when Ellen put pen to paper. The officers had been directed to focus initially on Iowa Territory, far to the west, but decided, probably on local advice, to look for land closer to their arrival point. On 27 April the men left Milwaukie and headed into the Wisconsin interior. The expedition began badly; the trio narrowly escaped injury when their stagecoach broke down, which caused the horses to take fright and escape. Proceeding on foot through

Prairie Ville (now Waukesha), they arrived at Spring Lake, where three years earlier a party of English emigrants led by a London radical, Thomas Hunt, had founded an Owenite colony which they named Equality. The men received a friendly welcome from the colonists, who put them up overnight, but were unforthcoming about the conditions they found there. On receiving their report, William Evans described the Spring Lake community as being in a 'highly flourishing' state. In truth, Hunt's experiment was in serious difficulty, and disbanded within a few months of the potters' appearance.[87]

Hunt's account of the visit, published in the radical journal *The Reasoner*, provides a glimpse into the officers' intentions. The men had been charged with purchasing 4,000 acres of land 'in Wisconsin or Iowa', he wrote, and were headed next for the 'Liverpool Temperance Society' community at Mazomanie.[88] Heavy rain and the atrocious state of the roads made progress agonisingly slow, and they were exhausted by the time they arrived in Dane County. It had taken five days to cover the thirty miles on foot from Spring Lake. At the Temperance Society settlement they were hospitably received by the agent, Charles Wilson. Before retiring for the night they discussed with him their respective projects which, as Hunt acknowledged, were based upon shared organisational principles. Wilson offered to help the potters in any way he could. However, he advised them that twenty acres were insufficient for settlement needs 'because we could not get the land all good, and thought that forty acres would be little enough'. He also warned them that they would find it difficult to 'get our land altogether'. The following morning the three men rode with him on his lumber wagon as far as the Wisconsin River. Continuing on foot, they headed northeast into the newly created Columbia County.[89]

Despite Wilson's cautionary comments, the men came away invigorated by their visit to the settlement. In their conversations the agent had revealed that their Society now owned 11,200 acres of land, and claimed that every pound invested had risen in value by 34 per cent. '*This is something to reason upon!*' enthused John Sawyer. But, having taken the temperance pioneers three months to find a suitable site, they were keen that the potters understood the challenges they faced. Most of the available land had been taken up by speculators, who were demanding between $5 and $6 an acre. Furthermore, no purchase could be completed without cash, which they did not have. 'But we must leave this part of the business with you to decide', they told Evans:

> only the sooner it is sent, by some means, the better, because some one might step in, and pay for the Location, which we had selected, before we did, or a part of it, and thus spoil our choice. And another reason is, that we shall be too late to do anything, this season, if it be deferred long, as the Land should be broken for wheat by July, at the latest.

Of more immediate concern were the treacherous conditions they faced as they made their way on foot through Columbia County. Approaching Portage, the three became separated in swampland, with Hamlet Copeland suffering painful abrasions to his legs. Before leaving Milwaukie, they had been advised that travelling this early in the season might prove hazardous, but, anxious to get on, felt they had little choice but to proceed.[90]

At Portage Prairie at the end of the first week in May, after trekking for more than 300 miles around southern Wisconsin, they found their government land. The location was ninety-five miles northwest of Milwaukie, close to the old military post of Fort Winnebago, abandoned the previous year. 'It is a very rich quick soil, with a sufficiency of timber on it, to suit our purposes. *It is a very healthy situation*, and has a pretty little creek running through it', Sawyer reported. Returning to Milwaukie, the men collected their families and by 21 May were back at the land. A young Scottish settler, John Smith, allowed the party of seven to bed down for the night on the floor of his newly built log house; the following morning, with his help, the men hauled timber from a local sawmill and built a rudimentary shanty – 'twelve feet square, six feet high in the front, and four at the back' – which became their temporary home. During the coming weeks they set about providing permanent dwellings for themselves and their families, hiring a local man to construct three two-storey log homes at a cost of $52 each (about £11 in English money). The plan was to complete all the building work in six weeks. Day-to-day survival aside, their principal worry remained the lack of funds. 'It has been, and still is, a source of great disappointment to us, on account of the money not being at hand to purchase the Land, which we have selected for our Colony', they wrote to Evans on 22 June. They were now in 'a very awkward' position, as new settlers crowded around them. One had already purchased eighty acres 'of the best wood-land' next to their shanty which they had previously claimed. In danger of losing the entire woodland, they went to the branch land office at Fox Lake in neighbouring Dodge County, where each filed a claim of 160 acres, the maximum permitted under the Preemption Act. The 1841 law established the 'squatter's' right to occupy government-surveyed land which they could then purchase at the fixed price of $1.25 per acre.[91] Receiving money to pay for the preempted land was now essential. Send it 'as speedily as possible', the men pleaded, 'so that the land can be secured before it is taken up by others and we are compelled to look out elsewhere'.[92]

Over the next few months the three families worked hard to ensure that the foothold at Portage Prairie would provide the basis of an enduring settlement. On one matter, at least, there was progress; following the officers' appeals, the Society agreed on 27 July at its monthly meeting to send £600 to Wisconsin for the purchase of land. The meeting was notable for an unsuccessful attempt by a small group present to delay dispatching the money until potters generally had given their opinion on the plan.[93] It also decided that the new colony would be called Pottersville. The name, Evans insisted, would descend through 'untold generations'. Acknowledging receipt of the funds, John Sawyer revealed how difficult their mission had become as local encroachments intensified. 'We have used every stratagem we could to keep as much land as possible', he reported at the end of September, 'but the neighbours would not back us in taking too much land to the exclusion of good settlers'. He was still optimistic about the future: 'Although we have been placed in the dilemma we have, I believe we shall be in a position to receive about three families next spring, so that you may begin to make preparations accordingly.'[94]

Preparations had been under way for some time. No sooner had the land officers left for America than the Society began planning the creation of an Estate Committee to oversee the new settlement. While it would be months before the officers could confirm that they had found a suitable site, Evans was anxious to sustain the momentum created by their departure. He wanted especially to see a rapid improvement in subscriptions and to forge greater unity within potters' ranks through branch investment in emigration. He proposed that branches raise subscriptions by 3d per week. Each branch would elect a member of the Estate Committee and fund their expenses to America, protecting both branch and Society interests.[95] He singled out the hollow-ware pressers for special attention. Although they had invested more than any other branch, he believed them capable of contributing more and setting an example to potters generally. 'More you might do; less you cannot', he told them bluntly. He also reminded them that 'two of the most honest men of your branch' were now scouting for land in their name across the Atlantic. He pricked similarly the consciences of the flat-pressers, calling on them 'to think of James Hammond, and the duties you have consigned to his care'.[96]

Endless exhortations aside, how could the Society generate more income? Although the spring of 1846 brought signs of improving trade conditions in the Potteries – partly through reduced fears of an Anglo-American conflict over Oregon – enthusiasm for additional contributions was bound to be muted.[97] Letters to the *Examiner* revealed a variety of opinions on resolving the problem. 'A Friend to Emigration' complained that the difficulty lay not with the operatives who failed to pay their dues, but with the Society itself for placing it beyond their reach to do so. Praising the setting-up of district committees, he observed that there were many who wished to take out shares but 'say they cannot afford to pay sixpence besides their other payments'.[98] Another writer, echoing Aaron Wedgwood's earlier criticism, suggested that a simplified 'system of continuous subscription' was needed.[99] But other correspondents reiterated the necessity for potters to bear current burdens in the cause of long-term security. A member of the Hanley's New Market Tavern lodge explained that he had resumed payment after listening to Evans talk about emigration at the party for the departing officers; 4,000 acres 'of good land, in a free country' was 'something on which to rest, that cannot be wasted', he told fellow unionists.[100]

The Hanley potter's admission that he had been swayed by Evans's remarks reminds us – if a reminder is needed – of the Welshman's pivotal role in sustaining emigration belief. Like his rival land colonisation advocate Feargus O'Connor, Evans was a charismatic, even mesmeric, figure – 'a vivid and rousing writer, and fluent and fierce speaker', according to Charles Shaw, who provided a memorable sketch of the editor in full flow.[101] Through the emotional and diagnostic power of his language, Evans sought to convince workers of the precariousness of their situation and of the means to extract themselves from it. They were casualties of the 'competitive principle, now prevailing in society', he lectured UBOP members in April. A 'superabundance of labour has been called into existence by the progress of science and the working of this principle, and every succeeding year must add to the evil thus generated, unless other means than those of strikes and turnouts, be resorted to for trade's improvement'. Evans was convinced that his prescription could apply throughout industrial society where 'the rottenness of existing things' prevailed. '*Land* should be the first thing sought for by the operatives of this country. That once obtained, and the physical means of life are secured', he reiterated.[102] By 1846, if not earlier, Evans had donned the mantle of land reformer, aligning himself with O'Connor, whose domestic version he contested, and with Anglo-American radicals such as George Henry Evans, about whose National Reform Association, founded in 1844 in New York, he kept potters informed through the *Examiner*.[103]

But, first and foremost, Evans was a working printer, editor and union organiser committed to defending the interests of potters, for whom, in Jamie Bronstein's phrase, he felt 'unaccountably responsible'.[104] In August 1846 Evans compiled and published from his Shelton office a seventy-page pamphlet titled *Art and History of the Potting Business*. The bulk of the work comprised a highly technical exposition of pottery making ingredients and processes, designed, as he explained in the preface, to teach potters about their profession's 'secrets'. The preface also served as a defence of his actions. Narrating recent developments, from the 'disastrous turnout' of 1836–7 to the machine controversies and emigration scheme, he maintained that he had no other motive than:

> to advance the intelligence and skill of those, amongst whom my life has been cast; to add to their societarian, social, and political power; to assist them

to remove, if possible, all difference, that may exist between them and their employers; to establish a just appreciation of the rights of labour, and a due respect for the interest and safety of capital.

He took special pride in the success of the union's printing establishment, 'one of the best in the Staffordshire Potteries'. Cheap literature was essential if workers were to free themselves from 'the state of mental darkness' to which they were traditionally confined. He was less proud of the failure to repay the Sheffield debt; with 'only a few paltry hundreds' returned, it was a permanent stain on the potters' character.[105]

Evans also felt vindicated by the fact that the union's successes had been achieved without the support of the majority of pottery workers. The present society 'have never exceeded, in numbers, two thousand members', he admitted. By the summer of 1846 retaining the allegiance of even this number was becoming increasingly problematic, with clear consequences for the emigration plan. On 11 August a general meeting considered how to improve prices and secure 'a regular and continuous contribution for the important purpose of peopling ' "Pottersville", the Union Estate'. The meeting's agenda had been set by the UBOP central committee, whose aims were now effectively inseparable from those of the Society.[106] At the end of April the hollow-ware pressers had resolved to devote half of their subscription income to emigration; the committee now recommended that all branches follow suit. At stake, it argued, was not just emigration but the union itself. The matter was simple: branches that had taken out shares in the Society were flourishing; those that had not were depressed like the turners and handlers or, like the packers, crate makers and slip makers, no longer existed. Emigration has become 'the very foundation of our stability, *and we must foster and protect it!*'[107] Union leaders were also adamant that the remaining portion of the operatives' dues would be sufficient to conduct its day-to-day business. The proviso was that the union would no longer squander its resources on 'foolish strikes' such as the bitter dispute over allowances with Samuel Barker's Don Pottery in Yorkshire, which had dragged on for a year and cost £2,000 in unemployment pay.[108] Some weeks earlier a sub-committee also suggested that branches might cut their costs by reducing the number of officers. The decision, it hastened to add, was entirely theirs.[109]

The majority of branches were quick to respond favourably to the half-subscription proposal. However, at this point there occurred, as Harold Owen put it, 'a curious development'.[110] The hollow-ware pressers, who first advocated it, now reversed their position, with the Hanley lodge taking the lead by a vote of thirteen to nine. A branch meeting on 17 August went a step further. The main resolution called for 'a separation of the Emigration Society from the proceedings of the Union'. Evans was disgusted. Although a decision on the resolution was deferred following a 'fiery' debate, he professed disbelief at a move that in his view would lead to the destruction of the potters' union as a permanent entity. Emigration 'has been the great bond that has held us together, when any other tie would have crumbled away like a rope of sand', he again asserted.[111]

The turn of events should not have surprised him. There had always been resistance to the union's strategy; what had changed was the emergence of a rival organisation competing for potters' support. In April 1846 the National Association of United Trades for the Protection of Labour, the body that Evans initially endorsed, began recruiting in the Potteries as part of a campaign to convince workers of the benefits of national unionism. (Evans had sought to retain links with the NAUT. At its June conference in Manchester, he spoke from the floor on his favourite themes, but was barred from further participation as he was not a delegate.[112]) Its agent was the Macclesfield weaver and Chartist John West. Over a four-day period West addressed workers in Hanley, Tunstall, Burslem, Longton and Stoke. Chairing the Hanley meeting was Mark Lancaster, the former potters' leader; the Stoke potter and veteran radical George Mart was also present. After the meeting unanimously endorsed the proposal that 'the working men of Hanley and Shelton' should form themselves into a branch of the NAUT, Mart announced that the painters and gilders had already joined, prompting applause. The other meetings followed the Hanley pattern. At Burslem's Temperance Hall, the presence of emigration supporters persuaded West to argue that the problem of surplus labour was best resolved by shortening the hours of work, rather than by leaving for America; at Longton audience members asked him about honouring the Sheffield debt.[113] The immediate results of the NAUT's foray into the Potteries were encouraging, and the following months saw numerous approaches to the association from within potters' ranks. At the end of September Edward Humphries, the corresponding secretary of the newly affiliated 'Staffordshire Potters Society', reported 150 paying members, with more expected to join soon.[114]

Evans and the central committee's response to the NAUT challenge was twofold. First, they proposed a reorganisation of the potters' union. Rather than the customary branch system, it would be based on the principle of 'miscellaneous' lodges. Second, they intensified efforts to persuade pottery workers that only through the acquisition of American land would they secure their futures. Evans took his case initially to the out-potteries. At the end of August he began his mission to the North, carrying with him copies of the *Art and History of Potting*. He stopped first at Swinton, Rawmarsh and Rotherham. 'The potters of these districts are all anxiety for the success of the Emigration Question', he claimed. At Leeds he found operatives in 'a depressed state', with one of the area's main manufactories having suspended production. Fifty miles to the north he met employees at the South

Stockton works, run by Potteries-born John Whalley. After commending the union's emigration plans, Whalley reassured his visitor that his use of machinery posed no threat to livelihoods. Evans was unconvinced: 'harmless' at the time, Whalley's pressing machine 'displays features of extension and improvement, that will prove of the most serious consequence to working potters'.[115] Continuing his journey northwards, at Middlesbrough and Newcastle he found the price of labour greatly depressed, while at nearby South Hylton he was shocked to find the 'curse and abomination of our trade – the Pilfering Allowance System' still operating. He ended his tour in Scotland, visiting works in Edinburgh, Glasgow and Greenock before returning home along the same route.

Exhausted by his trip, the editor's 'sudden indisposition' forced the *Examiner* to replace its lead article with a memoir of the American abolitionist William Lloyd Garrison. Evans needed all the strength he could muster. During his absence the Hanley hollow-ware pressers had finally determined to leave the potters' union and affiliate with the NAUT. In a lengthy article on 3 October under the heading 'Our Old Foes in New Guise', he vented his anger at the decision which he saw as the culmination of a long-term campaign to weaken the UBOP and destroy the *Examiner* – whose circulation he admitted was 'falling' – and 'its poor and humble servant'. He was especially scathing about the Hanley men's claim that they were organising a union 'on better principles' when all they sought was '*division*'. And he coined a new word for them: seceders.[116] Vilification of their actions now littered the *Examiner*'s columns. To rebut the challenge, the UBOP committee mobilised every available weapon. In mid-October it published a series of tracts, their titles indicative of a determination to expose their case: 'Deception Exploded'; 'Hypocrisy Unmasked and Falsehood Laid Bare'; 'Folly and Inconsistency, Displayed by Those Who Call Themselves "The Pottery District of the National Association of United Trades"'; and, more affirmatively, 'The Emigration Society, The Only Hope of Working Potters'.[117] It simultaneously issued a prospectus for the union's reorganisation.[118] On his northern tour Evans had witnessed the growth of the miscellaneous system, and he urged Staffordshire workers to follow the out-potteries' lead as the means of averting the union's fragmentation and resisting mechanisation. ' A crisis has arrived in the progress of our trade', he wrote at the end of October, 'which if not met with one unanimous stand, must inevitably end in our utter desolation. Machinery is upon us; whether for good or ill, *we* must decide.'[119]

Evans's deployment of the machinery threat had somewhat subsided over the past year; faced with an existential challenge to the union and emigration scheme, he vigorously revived it. In mid-October he lectured to audiences at Burslem, Tunstall and Stoke, during which he displayed specimens of the machine-made ware collected on his travels. According to a report in *The Staffordshire Advertiser* – a rare notice for the union – Evans traced the history of northern mechanisation to Andrew Scott, proprietor of the Southwick Pottery near Sunderland, who in the wake of the 1836–7 strike had invented a machine for the manufacture of flat- and hollow-ware that eliminated many defects of earlier prototypes. Versions of Scott's machine had infiltrated potteries in Newcastle, Middlesbrough and particularly South Stockton, where John Whalley had 'brought it to the greatest perfection'. In the reporter's view, Evans's specimens 'seemed to be of a high order of excellence' and 'equal to the best productions of the old skilled manipulating process'. The potential consequences were enormous: 'Skilled manual labour in the fabrication of many sorts of ware is almost superseded by this invention.'[120]

For the remainder of 1846 there would be no let-up in Evans's efforts to warn potters of the mechanisation threat, nor in his determination to discredit those seeking to subvert his emigration plans. Addressing a meeting on 19 November at the Christian Brethren's rooms in Hanley, he insisted that should Scott's machine be brought into general use, 1,000 adult potters 'would immediately be thrown out of employ, and their places filled by women and children', a comment that incidentally revealed much about the gender-based and hierarchical nature of relations at the potbank. He next provided a detailed description of the Potters' Emigration Society and 'its power, properly directed, to oppose machinery'. He again concentrated on cost, reiterating what could be achieved through the acquisition of American land when compared to England. Following his remarks, supporters proposed a resolution enjoining every worker to obstruct the introduction of Scott's machine; but before it could be voted on, a local representative of the NAUT (the *Examiner* described him as 'a leading Chartist') intervened to question the potters' leader's integrity and accuse him of perverting the truth about land costs. The interloper also insisted on the futility of 'sectional' trade societies and on the injustice of opposing the progress of mechanisation. In response, Evans argued that he was not hostile to a national union or to 'the proper application of machinery' but to its misapplication, and that so 'long as he had health and strength to oppose it', he would do so.[121]

Thousands of miles away in Pottersville the land officers must have viewed these developments with dismay, but were in no position to affect them. Communication between Staffordshire and the Wisconsin frontier was proving far from straightforward. Five months after the party's arrival, letters were still going astray as a result of confusion over postal addresses; others took an inordinate time to arrive, including one from John Sawyer's family dated 15 June which did not reach him until November.[122] Cataloguing the errant correspondence, Hamlet Copeland advised the Society to direct everything in future to ' "Fox Lake, Dodge County". It is Columbia County that we are in, but Fox Lake is in Dodge County; it is about the same distance as Portage from us, and, in my opinion, will be less liable to mistake.'[123] Despite these difficulties, the men and their families kept abreast of events in the Potteries through letters that did arrive and through the *Examiner*, which Copeland described as 'indispensably necessary to the successful working of our Society'. They were thus aware of the challenges that Evans and the union faced in sustaining support for a scheme for which they were the transatlantic standard-bearers. 'I should like to hear of the potters taking up the cause with a better spirit, for I believe it is the best cause that they ever undertook', wrote James Hammond two days before Christmas from his snowbound home.[124]

Arguably the most important communication after the men's arrival was that containing the draft for £600 agreed by the Society in July. Unfortunately, optimism that this would resolve their problems proved false. Writing home in the New Year, they described their efforts to use the draft to pay for preempted land. On the advice of a prominent Fox Lake pioneer, Dr Stoddard Judd, they set off at the end of September by hired wagon for the district land office at Green Bay, 120 miles to the northeast. Judd, who acted as an agent for those acquiring property in the area, reassured them that the office there would accept the unconverted draft, thus avoiding a detour to Milwaukie.[125] They reached Green Bay after a three-day journey and discovered to their annoyance that Judd was mistaken. The land office functionary refused the draft, telling them that with such a large acreage, it was 'a great pity we had not brought specie, and he could not receive any kind of paper money, not even their own treasury notes'. Returning to their lodgings, the men retrieved their wagon and set off immediately for Milwaukie. The journey south over rough roads proved gruelling and included a tense encounter with two armed Native Americans, who appeared disappointed by the travellers' lack of whisky. Arriving at the lakeside city, their education continued when they were forced to pay a 1-per-cent discount to convert the draft into hard currency. 'We were very much grieved at having to pay anything ... but trust that you will give us credit for having done our best', they reported. After concluding their business, the men went to the district court, where they registered their intentions to become US citizens, a prerequisite for acquiring land under the 1841 law. As neither they nor their oxen were in a condition to make the trek back to Green Bay, they returned directly to Pottersville. Despite his earlier advice, they had decided to pursue the Society's business through Dr Judd, 'but at different times, so that he would not have any great sum in his hands at once'.[126]

The land officers' narrative of their Green Bay expedition reveals them anxious to demonstrate how hard they were working to honour the trust placed in them by fellow potters. And they had a great deal of which to be proud. Progress at the settlement had been impressive, with homes constructed, wheat sown and preparations having begun for the anticipated arrival of new members in the spring. Reporting at the beginning of November, James Hammond enthused about their achievements thus far, including the choice of location, which he described as 'healthy as any in the States'. With his farming background, he sought to reassure prospective migrants about conditions in America. 'You wish to know whether a potter can make a farmer, or not. A potter *can* make a farmer; for the land does not require much farming in this country', he told them. He also eased the worries of those reared on frontier stories that no wolves had been seen lately and that '*there is nothing to be feared at Pottersville*'. He concluded by noting the growth of neighbouring settlements, including one of Welsh farmers four miles away,[127] and by extolling the freedoms that the potters and their families now enjoyed in the western republic: 'We have no rent-days here; no tax-gatherers; no coal-carriers calling every Monday-morning, for their pay; no person here calling for his tithe; no beggars here; no bastille staring you in the face; BUT ALL WE RAISE IS OUR OWN.'[128]

Such language was music to William Evans's ears, a vindication of everything he had striven for since the creation of the emigration scheme. But the progress in America masked an indisputable fact; after nearly three years of planning, the Society had acquired only a fraction of the land needed to fulfil its surplus labour and other goals. Part of the problem was the lack of financial support from working potters; but naivety and poor preparation, particularly in regard to land payments, also contributed to the shortfall. Intermixed with the officers' descriptions of their achievements in Wisconsin was the continuing lament about finding and retaining suitable tracts of productive land. Demand for land in Wisconsin was rising rapidly after a period of depression; the years after 1845 were the 'halcyon days' of the state's land market.[129] Writing on the eve of setting out for Green Bay, John Sawyer claimed that before his letter left America, he expected them to have purchased 2,000 acres, 'proof that our plans are not altogether a failure'.[130] In his updated report, published in the *Examiner* on 26 December, Hamlet Copeland was anxious not to be misunderstood. He doubted whether a 'compact colony' of 4,000 acres was achievable 'without having other land interspersed amongst it'. It was 'a matter of deep regret to us', he wrote, 'that a large portion of our original selection is now taken up by others, and which we had not the slightest possible means in our power of preventing'. Without the resources to pay for it, much of their claimed land had been lost, so that 'our Estate cannot now be gotten in that regular form, which we at first anticipated it would be'. So uncertain was the situation that, five months after their arrival, Copeland was unable to furnish the Society with a map of the potters' estate, although he promised to send one once the land was properly purchased.[131]

If Evans was disheartened by Copeland's remarks, he chose to conceal it, calling his letter a 'Christmas box' for the paper's readers. There was actually much to celebrate in its contents. Despite the admission that the Society's plans could not be fully realised, his description of the building of the land officers' houses revealed a community of shared endeavour, of cheerful cooperation between old and new settlers, which augured well for Pottersville's long-term prospects. To raise spirits further, he reported an addition to its population: Martha Hammond had given birth to a son, the first to be 'born in the colony'. Mother and child were doing well. But there was another reason for Evans's optimism. Accompanying the publication of Copeland's letter were the results of the Estate Committee elections. Eight men, representing six different branches of the trade, would leave for America in the spring with their families; all were in good health and 'ready to enter on the estate of working potters'. At a stroke, the settlement's population would increase by a further forty-four. As 1847 dawned, there was good reason to believe that many more would soon follow.[132]

Notes

1 *PEWA*, 21 December 1844.
2 Andrew R. Heaton, *Hannah's American Dream* (Glaisdale: Fryup Press, 2016), pp. 1–8, 19–24, 65, 71–4.
3 *PEWA*, 7 December 1844.
4 *PEWA*, 28 December 1844. Dodge served as Wisconsin's territorial governor in 1836–41 and 1845–8.
5 *Sheffield Independent*, 16 December 1843.
6 John B. Newhall, *The British Emigrants' 'Hand Book' and Guide to the New States of America, Particularly Illinois, Iowa, and Wisconsin* (London: T. Sutter, 1844), quoted in Jacob Van der Zee, *The British in Iowa* (Iowa City: State Historical Society of Iowa, 1922), p. 20. See also Shepperson, *British Emigration to North America*, pp. 62–3, 127.
7 Accounts of the Society are William Kittle, *History of the Township and Village of Mazomanie* (Madison, WI: State Journal Print Co., 1900), pp. 9–47; Shepperson, *British Emigration to North America*, pp. 127–8; and Vivien Vale, 'English Settlers in Early Wisconsin: the British Temperance Emigration Society', *Bulletin of the British Association for American Studies*, 9 (1964), 24–31.
8 *The Emigrant's Instructor on Wisconsin and the Western States of America* (Liverpool: British Temperance Emigration Society, 2nd edn, 1844), p. 3.

9 I am keeping the older spelling of the Wisconsin city, the one most frequently used in contemporary reports. Not until 1862 did it finally settle on 'Milwaukee'.
10 See the two letters from Charles and Elizabeth Wilson in *The Emigrant's Instructor*, pp. 35, 38.
11 *Ibid.*, p. 46.
12 *PEWA*, 18 January 1845.
13 *PEWA*, 1 March 1845.
14 *PEWA*, 15 March 1845. For reports of discontent among the Temperance Society's members, see Edwin Bottomley to his parents, 17 June 1845, in Milo M. Quaife (ed.), *An English Settler in Pioneer Wisconsin: The Letters of Edwin Bottomley, 1842–1850* (Madison: State Historical Society of Wisconsin, 1918), p. 94.
15 *PEWA*, 26 April 1845. See *Sheffield Independent*, 26 July 1845 for details of its founding. The Society's plans do not appear to have come to much fruition.
16 *PEWA*, 8 February 1845; *Northern Star and National Trades' Journal*, 29 March 1845. See also *PEWA*, 15, 22 February 1845. See the outstanding article by Gregory Claeys, 'John Adolphus Etzler, Technological Utopianism, and British Socialism: The Tropical Emigration Society's Venezuelan Mission and its Social Context, 1833–1848', *English Historical Review* 101:399 (1986), 351–75.
17 *PEWA*, 19 April 1845.
18 *PEWA*, 18 January 1845.
19 *PEWA*, 1 March 1845.
20 *PEWA*, 1 March 1845.
21 *PEWA*, 25 January 1845.
22 *PEWA*, 11 January 1845.
23 Owen, *The Staffordshire Potter*, p. 78.
24 *North Staffordshire Mercury*, 14 December 1844.
25 *North Staffordshire Mercury*, 25 January 1845.
26 *North Staffordshire Mercury*, 28 December 1844.
27 *PEWA*, 4 January 1845.
28 *PEWA*, 12 April 1845.
29 *PEWA*, 18 January 1845.
30 *PEWA*, 19 April 1845.
31 *PEWA*, 12 April 1845.
32 *PEWA*, 19 April 1845.
33 *PEWA*, 26 April 1845.
34 *PEWA*, 10 May 1845.
35 *PEWA*, 10 May 1845.
36 *PEWA*, 17 May 1845.
37 *PEWA*, 3 May 1845.
38 *PEWA*, 24 May 1845.
39 Stephen Roberts, *Radical Politicians and Poets in Early Victorian Britain: The Voices of Six Chartist Leaders* (Lewiston, ME: The Edwin Mellon Press, 1993), p. 94.

40 *Northern Star and National Trades' Journal*, 31 May 1845.
41 *Staffordshire Mercury and Potteries Gazette*, 14 June 1845. The paper reverted to its original title of *Staffordshire Mercury* in April 1845.
42 *Northern Star and National Trades' Journal*, 28 June 1845.
43 *Northern Star and National Trades' Journal*, 29 March 1845.
44 *PEWA*, 7 June 1845.
45 Evans refers to two short-lived Owenite communities, at Orbiston in Lanarkshire and Harmony Hall in Hampshire.
46 *PEWA*, 21 June 1845.
47 *PEWA*, 12 April 1845.
48 *PEWA*, 7 June 1845.
49 *PEWA*, 6 September 1845. See also 27 September 1845.
50 *PEWA*, 16 August 1845.
51 *PEWA*, 23 August 1845.
52 *PEWA*, 6 September 1845.
53 *PEWA*, 20 September 1845.
54 *PEWA*, 18 October 1845.
55 *PEWA*, 11 October 1845. Evans's 'four great Branches' comprised the hollow-ware pressers, flat-pressers, printers and ovenmen.
56 *PEWA*, 11 November 1845.
57 *PEWA*, 13 December 1845.
58 *Northern Star and National Trades' Journal*, 2 August 1845.
59 *PEWA*, 16 August 1845.
60 Warburton, *The History of the Trade Union Organisations*, p. 129.
61 *Staffordshire Mercury and Potteries Gazette*, 13 December 1845. See also *The Staffordshire Advertiser*, 13 December 1845.
62 *PEWA*, 27 December 1845.
63 MacDonagh, *A Pattern of Government Growth*, p. 163.
64 *The Staffordshire Advertiser*, 28 June 1845; *Liverpool Mercury*, 18 November 1844. The family were lucky to survive; the hurricane destroyed life, crops and property in Cuba as well as numerous vessels off Key West. *St Landry Whig* (Louisiana), 24 October 1844.
65 *PEWA*, 10 January 1846.
66 Walter Sawyer Hopkins and Andrew Winkle Hopkins, *The Richard and Harriet Hopkins Family: Empire Prairie Pioneers* (Denver, CO: Big Mountain Press, 1963), pp. 26–31.
67 *PEWA*, 11 July 1846.
68 *PEWA*, 17 January 1846.
69 *PEWA*, 27 September 1845.
70 *PEWA*, 17 January 1846.
71 *PEWA*, 7 February 1846. The officers also took with them £100 for expenses.
72 The *New York* was owned by the Black Ball Line. http://shipbuildinghistory.com/shipyards/19thcentury/webb (last accessed 19 November 2022).
73 The vessel, *Leonidas*, was on its way from Quebec. *Lloyd's List*, 12 January 1841; *Belfast Commercial Chronicle*, 16 January 1841; *Boston Post*, 30 August 1842.

74 Edwin Atlee Barber, *Historical Sketch of the Green Point (n. y.) Porcelain Works of Charles Cartlidge & Co.* (Indianapolis, IN: The Clay-worker, 1895), pp. 4–12.
75 *PEWA*, 9 May 1846. The daily journal was sent home under the signature of all three officers, but this section, at least, is Hammond's voice.
76 *PEWA*, 13 June 1846.
77 *Liverpool Mercury*, 6 February 1846.
78 *PEWA*, 27 June 1846.
79 *PEWA*, 7 December 1844. Maddock emigrated to New York in the spring of 1844.
80 *PEWA*, 6, 13 June 1846. The number of pottery crates is identified from a later set of accounts. *PEWA*, 12 December 1846. On the formation of American preferences, see Ewins, ' "Supplying the Present Wants of our Yankee Cousins …" ', pp. 38–55.
81 *PEWA*, 23 May 1846.
82 *PEWA*, 16 May 1846.
83 The Oregon boundary dispute threatened an Anglo-American rupture. The June 1846 treaty ended the joint occupancy and established the forty-ninth parallel as the boundary between the United States and British North America in the northwest.
84 The brothers are identified in a biography of their father: Allen C. Clark, *James Heighe Blake: The Third Mayor of the Corporation of Washington [1813–1817]* (Washington, DC: Columbia Historical Society, 1921), pp. 162–3.
85 The account of the Washington visit is from *PEWA*, 6 June 1846.
86 *PEWA*, 27 June 1846.
87 On Hunt's colony, see Harrison, *Robert Owen and the Owenites in Britain and America*, pp. 174–5; Montgomery Eduard McIntosh, 'Cooperative Communities in Wisconsin', *Proceedings of the State Historical Society of Wisconsin* 51 (1903), 113–15; and John C. Langdon, 'Pocket Editions of the New Jerusalem: Owenite Communitarianism in Britain, 1825–1855' (DPhil dissertation, University of York, 2000), pp. 323–30.
88 The extract from *The Reasoner* was published in *PEWA*, 11 July 1846.
89 Columbia County was created from Portage County on 1 May 1846.
90 *PEWA*, 20 June 1846.
91 Roy M. Robbins, 'Preemption: A Frontier Triumph', *Mississippi Valley Historical Review* 18:3 (1931), 331–49. The full text of the Act is available at '1841, September 4 – 5 Stat. 453 – Preemption Act of 1841' (2016), *US Government Legislation and Statutes*, 8, https://digitalcommons.csumb.edu/hornbeck_usa_2_d/8 (last accessed 22 November 2022).
92 *PEWA*, 22 August 1846. Their anxiety partly derived from uncertainty regarding contractual obligations. Curiously, they failed to take a copy of their contract with them. 'I think that I perfectly understand it; but John thinks otherwise', wrote Hamlet Copeland, in requesting a copy. *PEWA*, 20 June 1846.
93 *PEWA*, 1 August 1846.
94 *PEWA*, 14 November 1846.
95 *PEWA*, 14 February 1846.

96 *PEWA*, 7 March 1846. See also 30 May 1846.
97 *The Staffordshire Advertiser*, 21 March 1846; *Staffordshire Mercury and Potteries Gazette*, 18 April 1846.
98 *PEWA*, 14 March 1846.
99 *PEWA*, 21 March 1846.
100 *PEWA*, 28 March 1846.
101 [Shaw,] *When I Was a Child*, pp. 34–5. On rhetoric and persuasion, see Stephen Fender, *Sea Changes: British Emigration and American Literature* (Cambridge: Cambridge University Press, 1992), pp. 46ff.
102 *PEWA*, 25 April 1846.
103 *PEWA*, 19 December 1846; Bronstein, *Land Reform and Working-Class Experience in Britain and the United States*, pp. 154–5. On the National Reform Association, see also Mark A. Lause, *Young America: Land, Labor, and the Republican Community* (Urbana: University of Illinois Press, 2005).
104 Bronstein, *Land Reform and Working-Class Experience in Britain and the United States*, p. 125.
105 Evans, *Art and History of the Potting Business*, pp. iii–xi.
106 Owen, *The Staffordshire Potter*, p. 84.
107 *PEWA*, 15 August 1846.
108 Burchill and Ross, *A History of the Potter's Union*, p. 97.
109 *PEWA*, 27 June 1846.
110 Owen, *The Staffordshire Potter*, p. 89.
111 *PEWA*, 22 August 1846.
112 *Northern Star and National Trades' Journal*, 6 June 1846. Evans's report of the meeting was still positive. As a sign of his standing, he was invited to address a general meeting of the carpenters' union at Carpenter's Hall, Manchester. *PEWA*, 13 June 1846.
113 *Northern Star and National Trades' Journal*, 25 April 1846.
114 Warburton, *The History of the Trade Union Organization in the North Staffordshire Potteries*, p. 134; *Northern Star and National Trades' Journal*, 3 October 1846. See also Fyson, 'Chartism in North Staffordshire', pp. 299–300. On the NAUT, see Chase, *Early Trade Unionism*, pp. 207–15. One historian has described the NAUT as 'Chartism's contribution to trade unionism'. David Goodway, *London Chartism, 1838–1848* (Cambridge: Cambridge University Press, 1982), p. 56.
115 The pottery at South Stockton, founded in 1825 by William Smith, was noted for its early use of machinery. See Oxley Grabham, *Yorkshire Potteries, Pots and Potters* (York: Coultas & Volans, 1916), p. 98.
116 *PEWA*, 3 October 1846.
117 *PEWA*, 17 October 1846.
118 Ibid.
119 *PEWA*, 31 October 1846.
120 *The Staffordshire Advertiser*, 24 October 1846.
121 *PEWA*, 28 November 1846.
122 *PEWA*, 27 March 1847.
123 *PEWA*, 26 December 1846.

124 *PEWA*, 27 March 1847.
125 On Judd, see *The History of Dodge County, Wisconsin* (Chicago, IL: Western Historical Company, 1880), p. 349; and a useful article, 'Fox Lake Was Site of Land Office Receiver', *Fox Lake Daily Citizen*, 4 March 2013.
126 *PEWA*, 27 March 1847.
127 Columbia County was one of the principal rural destinations for Welsh emigrants. See Phillips G. Davies, *Welsh in Wisconsin* (Madison: Wisconsin Historical Society Press, revised and expanded edition, 2006), pp. 7, 12.
128 *PEWA*, 12 January 1847.
129 Paul W. Gates, 'Frontier Land Business in Wisconsin', *Wisconsin Magazine of History*, 52:4 (1969), 320.
130 *PEWA*, 14 November 1847.
131 *PEWA*, 26 December 1846. Signed by all three officers, the letter was clearly written by Copeland.
132 *Ibid*.

4

1847–8: Settling the land

William Evans was determined to begin the new year as he ended the old. In marking the advent of his paper's seventh volume, he gave no hint of the difficulties he and his co-workers faced in implementing the emigration plan. His message was one of confidence, buoyed by the ongoing reorganisation of the potters' union. 'Our society is progressing, – steadily progressing! and every week sees the investment of some £10 in *bona fide* property, for the good of the trade', he trumpeted. Despite the realisation that the Society would have to abandon its original design of compact settlement, Evans was certain that before June next it would add a further 1,200 acres to its present holding of 2,000, and that, remarkably, it would achieve this '*without the addition of a single extra farthing to our present funds*'. His explanation was simple. The Society would require each Estate Committee member to preempt 160 acres, 'costing no more than some twelve or fourteen dollars'. Compare this to £50 an acre 'for over-taxed British Soil!' proposed by our 'Chartist *friends*', he could not resist adding.[1] The land would of course still have to be paid for, and emigration expenses met, and nothing in Evans's message indicated any new thinking on how these were to be accomplished. Monies continued to trickle in, and it was hoped that the election and departure of the Estate Committee would rekindle subscriber interest. But the economic climate remained uncertain, tempering a likely surge in income. In early November 1846 trade was reported as flat, with short-time work already in evidence; by January *The Staffordshire Advertiser* was noting 'a degree of depression' in the Potteries, with most firms restricting hours. A decline in orders from America was again adduced as a factor in the downturn.[2]

On 11 January 1847, at the Sneyd's Arms in Tunstall, the Potters' Emigration Society held its first farewell event, a 'Concert and Ball' for the newly elected Estate Committee. Others would follow: at the George and Dragon, Hanley (18 January); the Three Tuns, Longton (25 January); the Star, Burslem (1 February); the Angel, Fenton (8 February); and the Wheat Sheaf, Stoke (15 February). The celebrations culminated in a grand party in Hanley Town Hall on 15 March, where resolutions unequivocally linked the emigration project to the struggle against machinery.[3] Conscious of the need to involve wives and other family members, the Society also hosted informal gatherings away from the usual public-house venues. A tea party at the union's printing establishment in Hanley on Sunday, 24 January was designed so that families travelling to America could get to know one another. The occasion began with a hymn; conversations ensued about the Atlantic crossing, the nature of the American log house and a host of other matters relating to the coming adventure. The emphasis throughout was on mutual assistance. The Estate Committee members gave this pledge: 'One could build, and plaster, with any man; another could make bricks; and a third could do anything in the building way except "carpeting", and that he could not do from want of tools; a fourth understood mining; – a fifth would open a school.'[4] The potters' settlement in Wisconsin would after all be a cooperative enterprise, but one stemming from practical necessity rather than any coherent ideology, Owenite or otherwise.

It was also announced that the Hanley ovenman and Primitive Methodist preacher Isaac Smith would serve as 'pastor of the flock', with the instruction to hold Sabbath-day prayers in the settlement's schoolroom. Pottery workers lived in communities steeped in Christian faith and practice – at least one family carried with them presentation Bibles from their local Sunday School[5] – and it was important that the Society made provision for their continuance on the frontier. The emigration scheme, however, was born out of secular dissent. Unlike Mormon converts, for whom the physical act of leaving North Staffordshire was inseparable from their spiritual quest,[6] potters were driven by a strong sense of the earthly benefits they would derive from a move to America. If there was to be a potters' Zion in Wisconsin, a workers' paradise on the prairie, independence and security would be its pillars; once these were erected, spiritual renewal was in their grasp. William Evans's own religiosity is difficult to gauge. Baptised an Anglican, he turned his back on religion in proper Owenite fashion before returning to the fold after 1839 and the family's move to the Potteries, where, influenced by his friendship with the prominent preacher James Bourne, he converted to Primitive Methodism.[7] As Jamie Bronstein has described, there was a strong religious and moral component to land reform beliefs, and a clear revivalist echo at the Society's meetings.[8] In an early defence of his emigration plans, Evans waxed powerfully on labour's natural right to the land. 'Where is *their* share of God's earth? – where is *their* sustenance for God's gift of life', he demanded.[9] Yet millennialist imagery, Old Testament quotation and natural rights arguments aside, there is no evidence that he invested his emigration scheme with any specific religious tenet or doctrine. In July 1846 he removed from his paper's masthead the motto 'God and our right' – it first appeared on 1 June 1844 set within an engraving designed by his father[10] – replacing it with a symbol of clasped hands. He offered no explanation for the removal, except to note that 'A love of change seems to characterize the spirit of the age; and the love must be gratified, even though it be in trifles'.[11]

There was little sign of intense religious feeling at the Sneyd's Arms, where potters gathered for the first of the weekly celebrations. The purpose of this and subsequent events was to raise support for emigration and, equally important, give those present the opportunity to hear directly from the men entrusted with managing the American settlement. Elected on a district basis, in the end only six trades – flat-pressers, hollow-ware pressers, mould makers, handlers, printers and ovenmen – were represented in the eight-man group.[12] Five of the eight – Henry Dooley, George Summerfield, William Bradshaw, Enoch Pickering and Isaac Smith – were chosen by district election; the remaining three – George Robertshaw, Samuel Fox and Joseph Clews – were appointed by the union's central committee. All three were currently unemployed, with Robertshaw and Fox supported by the 'Fund for Persecuted Cases' and Clews by the central committee. Announcing the men's nominations, Evans stressed the sacrifices made through their inability to work. Twelve months earlier Samuel Fox had lost 'a good situation for standing up for a general good and for labour'. Although he eventually found employment, it was short-lived, and he was now 'discharged again, without further hope'. Like Fox, George Robertshaw, a hollow-ware presser from Burslem, was praised for his sobriety and his 'devotedness to the union objects'. Joseph Clews, also from Burslem and a handler, was held in 'high esteem' by his fellow workmen. Out of work for nearly twelve months, he was noted for his 'patience, fortitude and perseverance' and his dedicated efforts 'without work and without pay' on behalf of his lodge. May he, like the others, find a better home in America 'than he has yet had on the overtaxed soil of his own country', wrote Evans.[13]

The eight men were diffident speakers, unused to public display; all were dedicated unionists, proud of their commissions and determined to hasten what the Tunstall flat-presser Henry Dooley called 'the era of potting redemption'. In an extraordinary surviving fragment written on the inside cover of an account book taken to Wisconsin, Dooley jotted down comments he would make as he prepared to address the farewell gatherings.

> Fellow Potters, There is nothing that I know of however Publicly or Privately important that could have induced me to assend a platform and stand before an audience but the present Buissness circumstances under consideration. A many people wonder whatever can have caused me to think of leaving this country they tell me I have a good situation a small family and possess the chance of doing as well or better than most of my class to such as these I answer can

you allways guarantee to me that i shall keep my present situation and give me positive satisfaction that I shall never do any worse than i now do again shall I always possess good health the favour of overlookers and employers is very uncertain and can i promise myself that i shall through all the ins and outs of Low craft and cunning.[14]

The first speaker at the opening event in Tunstall was Enoch Pickering, a mould maker from Stoke. He talked of 'every man's duty to assist in creating the greatest amount of happiness to the greatest number', and guaranteed to do all in his power 'to promote the happiness of those whose interests he was sent to watch over, on their land abroad'. In similar vein, Isaac Smith claimed that he and his colleagues had done their best 'to forward union in these districts; and he hoped that he should continue in the same honest course as heretofore, ever promoting the best interests of the trade'. Other speakers echoed Smith's sentiments, including Samuel Fox. The unemployed flat-presser had always stood up 'in defence of labour', actions that had cost him his job, and he now pledged 'to continue his exertions in the new sphere'. Surely 'the time was not far distant, when all would be moved beyond the fear of want, and in full possession', he told fellow potters. Another staunch union supporter who promised to continue that work across the Atlantic was 30-year-old George Robertshaw. This was the first time he had appeared 'before a public company', and his only regret was that eighty, not eight, potters might travel to America.

So far, these reported comments betray little bitterness towards the employer; indeed, one member, George Summerfield, a printer, claimed that not all manufacturers were 'tyrants' and that he 'had conversed with some who wished him every success and our land plan every prosperity'. However, there was manifest resentment at an industry that continued to deprive workers of the full fruits of their labour. William Bradshaw, a mould maker elected by the Hanley district, spoke for many in rejoicing at the prospect of leaving good-from-oven behind him, describing it as 'a most wretched system' with 'more robbery and tyranny practised under it, than under all the other practices of the trade, put together'. But what sort of personal transformation did the men desire or expect by swapping the potbank for the prairie? Henry Dooley, at least, was realistic: 'He knew that he should have to labour; but the produce of his labour would be his *own*! ... and he did not care how soon he set his foot on the vessel that was to convey him from this slave-ridden soil'. Instead of good-from-oven, agreed Bradshaw, 'he should now have his twenty acres of land, a good substantial dwelling, and five acres cultivated, without parsons, tithes, taxes, and poor-rates'. Besides, he added with a smile, 'there were wild dear [sic] running up and down the land asking for someone to come and shoot them!' The same vision drove Isaac Smith, who could not wait for the group's departure and whose large family – 'six children all under fourteen years of age' – was central to his goal of independent proprietorship. His wife Sarah was also 'deeply anxious to go'; she was in fact ' "the best man of the two" '. It was left to the final speaker, Joseph Clews, a father of four, to sum up with simple eloquence the sentiments of all of the men: 'He was tired of this country; and he felt assured that he was about to depart to a land of freedom, and one that would give a just reward for all honest toil.'[15]

On the Tunstall evidence, the yeoman ideal was alive and well in North Staffordshire. The men chosen to oversee the Wisconsin settlement were not driven by narrow materialism – potters were among the better-paid manufacturing workers in the 1840s – but rather by the prospect of acquiring in America the security, freedom and independence that English industrial society could no longer furnish. In opting to become farmers, potters revealed attitudes that Malcolm Chase has identified as core components of popular agrarianism, especially the emphasis upon control over one's own labour.[16] Yet how far Smith, Dooley and the others saw themselves as subscribing to a radical back-to-the-land ethos is doubtful; after all, rural settlement might still allow them to ply their old trade as a small-scale supplement to farming, yet freed from the exploitations and degradations of industrial production. Finally, we should not underestimate the men's belief in a duty owed to fellow trade unionists left behind in the Potteries. As their remarks demonstrate, relocation to the American frontier embodied both a personal quest for renewal and an unselfish attempt to enhance the welfare of a trade to which they remained strongly attached. Dooley's phrase, 'potting redemption', neatly sums up this aim; that it went unfulfilled should not blind us to its sincerity.

Three months would elapse between the Tunstall celebration and the Estate Committee's departure. Evans continued to beat the editorial drum for emigration, aided by another 'victory' over Scott's machine, this time at Copeland and Garrett's works in Stoke, prompting yet another proposal for a new fund, 'for the obstruction of machinery', with half-crown levies payable by instalments of as little as threepence. 'Even the female branches of the trade will not refuse to assist in this great work of Labour's protection', he insisted.[17] He also tried to persuade more potters to join the pioneer party. In an article on 13 February headed 'When Do They Depart?' – about 24 March was the current idea – he reiterated the attractions of the emigration scheme, fleshing out details about accommodation and credit and repeating his plan to expand the Society's landholding through further preemption. Although his focus was family migration, he also appealed to single men who could 'cross the water, and get up to the estate for about £7'. Again, Evans felt it necessary to remind potters of the scheme's core aim: the removal of surplus labour, given new charge by the threat of mechanisation.

He ended with a familiar flourish, a pulling together of emigration's ideological and emotional threads.

> There will be no fear of employers here; – there will be no persecuted cases; – there will be no draining of funds, to keep men in idleness; – there will be no 'pickets' on the watch for strayed 'nobsticks'; all will be a clear remove, by the most simple and quiet machinery, from the pot-works, to the field; – from dependence, to independence; from the dust and disease of a poisonous workshop, to the healthy and plenty-supplying home of a twenty-acre farm![18]

By the end of February Evans could report that the Estate Committee party had increased to 'some dozen families, numbering about sixty individuals, one half adults'. Enrolment in the Society was also improving, notwithstanding the 'deplorably wretched' state of the pottery trade.[19] Confident that the scheme was off the ground, the editor was in no mood for concessions to its critics. In January the central committee rebuffed an advance by the Hanley seceders to settle their differences and recombine for the 'common purpose of trade protection'.[20] A proposal from the Hanley branch of the Chartist Cooperative Land Company for three public debates also came to nothing when the Company rejected the potters' demands for publication of accompanying letters in the *Northern Star*. The *Star* is 'a national organ', intoned its secretary, and cannot be expected to 'lend its aid to little emigration questions'.[21]

The backdrop to these exchanges was the wider competition for workers' allegiances. In February 1847 the National Association of United Trades for the Protection of Labour (NAUT) resumed its recruiting mission in the Potteries. Its agent was the Chartist secretary of the London tailors, John Whitaker Parker. Parker spent several weeks in Staffordshire addressing trades' meetings about the advantages of a national organisation 'as being superior to local efforts'.[22] On 16 February he met with painters and gilders at the Royal Oak, Hanley; two days later at the Golden Lion in the same town he spoke to a general meeting of pottery workers, where a lone voice, a Mr Adams of the Potters' Emigration Society, dissented from the resolution pledging that 'we, the operative potters of Staffordshire' would cooperate with other trades to carry out the NAUT's plans.[23] Parker pressed his case the following week in Stoke and again in Hanley and two days later in Longton, where he met crate makers. These efforts had some success. A new district meeting of the various trades was set up, with the potter Edward Humphries, who had accompanied Parker throughout his visit and would go on to achieve national office in the NAUT, appointed secretary. Although potters' responses overall are difficult to gauge, the *Northern Star* reported that upwards of 100 names had been sent in to join the new lodge in the wake of the painters and gilders' meeting.[24]

Few pottery workers actually joined the NAUT. As Robert Fyson notes, crowded meetings did not guarantee increased membership, especially at a time of deepening depression.[25] Hanley seceders aside, recruitment was strongest among the crate makers, an auxiliary occupation, and the painters and gilders, a relatively new society. The NAUT also made little headway in the out-potteries.[26] Nevertheless, with its greater resources and broad strategy, it posed a challenge to a union irretrievably committed to emigration as the principal means of resolving the surplus labour problem. The NAUT returned to the Potteries at the end of April. This time it targeted individual firms, including Wedgwood's, whose workers met at the Etruria Inn to hear its 'principles and objects' explained by its agent William Peel.[27] The Emigration Society had barely deigned to notice Parker's mission, but the renewed initiative drew Evans into responding. On 26 April, at the Golden Lion, he debated with Peel before an audience of workers from Charles Meigh's Old Hall Pottery, who, undecided between the rival organisations, invited each to make its case. In his half-hour speech, Evans insisted that he was 'highly favourable' to the National Trades' movement – but only after the potters had carried out their emigration plan. The decision of these present, – less than a third of the workforce – was victory for the NAUT by a vote of twenty-eight to thirteen.[28] Further exchanges followed as the NAUT continued its activities in the Potteries, including involvement in September in a strike by Longton crate makers.[29] While sympathetic to many of its aims, Evans viewed its opposition as part of a long-term design dating back to O'Connor's interventions nearly three years earlier: 'In the Sheffield Debt movement, in the Home Colonization movement, and now in the National Trades Association movement, the one great purpose is "Break up the Potters' Emigration Society, and destroy the Examiner!"'[30]

By the time Evans spoke at the Golden Lion, the Society's plans had entered a new phase. On Tuesday, 6 April the Estate Committee party left the Potteries for Liverpool and the New World. We cannot be certain about the numbers that turned out to witness the departure, but they were undoubtedly in excess of the previous year's send-off. According to the *Examiner*, between 8,000 and 10,000 gathered at the Etruria Wharf, where, to the tunes of the Hanley Temperance Band, pledges of remembrance and 'promises to follow at the next spring were made in every direction'. The excitement at the party's leave-taking was confirmed by the *Mercury*'s account: 'Thousands assembled at Etruria, Burslem, and Tunstall – the banks of the canal were lined by spectators – great numbers accompanied the emigrants as far as Wheelock.'[31] Even the *Advertiser* talked of the 'considerable numbers' who assembled to bid the emigrants farewell.[32] The event also created interest outside of Staffordshire, with newspapers as far away as Fife in Scotland reporting it.[33]

Despite the Society's efforts to capitalise on the impending departure, there had been no large increase in the numbers joining the Estate Committee families on their journey to Pottersville. As Evans reported in February, the party as a whole comprised about sixty individuals. Migrants to America in the mid-nineteenth century were generally young, and the potters' party was no exception.[34] Only one member, George Robertshaw's father-in-law William Chatley, in his late sixties by the time of the departure, was born in the eighteenth century. The largest families were those of Isaac Smith and Enoch Pickering, with eight members each. One member, Samuel Fox, would travel alone, his wife Anne, whom he wed at St John's, Burslem on Christmas Day, having died some weeks earlier; another, George Summerfield, was also a widower. Two of his five adult sons would go with him. Reports of the April departure speak of fourteen families; however, Estate Committee members aside, only two other family groups seem to have been involved. Forty-year-old Benjamin Hopkins from Burslem had served apprenticeships in glass blowing – he carried with him to America six glass goblets crafted twenty years earlier – earthenware printing and pawnbroking before failing to establish himself in business. He would struggle with alcohol for much of his adult life. Accompanying him were his wife Elizabeth and their five children.[35] The other non-Estate Committee family was that of William Evans's brother Alexander, like him a painter and gilder; he travelled with his wife Elizabeth and their four young children. As paid-up members, both were entitled to a twenty-acre lot of Society land and twelve months' provisions.[36]

Single men made up the remainder of the party, including George Hammond, younger brother of the Society's conductor. Also in the departing group was Thomas Maddock of Burslem, whose brother William had assisted the land officers in New York a year earlier. He remained in the city, where he established a highly successful china decorating business. There were two late recruits: Richard Whitmore and William Skinner. While we cannot be certain of individual motives, unhappiness at their recent treatment undoubtedly shaped the men's decision to leave. The circumstances of Whitmore's case are unclear, but a well-attended meeting in Burslem on 3 March pledged to contribute sixpence each to the persecuted fund to help the 27-year-old potter claim his American farm.[37] (It is unknown whether he reached Wisconsin; the 1850 census records him working in East Liverpool, after which he would forge a distinguished career as a pottery manufacturer in Akron, Ohio, amassing 'a fortune' before his death in 1897.[38]) Skinner's history is better documented, and shows the exasperation felt by pottery workers at their employment terms and more general disenchantment with conditions in industrialising Britain. Skinner worked as a cup maker at Joseph Clementson's Shelton factory. In March he sued his employer for dismissing him in violation of their agreement. Appearing before Thomas Bailey Rose in Longton, he explained that he had for some time been short of work, and when a situation offered itself in Scotland, he was minded to accept it. Clementson, however, delayed replying to his request for a discharge, by which time the position had been filled. He then dismissed Skinner for reasons which are not given. Rose, belying his reputation, was sympathetic to the journeyman's claim, pointing out that the employer was bound 'under present circumstances, to find the complainant employment, and if his conduct was bad, to bring him before the magistrates'.[39] At a subsequent hearing Clementson withdrew the dismissal, claiming he had been given wrong advice by his foreman, and offered Skinner his job back. The potter's response left no doubt of his state of mind; he would give a month's notice and 'as he was tired of this country, he should leave it for another and a better'. The previous week, anticipating and perhaps influencing his decision, the Society's committee agreed to assist him 'for the persecution he has undergone, to a Twenty-acre Farm, on their estate at Pottersville'.[40]

Manufacturers generally reacted well to their workers' departure, with only one, William Bradshaw's employer, James Edwards of Dale Hall, coming in for criticism. Among those praised for their 'spirit of liberality' was Copeland and Garrett of Stoke which, fresh from its recent machinery dispute, permitted Enoch Pickering to work 'up to the last hour' and to take with him 'what ware he pleased for his family's use'. William Adams of Tunstall granted the same favour to another of the departing group. Special mention was afforded the Hanley manufacturer William Ridgway. A few days before the departure, the *Examiner* reported that Ridgway, who had strong American connections and was about to leave for New York, had sent for one (unnamed, but Isaac Smith) member of the Estate Committee and offered him 'much valuable instruction as to the requisite frugality and industry to be attended to in a new country and a new clime'. He also presented him with medicine for the voyage, 'some books for instruction' and a crate of earthenware, generously paying the latter's freight costs to Liverpool. He made the same present of ware to Alexander Evans and possibly others. Ridgway, reported William Evans with satisfaction, was 'much in favour of our land operations and wished the emigrants every success'.[41]

The group's departure from the Potteries was nothing if not colourful. The three boats carrying them and their baggage to Liverpool left Etruria Wharf festooned with flags proclaiming the dream of a landed home in America, 'Free from Rent, Taxes, and Tithe', as one had it. Evans was again in attendance, busy with last-minute travel and lodging arrangements. They were originally booked on the *Orezaba*, but its sailing was delayed; it had also just discharged a cargo of train oil, and the accommodation was deemed less than ideal. A sudden rise in its charges – steeper partly because the Society had failed to remit the required £25 deposit – encouraged the decision to seek an alternative passage. Evans pleaded the potters' case at the offices of the ship-brokers Harnden & Co and was rewarded with a booking at the original charge of £4 for adults and £3 5s for children on the Boston-built *Clifton*, captained by J. B. Ingersoll, which was due to sail in four days' time. Seven years earlier Ingersoll and the *Clifton* had received widespread commendation following a rescue of passengers and crew from a Le Havre-bound vessel, the *Poland*, which had been struck by lightning five days out from New York.[42]

The potters' crossing produced no such drama. The *Clifton* slipped out of the Mersey on the morning of 13 April with the party all reported in good health. Brisk northwesterly winds contributed to early bouts of sea sickness, but by the end of the first week only Samuel Fox and Sarah Smith continued to suffer the effects. On board were large numbers of Irish emigrants, and there were occasional incidents of friction, including, a few days in, an 'affray' over cooking. The Irish are 'a very passionate and unreasonable lot; but kind treatment soon cooled them down', wrote Enoch Pickering after a later occurrence. Accommodation was also required over religion. The group's pastor, Isaac Smith, was keen to commence his duties, but forbore doing so after consulting the first mate 'for fear of a dispute with the Irish or Catholic part of the passengers'. Otherwise, the main distraction was the unpredictable wind, with two days of 'dead calm' in the second week in May causing anxiety. Finally, in the early morning of 16 April, after thirty-three days at sea, the *Clifton* entered New York waters. Soon after breakfast doctors boarded the ship to inspect the passengers. Seven of the children had come out in a rash which the doctors decided was measles and they ordered the whole party to remain quarantined on board until the next day. Children and their mothers were then conveyed to a nearby hospital, where they were treated 'with every kindness'. All quickly recovered. Once disembarked, of greater concern was the shortage of funds. After apologising for the failure to remit accounts, Pickering explained that provisions were 'very expensive' in New York. He advised future parties to purchase as much as they could at home before departing.[43]

Evans and his co-workers had again revealed their innocence of transatlantic conditions. 'When we left Liverpool', reported the Estate Committee, 'we had but a little above £50, which we then thought would be amply sufficient to carry us to the land at least; and which would, in fact, have done so, if our passage had been paid no farther than New York'. The problems arose from the excessive costs incurred through the emigrants having placed themselves in the care of shipping companies rather than negotiating their travel needs locally. There were also complaints about the goods provided in Liverpool, many of which were deemed substandard. The captain of the *Clifton* 'often upbraided us with being "Harnden and Co'd"', they wrote. Luggage charges were especially steep, and future parties were advised to restrict what they took with them to America. Matters came to a head on arrival in Milwaukie, where they were compelled to pay an 'extravagantly high' landing fee of which they had been previously ignorant.

For some families the costs of migrating to America were far higher. Three of the party, including Charlotte Clews, wife of the Burslem handler, died en route from New York. The other victims were infants. Two-year-old Elizabeth Dooley fell ill on the steamboat from Buffalo. Her parents' only consolation was the captain's reluctant decision to allow the child's body to remain on board so that she could be buried in Milwaukie.[44] The third victim was Alexander and Elizabeth Evans's youngest child, Alexander, who succumbed two hours after their arrival at the lake port. The experience of emigration proved extremely testing for the family. Lack of money forced them to remain in New York as the rest of the party continued their way west. Much of the ware they had taken with them was broken due to poor packing; Alexander lamented that it would have made him 'independent for life'. To make ends meet, he exchanged his watch with Isaac Smith for a gold half-sovereign, to be redeemed when funds permitted. Further help came from the recently arrived William Ridgway, who converted the coin into usable money. The family also benefited from the compassion of strangers. On the boat from Buffalo, a clergyman doctor and his wife took the stricken family in hand, and, among many kind acts, persuaded the captain to waive all passage and freight charges, and gave them nearly $20 to tide them over. Their fortune continued in Milwaukie when they met a man who transported them free of charge to the Society's lands.

In Milwaukie the Evanses caught up with the main party, which had been delayed there due to shortage of funds, requiring the families to sell their ware, including items for personal use. Meeting the group was James Hammond, who would conduct them to the Society's lands 100 miles distant. Hopes that the former Shelton potter would ease their financial worries were quickly dashed; he had no money and was expecting to receive some from them. To depress them further, Hammond revealed that the estate was in debt 'some hundred dollars' for the building of two houses. He also told them that the only land cleared and planted with wheat was an acre and three-quarters on a lot allocated to William Bradshaw, 'which, he is determined to hold for his own exclusive use, and on which we request your opinion and decision'.[45] When the party finally reached Pottersville, they found only four houses built, none of them finished, and two more under construction, poor progress in light of the land officers' promise in

February that they would 'soon have Eight more buildings up'.[46] They were most exercised by the lack of agricultural improvement. 'The land not being broken up has thrown us completely back for the next 12 months; for the season is too far advanced to do anything this year', they advised.[47]

The Estate Committee's first report to the Society from Pottersville, dated 4 July and published in the *Examiner* on 18 September, was dominated by money, or rather the lack of it. Forced to leave part of their luggage in Milwaukie, the men complained that it would likely remain there some time, 'and that time will depend upon you', for they had no funds to retrieve it. These short-term difficulties would soon be resolved; the chronic issue was the effect of lack of money on the Committee's ability to fulfil its instructions. The land officers, Hamlet Copeland, John Sawyer (whose wife Elizabeth died shortly after the Committee's arrival) and James Hammond, had struggled to realise the Society's ambitious preemption plans, and consequently the newcomers were uncertain how best to deploy their scarce resources. 'They contend that they had not the money to purchase for the society', Pickering and the others wrote, 'and that if they did not purchase, other parties would … which we believe to be true; as all the land, round the society's land, is taken up'. Uncertainties about contracts added to the anxiety. These included the procedures for termination, a matter they raised because of the expectation that James Hammond 'will cease his services with the society'. There were also questions about ownership of crops, and about conditions of service.

> When we were in the Potteries, it was our impression, that five acres of our land was to be sown, and fenced out; for which we were to give in return, one day per month in labour, for the period of ten years on the Estate; but since we came here, we have learned that we must pay for it; if not now, at some future period. Please to say which is correct.[48]

Over five months had elapsed since the Estate Committee's departure and William Evans was keen to confound rumours about the party's fate. He admitted that there had been deaths on the long passage from New York, but casualties such as these 'hourly transpire around us; and must be expected in any part of the known world'. He also conceded the difficulties suffered through higher-than-expected costs, and assured members the Society had taken remedial steps, with the dispatch of a banker's draft of £100 and further money sent with the Shelton potter Joseph Clark, who had just left for Wisconsin.[49] Sustaining the momentum had proved a challenge in the weeks after the group's departure. It had begun inauspiciously; on the same day the *Examiner* reported the send-off, it announced the death after a long illness of one of the Society's founding members, Aaron Wedgwood. Born in Burslem in 1803 the son of a New Connexion Methodist preacher and potter, Wedgwood started work as a handler and at an early age was active in support of his fellow operatives. It was his literary talents – honed by early immersion in New Testament prose – that he employed to greatest effect on behalf of emigration and the union. 'Night after night has he been labouring, both with his pen, and in person, to achieve a fair day's wages for a fair day's work', wrote the editor in a brief memoir.[50] In March 1846 illness forced him to stop work; in October the union organised a fund for the relief of a man it described as a 'fearless defender' of potters' rights.[51] Across the Atlantic the land officers prayed that he would soon be restored 'to health and usefulness'.[52] It was already too late. Wedgwood's voice, regularly heard in the *Examiner*, was as reasonable as it was ardent, and his death deprived potters of a valuable counterpoint to Evans's rhetorical excesses.

On 24 April Evans set out the Emigration Society's prospects. Having overseen the Estate Committee's departure, it was time to remind supporters and sceptics alike of what had been achieved in the three years since its launch. The editor was sure that the tide had turned. With more families about to arrive, the future looked bright, and it remained for the parent society 'to give method to the proceedings of the colony, and to secure, if possible, its spiritual, moral, intellectual, and physical prosperity'. He identified four 'great requisites': a place for religious instruction, a school, a well-stocked store and, most pressing, more land. Evans anticipated – he talked of 'reading rightly the signs of the times' – that in the spring a large number of shareholders, paying their own expenses, would make their way to Wisconsin. To accommodate them, the Society should not only preempt more land; it 'must *purchase*, in the names of the Trustees, as much land as we can possibly spare the money for'. He proposed that a specific amount be set aside each month for the 'sacred' purpose of land acquisition. All this would be accomplished without it affecting the monthly ballot or lottery, the first drawing of which was imminent. The rest of the article detailed how the ballot should be conducted. Transparency was vital to avoid the taint of corruption. His solution was a lottery wheel, comprising six hoops of two feet in diameter representing the six sections of the society and recording the number of every paid-up share. A seventh hoop would identify the separate sections: 'It is an open, plain, and child-like process, which all might *see*, and all might *understand*'.[53]

The following week the Society's committee resolved to hold the first ballot on Whit Monday in Hanley's Covered Market, and, since the date coincided with its anniversary, to top off the proceedings with a celebratory ball. It also agreed to reserve £20 each month for the purchase of land. Commenting on the decision, Evans calculated that in a year's time, receipts would allow the Society to send out thirteen families and acquire an additional 1,300 acres, bringing its total to 2,900. After deducting occupied and reserved land, nearly forty twenty-acre allotments would be 'ready for peopling'. Some members thought the number too few for its growing needs. The issue was complicated. For months, the Society had been urging shareholders to take up allotments in Wisconsin on a self-paying principle. However, if too many took up the offer, it could consume all the spare allotments and infringe on the reserved land. Evans refused to believe that this was a matter of serious concern: 'Hold fast by the reserved land for the benefit of those at home; and let the other lands of the society be taken up as fast as shareholders can be found to people them. The more the better.' He also rejected the suggestion that non-union men – 'nobsticks' – would take up allotments; even if they did, the required labour of one day a month for ten years would render a decent profit. Who knows, he quipped, emigration might even turn bad men into good.[54]

The ballot duly took place on 24 May, a week after the Estate Committee's landing in New York. Announcing the event, the *Advertiser* noted that it was one of many activities for 'pleasure-seekers' in the Potteries over Whitsun that included an ascent by the celebrated balloonist John Hampton.[55] Upwards of 1,000 people, 'principally operatives',[56] attended the potters' event, the commencement of which was signalled by a peal from the Hanley Church bells. After the conclusion of the ballot, the festivities began in earnest. Marsden's Band had been engaged to entertain the huge crowd, alongside an eight-man choir. At some point Evans interrupted the entertainment to say a few words about emigration; otherwise, it was non-stop song and dance, with many revellers surviving until well after midnight. At 'a late, or rather an early hour', the *Advertiser* noted approvingly, 'the party peaceably separated'.[57] The *Examiner* confirmed the occasion's respectability.

> At an early hour on Tuesday morning, the glee-singers gave 'God save the Queen', as a *finale* to the proceedings; and in perfect order and soberness, without the display of the slightest bad feeling on the part of a single individual, the large assembly sought their homes, and their beds.

While there was no expectation of trouble, the Society took no chances, employing twenty-four doorkeepers to police the Market's entrances and bar anyone of a 'disorderly character'.[58]

The ballot passed off without a hitch, although not without tension. Three delegates from the out-potteries were asked to supervise the proceedings. The first stage, selecting one of the six sections, was quickly done; however, with numerous blank spaces, it needed several turns of the wheel to find the winner. The pendulum finally came to rest on number 246. Scrutiny of the books revealed that the share was one of fifty collectively owned by the ovenmen, who had rejoined the potters' union after a brief dalliance with the NAUT.⁵⁹ Two weeks later branch members met in Hanley to decide on the lucky recipient of the winning share, but deferred the final choice until the following week. Evans now made a surprising suggestion; they should offer the prize, which included all travel expenses, to the Burslem-born Enoch Bradshaw, who was already in the United States. Bradshaw, it will be recalled, had emigrated in 1844 after suffering dismissal as a result of his union activities, and Evans clearly wanted to remind the ovenmen, and operatives generally, of his heroic example. Arriving in New York, Bradshaw had gone to East Liverpool, where he immediately found employment in the town's embryonic pottery industry.⁶⁰ By the summer of 1847 the 29-year-old, now married into a prominent local family, was an established member of the East Liverpool community – he would become its mayor at the end of the following decade – a status he was unlikely to surrender for twenty acres of Wisconsin soil. The ovenmen wisely chose to disregard Evans's advice. Reconvening, members drew lots to determine the fate of the winning share. Successful in the ballot was John Barlow, a 31-year-old married man whose wife Elizah was expecting their first child. A long-time union and Society supporter, Barlow was immediately offered sums of £15 and £20 for the share, but insisted he would not sell 'under any consideration'.⁶¹

The second ballot followed in the last week of June; it too failed to produce an individual winner. The victors on this occasion were the hollow-ware pressers, the share being one of 168 taken out by the branch.⁶² They were also successful in the third ballot on 6 August, which also saw the resumption of the lottery as popular entertainment; an estimated 1,200 people packed into Hanley's Covered Market, where, following the draw, they danced to the strains of the North Staffordshire Waltz and Quadrille Band. The *Advertiser* again went out of its way to praise the conduct of proceedings: 'Intemperance, we are told, was a stranger to the festival, and the greatest decorum was observed.'⁶³ In October it was the flat-pressers' turn to be successful in the ballot conducted at the Mason's Arms, Burslem, where a 'crowded party' attended the event, according to the *Mercury*.⁶⁴

With the ballot's implementation, the Society appeared to have taken a significant stride towards realising its plans for the redemption of the trade. Evans naturally saw it in that light. Whit Monday, 1847, he wrote, 'will become a jubilee-day in the proceedings of working potters!'⁶⁵ But barely had the strains of Marsden's Band receded when the Society made an important announcement. On 5 June it issued a prospectus for the establishment of new Emigration Clubs. On offer were twenty-acre farms 'with good substantial Log Buildings' on the Society's lands in Wisconsin, together with two years' credit at the colony store. The price of each farm was £30, to be paid by instalments of wheat over ten years. The prospectus specified the costs of passage to Pottersville: a single man, £7; husband and wife, £14;

with two children, £21; with four, £28. To fund their passage, shareholders would make weekly contributions starting at fourpence for a single man and rising to 1s 4d for a family of six. The duration of each club would be eight years; if membership reached 100, one family per month could be accommodated on a twenty-acre allotment. In any event, all paid-up members would secure their land and building by the time of the club's expiry.

There was nothing on the face of it unusual in this new effort at fundraising; what made it so was the target audience. No longer would the Society appeal solely to pottery workers, but would, through the shareholders' clubs, embrace other trades. We are happy to state 'that any working man, of this country, or any set of working men, might become independent in the course of a few years, by taking advantage of the plan, now offered by the potters' society', the *Examiner* announced.[66] The following week it reported the formation of the first club. Workers from various trades had assembled at the Fox and George, Hanley, and promptly elected a secretary and began taking subscriptions, 'upwards of twenty names' being initially entered. It was truly gratifying to witness 'the collier, the stonemason, the bricklayer, the tailor, the shoemaker, the brickmaker, the cratemaker, the agricultural labourer, and, indeed, the middle-class shopkeeper, each and all anxious to become possessed of twenty-acre farms', the paper noted. There had also been inquiries from the other Potteries towns about starting similar clubs. All that remained was to encourage working men everywhere to grasp the opportunity for self-advancement through emigration. The second Hanley meeting was scheduled for the following Monday; with membership capped at 100, there was no time to lose.[67]

Historians have largely failed to register that the Society decided as early as June 1847 to extend its activities to other trades.[68] The failure reflects the uncomfortable truth that by the time the decision was taken the main focus of their interest, the potters' union, was struggling to survive. A federation of branches, the 1843 union lacked the robust quality and size of its better-known predecessor. With Evans and other leaders adamant that potters could only achieve security through emigration, its fragility was gradually exposed, resulting in its reconstitution and subsequently its demise. Signs of its reduced authority were evident in September, when operatives attended meetings to discuss the likely impact on wages of the deteriorating economic situation. Although the union, now made up of district lodges, was involved in the meetings, it failed to garner a mention in the *Mercury*'s report of the opening event, held at the Talbot Inn, Hanley on 20 September, and chaired by 'a working potter, in the employ of Mr. John Ridgway'.[69] Union activists would not go down without a fight. In mid-October the *Examiner* reported the setting-up of new lodges in Burslem and Tunstall: 'The spirit of combination is now rife in the Potteries; and all that is required are a few good and true men to gather in the harvest on behalf of the trade.'[70] Promotion of Emigration Society objectives continued to loom large in discussions. In Hanley speakers eulogised about Pottersville's potential to provide 'independent landed homes' for all. The following month Evans addressed a dozen meetings during which he urged operatives to support the 'steady, growing, moral-force, press-assisting, land-acquiring' union.[71] Despite these efforts, the union did not revive, and by the end of 1847, according to Harold Owen, 'there was no longer any trade organisation worthy of the name'.[72]

Over a period of two years, from the summer of 1847 until August 1849, when copies of the *Examiner* are again available, the Emigration Society was transformed from a vehicle for reducing surplus labour in the pottery industry to a national organisation with branches that stretched from Cornwall in the Southwest to Kirkcaldy and Ayrshire in Scotland. Although pottery workers continued to make up a substantial proportion of its membership, their support alone was insufficient to sustain its ambitious plans. Potters enthusiastically attended the various Society functions and turned out in large numbers to wave the departing families goodbye, but were less ready to commit themselves financially to the emigration project. One reason for their reluctance immediately suggests itself. By late 1847 economic conditions had started to deteriorate. In November the *Advertiser* reported that trade in the Potteries was in 'a state of depression not anticipated a few months ago'.[73] Twelve months later the paper found little sign of an end to the slump. The depression has caused 'a vast amount of suffering through want of employment, and all the efforts of the benevolent will be required to alleviate distress during the winter', it noted.[74] Although the opening weeks of 1849 saw some improvement, the setting-up of a Pottery District Relief Society evidenced the continuing misery wrought by the downturn, with many manufactories still dormant and 'a large proportion of the operative population' unemployed.[75]

If, as seems likely, economic conditions adversely affected the Society's money-raising plans, we can be less confident that they discouraged emigration itself. Throughout 1848 a move to America, with all its costs and uncertainties, remained a viable option for workers affected by the sharp contraction in trade. 'The depressed state of the staple manufacture of the north of the county is causing the tide of emigration amongst operative potters to flow steadily to the "Far West"', the *Advertiser* commented at the end of May.[76] Yet so meagre is the documentary evidence that any judgement on motivation, and on the economic and other factors that shaped emigration choices, is speculative. We might consider, for example, the distinctive society and culture of the Staffordshire Potteries. Potters inhabited localised, close-knit communities where high levels of residential and occupational persistence reflected unusually strong identifications between work and home. It should be no surprise that the separation and risk involved in transatlantic emigration was too daunting for many families to contemplate.[77] On the other hand, many potters did leave Staffordshire for America in the middle decades of the nineteenth century, establishing themselves in the new manufacturing centres of East Liverpool and Trenton, where, to mitigate the pain of separation, they recreated many familiar practices, rituals and relationships.[78]

For those families anticipating transatlantic travel, New Year 1848 brought sobering news. In September 1847 the Society despatched Joseph Clark, a hollow-ware presser employed at Ridgway's pottery in Shelton, to Wisconsin. Accompanying him were his wife Mary and three young children. The sea crossing proved uneventful; what followed was unimaginable. After leaving New York, one of the children fell sick and died, forcing the family to interrupt their journey at the Hudson River town of Troy. This delay to bury their child was critical; missing their original departure from Buffalo, the Clarks took passage on the steamship *Phoenix*, built two years earlier and regarded among the leaders of its class. On 11 November it headed west on its regular run to Chicago. Despite rough conditions and a captain confined to his cabin with an injured knee, the twin-propeller vessel made good speed and ten days later reached Manitowoc, Wisconsin on Lake Michigan's western rim. Early the next morning, Sunday, 21 November, approaching Sheboygan, a fire broke out in the engine room. After initial confusion – reports point to drunkenness among the crew – two lifeboats were launched, and forty-three people, including the immobilised captain, were rowed to safety in the darkness. There would be no deliverance for most of those on board. Within two hours fire consumed the wooden vessel. The result was one of the worst inland waterway disasters in American history. At least 250 passengers and crew perished on the lake, most drowning or freezing to death in the icy black waters. The majority of the victims were Dutch emigrants, seceders from the Reformed Church from the eastern provinces of Gelderland and Overijssel, but the dead also included Joseph and Mary Clark and their two remaining children.[79]

Although news of the *Phoenix* tragedy reached England in mid-December,[80] the people of the Potteries did not learn of the Clarks' fate until the first week of January. Aside from the obvious shock and grief, it is impossible to say what effect the news had upon local sentiment, including those families considering emigration. Disaster at sea was not unknown in the 1840s, its occurrence widely reported in the provincial press. In February the emigrant sailing vessel *Omega*, en route to New York from Liverpool, suffered catastrophic damage that ultimately caused the loss of 200 lives.[81]

But the horrific nature of the Clarks' deaths, and the fact that they occurred after their safe arrival in the United States – a 'happy and encouraging' letter home from New York added to the poignancy – made the tragedy all the more affecting. It was also a setback for the Society. Writing home from Pottersville on Christmas Eve, the Estate Committee members were anxious about the non-appearance of 'friend Clark'.[82] Sent to Wisconsin for the purpose of alleviating their financial woes, he carried with him an £80 bank draft, which was redeemable, and £30 in cash, which was not, together with a crate of earthenware, some haberdashery goods and a further £4 for the beleaguered Alexander Evans.[83] With potters' resources thinly stretched, such losses were hard to bear.

Pressure on the Emigration Society took many forms, including competition from the Chartist Land Company, which had begun recruiting in the Potteries following Thomas Clark's visit in 1845. Rivalry between the two land schemes persisted throughout 1846 and 1847. Personal insults aside, arguments largely centred on whether foreign or domestic colonisation offered the most practical value. As Robert Fyson has described, support for the Chartist plan was strongest in Hanley, but the Company also established branches in other towns, including Burslem, the emigration stronghold. The peak year of recruitment was 1847, when the first allotments were occupied at estates in Hertfordshire and Worcestershire. Unsurprisingly, given the industry's dominance, pottery workers made up a large proportion of North Staffordshire members: of the 600 shareholders in 1847–8, just over half were potters. How many of these would have supported the Emigration Society in the Company's absence, on the other hand, is impossible to say. After the publication of a critical Parliamentary report in August 1848, Land Company recruitment went into sharp decline, and by 1850 the flow of subscriptions from the Potteries had dried up. Beset by legal, financial and administrative difficulties, Feargus O'Connor's smallholding plans finally petered out in 1851.[84]

In the spring of 1848, however, recruitment was still buoyant. O'Connor returned to the Potteries in early March. At Hanley's Covered Market on Shrove Monday he lectured to a crowd of several thousand about the new Chartist petition and the recent dethronement of the French monarchy as well as the land plan, but made no reported mention of the potters' scheme.[85] Over the coming weeks, as the day of the mass presentation of the petition to Parliament approached, the political temperature rose. On 31 March between 3,000 and 4,000 attended a meeting on Crown Bank, where, following a speech by the Manchester activist Daniel Donovan,[86] delegates were elected to the National Convention. In North Staffordshire, as in other places, the Chartist resurgence aroused fears of revolutionary violence from those in authority. Leading the reaction was the magistrate

Thomas Bailey Rose, for whom the memories of 1842, when his house and library were destroyed, were doubtless still vivid. On 10 April, as thousands gathered in the capital on Kennington Common, companies of infantry, enrolled pensioners and local yeomanry, augmented by more than 3,000 special constables, stood ready to quash any disturbance in the Potteries. In the event, no disorder or large demonstration occurred, but for two months thereafter Chartist activity and close surveillance by local authorities continued 'at a high level of intensity'.[87]

By the beginning of April 1848, in John Saville's words, a 'sense of alarm and apprehension was accumulating steadily in the minds of all those who, for various reasons of self-interest, ideology and an awareness of property rights feared for the stability of the established order'.[88] Among those anxious about the threat of insurrection was the MP for Staffordshire North, Charles B. Adderley. On 18 April, in a debate over a proposed security bill, Adderley told the House of Commons that he feared the 'age of chivalry' had been replaced by the 'age of treason', and insisted that the gentry and middle classes 'would not be slow to take up arms if the safety of the Queen and the integrity of the constitution were invaded'.[89] Such sentiments came naturally to the Tory politician who as a child inherited large estates in Warwickshire and Staffordshire. A week before the debate he had mobilised his yeomanry troop in defence of local order. But Adderley also revealed a more enlightened side, one indicative of strong evangelical beliefs. Although adamant that liberty would not be advanced 'by outbreaks, or the clamour of disorderly mobs', he felt that the 'condition of the people in this country was such that a good man could not look upon it without sorrow'. Extreme wealth coexisted with extreme poverty, he told MPs, and the 'richer classes' should make every sacrifice 'even to their last shilling' to 'diminish the distresses around them'.[90]

Among the remedies Adderley considered was emigration. 'Pottery schemes, School of Design, Emigration to Pottersville, Mendicity, Friendly Society. Seeing all this quarter in worse state, and being connected with it myself, gave me much to know and feel', he wrote in his notebook.[91] In early May, prompted by the 'great and unparalleled distress now prevailing in the Staffordshire Potteries', the Emigration Society petitioned the county's gentry, Adderley included, for financial assistance. Issued under the name of its chairman, William Mayer, the letter offered a defence of the potters' actions over the past decade that was designed above all to reassure conservative opinion. 'We are a progressive, peaceful, legalized body', it insisted. The narrative began with the strike of 1836–7 – a 'sorrowful display of operative folly' – and continued with the fight against the allowance system and the establishment of the emigration scheme. In addition to 1,600 acres of Wisconsin land and the plan to acquire 800 more, the Society now boasted its own printing establishment and weekly periodical. But the current downturn had left operatives 'literally starving from the want of bread', and it appealed to the better-off classes to join it in this 'peaceful work of social transformation'. The letter concluded with a veiled warning: 'In this time of great tribulation, the Operative Potters' Emigration Society is a hopeful beacon, soothing the harsher feelings of its members, — fostering hope and good-will, where otherwise might prevail despair and anarchy'.[92]

The appeal resulted in contributions from some of the area's wealthiest and most influential individuals, their support likely made easier by the demise of the potters' union. The initiative was not without jeopardy, and most mutual improvement ventures in the Potteries in this period were resistant to middle- and upper-class patronage.[93] Adderley himself headed the published list – titled 'Gratuities of the Rich to the Destitute Poor'. Other names included the future Liberal MP John Ayshford Wise; Tunstall-born Smith Child, who would join Adderley in the Commons in 1851 and become one of the Potteries' most prominent benefactors; the businessman and landowner Charles Bourne Lawton; and the wine and spirit merchant George Baker, whose public roles included chairmanship of the Burslem and Wolstanton Board of Guardians.[94] Adderley's patronage did not end there. Meeting in Hanley on 14 May, shareholders discussed the propriety of opening up the Society to other trades. The proposal was carried with only three dissenting votes. According to the *Advertiser*, the step was taken 'in accordance with the expressed wish of our respected county member, C. B. Adderley Esq., who, it is understood, intends using his influence in obtaining a grant of colonial land for the services of the society'.[95] A few weeks later the MP's motives were again on display during a Commons debate on a proposal to assist the emigration to the colonies of boys from so-called 'ragged schools'. In noting the rise of workmen's emigration initiatives, he drew particular attention to the potters': 'These men had originally formed themselves into an association with the Chartist object of organising strikes for wages; they had dropped that, and now had one simple object in view, *viz.*, to enable each other to emigrate to other countries'. Although the Society's leaders doubtless welcomed Adderley's backing, they may not have appreciated his account of their self-help efforts. The potters 'did not understand the matter', he claimed;

> they were subject to every species of fraud; they went to the nearest country — to the United States of America, on the smallest outlay, and thus by acting in this imperfect manner their views were almost certain to end in disappointment, and they were thrown back on their native country, and became dangerous to its peace and welfare.[96]

Whatever Adderley's precise role, the Society's decision to open its doors to other trades – and to communities far beyond the Potteries – marked a major shift in its appeal, one previously signalled by the setting-up of shareholders' clubs. Access to its lands in Wisconsin would henceforward be available to everyone on equal terms. Writing in August in his introduction to the revised rules and regulations, William Evans celebrated the fact that the 'confinement of the Potters' important plan to the limits of one small trade' had been abandoned, 'and the arms of the society are now open for the embrace of all!' Among the 'many important modifications' made by the Society's general meetings, one stood out: a 'self-supporting principle is now introduced, which cannot fail to give permanency' to its proceedings. In future, all 'allottees, whether balloted or otherwise', must return to the Society 'the precise amount' they receive from it: 'Couple with this the profit on the sale of reserved land, and the whole machinery of the society is understood at once.'[97]

Emigration from the Potteries had resumed well before the radical change in the Society's appeal. For the first time since its founding – the ill-fated Clarks being the exception – single families headed to Wisconsin. At the end of March James Thomas, a 34-year-old saggar maker, crossed to New York with his wife and four children on the giant American packet *Rappahannock*, before journeying on to Columbia County, where they would remain for the next three decades.[98] Most emigrants chose to travel in groups, where organisation could be coordinated and resources pooled. The first party left Liverpool for New York on 7 May, and comprised about forty individuals. Familiar scenes attended the send-off. 'The emigrants took their departure amid the greetings of their friends and a large concourse of spectators', reported the *Mercury*. Through the generosity of the innkeeper at the Swan, Burslem, they were conveyed free of charge, 'accompanied by a cornopian band', to Madeley, where they boarded the train to Liverpool. There to meet them was William Evans, who had arranged passage on the Black Star packet *Republic*.[99] Among the departing group were John Barlow and family, winner of the Society's first ballot nearly twelve months earlier. Others included William and Edna Smith and four children from Newcastle-under-Lyme (their eldest child Hannah remained at home; two decades later she would join the family in Wisconsin); and Burslem hollow-ware presser Edward Parker, his wife Sarah and their five children. There were also an undetermined number of single travellers. They included another Burslem presser, Sheffield-born Matthew Mason, who in 1853 would marry Emma Smith, daughter of the Pottersville pastor; and Robert Mountford, who left his young wife behind in Staffordshire. Mountford was one of several members of the party who failed to settle across the Atlantic, returning to England before the 1851 census.

Three weeks after the *Republic*'s sailing, more emigrants departed for America. The composition of this second group is less clear. We know that

1847–8: Settling the land

on 22 May, 'a number of individuals, chiefly from Burslem, Longport, Cobridge, and Shelton, left the Potteries in several vehicles, preceded by a band of music, and passed through Newcastle to the Whitmore Station to proceed to Liverpool, for embarkation to the United States'. According to the *Advertiser* report, some of the group were headed for Pottersville; others the Society dispatched with the aim of preempting land for a new colony near Lake Puckaway, sixteen miles away. They left Liverpool on 29 May in another Black Star vessel, the *Marmion*, berthing in New York five-and-a-half weeks later. As with previous send-offs, their departure 'excited considerable interest', with spectators hoping that their prospects 'might be as bright as the fine sunny day on which they left their native homes'.[100] Progress after their arrival in New York is harder to track. Of the thirteen passengers, all male, recorded as potters in the ship's manifest, only two definitely made it to Wisconsin. They were John Peake, a hollow-ware presser from Burslem, and Thomas Simpson from Tunstall. Peake remained in the area, but Simpson returned to the Potteries sometime after October 1849. The oldest member of the party was James Finney, also from Tunstall, whose wife and teenage daughter later joined him in America. By 1850 the Finneys were running a pottery store in Philadelphia. At least one member, Thomas Moloneaux from Burslem, who travelled with his young son, settled in East Liverpool; another Burslem man, Hamlet Greatbach, ended up farming in Franklin County, Indiana, although by what route is unknown. As to the 'Puckaway Pioneers', clues to their fate can be found in a later comment by William Evans. Describing the disappointment suffered by his brother in the wake of the Clark tragedy, the editor recalled that he had entrusted the Pioneers with 'wedges, beetling rings, and other useful articles, together with a rifle', but that nothing had reached him 'as the party never got beyond [New] York State'.[101] Confirmation that the men became diverted soon after arriving in America comes from the Hanley potter Charles Hall, who had recently settled with his family in Bennington, Vermont. Writing home in September, he criticised members of the Emigration Society 'who instead of going right away to the land have turned their attention to something else, some of them staying in new York and up and down until their funds are almost gone'. He added that the conduct:

> of some that have been sent out this year is murdering the Potters Emagration Plan, which in my Opinion promises no more then it is possible to be realized, if the men sent out be made of the right meteriel and the men at home as determined to support them in it as they were when I left home.[102]

On 8 August a third Staffordshire party left Liverpool for New York aboard the *Constitution*. According to a report, thirty-one of its fifty-one members were travelling to Pottersville under the auspices of the Emigration

Society. The remaining twenty were headed for 'various destinations' in the United States, their passage no doubt arranged by the resourceful Evans, who in March began advertising his agent's services 'at the most reasonable cost' to anyone travelling to America.[103] Unlike the *Marmion* emigrants, the party comprised several established families, including that of William and Hannah Mountford from Hanley; and 52-year-old Peter Watkin, the Burslem potter who in 1844 had first raised the prospect of putting unemployed operatives to work on the land. Accompanying him to America were his wife Rachel and their adult daughter Margaret, blind since birth.

While the August departure appears to have been relatively low-key, there was no sign that interest in emigration generally in the Potteries was abating. A few weeks after the group left, J. C. Byrne, author of *Twelve Years' Wanderings in the British Colonies*, drew a large audience to Hanley Town Hall, where he promoted the prospects for emigration to Australia.[104] But by then Evans and his colleagues had begun to expand their activities into adjoining areas. Among the first places targeted were the Cheshire silk towns of Congleton and Macclesfield. On 25 July, at Congleton Town Hall, the Burslem potter William Coates lectured the audience on the Society's emigration plans. At the end of the meeting, ten people, headed by the town's mayor, registered their interest in the scheme.[105] The Society also circulated its prospectus in Macclesfield, inviting workers there to enrol as members and qualify for 'a home in the west'.[106] Other nearby towns where it was active included Leek, a dozen miles to the northeast of the Potteries, where a meeting in August at the Temperance Hall attracted about 300 people and led directly to the establishment of a new branch;[107] and Crewe to the northwest, where in September Evans addressed 'a large meeting' of coachmakers, after which 'a unanimous vote was carried to assist and forward the objects of the society'.[108]

Evans's personal campaign had begun in industrial Warrington on the Cheshire–Lancashire border. On 24 July he addressed a hastily arranged gathering to discuss emigration and the principles by which the Society was conducted. His talk provided a script for future meetings. Each enrolled member, he stated,

> on paying the sum of £1 1s 6d, had a right of ballot for a farm, consisting of 20 acres; each member who succeeded in the ballot, and after entering on the land, would have to pay, in the course of six years, a further sum of £4 8s 6d, making £5 10s, the first cost of the land to the society.

Evans explained that the Society would assume the migration expenses of balloted members and also provide a log house, cultivation and fencing and prior planting of five acres, together with two years' credit for provisions, the whole cost to be repaid over ten years in cash or wheat. Outlining the logic behind the project, he urged all trades to follow the potters' example; the societies thus established 'would enable them to lighten the country of the surplus population to a very great extent'. Better this strategy than the present one of expending large sums of money 'in supporting "strikes" against capital', he contended. It was reported at the meeting that three branches of the Society had been formed in the town, with forty members already enrolled.[109]

Evans's lecture in Warrington was the prelude to a major recruitment effort in the Lancashire textile districts, where persistent economic insecurity helped fuel the appetite for emigration. In March a Manchester paper noted that in Stockport 'able bodied men and their families, with their savings' were continuing 'to expatriate themselves' to America; at the end of April it reported that the previous week eighty-six families had left Ashton-under-Lyne for the same destination.[110] A week after his Warrington lecture, the potters' leader appeared at the Temperance Hall in Preston, where he sought to encourage the establishment of a town branch. Detailing the Society's assets, he revealed the imminent purchase of 2,000 acres of Wisconsin land to supplement its existing 1,600 (later reports of the tour indicate that the Lake Puckaway area remained its preferred location[111]). At the end Evans invited questions from the audience. His answers were sufficient to persuade the local paper that the Society 'was no speculation, but a practical undertaking, and one that offered every advantage to emigrants'.[112] Such endorsement was not always forthcoming. After his Warrington appearance one editor warned that 'the working classes' should be very careful 'how they join themselves to any such society, or place their hard earned guineas in the hands of plausible talkers'.[113] Several months later Evans again aroused the *Manchester Courier*'s suspicion after a 'thinly attended' lecture in Todmorden: 'The prospects held out by him were very tempting if what he stated can be realized, but so many quacks prescribe cures for the depressed condition of the labouring classes, that it would require the wisdom of a Solomon to say who is honest.'[114]

Such comments were rare; most reports of the Society's meetings at this time were free from reproach, with newspapers acknowledging the potential benefits of emigration. They also reveal how much the Society owed to its indefatigable agents. The most detailed account of Evans's Lancashire tour comes from his appearance in Manchester. On the evening of 24 August he addressed a crowded meeting 'exclusively composed of working men' at the Bird in Hand public house in Great Ancoats Street. It was an eloquent and confident performance. Although he had long abandoned hopes that the Wisconsin colony would be contained within a single tract, his belief in rising land values was undiminished. Evans claimed that the Society had in its first two years raised £2,000 from its 7,000 members, 'comparatively a small sum', with the result that 'only 134 settlers' had relocated to Wisconsin. Had potters invested in American land the estimated £8,000 they had spent in 'charity', their situation would have been very different. The rest of his lecture trod familiar ground. Among the subjects covered were migration costs, agricultural productivity, education, climate and the legal processes for acquiring land in America. In noting the success of other transatlantic initiatives, Evans confirmed that it was George Flower, 'founder of a flourishing colony in Illinois', who 'first originated the scheme which he was there to advocate'. He ended his talk by insisting that he had no wish to compromise other working-class projects. He was here 'to explain clearly defined principles, to show what could be done, and the means by which the working men could be improved in condition, and rendered able to live under their own vine and fig tree, none daring to make them ashamed or afraid'. The questions that followed showed an audience alert to the demands of migration and settlement. The meeting then carried by acclamation a motion 'thanking Mr. Evans for his explanations'.[115]

The main aim of the Lancashire tour was to raise funds for the purchase of additional land. In Manchester Evans reported the establishment of twenty-four branches in the past few months, including four in the city itself. The weeks to follow saw more evidence of the growing enthusiasm for the scheme among Lancashire workers. Reporting on meetings in Bolton, Manchester and Patricroft in September, the *Manchester Times* suggested that it was 'highly probable that some 3000 spinners will connect themselves to the potters' movement'. Evans was particularly well received at the Mechanics' Institution in Patricoft, where his three-hour lecture brought a vote of thanks and 'and several rounds of applause'. Similar scenes played out in towns across the industrial Northwest. Introducing him to a dense crowd at the New Bull Inn, Blackburn, the chairman, R. W. Smiles, said that 'the subject of emigration was one that forced itself on the consideration of all thinking men' as they sought to redress the 'evils of redundant population'. It was noted after the talk that a branch of the Society had been formed in the town.[116] Lectures in Oldham and Burnley produced the same outcome.[117] The mission to Oldham was especially fruitful. Two months after his first visit to the important mill town, Evans returned to its Working Man's Hall, encouraged by the success of the newly established branch, which had enrolled upwards of ninety members. Even the doubting *Courier* was forced to acknowledge the Society's progress. The Oldham meeting attracted 'a very numerous attendance', it conceded, 'and the scheme seems to be rapidly obtaining favour among the operative population'.[118]

By October the Emigration Society's reach had extended into other industrial areas, with branches in Leeds, Birmingham, Liverpool and Nottingham (Evans would lecture there in November and December)[119] among those listed in a widely circulated advertisement. Accompanying the notice in the *Leeds Times* was a lengthy article on Iowa and Wisconsin as settler destinations which profiled the British Temperance and Potters' Emigration schemes. The writer noted that similar associations were under consideration in West Yorkshire, and while caution was always advisable, 'the success of the two societies above named is, on the whole, of a very encouraging kind'.[120] In November William Coates made a brief tour of the county, beginning in Leeds on the 20th. The event was notable for the interjection of a working man who had travelled through Wisconsin and challenged a number of the speaker's claims, including the costs of land preparation. Rather than join a society, those desirous of emigrating should do so under their own resources, where the 'choice of land and situation' would be theirs to make. Even so, he admitted that the potters had 'selected one of the healthiest and best parts of America'.[121] Coates seemed undaunted by the exchange and the next evening continued his tour in neighbouring Bradford. Despite the small numbers present in the Temperance Hall, the meeting agreed to establish a branch in the town.[122] Two days later he lectured to 'a numerous and respectable audience' in the Guild Hall, Huddersfield.[123]

Notice of the emigration scheme was now being taken in places far removed from its original home. In early November an Arbroath man, Peter Fettes, contacted the Scottish-born radical MP Joseph Hume to gain his opinion on the Society. He enclosed a copy of its prospectus. Responding from his seat in Norfolk, Hume admitted that he had not heard of the potters' project, but that he was a strong advocate of emigration, advising only that it was better to go to America not bound to any particular location.[124] (Hume also suggested that Fettes write to Robert Owen, who replied that he too knew nothing of the Society, had not visited Wisconsin and recommended northern Texas as a site for settlement.[125]) More significant for the Society's subsequent history was the growing interest in emigration among the London trades. On 13 November, before embarking on his Yorkshire tour, William Coates outlined its plans at a meeting at the White Conduit House, Islington.[126] He repeated the talk two nights later in Holborn, where the *Morning Advertiser* reported that the audience in the National Hall 'loudly cheered the plain statements made by the lecturer, whose object was to show how combined efforts would not only release this country of a vast quantity of surplus labourers, but materially assist and better the condition of those emigrating'.[127]

Over the next twelve months support for the Society would increase in industrial communities in London, Scotland, the Midlands and Lancashire. Confidence in the emigration scheme was becoming infectious. On New Year's Day, 1849 several thousand supporters gathered for a 'grand tea party' in Manchester's Free Trade Hall.[128] Both of the Williamses, Evans and Coates, spoke at the meeting, whose main purpose was the drawing of the Society's ballot. The ballot table was taken to the hall early, so that delegates from the out-districts could inspect its workings and ensure an honest outcome. At four o'clock 'a full orchestra, in military uniform' assembled on the platform. Seventeen delegates were chosen to superintend the draw, with a man called Scott from Paisley – whom we will encounter again – given the honour of turning the wheel. Scott had lived in the United States for nearly thirty years, including 'some time' in Wisconsin, and spoke 'in the highest terms' of the state's climate and soil. To whet shareholders' appetites with the flavour of pioneer life, he had brought with him 'several Indian curiosities, together with some excellent maps'. The ballot then commenced. The winner of the first allotment was William Scholes from Oldham, holder of ticket number 2647. There followed three from Burslem (George Cartledge, Aaron Hawthorn and George Cooper); one from Crewe (Henry Stubbs); and finally, another Oldham member, George Robinson.[129]

Eight months had passed since the Society's decision to expand participation in the emigration scheme to other trades. The move was a pragmatic response to its failure to raise sufficient funds for the scheme's continuance, and should be seen in the context of widespread economic distress and the vulnerability of working-class activism across industrial Britain. The collapse of the potters' union in 1847 largely absolved the Society from the taint of radicalism, paving the way for its wider acceptance and patronage by middle- and upper-class interests. Expansion entailed risk, however. Although the Society retained its working-class appeal, breaking free from its occupational moorings had implications for the scheme's governance, financing and identity. Nearly five years after its founding, the Potters' Emigration Society had become a catch-all organisation with a branch network that would extend the length and breadth of the country. With half of the New Year's Day ballot winners coming from outside of North Staffordshire, a project designed as a vehicle for the pottery industry's salvation was already being transformed.

Notes

1 *PEWA*, 2 January 1847.
2 *Staffordshire Mercury and Potteries Gazette*, 7 November 1846. *The Staffordshire Advertiser*, 23 January 1847 noted that smaller firms were chiefly suffering, while *PEWA*, 7 November 1846 reported Burslem and Tunstall potters on 'barely half employ'.
3 *PEWA*, 20 March 1847.
4 *PEWA*, 30 January 1847.

5 *PEWA*, 17 April 1847. The family was that of Joseph Clews.
6 Catherine Cartwright writes that emigration was often seen as 'a religious duty'; 'Early Mormonism in Staffordshire, 1839–69', *Staffordshire Studies* 19 (2008), 58. See also David Michael Norris, 'The Emergence and Development of the Church of Jesus Christ of Latter-Day Saints in Staffordshire, 1839–1870' (PhD dissertation, University of Chichester, 2010), pp. 152–79.
7 Boston, 'William Evans and the Potters' Emigration Society' offers the only detailed discussion of his religious beliefs.
8 Bronstein, *Land Reform and Working-Class Experience in Britain and the United States*, pp. 63–8, 149–50.
9 *PEWA*, 13 July 1844.
10 *Cooperative News*, 1 June 1878.
11 *PEWA*, 4 July 1846.
12 See the letter from 'A Brother Brush' in *PEWA*, 5 December 1846, which notes the absence of any representative from the painters and gilders and suggests that a certain individual could worthily fill the position. There is circumstantial evidence that the writer and/or suggested candidate may have been Alexander Evans. My thanks to Mike Beckensall for alerting me to the letter's curious content.
13 *PEWA*, 28 November 1846.
14 Carol Dooley Strong, *A Strong Family Tree* (Columbus, WI: Town and Country Printers, 1993), p. 101.
15 *PEWA*, 16 January 1847.
16 Chase, *'The People's Farm'*, pp. 183–4.
17 *PEWA*, 3 April 1847.
18 *PEWA*, 13 February 1847.
19 *PEWA*, 27 February 1847.
20 *PEWA*, 23 January 1847.
21 *PEWA*, 27 February 1847.
22 *Northern Star and National Trades' Journal*, 20 February 1847.
23 *Northern Star and National Trades' Journal*, 27 February 1847. Probably Charles Adams, a trustee.
24 *Northern Star and National Trades' Journal*, 6 March 1847.
25 Fyson, 'Chartism in North Staffordshire', p. 302.
26 Warburton, *The History of Trade Union Organisations*, pp. 134–5.
27 *The Staffordshire Advertiser*, 8 May 1847.
28 *Northern Star and National Trades' Journal*, 1 May 1847; *PEWA*, 1 May 1847. A week later Evans claimed the thirteen recruits to the Society from the factory had increased to twenty. *PEWA*, 8 May 1847.
29 Fyson, 'Chartism in North Staffordshire', pp. 303–4.
30 *PEWA*, 22 May 1847.
31 *Staffordshire Mercury and Potteries Gazette*, 10 April 1847.
32 *The Staffordshire Advertiser*, 10 April 1847.
33 *Fife Herald, and Kinross, Strathearn, and Clackmannan Advertiser*, 6 May 1847. Other papers reporting the departure included *Leicester Journal*,

16 April 1847; *Derbyshire Advertiser and Journal*, 16 April 1847; *Berkshire Chronicle*, 17 April 1847; *Morning Post* (London), 19 April 1847; *Manchester Times*, 23 April 1847; *The Globe* (London), 24 April, 1847; *Gore's Liverpool General Advertiser*, 29 April 1847; *Cheltenham Journal and Gloucestershire Fashionable Weekly Gazette*, 19 April 1847; *Stamford Mercury*, 30 April 1847; *The Spectator*, 1 May 1847; and *Lloyd's Weekly Newspaper*, 2 May 1847.

34 For data on age (and gender), see Van Vugt, *Britain to America*, pp. 17–18; and Cohen, *Mass Migration Under Sail*, pp. 99–100.

35 *The History of Columbia County, Wisconsin*, p. 1051; Hopkins and Hopkins, *The Richard and Harriet Hopkins Family*, pp. 19–21.

36 It is clear that William Evans funded Alexander and his family's emigration expenses.

37 *PEWA*, 6 March 1847.

38 *Pittsburgh Daily Post*, 21 February 1897.

39 *Staffordshire Mercury and Potteries Gazette*, 6 March 1847.

40 *PEWA*, 6, 13 March 1847. Skinner's fate is unknown. In 1850 he was boarding with his brother George and family, who had emigrated the year after him, on the 'Indian lands', after which he disappears from view.

41 *PEWA*, 3 April 1847.

42 *Liverpool Mercury*, 26 June 1840 and other reports.

43 *PEWA*, 26 June 1847.

44 'The Last of the Potters' Society', dated 10 June 1890, 2pp. manuscript, Wisconsin State Historical Society, copy in Hobson Collection, PA/HOB/1, Stoke-on-Trent City Archives.

45 Bradshaw's signature was absent from the Estate Committee's first letter home, suggesting friction over the issue.

46 *PEWA*, 8 May 1847.

47 *PEWA*, 18 September 1847.

48 *Ibid*.

49 *Ibid*.

50 *PEWA*, 17 April, 8 May 1847; *The Staffordshire Advertiser*, 17 April 1847.

51 *PEWA*, 10 October 1846.

52 *PEWA*, 3 July 1847.

53 *PEWA*, 24 April 1847.

54 *PEWA*, 1 May 1847.

55 *The Staffordshire Advertiser*, 22 May 1847. Whitsun pleasure-seekers would be disappointed; Hampton, the first Englishman to make a parachute jump, had to postpone. He subsequently made two ascents in the Potteries, the second of which, on 12 July, almost ended in disaster as rapid condensation caused the balloon to descend too quickly. *The Staffordshire Advertiser*, 5, 19 June, 17 July 1847.

56 *Staffordshire Mercury and Potteries Gazette*, 29 May 1847.

57 *The Staffordshire Advertiser*, 29 May 1847.

58 *PEWA*, 29 May 1847.

59 Ibid.
60 Gates, Jr., *The City of Hills and Kilns*, pp. 36–7. Three days after arrival, Bradshaw was taken on by the former Burslem potter John Goodwin.
61 *PEWA*, 26 June 1847.
62 Ibid.
63 *The Staffordshire Advertiser*, 14 August 1847.
64 *Staffordshire Mercury and Potteries Gazette*, 30 October 1847.
65 *PEWA*, 29 May 1847.
66 *PEWA*, 5 June 1847.
67 *PEWA*, 12 June 1847.
68 Harold Owen noted the establishment of the new clubs but did not mention the change in policy. Owen, *The Staffordshire Potter*, p. 97. There is a brief reference in Fyson, 'Chartism in North Staffordshire', p. 208.
69 *Staffordshire Mercury and Potteries Gazette*, 25 September 1847. The *Examiner*'s own report also points up the union's reduced role. *PEWA*, 25 September 1847.
70 *PEWA*, 16 October 1847.
71 *PEWA*, 25 September, 16 October 1847.
72 Owen, *The Staffordshire Potter*, p. 99. The union formally terminated in June 1848. *The Potters' Examiner and Emigrants' Advocate* (hereafter *PEEA*), vol. 9, no. 68 (20 October 1849). *PEEA* publication dates have been established from the printing information at the end of each issue.
73 *The Staffordshire Advertiser*, 20 November 1847.
74 *The Staffordshire Advertiser*, 18 November 1848.
75 *The Staffordshire Advertiser*, 6 January 1849.
76 *The Staffordshire Advertiser*, 27 May 1848.
77 On persistence, see Dupree, *Family Structure in the Staffordshire Potteries*, pp. 83–6. Whipp, *Patterns of Labour*, esp. pp. 43–84, provides insight into the relationship between work and home.
78 See Gates, Jr., *The City of Hills and Kilns* and Marc Jeffrey Stern, *The Pottery Industry of Trenton: A Skilled Trade in Transition, 1850–1929* (New Brunswick, NJ: Rutgers University Press, 1994).
79 The only extant references to the family's fate are *Staffordshire Mercury and Potteries Gazette*, 8 January 1848; and *PEEA*, vol. 10, no. 5 (3 August 1850). The most authoritative discussion of the tragedy remains William O. Van Eyck, 'The Story of the Propeller *Phoenix*', *Wisconsin Magazine of History* 7:3 (1924), 281–300. John Textor, *Phoenix: The Fateful Journey* (Sheboygan, WI: Sanderling Press, 2006) is well-researched, if marred by an absence of documentation and invented dialogue.
80 See *Leeds Times*, 18 December 1847, among many reports.
81 Among numerous reports of the disaster, see *Lloyds Weekly Newspaper*, 16 April 1848.
82 Evans reprinted their letter in *Co-operative News*, 1 December 1877.
83 *PEEA*, vol. 10, no. 5 (3 August 1850). No copy survives of the Clarks' New York letter, presumably published in the *Examiner*.

84 Fyson, 'Chartism in North Staffordshire', pp. 192–213. For the wider history, see Joy MacAskill, 'The Chartist Land Plan', in Asa Briggs ed., *Chartist Studies* (London: Macmillan, 1960), pp. 304–41; Alice Mary Hadfield, *The Chartist Land Company* (Newton Abbot: David & Charles, 1970); Malcolm Chase, '"We Wish only to Work for Ourselves": The Chartist Land Plan', in Chase and Ian Dyck (eds), *Living and Learning: Essays in Honour of J. F. C. Harrison* (Aldershot: Scolar Press, 1996), pp. 133–48; and Chase, '"Wholesome Object Lessons": The Chartist Land Plan in Retrospect', *English Historical Review* 118:475 (2003), 59–85.

85 *Staffordshire Mercury and Potteries Gazette*, 11 March 1848; *Northern Star and National Trades' Journal*, 11 March 1848.

86 On Donovan, see Paul A. Pickering, *Chartism and the Chartists in Manchester and Salford* (Basingstoke: Macmillan, 1995), p. 194.

87 Fyson, 'Chartism in North Staffordshire', p. 221.

88 John Saville, *1848: The British State and the Chartist Movement* (Cambridge: Cambridge University Press, 1987), p. 102.

89 *The Staffordshire Advertiser*, 22 April 1848.

90 *Ibid*.

91 William S. Childe-Pemberton, *Life of Lord Norton (Right Hon. Sir Charles Adderley, K. C. M. G., M. P.), 1814–1905: Statesman and Philanthropist* (London: John Murray, 1909), p. 63.

92 *The Staffordshire Advertiser*, 13 May 1848.

93 R. A. Lowe, 'Mutual Improvement in the Potteries', *North Staffordshire Journal of Field Studies* 12 (1972), 75–82 (quotation p. 80).

94 *The Staffordshire Advertiser*, 13 May 1848; Dennis Stuart (ed.), *People of the Potteries: A Dictionary of Local Biography, Volume 1* (Keele: Department of Adult Education, University of Keele, 1985), pp. 26–7, 60–1, 232. Other donors Evans acknowledged included the Earl of Dartmouth and Lady Lyttelton (*The Staffordshire Advertiser*, 9 September 1848) and Admiral Henry John Rous (*Cotton Factory Times*, 19 June 1885).

95 *Staffordshire Mercury and Potteries Gazette*, 13 May 1848; *The Staffordshire Advertiser*, 20 May 1848. Nothing came of the colonial land suggestion.

96 *Morning Chronicle*, 7 June 1848. On Adderley's 'ecclesiastical' paternalism, see David Roberts, *Paternalism in Early Victorian England* (London: Croom Helm, 1979), p. 218.

97 *Rules and Regulations of the Potters' Joint-Stock Emigration Society and Savings Fund*, revised edition, August 1848. Thanks to Roger Bentley for providing me with a copy from the original left behind at Fort Winnebago and now housed in the Surgeons' Quarters Museum.

98 The *Rappahannock* was the largest US-built ship at the time of its launch in 1841.

99 *Staffordshire Mercury and Potteries Gazette*, 13 May 1848.

100 *The Staffordshire Advertiser*, 27 May 1848.

101 *PEEA*, vol. 10, no. 5 (3 August 1850).

102 Charles Hall to his mother, 27 September 1848, Hall Family Letters, Stoke-on-Trent City Archives.

103 *The Staffordshire Advertiser*, 12 August 1848; 25 March 1848.
104 *The Staffordshire Advertiser*, 23 September 1848.
105 *Macclesfield, Stockport and Congleton Chronicle*, 29 July 1848.
106 *Manchester Examiner & Times*, 22 July 1848.
107 *The Staffordshire Advertiser*, 26 August 1848.
108 *Manchester Examiner & Times*, 19 September 1848.
109 *Manchester Courier and Lancashire General Advertiser*, 29 July 1848.
110 *Manchester and Salford Advertiser and Chronicle*, 4 March, 29 April 1848.
111 *Bolton Chronicle*, 4 November 1848.
112 *Preston Chronicle*, 5 August 1848.
113 *Manchester Courier and Lancashire General Advertiser*, 29 July 1848. The *Courier* was established in 1825 as a Conservative rival to the *Manchester Guardian*.
114 *Manchester Courier and Lancashire General Advertiser*, 8 November 1848.
115 *Manchester Examiner & Times*, 2 September 1848.
116 *Manchester Examiner & Times*, 23 September 1848.
117 *Manchester Courier and Lancashire General Advertiser*, 4 October 1848; *Blackburn Standard*, 8 November 1848.
118 *Manchester Courier and Lancashire General Advertiser*, 18 November 1848.
119 *Nottingham Review and General Advertiser*, 24 November 1848; *The Lady's Newspaper*, 16 December 1848.
120 *Leeds Times*, 21 October 1848.
121 *Leeds Times*, 25 November 1848.
122 *Bradford Observer*, 23 November 1848.
123 *Manchester Examiner & Times*, 25 November 1848.
124 *Arbroath Guide*, 18 November 1848; *Montrose Standard and Angus and Mearns Register*, 17 November 1848. For a similar inquiry about the Society, see *Glasgow Saturday Post and Paisley and Renfrewshire Reformer*, 17, 24 February 1849.
125 *Dundee Courier*, 22 November 1848.
126 *London Daily News*, 15 November 1848 and other papers.
127 *Morning Advertiser*, 17 November 1848; *Shipping and Mercantile Gazette*, 17 November 1848.
128 *The Staffordshire Advertiser*, 13 January 1849.
129 *Nottingham Review and General Advertiser*, 16 February 1849, quoting a lengthy description of the event from the *Examiner*. It numbered attendance at between 3,000 and 4,000; the *Advertiser* reported 2,000.

5

1849: Expansion and scrutiny

The late 1840s saw the number of people leaving Britain reach new levels. 'There is at this moment a powerful and instinctive desire for emigration in the United Kingdom, especially in England', commented the liberal *Morning Chronicle* in April 1848.[1] Discussion of the subject was ubiquitous. While many endorsed the *Chronicle*'s view that the aim of emigration was 'the preservation of the working-classes from distress', there was less agreement about how this was to be accomplished and what role, if any, the state should assume. At a meeting called later that year in Stafford to establish a branch of the recently founded Society for the Promotion of Colonization, the MP Charles B. Adderley tried to bring order to a subject that touched all areas of public policy. Adderley declined to consider the matter of whether Britain was overpopulated or not, but he thought it undeniable 'that from time to time the pressure of the people had been felt, and prompt measures had been required to prevent them from famishing, while on the other side of the ocean there was a demand for the population, which this country required to be relieved of'. Noting the appearance of voluntary emigration societies, including one in the Potteries, he said that if the government held back, 'the operative classes of this country would do the work for themselves', a prospect the Tory politician did not regard as ideal.[2] A different level of debate unfurled several weeks later a few miles to the north, when voters in Wolstanton rejected a proposal that the parish raise money to send fifty-nine paupers to Canada, Australia and the Cape of Good Hope (the individuals were asked to choose their preferred destination). The question at stake was not demography, the national interest or British colonial policy, but how much the costs would add to the poor rates. Following the decision, Joseph Lowndes, the clerk to the Wolstanton and Burslem Union, continued his efforts to borrow the £800 necessary to fund the parochial scheme, but apparently to no avail.[3]

Although state or parish assistance was not an issue for those seeking a move to the United States[4] – where by the end of the decade three-quarters of those leaving Britain were headed – reports of associational schemes continued to appear. Among them in early 1849 was the London-based California Emigration Society, which sought to capitalise on the recent discovery of gold in America's Far West. In a widely circulated advertisement, it claimed that its procedures for selection would be made 'on the same plan as that exercised in Building Societies, and those established in the Potteries'.[5] By 1849 the Potters' Emigration Society was by far the best-known of the voluntary schemes, and a model for those planning similar ventures. The Scottish reformer Robert Fleming Gourlay invoked the Society in presenting his own Canadian settlement plan. 'I am glad to see such a work', he wrote after examining its prospectus, 'for, although it may not be all we could wish now, it may so far advance to what is desirable'.[6] Another who took the Society's progress seriously was John Dunmore Lang, the indefatigable Greenock-born 'clergyman, politician, educationalist, immigration organizer, historian, anthropologist, journalist, [and] gaol-bird' who left Scotland for Australia in 1822.[7] During a three-year visit to Britain beginning in 1846, Lang strove tirelessly to promote Protestant emigration to his adopted country, and it was in this context in April 1849 that he felt impelled to take notice of the potters' project of which he had been repeatedly asked his opinion.[8] Writing to a Birmingham paper, Lang praised the Society's 'noble objects', but begged to inquire what advantages the United States, and Wisconsin in particular, held over Australia, to where, he calculated, relocation could be effected at substantially lower cost.[9] Lang's intervention prompted several replies, including one from the Hull editor George Sheppard. Disclaiming any connection to the potters' scheme, Sheppard wrote that its members 'have been, and are, quietly engaged in the performance of a great work, while Dr. Lang rests content with mere preaching'.[10] Three months earlier Sheppard's paper, the *Eastern Counties Herald*, had run an appreciative article on the Society, which had recently established a branch in Hull, and he remained a strong supporter.[11] At the end of 1849 he was the leading spirit behind the Iowa Emigration Society, a semi-communal initiative that, like the potters', sought to transplant English workers to the American prairie.[12]

As the Potters' Emigration Society spread its wings, controversy was bound to follow. At the end of a lecture by William Coates on 23 January in Sheffield Town Hall, audience members raised the historic grievance of the debts incurred during the 1836–7 strike. A saw maker, Mr Rawlinson, noted that the Sheffield trades had visited the Potteries many times to pursue their claim, but were now of the opinion that 'this emigration society had been pushed forward by Mr. Evans, its founder, purposely to divert the attention of the potters' from their just demands. The next evening Coates sought privately to reassure trades' representatives that the late union's committee had forwarded their claims 'to the utmost of their power', but they remained unpersuaded.[13] There was more rough weather in Stockport, where a branch had recently been formed. In January branch leaders decided that there were problems with the potters' scheme that rendered further support impossible. The main issue, according to the secretary, Dr J. Jeffrey, was the scheme's 'indefinable notion of rendering labour as scarce as possible'. By applying all profits to 'the deportation' of workers, it operated as 'a bounty on emigration, after it may have ceased to be enjoined by natural causes'. The result could see employment checked and wages decline. He proposed instead a new organisation, the Stockport Emigration Society, which would enjoy the advantages of the potters' scheme and eschew its faults.[14] In a lengthy rejoinder William Evans suggested that the dissolution of the Stockport branch had nothing to do with the reasons Jeffrey had given. The primary cause, he wrote, 'exists in the circumstance that the branch contained, as members, two professional gentlemen and a minister of the established church, who could not fraternize with a few working men that comprised the majority'. Jeffrey, 'and those in his station', had no sympathy with 'a working-man's movement'.[15]

The Society's operations were now subject to increasing scrutiny. An article in April in the London-based *Spirit of the Times* was prompted by requests for information from readers desirous of emigrating to America. After examining 'the data' from the potters' scheme, the paper decided that it could not 'advise any of our friends to make a venture in that direction'. The problem was the Society's 'inadequate' funding arrangements, coupled with its underestimation of the costs of migration and settlement. From the evidence of its prospectus, sections of which the article printed, its only source of capital was the 6d a week in subscriptions from members, the vast majority of whom would be unsuccessful in the ballot. To make matters worse, the rules specified that anyone who had paid the sum of £1 1s 6d could 'go out to Wisconsin and claim his twenty acres of land on credit with a year's provisions'. The paper pointed out that in four years only fifty families had gone out under the scheme, with many discovering on arrival that 'no resources whatever' had been prepared for their sustenance. As a final barb, it included a 'unique morsel' from a recent *Potters' Examiner*. Publication of the extract, which advertised pre-embarkation arrangements in Liverpool in which families had '*the liberty of sleeping as many in one bed as they please*', was designed to point up the low domestic and moral standards set by the Society's managers. 'We trust they manage things better in Wisconsin', the paper added.[16]

The *Spirit of The Times*'s article identified William Evans as responsible for the emigrants' sleeping arrangements, and he inevitably became the focus of the criticism being levelled at the potters' scheme. Evans was by nature a controversialist, incapable of letting any censure or perceived slight pass unnoticed; he now met his match in the mercurial preacher-printer-abolitionist Joseph Barker. After initial scepticism, the Yorkshire-born Barker, who had strong connections to North Staffordshire, had become convinced of emigration's value as a solution to labour's problems and equally of the United States as the optimal destination. In June 1848 he began publishing a new one-penny paper, *The People*, the pages of which he filled with letters from British immigrants in America. His earliest reference to the Potters' Emigration Society was favourable. 'I believe it to be one of the best Societies of the kind', he told a Manchester correspondent, adding that he knew 'some of the parties connected with it' and believed them to be 'honest and well-meaning men'. He also considered the climate of the region where the potters had settled to be 'friendly to health' and the land 'rich and productive'.[17]

He returned to the subject a few weeks later. A friend, Charles Heath, a pottery worker from Shelton, had written to caution against investing money in the Society as the money would 'not be safe'. Heath enclosed a letter from a Thomas Bull that painted a bleak picture of conditions at the Pottersville settlement. Bull complained that he and his family had received virtually nothing from the colony's store, and that 'only three of those that have gone up to that place, since he and his family went' were still there. Also damaging was his report that the agent's credit was gone, and that the land was 'in jeopardy for debts which have been contracted'. Commenting, Barker wrote that the things of which Bull complained 'would not, to me, be very great calamities', but still advised anyone thinking of joining the Society to obtain satisfactory information before doing so. He had recently heard from William Evans, who spoke favourably of its operation and prospects. All his paper could do was to provide as much correct information as possible, leaving readers 'to choose their own course'.[18] Evans inevitably took offence. In what Barker described as some 'very angry remarks' in the *Examiner*, he called Heath a 'bigoted *boy-follower* of Mr. Feargus O'Connor', who had not paid a penny to his trade's society, a charge his friend quickly refuted. Barker countered Evans's claim that there had never been a colonist called Thomas Bull in Pottersville by suggesting that the name had been subject to a printer's error, 'putting *u* instead of another vowel'. (The letter-writer was almost certainly the Burslem potter Thomas Ball, a member of the *Constitution* party that left Liverpool the previous August.) He also reported that he had recently been in North Staffordshire and found 'that many have a good opinion of the *principles* of the Potters' Emigration Society, but not of its manager, Mr. Evans', whom he now described as 'prone to arbitrary and violent conduct'. If the Society was a good one, he wrote, 'as I am inclined to believe, it is a pity it has not a more truthful and trustworthy guardian'.[19]

So the exchanges continued, bringing diminished credit to both sides. Evans vigorously defended his role as the Society's agent, including his remuneration of 2s a week, and suggested that opposition in the Potteries arose from 'a bitter animosity to the principles of emigration as a means of trade's improvement', a statement Barker derided as false.[20] Two weeks later *The People* printed a letter from a former union official, Enoch Mountford, who told stories of Evans overcharging for travel expenses and other transgressions. His letter portrayed a man (he 'sat at the end of the table, with his gold ring on his finger') more concerned to line his own pockets than advance the welfare of working potters.[21] Evans's next assailant was another Barker acquaintance (and future mayor of Stoke), George Turner, who charged Evans with several crimes, including inflating the circulation of the *Examiner*. Turner also found Society membership to be far short of the alleged 3,000.[22] The personal assault deepened in a letter from John Green of Tunstall, dated Liverpool, 12 February, who had 'lately left the Potteries for America'. Green had been warned of the 'sharks' that lay in wait at the Mersey port, but never suspected that the greatest shark of all would be 'the emigrant's friend', the 'paid agent' of the Potters' Emigration Society. The upshot of Green's tortuous tale was that he had given Evans money to arrange passage to New Orleans, but on presentation of his ticket at the shipping office was informed that they had no connection with the vessel named. The whole business is 'nothing but a piece of villany [sic] and robbery', he wrote.[23]

Although Evans's supporters were adamant that these attacks emanated from 'a knot of men who have been expelled from the Society',[24] some of the arguments were not easily dismissed. Mountford, for instance, questioned the effect of the Society's expansion on its legitimacy and legality, and urged members in the out-potteries in particular not to be deceived by the agent's assurances. The laws under which the Society was enrolled 'are broken up and scarcely one is acted upon', he told them, and were null and void in the opinion of 'certain attornies'. Members could only get their money back if the parent society chose to return it: 'The idea of a few individuals in the Potteries, who contribute only some £3 10s. a week, transacting the business of out-districts who are contributing £100 a week, is monstrous'. One member no longer worried about his investment was W. Haywood from Oldham's 'Labour Refuge' branch. He wrote to say that he had decided to sell his paid-up share. Although the 18s he received from the sale left him out of pocket, he would in the long term be the gainer, as his 'weekly pence' were safer in the savings bank, 'where I can get a little interest for them'.[25]

Without access to the *Examiner*, the day-to-day workings and finances of the Society are almost entirely obscured. Equally hard to find is information on the progress made at its lands in Wisconsin. From the late summer of 1848 until the spring of 1849, its agents repeated the same encouraging statistic – the Pottersville colony comprised 134 individuals, made up in various accounts of 50, 40 or 34 families – but they offered no details about conditions there.[26] Given that an unknown number of emigrants had left the settlement, some returning to England, Pottersville's population was undoubtedly fluid. Adding to the uncertainty were those members who never made it to Wisconsin, deflected by opportunities en route or simply lacking the resources to proceed. In at least one case, the Society's own administrative shortcomings helped shape a family's progress. David Bridge, a 30-year-old mechanic from Macclesfield, and an early responder to the Society's recruitment drive, arrived in New York on 16 September 1848 with his wife and two children. From a letter home the following August, we learn that the Bridges left Paterson, New Jersey at the end of April 1849, stopping off for three weeks at a friend's in Cleveland, where David failed to find employment, before travelling on to Detroit, where he was taken on at a railway works. In his letter he asked his parents to pursue with Society officials the status of his land certificate, dated 10 August 1848. He had written twice to the 'land steward' but had received no reply. A young man from Manchester, whom he had recently met, had experienced the same problem. Despite this setback, the family were not discouraged. David had learned of a property sixty miles north of Detroit where he could realise his ambition to farm. Ultimately, it was God, not William Evans, who would deliver them: 'He has brought us safe over five thousand miles from our native land, to a place where we can get all the necessaries of life,—many of its luxuries if we wish for them, and something to spare for a future day.'[27]

Little by way of luxury greeted those families that did reach the Society's lands. Conditions had been particularly difficult for the members of the Estate Committee party who arrived in Pottersville in July 1847 with their funds exhausted. Finding only four homes built – and those missing doors and windows – some families took refuge in the abandoned barracks at nearby Fort Winnebago; others erected make-do shelters while the work was finished. The planting season was already advanced, and with little land cleared they struggled for survival.[28] One disgruntled member, Enoch Pickering, wrote two years later that without 'anything to cultivate our land with ... we were set down in a new settled country, with our hands tied behind our backs, by being robbed of our first winter's labour, and of the last fraction which charity had given us at home'.[29] Hunger was a regular companion, and families were forced to range far and wide in search of provisions. Isaac Smith recalled that once during the first winter, 'we never saw any bread of any description, and the only means of our subsistence was a few heads of wheat rubbed out with our hands, then boiled, which answered for our food for nine days'.³⁰ They also confronted an unfamiliar climate. At the Temperance Emigration Society's colony at nearby Mazomanie, one newcomer recorded on 21 December 1847 that the snow had started falling at the beginning of the month and was not expected to clear until April. The following day the thermometer plummeted to '28 below freezing'; two weeks later it registered 39 below freezing, the cold mitigated by the near-incessant sunshine.³¹ Many years later Isaac Smith recalled the fierce snows of that first winter when he was employed chopping wood 'for the late Henry Merrill at 25 cents per cord', when temperatures frequently fell to between 20 and 28 below freezing.³² Such extreme conditions could have fatal effects; in February 1850 James Hammond's brother George froze to death in circumstances we can only imagine.³³

Incomers either adapted to the harsh conditions and privations or left. Among those who endured were the Tunstall presser Henry Dooley and his wife Maria, who had worked at the potbank as a transferrer, and their 9-year-old daughter Harriet. The Dooleys had good reason to be discouraged by their experience of emigration; their youngest child Elizabeth had failed to survive the Lake Michigan crossing. Arriving in Pottersville, they found their allotted land 'in a wild state, in the midst of an unbroken forest'. The result was that for much of the first year they shared a 14-by-16-feet cabin with a Scotsman, Robert McConochie, who had recently crossed from Canada to join his brother Sam, who had settled in the area three years earlier. Sam provided the Dooleys with vital employment; Maria kept house in return for board, while her husband chopped wood and split rails for $8 a month.³⁴ On 18 March 1848 the couple celebrated the birth of another daughter, whom they named Elizabeth Ann. Spring also saw them move into their own home on the twenty-acre plot which they began to clear for cultivation. It had been a harsh baptism, but there were compensations. Henry frequently said that 'he enjoyed himself during that winter as well as he ever did in Wisconsin'. As he went to his daily labour, 'with his dinner and ax, he often saw the sun peeping over the hills'.³⁵ The prairie's natural bounty also impressed Maria, with the abundant game and wild berries providing valuable supplements to the family's food stocks. She also recalled the 'visits from Indians as they followed the trail from Fox Lake to Portage'.³⁶

These glimpses into pioneer days in Pottersville come to us mediated by the filter of memory – of nostalgia, even. Contemporary evidence of the hardships faced by the early settlers is provided by Alexander Evans and his family, who also lost a child en route to Wisconsin. Chronically short of funds and with no home built or land cleared, they spent their first winter in a temporary shelter. In November 1847, as previously described, they suffered a serious setback when money and goods were lost in the *Phoenix* disaster on Lake Michigan; their ill-luck continued the following year when a further consignment, dispatched with the Puckaway-bound party, also failed to reach them. To help ensure their survival, the family distributed their three young daughters as live-in servants among various farm households. Throughout 1848 Alexander was employed 'on shares'; the following spring he left the settlement for a season, returning in March 1850, when he resumed working for others under the same arrangements. In the meantime the family's twenty-acre allotment remained unbroken, and Alexander was again forced to request financial help from home.[37]

Also struggling to establish himself was John Peake, a 28-year-old presser from Burslem, who arrived at Pottersville in the late summer of 1848. In a letter to his brother the following September, he described what he had done over the preceding year 'so that you will be enabled to form a pretty good idea as to whether a man can get along or not'. Peake began work at Portage for 50 cents a day. After a spell digging potatoes, he joined up with another Burslem settler, William Mountford, working mostly for board. In the spring of 1849 he hired out for $15 a month, but was forced to give up the work as 'my legs were breaking out all over sores, from being in the water so much'. He found better employment with the Society, chopping wood and helping to construct homes, which enabled him to pay for the clearing of five acres of land on his newly staked claim. He also resumed work for Mountford, cutting and stacking hay and helping him build his log house. Unfortunately, the house burned down on completion, consuming Mountford's bedding and tools. Peake himself was undeterred. By September 1849 he had five acres of wheat sown and paid for. 'I am going to get my house up right off hand, get married and go into it', he told his brother (his bride-to-be was Mountford's daughter Eliza). He had also purchased a cooking stove, 'so that you see a man may get along if he will'.[38]

Peake's improved fortunes owed much to the work of the Society's agent, Thomas Twigg, who greatly expanded settlers' employment opportunities.[39] Twigg's arrival in April 1849 was a significant moment in the colony's history. As a circular explained, the 38-year-old potter (and former president of the Society) had been sent to Wisconsin to oversee the colony's expansion 'with full power to purchase land; and to build a Store, and to stock the same with food and agricultural implements'.[40] But Twigg had another task to perform, unmentioned in the circular, and that was to sort out problems at the Pottersville settlement. Thomas Ball's admittedly unverified comments on the dire state of things there have been noted; further evidence of the lack of progress – and a possible explanation for it – comes from the Yorkshire machinist John H. Broadbent, who reached Columbia County in June. Pottersville is 'one of the most miserable places you can imagine', he told his parents; 'the people there have been too lazy to work; they would do nothing but shoot for a living, the same as wild men'.[41]

Addressing a meeting in Hanley Town Hall in December 1849, Twigg talked of how he arrived at Pottersville in April 'and found irregularities there which required correcting'. While many settlers had followed the rules regarding credit, some had left without refunding their advances.[42] With too little collective progress and too many unpaid debts, the situation was highly unsatisfactory, and in his report dated 26 August he outlined proposals to remedy it. 'You wish me to make Pottersville a flourishing place', he advised the Society's committee. 'That will require a little time, and new arrangements, so as to give confidence and encouragement to the settlers to set to work and improve their homes.' The first step was to change a core element of the scheme's design. Twigg recommended that each colonist now be given forty acres of land, 'as 20 acres are not sufficient to enable a man to pay a large debt in any thing like a reasonable space of time'. Agreeing to put Pottersville on 'the 40-acre principle' will be the means 'of getting in a large amount of debts now outstanding', and he urged the committee to settle the question quickly. His second proposal addressed settler behaviour, and specifically the failure to honour the colony's labour requirement: 'There is not one of the settlers who has performed one day's work towards his day per month for ten years, according to agreement, and which must be done before their deeds can be granted.' Enforcing the rule would 'secure them as permanent settlers; and will bring you back at least part of the capital laid out, with interest'.[43]

The person responsible for ensuring compliance with the Society's rules was the estate steward, Hamlet Copeland, 'a truly kind and honourable man', according to its circular. Twigg made no public criticism of Copeland's management; he did, however, comment on his having acquired an extra twenty acres of land for which 'he only paid 40 dollars'. 'I was obliged to let him have it', he wrote, although he thought twice that sum a fairer price. A more satisfactory negotiation involved the deeds of the Pottersville estate. On 5 July these were transferred from the land agents, Copeland, John Sawyer and James Hammond, in whose names the property was purchased, to Twigg and his fellow trustees, Charles Adams and John Johnson, who had accompanied him to Wisconsin. The transaction was properly registered, and the deeds carried to England by Twigg himself and lodged with the Society's bank, Thomas Kinnersley & Sons of Newcastle-under-Lyme.[44] For Evans and his co-workers, their receipt represented another milestone in the struggle for acceptance. 'It has been said by our enemies, that The Title Deeds of Pottersville would never come to England', headlined the *Examiner* in December. 'Like most other vindictive statements, we can point to its falsehood.' To confirm their arrival, the paper printed verbatim copies of the various documents, all duly signed, sealed and delivered in the presence of Columbia County justices and witnessed by the Society's surviving pioneer settlers: Hamlet and Ellen Copeland, John Sawyer and James and Martha Hammond.[45]

Having played no part in its birth and disparaging of the settlers' conduct, Twigg never really took to Pottersville. By August he was complaining that there were 'parties' there 'who would glory in our destruction, and are working for that end'.[46] Sorting out its problems was always subordinate to his main goal: the establishment of a new colony based on the principle of forty-acre farms. Twigg seems to have had considerable room for manoeuvre regarding land acquisition. Snapshots of his progress come from the Society's lecturers. At Sheffield Town Hall in January, William Coates reported that having acquired 1,600 acres in Wisconsin, the Society was 'now taking steps' to obtain 2,000 more.[47] Four months later, in Sunderland, he advised that the Society was 'at present in treaty with the American government for twenty-three thousand acres' of Wisconsin land.[48] Finally, on 4 July at the Carpenters' Hall, Manchester, William Evans proudly announced that the Potters' Emigration Society possessed three separate estates.

> The first estate, comprising 1600 acres, is now peopled; it is named Pottersville. The second estate, comprising 2000 acres, and named Emancipation, is in the course of peopling. It is on the south bank of the Fox River, and is said to comprise a succession of 'oak openings', and to be rich in minerals. The third estate, comprising the large quantity of 12,000 acres, is situate [sic] on the north bank of the Fox River, and runs parallel with the Emancipation purchase. Two hundred families are now located on the last purchase, and from the remarks of the lecturer it would appear that the colonists are well satisfied with their change of country.[49]

Without access to Twigg's early correspondence, it is impossible to track the movements and dealings that produced these outcomes. One unverified local account, written in 1876, tells how Twigg and the Burslem potter Peter Watkin, later Twigg's deputy, landed at Fort Winnebago in the fall of 1848 and were conveyed down the Fox River by Isaac Smith and William Mountford. Smith and Mountford then scouted for land 'but were prevented from venturing far from their stopping place for fear of being lost in the wilderness'.[50] Although we cannot verify when Twigg travelled to America, Smith and Mountford's involvement is certainly plausible, as both played prominent parts in the colony's early development. In 1848, anxious to avoid a round-trip walk of twenty-eight miles, Rev. Smith had moved his family to Fort Winnebago, where he performed a weekly service following a first appearance there on Christmas Day. From the beginning he was busily involved in local communications projects, including, during the first winter, helping to build a bridge across the Fox River and afterwards digging the first sod in the excavation for the canal to connect the Fox and Wisconsin rivers.[51] Mountford, who arrived in September 1848, was also active in the settlement's development. He owned one of its first ox teams, which he used to transport supplies from Milwaukie; Twigg later employed him to haul timber and provisions from Fort Winnebago.[52]

Twigg's surviving account, given at Hanley in December, makes intriguing reading.

> Seeing the propriety of founding a new colony upon somewhat different principles, he proceeded to the Fox River, and having obtained an interview with the Governor, and stated the object of his visit, a site of land was fixed upon of 50,000 acres in extent, and was now called Emancipation Ferry.[53]

The area allegedly allocated by Governor Nelson Dewey formed part of the 'Indian Lands', a designation that remained in usage for some time. In October 1848, five months after it achieved statehood, Wisconsin ceded its last remaining tribal territories to the federal government. It was the final act in a long process of appropriation that reached its peak between 1829 and 1833 when all Native American lands south of the Fox–Wisconsin waterway were transferred to the United States, paving the way for an inrush of white settlers. The Menominee cession of 1848 was the tribe's second in twelve years, and comprised 4.5 million acres between the two rivers. It received in return $350,000 and a new homeland in Minnesota. An important stipulation permitted the Menominee to remain in Wisconsin for a further two years. (The tribe refused to move at the end of the period, petitioning that they had been coerced into selling the land. In 1852 they were granted a temporary reservation along the Wolf River in northeastern Wisconsin. It became their permanent home two years later.[54]) To those critics who objected to the Native presence, Twigg had a firm response. In December he assured a Liverpool meeting that the 'kindliest feeling subsisted between the colonists and the Indians' and that 'he had never known a single act of depredation committed by them'. Their only failing 'was an insatiable love of whisky', a vice, he reminded his audience, 'in which many more civilized people nearer home participated'.[55] Other settlers endorsed Twigg's view. 'We are placed in the midst of Indians, who are to leave this land in about 18 months; they are very civil and kind', wrote John H. Broadbent.[56] Less impressed with their demeanour was Martin Ellison, who arrived with his family at the end of August. He noted that they had shot several deer on his land and lived 'solely by hunting, begging, and stealing'.[57] Native American testimony is in short supply. But another newcomer, John Frankland, reported that one armed visitor to the store had 'wished me to "puckagee," that is "Go away"'. Refusing the offer of whisky, he partook of bread and pork before shaking hands and departing. 'I have not seen him since', the Yorkshireman wrote.[58]

As Evans described, the lands chosen for the Society's new colony straddled the Fox River to the west of Pottersville on the border between Columbia and Marquette Counties. At a river crossing a few miles north of Fort Winnebago that became known as Twigg's Landing, the agent established the Emancipation Ferry, named, as a local history put it, because the colonists felt liberated 'from the virtual position of serfs in the mother country and here were made freemen'.[59] He also built and operated a store and a blacksmith's shop. The location would arouse criticism from numerous settlers who complained of the area's poor sandy soils, but Twigg had no doubt of its potential. Less than two miles separated the Fox from the Wisconsin River. In 1849 work began on a canal to bridge the historic portage, with the aim of connecting the Great Lakes to the Mississippi and Gulf of Mexico.[60] Reporting in August, Twigg spelled out the advantages he believed would accrue from the navigational work currently underway. 'In twelve months the boats will be flying past our doors', he insisted.

> Our emigrants can then be landed on our estate, direct from Liverpool, by water conveyance, at one-half the present cost ... Groceries, Sheffield cutlery, Staffordshire crockery, Manchester dry goods, Nottingham stockings,—all these can be brought to our doors in some six weeks hence, and our grain and pork can be taken back to England in return.[61]

Twigg's immediate task was to prepare for the influx of new settlers. Among the earliest arrivals in 1849 – he may have been the first – was the aforementioned John Frankland, a member of Bingley's 'Industry' branch. In a belated letter to his family, he lamented the 'expense and trouble' incurred during a forty-five-day crossing to New York followed by two weeks in Buffalo awaiting the break-up of ice on the lakes. 'I left home a month too soon', he admitted. Frankland reached the potters' lands on the same day, 28 April, as Twigg. After an unpromising start – he had to abandon a partially built cabin after objections from local 'Yankees' – he was soon employed 'chinking and plastering' the houses for the arriving members. The Yorkshireman had nothing but praise for the Society's agent; he had no complaints either about his allotted forty acres of land, 'richer than any I have seen in England'.[62] Frankland was not the only member to make an early start for America. On 9 March five textile workers from Preston in Lancashire, Leonard Lodge, Thomas Beckett, brothers James and Charles Clitheroe and Charles Ayrey, sailed from Liverpool aboard the *Charles Chaloner* bound for New Orleans, where they landed on 23 April.[63] Also opting for the warmer southern route was 35-year-old George Cocker, a cotton spinner from the Ashton-under-Lyne area, who crossed the Atlantic with his wife Margaret and two young children. Departing from Liverpool the day after the Preston men, their voyage on the *Hindostan* lasted a gruelling eight weeks. 'We left our old worn-out country on the 10th March, and we landed at New Orleans on the 5th of May', Cocker wrote to William Evans. It took them a further two weeks to ascend the Mississippi and reach the settlement. Like Frankland, Cocker was unstinting in his admiration for Thomas Twigg, who 'deserves the praises and blessings of every working man in England'.[64]

Most emigrants preferred the shorter crossing to New York.[65] The spring and early summer of 1849 saw a steady trickle of families heading for the interior through the booming East Coast port. They included the first members from London. Arriving from the capital on 23 April aboard the *Burlington* was 24-year-old Thomas Ciscel and his wife Elizabeth. Thomas's skills as a butcher would stand him in good stead across the Atlantic. From South London came the Hatchers, George, Elizabeth and baby son, who sailed from London on the Baltimore-based *Wenham*, landing on 5 May. By trade a baker, Hatcher was recorded in the ship's passenger list as a 'macaroni maker'. Travelling with them was a law student, John Turner, and his sister Elizabeth. Despite his age – he would not turn 21 until the following November – he quickly assumed a prominent role in the settlement's affairs.[66] Three weeks after the *Wenham*'s arrival, the *Silas Richards* docked in New York, bringing two more families from the capital. George and Mary Denby were from Hackney. Settling in Marquette County, George reported his occupation as that of 'wheelwright', an invaluable trade on the pre-industrial frontier. With the Denbys were John and MaryAnn Pettepher and their son Richard from Central London. John, a carpenter, would find ready employment in Wisconsin.[67]

They were joined by the first emigrants from Scotland: Alexander Sim, a stonemason, his wife and four children, and two single men, John Thomson and the younger George Mitchell, who worked in the Abbotshall linen mills in Kirkcaldy. They sailed from Greenock on 2 April on the barque *Cuthbert*, which aside from its nearly 400 passengers carried 1,000 tons of pig-iron for use in the republic's burgeoning railroad industry.[68] 'I do not think any set of passengers ever enjoyed more health, felt more agreeably, or exhibited more of a friendly disposition to each other than we did', Mitchell wrote of the twenty-seven day crossing. His widely circulated letter home described the group's 1,300-mile journey to Milwaukie, where he and Thompson worked for a few days before setting out on their final stage. The letter also revealed an improvised side to the scheme's operation. The two men were not members of the Society and may only have learned about it from Sim. They still received a warm welcome at Fort Winnebago, where the agent accepted them 'as members, as far as he can'. As it was not possible to join the Society at the settlement, Mitchell asked his family to pay the required subscription at their local branch in Kirkcaldy.[69]

Two days after the *Cuthbert*'s departure from Greenock, the Black Star packet *Marmion* left Liverpool for New York, arriving on 30 April. Of its 430 passengers, at least 50 were destined for the Wisconsin lands. Among them was 34-year-old William Scholes from Oldham. His had been the first share drawn in the New Year's Day ballot at Manchester's Free Trade Hall. He was accompanied by his wife Ann and six children (the couple would go on to have five more). The youngest child of thirteen, Scholes cut his teeth in the silk trade before transferring to the cotton mill, where he rose to become superintendent of the carding-room. As a carder, he was exposed daily to the room's fibrous dust, free-floating particles that attacked the lungs with poisonous effect. 'Some constitutions can bear it, some cannot; but the operative has no choice', wrote Friedrich Engels in 1845 of the carder's life.[70] Little wonder the newly arrived settler was glad to exchange the 'stinking factory' for the pure air of the backwoods. He only wished that more workers could 'leave their sickly toil and come to one of the healthiest places on earth'.[71]

There were several other Oldham men in the party. Henry Mattley was a 54-year-old hatter. Boarding with the Scholes family, he was still waiting to hear from his wife and two sons several months after arriving in Wisconsin. Also leaving his family behind in Oldham was John Goulding, a spinner. He too became frustrated by the lack of news from home; despite repeated inquiries, a letter from his wife had lain undetected for a month at the Portage post office.[72] Other single travellers included the Leeds machinist John H. Broadbent; John Tordoff, a gardener, also from Yorkshire; Joseph Brentnall, a Nottingham lace maker; and a 22-year-old tanner, John Robbins, from Bermondsey in Southeast London. New families arriving on the *Marmion* included the Wilsons, James and Margaret and their two sons, from Clitheroe in Lancashire, where James was employed as a bleacher; and, from Birmingham, the Wells and Horton families. Henry Wells worked in the gun trade; William Horton was a scale maker. Writing home in July, the latter reflected that his brother, a barber, would do very well in Wisconsin, 'for we have no barber near, nor have I any razors'.[73] There were several families from the Potteries, among them that of George Cooper, a Burslem potter who had also been successful in the New Year's Day ballot; he travelled with his wife and five children; Stephen Murray, also from Burslem and a hollow-ware presser, his wife and three children; and John Hammond, older brother of the Society's pioneer settler, who was accompanied by his wife and two daughters. Anticipating their new lives in Wisconsin, both Cooper and Murray were listed as 'farmer' in the *Marmion*'s manifest.

As with any group of migrants, individuals reacted to their new environment in varying ways. The Oldham friends William Scholes and John Goulding were soon enthusing about their experience of prairie settlement.

Having 'five acres of fall wheat sown' and a larger crop expected next season, the former hoped in a year or so to put his family 'out of the reach of want'. Hard work was all that was required. 'How many of our friends in Oldham can say the same', he asked. 'Not many, I think'. Goulding was also pleased with his progress, and informed his wife that he had 'no thoughts of coming to old England again'. Above all, the men were determined to counter the stories of those who 'would rather grumble than work', as Scholes put it. The naysayers included Enoch Pickering, who told 'dismal tales' of the conditions awaiting the Oldham men in the 'Indian land'. Particularly disappointing was the conduct of a fourth emigrant from the town, James Grey. In a letter to branch members, Scholes posed the question as to how Grey 'got away from here after a stay of three months, for he had not a cent when he came, but he was indebted to others for getting up at all'. He was similarly scornful about another member of the *Marmion* party, George Farmer from Birmingham, who had emigrated with his wife Emma; he 'only used his axe once, when he threw it down and would work no more, and he is telling the most pitiful tales about the settlement'.[74] Farmer had started back, confirmed fellow Brummie William Horton on 10 July, 'as he cannot do as he likes here'.[75]

Throughout June, July and August emigrants continued to descend on the Society's lands. They came from all sections of the country, with little connecting them save a desire to escape to a new and better life in America's virgin West. From Renfrew came Alexander Pinkerton, a weaver, with his wife Marian and their infant daughter. They landed in New York from Greenock at the end of June. They were followed soon after by one of the oldest emigrants, Thomas Keen, a 60-year-old widower from Burslem, who worked as a joiner, and his son Robert and daughter Mary. Arriving in New York from Liverpool on the *Kate Hunter* on 7 July, they made their way to Milwaukie, where they encountered a man from Birmingham (probably George Farmer) who 'gave such a bad account of the estate, that Robert thought of getting work, while I went up to see if such accounts were true'. At Fort Winnebago father and son found employment easy to come by, sufficient at least to tide them over. A shrewd observer, Thomas had no time for those unwilling to work. However, he admitted that frontier agriculture was more labour-intensive than he expected: 'Things, you know, up here, cannot be very promising at present, when a man has to go into a place something like Bradwell Wood, and cut down all the timber before they can plough up the ground' and prepare for planting. He added that they had 'got up here too late to have anything of that sort done for this year'.[76]

By contrast, Accrington-born engraver Martin Ellison and his family, who arrived a month after the Keens, showed that the season was never too advanced to begin work on the land. The Ellisons were among several migrants from the Accrington area travelling on the *Queen of the West*, which left Liverpool on 8 July; they included Martin's friend James Barnes and his son, also James, both shoemakers. During the crossing James senior fell sick, prompting advice from the ship's doctor to prepare his will. He thankfully recovered, as did another member of the party, George Penrice, a tailor, who was emigrating with two young children.[77] After disembarking on 10 August in New York, the group made swift onward progress, reaching Buffalo on 21 August and Milwaukie four days later. As Ellison reported with typical exactitude: 'Got to Fox Rover at 11 a.m. on Wednesday the 29th, crossed the river by the society's boat; saw Mr. Twigg, the society's agent, same day, presented our "land certificates", got the necessaries of life and lodgings at the society's store.' With five children whose ages ranged from 4 to 22, the Ellisons could draw upon considerable domestic resources, which they soon deployed on the tasks of improvement (the eldest son, James, had also been allotted forty acres abutting his parents' property). 'We have about three acres of ploughed land, and are busy grubbing it, viz. clearing it of tree roots, brushwood, &c. and burning them', Martin wrote on 16 September. Other vital jobs included mowing and stacking grass, digging wells and clearing a road.[78] By 24 August they had sown their wheat; three days later they had harvested the hay; and two weeks after that they had finished work on their kitchen and built a 'fowl house'.[79] In his letter Martin provided a detailed summary of the new estate's progress. There were 'about 60 houses built, inhabited by nearly one hundred families'. The family's own dwelling was 'ten miles up the country from head-quarters ... the very west end of civilization; but there is a chain of colonists down to the river, and one of our society's stores is not quite two miles distant, and there [are] two houses within half a mile of us inhabited by London Members'.[80]

Other settlers arriving without fanfare at the Society's lands in late August and September included John Lymburn, a young baker from Paisley in Renfrewshire; Thomas Parr, a carpenter from Newcastle-under-Lyme, whose wife Lydia and four children would follow two months later; and Joseph Twycross and his family from London. The continuing arrivals posed a challenge for Thomas Twigg, who had little idea of the numbers heading his way. Advance notice was crucial in regard to the balloted members, who expected to find a home erected and five acres of land 'broken-up, fenced and sown'.[81] In July the Society despatched a 24-year-old carpenter, Frances Orme, to build six log houses for balloted members arriving in the fall. On learning of his imminent appearance, Twigg informed the committee that the work was already complete, but if permitted he would employ Orme to construct homes for those arriving the following spring. Barely concealing his frustration, he also asked it to apprise him of the numbers expected in the spring 'or any other time you may wish to go to ballot'. Sadly, Twigg faced no dilemma over the carpenter's duties. On 26 August he reported that Orme had succumbed to cholera nine days out from New York. He was one of at least thirteen passengers to die on the *Patrick Henry* (see Figure 5.1), which had docked three weeks earlier. He left behind in the Potteries a widow and three children.[82] (Orme was a victim of a global epidemic, one of several in the nineteenth century. Cholera arrived in New York in December 1848; by May 1849 it had extended as far north as Kenosha, Wisconsin. There is no evidence that it reached the potters' settlement.[83])

On 7 September the Blue Swallowtail packet *Aberdeen* arrived in New York after a thirty-day passage from Liverpool. On board were a large number of emigrants headed for the Society's lands. Reports differ on exactly how many; one newspaper noted that fifty families amounting to 'two hundred persons' had left Liverpool for Wisconsin, while the *Examiner* claimed on 29 September that 'some 130 souls belonging to the society' had arrived safely in America.[84] Among the *Aberdeen*'s passengers were a Manchester stonemason, Joshua Winterbotham, and his friend Ainsworth Slater, a joiner, who was travelling with his wife and young daughter. Reaching Fort Winnebago, the men were impressed with the estate's potential, noting the local improvements being undertaken by the state government. However, in

Figure 5.1 Blue Swallowtail Line transatlantic packet *Patrick Henry*, which suffered a cholera outbreak in 1849 (oil painting by Philip John Ouless, c.1859).

a letter to branch friends in Salford, Winterbotham maintained that future progress required a continuing flow of money from home and a change in behaviour. 'The laziness of some, and the roughness of others, will do much towards counteracting all good that may be done by the industrious', he wrote. He ended by praising Thomas Twigg, 'a sensible man ... doing his best', who was due to depart for England.[85] Two months later Joshua's parents Thomas and Eliza arrived at the settlement. In the early 1850s the family migrated the short distance to Dane County, where in April 1859 Thomas was killed by a falling tree while out ploughing.[86]

The *Aberdeen* party represented all main areas of Society recruitment: Lancashire, London, Scotland, Birmingham and the Potteries. How many of its members made it to the settlement or stayed there more than a short period is difficult to establish. Among the families who did were the Stantons from Birmingham. Henry Stanton worked as a toolmaker in Birmingham's arms industry; with him were his wife Rhoda and six children. The family remained in the Marquette and Columbia Counties area, with Henry living to the exceptional age of 95. Also leaving Birmingham with seven of their children were William and Hannah Betts. The couple had a nomadic history; one accompanying son was born in Corfu, another in Malta. Sometime during the 1850s the Betts left Wisconsin and crossed into Canada, settling in London, where in 1861 William was working as an innkeeper. Describing their journey to Fort Winnebago in 1849, he especially regretted the loss of his spectacles on the road from Milwaukie.[87] Families from Staffordshire on the *Aberdeen* included William Hopwood, a crate maker, his wife Hanna and five children, who would remain in the area; Samuel Machin from Tunstall, his wife Jane, a bonnet maker in the Potteries, and their two children; and a balloted member from Burslem, James Kirkham, who would return with his wife and family to England the following year.

While the end of summer brought fewer emigrants to Wisconsin, some were still willing to risk the late season's crossing. On 24 September the Black Star packet *Ivanhoe* left Liverpool for New York, arriving there on 19 October. Its passengers included 'several members of the society', according to the *Examiner*.[88] Two vessels carrying Society emigrants arrived in New Orleans on the same day, 7 November. Passengers on the *E and E Perkins* included Hanley potter David Boulton, his wife Olive and two children; aboard the *Joseph Badger* were two Nixon families, James and his three children (his wife Mary and eldest son died during the voyage); and Enoch, Ann and their five children. Both James and Enoch worked as potters. Late travellers to Wisconsin also included family members of men already in America, among them Maria Cadman from Burslem, whose husband Samuel had accompanied the ill-fated Francis Orme on the *Patrick Henry*. With her were John and Jane Scott from the Bucknall area of Stoke. On reaching Milwaukie on 10 October, the couple found their resources depleted. After paying $7 to transport his wife and luggage to Fort Winnebago, John was left to make his way to the settlement on foot, a four-day trek. With no prospect of income from the land, finding work was a priority. Two months' contracted labour 100 miles away at Stevens Point ended prematurely in a dispute over money, prompting the 38-year-old bricklayer to branch out on his own. He had soon earned enough to 'keep us all winter, for we get paid for our work in this country'. Like others, he valued the opportunities available in the developing frontier society and condemned those who spurned them. He also valued its egalitarianism: 'I put up a oven last week at a tavern, where I dined with a magistrate, two doctors, and two lawyers, and I was as good as any of them; you could not do this in England', he wrote to his relatives in the Potteries.[89] Another late arrival who quickly found work was Joseph Tempest, a Yorkshireman in his late forties who did not reach the settlement until mid-November, having also walked most of the way from Milwaukie. He told a friend that he had no fear of doing well: 'This is a New Settlement, and we cannot expect to have everything we want; but we must look forward with hope.'[90]

Fulfilling that hope required energy and perseverance but also a measure of support. The spring of 1849 saw the Society embark on its most successful phase. Between March and October several hundred migrants left Britain for the Wisconsin lands. Beginning as an arm of the potters' union, the Society had grown in five years into a national movement, with over 100 branches located throughout industrial Britain, their names redolent of working-class faith in America's restorative powers: 'Land of the Free' (Preston); 'New Paradise' (Ashton-under-Lyne); 'Poor Man's Refuge' (Hyde); 'Slave's Hope' (Hull); 'Speed the Plough' (Wishawtown).[91] Expansion, however, brought tensions as differing views emerged on the best use of the Society's resources. At a meeting in the Potteries in August, delegates resolved that ballots should only take place when £650 in funds was in place. Any money left over after paying balloted members' expenses should go towards the purchase of new land. The delegates' intent was clear: acquiring full title to the preempted land must be the priority. The resolution was proposed by an East London delegate called Taylor and reflected the concern that on present course the land would never be purchased. Responding, the *Examiner* described the resolution as 'in prospective ... feasible and well'. The problem was that in their recent letters Twigg and his de facto deputy Peter Watkin had made urgent requests for funds to buy supplies for the winter, which, as the latter put it, was likely to be 'long and severe'. Feeding those who are here 'must by the *first* care of the society', Watkin advised. In the wake of the agents' appeals, the leadership decided to rescind the Taylor resolution and forward all available monies to Wisconsin. 'This is not a consequence of diversified opinion, but of absolute necessity', the paper affirmed.[92]

However justified the need, the rescinding could only fuel concern about the authority of the so-called 'Parent Society'. At the delegates' meeting Taylor had further suggested reorganising the Society along 'sectional' lines, but he failed to attract support. The seed of rebellion had nonetheless been planted. Delegates at a district meeting in Manchester on 26 August unanimously approved a motion to implement a sectional plan which involved closing the Parent Society and reconstituting it as a section of the reformed body. In a widely circulated letter, 'A Member of the Prairie Branch, Salford' proposed converting the Society into sections of no more than 3,000 or 5,000 members. Each section would have 'sole management of their own affairs'.[93] The Manchester move brought a sharp rebuke from the Potteries leadership. In a leading article William Evans argued that if adopted, the sectional system would eventually destroy 'our great and good cause', and that branch representation was properly accommodated through the establishment of a delegate meeting. The Society's governance was fixed by law, and delegates 'overstepped their duties' in passing the resolution for the accumulation of a land fund: 'Why agitate the whole society for that which cannot be granted,— and will not be granted?'[94]

It would be wrong to overstate the magnitude of this opposition. Most members accepted the argument that funds should be set aside to ensure the settlers' survival; and if some Lancashire branches withheld contributions over the sectional plan, there were no large-scale defections. Support for the leadership was widespread. Members of the 'City of Glasgow' branch issued a strong statement condemning the Manchester action and applauding Evans and Twigg 'for the noble exertions they have made, and are still making, to elevate the working classes of this country to landed independence'.[95] There were similar expressions from branches in London, Birmingham and Halifax.[96] Evans himself recognised that there was a legitimate debate to be had on how the Society should utilise its resources; his concern was the spirit in which criticisms were offered and the degree to which they threated its unity and progress. At the beginning of September the *Examiner* published on its front page a letter from Charles Chubb, the 'South London' branch chairman. Chubb, like others, was unclear how the Society would pay for its preempted land which, if not redeemed, would be lost, together with improvements made to it. His advice was to leave nothing to chance, and 'secure the money against the time it is wanted, and when the land is paid for and in producing order, we may ballot for fifty families instead of six'. In an editorial note Evans rejected Chubb's counsel, but praised him for his good sense and the 'kind and gentlemanly' tone of his communication.[97]

Evans must also have been pleased by Chubb's enthusiasm for the campaign to fund the erection of a grist mill. Grist mills were important practical and symbolic components of community development on the American frontier, 'the natural centre of social and economic life', according to one historian.[98] The initiative for building a mill on the Society's lands came from Thomas Twigg, who saw the benefits it would bring to the area's growing farm population. 'Let me have cash for the Grist Mill!' he pleaded on 26 August. 'We must and will have one, if I go in debt for it.'[99] For Twigg and shareholders like Chubb, the project opened up great prospects for future growth, particularly if combined with a sawmill. Sited near the ferry, it 'will be sure to cause a town to spring up by magic', the latter claimed. To pay for the mill's construction, the Society established a voluntary fund which soon drew regular contributions from members across the country. Leading the drive was Hanley's 'William Evans' branch. In September it issued penny contribution cards and organised a concert and ball, with all proceeds going to the fund. As further evidence of the grist mill's appeal, that month Evans received a donation from a Birmingham artist (he was by trade a japanner[100]), William Bidwell Henley, of a framed oil painting valued at £4. He also enclosed a subscription. Accepting the 'excellent work of art', the Society offered it as first prize in a national raffle, with tickets priced at 1s; it even promised to pay for delivery should the lucky winner live outside the Potteries.[101]

If Evans was gratified by the response to the grist mill appeal, he was relieved by the outcome of an audit of its accounts, a summary of which the *Examiner* published on 13 October. The auditors, George W. Robinson, James Rowbottom and Thomas Nichols, had been appointed by the London, Manchester and Birmingham districts respectively. A clue to the audit's origins can be found in the men's comment that they began 'with no slight amount of prejudice against the managers of the society, and some misgivings as to its real position'. But after wading through five years of paperwork, they came to a different view, exonerating Evans and his fellow directors of any wrongdoing and offering a positive prognosis of the Society's long-term health.

> Our prejudice is removed, our misgivings are gone to the winds, and we have strong confidence in the power of the society to accomplish the objects for which it was established, as well as in the honesty and ability of its conductors fully and efficiently to work those objects out.

Singled out for praise were the printing office – which had realised a 20-per-cent return on original capital and provided what 'all working men most desire', the means 'of publishing their own grievances, and clearly and fully advocating their own just rights' – and the *Examiner*, which had also turned 'a positive profit'. However, the three were highly critical of the Society's bookkeeping. Although there was no suspicion of dishonesty, they found 'an amount of confusion and disorder' that they wished to see removed in the future. They reminded the Society that it was now 'a large and very important national organization' (current membership was recorded as 3,500), whose affairs should be managed 'with all the care, regularity, and vigilance' of a commercial house or bank.

The auditors reflected in a postscript on 'the real position of the society's affairs in the Far West'. The Pottersville estate was secured, they noted, with the land now worth four times its original cost and certain to recoup all of the funds spent on it. Admittedly, a large portion of the money and provisions advanced to the colonists remained unpaid, but with the deeds now in trustees' hands, 'payment CAN and WILL be enforced in accordance with the laws'. They were equally sanguine about Twigg's colony, which was progressing as favourably as could be expected: 'The foundation is laid for future and extensive operations; a large and flourishing town will, ere long, be erected on the site, and an example will be set worthy of imitation by all bodies of working men.' Finally, they paid tribute to the Society's founder: 'May he live long to witness his proudest dreams fully realized in the emancipation of thousands of the sons of toil from the over-populated, tax-ridden country to happier, more free, and independent homes in the Western World.' Evans could hardly let such vindication pass without comment. In triumphal voice, the *Examiner* claimed that the report proved that the libellous attacks upon the Society had been of 'the most false and despicable' character. Nevertheless, it was important that the Society acknowledge the criticisms of its chaotic accounting. On 9 October the committee unanimously endorsed the recommended changes, including the use of cheque books and the employment of one treasurer, not two. It also authorised the printing of 1,000 copies of the auditors' report.[102]

Proper bookkeeping was also a priority for Thomas Twigg. In August he explained that he was preparing 'a balance-sheet of the New Estate' and pledged to provide quarterly reports. Keeping accounts was one of many tasks the overburdened agent was compelled to undertake, and in the same breath he asked the committee whether it would consider sending out someone to assist him: 'He must be a man that can stand some little hardship, and that understands how to survey land, and work by the compass in the woods; and take a log for his pillow occasionally.' Such an appointment could also help facilitate a visit home to England. 'There are a many points that I could for ever settle, which are impossible for me to explain by letter', he wrote, 'but I am content myself, and shall leave the matter for you to decide'. He also requested 'a small remuneration' for the Burslem potter Peter Watkin so that he could hire him for winter work: 'He is the most honest, straightforward man he was when in England, and I feel assured he will remain so.'[103]

Not the least of the reasons for Twigg returning home was the opportunity to counter the adverse reports of the colony's wellbeing. Although the summer of 1849 saw a lowering of the critical temperature – helped by Joseph Barker's absence in the United States – stories from disgruntled emigrants continued to cloud the Society's reputation. The effect of such stories at this stage on local opinion, whether publicly or privately related, is hard to judge. Addressing working men in Macclesfield in August, William Evans was warned to expect a 'discussion' following the news that a branch member had left Wisconsin for England three days after arriving, although in the end the lecture passed off without opposition.[104] Among the most negative testimony was that of a Blackburn man, William Coates (not to be confused with the Society's agent). In a letter home from Milwaukie on 26 August and published in the *Preston Chronicle* – the paper claimed it never had faith in the Society 'or the principles upon which it professes to act' – Coates painted a bleak picture of the colony's future: 'Tell Mr. Hargreaves I have been in Pottersville, and find things very bad there. The first lot that came out—that is, the committee, twelve in number,—three of them are there yet, the others are gone, and those who remain would go too if they could get off.' Leaving Pottersville, he went to the 'English settlement (5,000 acres purporting to have been purchased by the Potters' Society)'; on the way he met five families returning home. Scores more had left, and many were going 'with the purpose of shooting "Evans," if ever they see him', he wrote. Prospects outside the Society's lands were no better: 'I have found things different to what I had expected at this place, so I intend going to St Louis in a day or two from this, for I find there are more people than work in the town of Milwaukie.'[105]

The best way to counter these reports was to provide first-hand evidence of the Society's progress in America. It found important validation in the Kirkcaldy linen worker George Mitchell. Mitchell's letter to his sister, dated Fort Winnebago, 9 June, was the most widely read account of the Wisconsin settlement in this period. Originally published in the *Fife Advertiser* on 21 July, by mid-September it had found its way into newspapers in London, Nottingham, Bradford, Leeds, Staffordshire, Perth and Limerick, and doubtless elsewhere. The letter's circulation was no accident. Evans actively promoted its republication – and even tried to have it published in the medical journal *The Lancet*.[106] As previously noted, in his letter Mitchell described the 'fine appearance' of the Pottersville settlement and the warm welcome given to him and his companions by Thomas Twigg. According to *Lloyd's Weekly Newspaper*, which had received 'innumerable' letters about the scheme, the value of Mitchell's account derived from it being 'an impartial statement, the writer having no connexion with the Potters' Society when he left his home for America'. Adding to its credibility was that he made no attempt to disguise the effort and costs of establishing himself on American soil. 'I am healthy and strong, and can get along, although at the same time, if I could get a little assistance from home, I could make a paradise here for you all whenever you should like to come out', he wrote.[107] Back in Fife, Mitchell's report was predictably welcomed. It will gratify 'those of our readers who are in connection with the Potters' Emigration Society, to hear such good accounts of their property in Wisconsin', observed the local paper. Fortuitously, in the ballot held on 24 September at Hanley's Covered Market attended by an estimated 2,000 people, the holder of winning share no. 4217, Daniel McGowan, came from Kirkcaldy.[108]

The Hanley meeting concluded with a vote of thanks to Thomas Twigg, another sign of his rising worth. By then Twigg's ambivalence about returning to England had begun to dissolve. The issue, inevitably, was money. In a brief communication to Evans, dated 14 September, the agent expressed his impatience that in his latest letter his 'dear friend' had asked the question: ' "Whether I can do without any more cash until spring?" ' He explained that 'to carry out my engagements' he required £800, half of which he must have by 30 November. 'I have commenced to build a good Store', he wrote, 'and shall make a Warehouse of the old one. I have also ordered Goods to the amount of 1200 dollars to stock the store, cash being promised upon delivery.' Asking Evans to let him know exactly what funds he could expect before the spring, he stressed that what he could achieve depended on how much he received. 'For God's sakes let us have no mistakes', he pleaded. Evans for his part saw the merit in publicising Twigg's frustration. Reporting that £200 had already been dispatched, he urged members to heed the agent's appeals and show him they had the 'hearts and minds' to assist him. He must be backed 'by all the power we possess; and in some twelve months hence, a goodly return on the capital now in course of investment on the New Estate, will be the result'.[109]

By 19 October Twigg had made up his mind. Having received no money for ten weeks, he now saw the 'necessity' of returning to England 'in order that a proper understanding may be established as to what the colony will need to make it what it ought to be'. Time was running out; if he did not leave in the next few days, the lakes would be frozen over. In his letter Twigg detailed the arrangements he had made regarding the estate's activities during his absence. Peter Watkin was entrusted to handle all finances, while 'Mr. Parks' (probably the carpenter Frederick Park from the *Aberdeen*) would 'look after the men'. Twigg had also arranged that building materials for the grist mill be made ready, at a cost of $5,000. The intention, if funds permitted, was to have it in operation by the autumn of next year. The mill's construction was central to Twigg's development vision. 'Get your meetings ready for me', he told the committee. 'Let there be no delay. Heaven and earth must be moved for this object;—it will give permanence to the society.'[110] Evans needed no prompting; however, he cautioned members that Twigg, who was scheduled to remain in England until late February, would not be able to visit every branch, and so branches would be divided into districts to give everyone the opportunity 'of seeing the little plain, rough, honest man'.[111]

Everything was now focused on the agent's return and the grist mill campaign. On 13 November a concert and ball was held at the Temperance Hall, Burslem, attended by 'a large and respectable audience'. The event, admission price sixpence, was organised by Burslem's 'Pottersville' branch for the purpose of 'forwarding the Grist Mill Fund' and involved the usual round of singing, dancing and recitation to the strains of a local quadrille band. At some point in the evening Evans addressed the audience about Twigg's visit and 'the honour and gratitude that awaited him for his manifold exertions on behalf of the society'. The other object of the event was the holding of a ballot. The winning share, no. 2861, belonged to Emanuel Dyson of Burnley. Reporting the draw, the *Examiner* detailed the benefits accruing to the holder, who next August 'will be removed, by the funds of the society, from this country to the potters' land on the Fox River, Columbia County, State of Wisconsin, United States, North America'. If he chose, he could also cash in his share, in return for which, 'if his family number four children, he may realize £20 to-morrow'.[112]

Twigg was already on his way home. The agent left Fort Winnebago for England on 21 October. The previous day 'a full meeting of all the settlers' unanimously thanked him for 'his able services and persevering conduct amongst us'.[113] Sailing from New York on 7 November aboard the *New World*, he landed in Liverpool less than three weeks later. (Coming up the Mersey, the vessel collided with the Bombay-bound *Eucles*, carrying away its bowsprit and forcing it to return to dock.[114]) On Monday, 3 December the agent delivered his report 'on the prospects and condition of the society's colonies' to a crowded meeting in the Potteries; the next night he returned to Liverpool for a members' dinner at the Flying Horse inn in Dale Street. It is hard to overstate the importance attached to Twigg's mission. Not only had he brought with him the Pottersville deeds, but his visit gave members their first opportunity to hear directly about the Society's progress and plans, and in turn gave him the chance to challenge the negative reports that continued to appear. Discovering on his arrival a venomous account of the Wisconsin settlement by a man called Hardcastle, Twigg pointed out that the writer had arrived at Emancipation Ferry $20 in debt for team hire, had stayed only a few days and then decamped, 'leaving his food, lodging, and everything else

1849: Expansion and scrutiny

unpaid'. More positively, also awaiting him was a letter signed by fifty-nine residents of the new estate, sent with the express purpose of assisting his campaign against the Society's detractors. 'Taking advantage, then, of your temporary absence', they wrote, 'we beg to express to you our unqualified admiration of the excellent and consistent course taken by you while here', which had allowed them 'to escape from the vile, grasping, and intolerant domination' of aristocratic England. 'We are getting on all right, determined to succeed, or die by it', added the former law student John Turner, who seems to have organised the address.[115]

To coincide with Twigg's arrival, Evans produced more evidence of the settlers' wellbeing. On 1 December the *Examiner* published letters from the Oldham cotton workers William Scholes and John Goulding. They had been forwarded to the editor by the branch secretary, John Heap, who hoped to counter the 'false and prejudicial statements' that had been 'published and extensively circulated, by interested and designing parties, respecting the selection of the New Estate of the Potters' Emigration Society, and the position of the Colonists'. The branch offered the printed letters for sale at a cost of a half-penny, and 'the parties being so well known in Oldham, nearly 500 copies were sold in four days'. In an accompanying editorial, Evans urged the pamphlet's widest possible circulation. He also reiterated his belief in the 'judicious' choice of land on the Fox River in regard to its location and fertility.

> Emancipation Ferry cannot fail to become a city of eminence in the progress of the great American Union; and with its rise, the poorest of England's poor that now dwell in the rough log cabins of a new colony, shall be elevated into the independent citizens of a free and independent country. At least, to such a consummation do our aspirations lead.[116]

The first leg of Twigg and Evans's tour began in Crewe on 6 December, and was followed by appearances in Macclesfield, Manchester and Hanley. *The Staffordshire Advertiser* described the attendance at Hanley's Town Hall on 11 December as 'tolerably good', although not as large as it might have been had not other 'popular lectures' been taking place on the same evening. Opening the proceedings, Evans described how the £3,000 so far raised had been used to purchase the Pottersville estate, where forty families were located, and to establish the new settlement on the Fox River, where 340 individuals were now living. But it was Twigg whom the audience had come to hear. The agent spoke at length about the Wisconsin lands, emphasising the advantages of the new estate's location in light of the ongoing navigational improvements. 'One matter was particularly required in the colony, and that was a grist mill', he said, and he 'trusted that the funds of the society would soon be in a position to admit of one being built'. He also wanted to counter the 'erroneous opinions' that when emigrants reached a new country 'they would have done with work'. With three years of 'diligence and perseverance', it would be a man's own fault 'if he did not find his affairs prosperous, by having a number of acres under good cultivation, and his farm well stocked with cattle'. The questions that followed ranged from hawthorn hedges, American property laws, the availability of brick clay and 'whether the settlers had suffered any molestation from Indians'. An individual named Tams, who claimed to have been in Wisconsin, made a number of suggestions, including 'that a man should never force his wife to accompany him' as she would soon become homesick and beg to return. Twigg replied that he would not advise any man to take his wife against her will.[117]

Twigg and Evans next headed for London, breaking their journey at Wolverhampton to speak at the town's Athenaeum. The local paper reported that the lecture was 'thinly attended, owing to the shortness of the notice'; however, in the *Examiner*'s opinion, it represented a wider failure: 'Wolverhampton and the surrounding districts comprise a large population of the industrious classes; and it is much to be regretted, that a spirited course of agitation has not been pursued in that populous neighbourhood.'[118] They also made a brief stop at Stafford to meet the secretary of the local tailors' association with a view to establishing a branch in the town. Arriving in the capital, on 17 December they addressed an 'overflowing' meeting of the 'First London' branch, where they were welcomed by the secretary and auditor, George W. Robinson, who was due to emigrate to Wisconsin. Twigg's detailed account of the Society's progress in America provoked several rounds of applause and a spontaneous collection that raised 15s for the grist mill fund. Similar scenes prevailed the following day at a meeting of the 'East London' branch. The next evening the two men appeared before an estimated audience of 1,200 'consisting of both sexes' at the National Hall, Holborn. On this occasion Evans took centre stage, providing a history of the Society's origins and organisation before turning to emigration. Instead of 'engaging in useless strikes', he reiterated, the Society aimed to convert 'superabundant artizans in England into comparatively thriving agriculturists in the United States'. There followed an account of the Wisconsin settlements and plans for future development. These included the establishment of 'two or three towns' on the Society's land, and the obtaining of a charter of incorporation 'which would entitle the settlers to all the privileges of self-government and of citizenship of the United States'. Then it was Twigg's turn. Reporting the event, the *Daily News* noted that the agent's 'personal observations' showed that the Society's settlers 'had not escaped some of the evils incident to the management of the committees, and to the want of adequate capital'. A voluntary collection produced another £2 3s 9d towards the grist mill.[119]

The Holborn audience listened with the 'utmost interest' to Twigg and Evans's account of the emigration scheme, as did, as far as we can determine, others they addressed on their tour. Leaving London, the pair made their way north, stopping at Preston on Christmas Eve and arriving in Glasgow in time for the New Year's Day soirée at the Merchants' Hall, during which six more names were drawn in the ballot for land.[120] It was exactly twelve months since the similar event at the Free Trade Hall in Manchester. During the intervening period the Society had undergone transformation following the decision to expand its membership to other trades and regions. Although its organisational heart remained within the Staffordshire pottery community, much of the impetus for growth and most of the individuals and families migrating to its lands in America now came from outside the Potteries, leaving a question as to how far it could continue to reflect the values and aspirations of its founding. On a practical level, there was the eternal issue of how the Society would finance its ambitious plans. In October an Oldham branch member inquired whether Twigg's zeal 'was greater than his judgment' in proposing to establish another colony in Wisconsin. 'I may be mistaken; but we cannot forget that many well-intended societies, have failed through striving too much with inadequate means', wrote John Booth.[121] The Society's 'means' would be tested to the limit in the months to come. As working men and women throughout industrial Britain continued to dream of exchanging a harsh and sometimes oppressive life for prosperity and independence in America, it was unclear whether the Society possessed either the resources or capability to satisfy them.

Notes

1. *Morning Chronicle*, 21 April 1848.
2. *The Staffordshire Advertiser*, 16 December 1848.
3. *The Staffordshire Advertiser*, 3, 10 February, 31 March 1849; Joseph Lowndes to Poor Law Board, 13 February 1849, National Archives, MH 12/11198/95.
4. There was some limited parish-assisted emigration to the United States. See Van Vugt, *Portrait of an English Migration*, p. 39.
5. See advertisements in *Carlisle Journal*, 16 February 1849; *Cambridge Chronicle and Journal*, 24 February 1849; *Wiltshire Independent*, 26 April 1849; *The Emigrant and Colonial Gazette*, 24 February 1849; and other papers. Much of the advice to would-be emigrants to California was far from positive regarding the conditions they could expect to find there. See Robert A. Burchell, 'The Loss of a Reputation; Or, The Image of California in Britain before 1875', *California Historical Quarterly* 53:2 (1974), 115–30 (esp. 123–5).
6. Robert Fleming Gourlay, *Emigration and Settlement on Wild Land* (Cupar, Fife: privately printed, 1849), pp. 3, 8. D. W. A. Baker, 'Lang, John Dunmore

(1799–1878)', *Australian Dictionary of Biography* (Melbourne: Melbourne University Press, 1967), vol. 2, pp. 76–83.
7 Baker, 'Lang, John Dunmore', p. 76.
8 For Lang's visit, see Rosemary Lawson, 'Dr. John Dunmore Lang and Immigration' (MA dissertation, Australian National University, 1966), pp. 115–34.
9 *Birmingham Mercury*, 28 April 1849. Lang was led to believe that the Society's headquarters were in Birmingham. For another contribution to the debate over America (as represented by the Potters' Emigration Society) and Australia as rival destinations, see the letter from R. W. Smiles (brother of the reformer Samuel) in *Manchester Examiner & Times*, 28 July 1849.
10 *Birmingham Mercury*, 5 May 1849.
11 In July he chaired a lecture by William Coates in Hull's Town Hall. *Hull Advertiser and Exchange Gazette*, 20 July 1849.
12 Brian P. Birch, 'The Editor and the English: George Sheppard and English Emigration to Clinton County', *The Annals of Iowa* 47:8 (1985), 622–42.
13 *Sheffield and Rotherham Independent*, 27 January 1849.
14 *Lloyd's Weekly Newspaper*, 4 February 1849.
15 *Lloyd's Weekly Newspaper*, 18 February 1849. According to a report, Jeffrey had been 'perfectly satisfied' with the answers he received after questioning Evans and Coates at a meeting in early January. *Manchester Examiner & Times*, 6 January 1849.
16 *The Spirit of The Times*, 14 April 1849. See also 2 June 1849.
17 *The People*, vol. 1, no. 25, p. 200. The issue appeared in November 1848. Barker abandoned dating his paper after the third issue. See Michael Brook, 'Joseph Barker and *The People*, The True Emigrant's Guide', *Publications of the Thoresby Society* 46:3 (1961), 331–78. See also the outstanding essay in Betty Fladeland, *Abolitionists and Working-Class Problems in the Age of Industrialization* (Baton Rouge: Louisiana State University Press, 1984), pp. 132–70.
18 *The People*, vol. 1, no. 30, p. 240.
19 *The People*, vol. 1, no. 34, p. 289.
20 *The People*, vol. 1, no. 39, p. 306.
21 *The People*, vol. 1, no. 41, p. 326. The letter was dated 18 February 1849.
22 *The People*, vol. 1, no. 44, p. 351. On Turner, see Stuart (ed.), *People of the Potteries*, p. 210.
23 *The People*, vol. 1, no. 46, pp. 366–7.
24 *The People*, vol. 1, no. 51, p. 406.
25 *The People*, vol. 1, no. 51, pp. 407–8.
26 See *The Staffordshire Advertiser*, 9 September 1848; *Sheffield Independent*, 27 January 1849; *Bradford Observer*, 22 February 1849; and *Nottingham Review and General Advertiser*, 27 April 1849.
27 PEEA, vol. 9, no. 64 (22 September 1849).
28 Dorothy G. McCarthy, 'Tales of Old Portage', *Portage Daily Register*, 2 August 1961, 1 August 1970, 25 May 1974 are useful accounts based on local memories.

29 *The People*, vol. 2, no. 89, p. 294. The letter, to George Bell, was dated Fort Winnebago, 16 November 1849.
30 Isaac Smith, 'Early Days in Columbia County: Potters' Emigration Society', *Wisconsin State Register*, 12 June 1880.
31 Josie Greening Croft, 'A Mazomanie Pioneer of 1847', *Wisconsin Magazine of History* 26:2 (1942), 215–16. The writer was John Greening, a Worcester boot and shoemaker.
32 *Wisconsin State Register*, 17 February 1883.
33 His death is recorded in the US Census (Mortality Schedule) of 1850.
34 The previous year Samuel and his brother John had erected the Blue Tavern on the Milwaukie-to-Portage road. Jones (comp.), *A History of Columbia County Wisconsin*, vol. 2, p. 426.
35 'The Last of the Potters' Society'; and Strong, *A Strong Family Tree*, pp. 98–101.
36 *Ibid.*, pp. 101–2. On the region's wildlife and trees, see Lowell J. Ragatz (ed.), 'A Swiss Family in the New World: Letters of Jakob and Ulrich Bühler, 1847–1877', *Wisconsin Magazine of History* 6:3 (1923), 324–6.
37 *PEEA*, vol. 10, no. 5 (3 August 1850).
38 *PEEA*, vol. 9, no. 78 (29 December 1849).
39 Twigg arrived in Pottersville on 28 April. See John Frankland's letter, *PEEA*, vol. 9, no. 63 (15 September 1849).
40 The circular was published in *Reynold's Miscellany of Romance, General Literature, Science, and Art*, vol. 2, no. 33, 24 February 1849, pp. 526–7 and, abridged, in *Sidney's Emigrant's Journal*, vol. 1, no. 18, 1 February 1849. The latter was sceptical about the scheme's funding, having earlier praised the initiative. *Ibid.*, vol. 1, no. 10, 7 December 1848.
41 *PEEA*, vol. 9, no. 63 (15 September 1849). The letter is dated 30 June 1849.
42 *PEEA*, vol. 9, no. 78 (29 December 1849).
43 *PEEA*, vol. 9, no. 66 (6 October 1849).
44 *Ibid.*, and vol. 10, no. 16 (19 October 1850).
45 *PEEA*, vol. 9, no. 76 (15 December 1849).
46 *PEEA*, vol. 9, no. 64 (22 September 1849).
47 *Sheffield and Rotherham Independent*, 27 January 1849.
48 *Daily News* (London), 2 June 1849.
49 *Manchester Examiner & Times*, 7 July 1849.
50 *Montello Express*, 27 May 1876.
51 *Wisconsin State Register*, 12 June 1880.
52 'Story of Moundville, 1849–1922', contributed by Mary Ann Miller from an original document by Mildred Jones Bennett, p. 2. Thanks to Roger Bentley for providing me with a copy. Mountford's letter home in *PEEA*, vol. 9, no. 78, provides a strong impression of his activities and character.
53 *PEEA*, vol. 9, no. 78 (29 December 1949). I have silently corrected an obvious error: '500,000 acres'.
54 An authoritative account of Native American land cessions in Wisconsin is Alice E. Smith, *The History of Wisconsin, Volume 1, From Exploration to Statehood* (Madison: State Historical Society of Wisconsin, 1973), pp. 122–61.
55 *PEEA*, vol. 9, no. 76 (15 December 1849).

56 *PEEA*, vol. 9, no. 62 (8 September 1849).
57 *PEEA*, vol. 9, no. 73 (24 November 1849).
58 *PEEA*, vol. 9, no. 63 (15 September 1849).
59 *The History of Columbia County, Wisconsin*, p. 738.
60 For the wider context of the canal's development, see Ronald E. Shaw, *Canals for a Nation: The Canal Era in the United States, 1790–1860* (Lexington: University of Kentucky Press, 1990), p. 143.
61 *PEEA*, vol. 9, no. 66 (6 October 1849).
62 *PEEA*, vol. 9, no. 63 (15 September 1849).
63 Ayrey's name does not appear on the *Charles Chaloner*'s manifest but he is clearly part of the same group.
64 *PEEA*, vol. 9, no. 76 (15 December 1849).
65 Still useful on the choice of American port destinations is Thomas W. Page, 'The Transportation of Immigrants and Reception Arrangements in the Nineteenth Century', *Journal of Political Economy* 19:9 (1911), 732–49.
66 For Turner's account of his journey and early efforts at the settlement, see his letter, dated 16 August 1849, in *PEEA*, vol. 9, no. 69 (27 October 1849).
67 *History of Northern Wisconsin, Containing an Account of Its Settlement, Growth, Development, and Resources ...* (Chicago, IL: Western Historical Company, 1881), p. 330.
68 On Scotland's dependence upon American exports, see R. H. Campbell, 'Developments in the Scottish Pig-Iron Trade, 1844–1848', *Journal of Economic History* 15:3 (1955), 209–26.
69 *Fifeshire Advertiser*, 21 July 1849.
70 Engels, *The Condition of the Working Class in England*, p. 181.
71 *PEEA*, vol. 9, no. 74 (1 December 1849). On William Scholes's early life, see *Portrait and Biographical Album of Green Lake, Marquette, and Waushara Counties, Wisconsin*, p. 757; and for further information, Harold Henderson, 'From the First Industrial City to the Wisconsin Frontier: William Scholes (1814–1864), Ann Mills Scholes (1814–1875), and Their Family', *Annals of Genealogical Research* 1:2 (2005) at www.genlit.org/agr/viewarticle.php?id=5 (last accessed 26 February 2023).
72 *PEEA*, vol. 9, no. 74 (1 December 1849).
73 *PEEA*, vol. 9, no. 67 (13 October 1849).
74 *PEEA* vol. 9, no. 74 (1 December 1849).
75 *PEEA*, vol. 9, no. 67 (13 October 1849).
76 *PEEA*, vol. 9, no. 73 (24 November 1849).
77 Information on the crossing comes from Martin Ellison's diary, transcribed by Nathan Weber at www.wiroots.org/wimarquette/ellisondiary.html (last accessed 4 June 2008). The other Accrington travellers were Robert Bold, a tailor, and John and Mary Sutcliffe and their five children. John worked as a print or block cutter.
78 *PEEA*, vol. 9, no. 73 (24 November 1849).
79 Martin Ellison's diary.
80 *PEEA*, vol. 9, no. 73 (24 November 1849).
81 The phrase is from the Society's circular. See n. 37.

82 Twigg learned of Orme's death from a fellow passenger, Samuel Cadman. The precise location is reported in *The Staffordshire Advertiser*, 29 September 1849. Orme's death was reported in *PEEA*, vol. 9, no. 66 (6 October 1849). Joseph Barker arrived in New York a week later and noted the *Patrick Henry*'s plight. *The People*, vol. 2, no. 69, p. 134.
83 Charles E. Rosenberg, *The Cholera Years: The United States in 1832, 1849, and 1866* (Chicago, IL: University of Chicago Press, 1962), pp. 101–20.
84 *Norfolk News*, 1 September 1849; *PEEA*, vol. 9, no. 66 (6 October 1849).
85 *PEEA*, vol. 9, no. 73 (24 November 1849).
86 *History of Dane County, Wisconsin, Containing an Account of Its Settlement, Growth, Development, and Resources* … (Chicago, IL: Western Historical Company, 1880), pp. 1074–5.
87 *PEEA*, vol. 9, no. 82 (26 January 1850).
88 *PEEA*, vol. 9, no. 66 (6 October 1849).
89 *PEEA*, vol. 9, no. 91 (30 March 1850).
90 *PEEA*, vol. 9, no. 87 (2 March 1850).
91 The maximum number of branches was 106, although the number active at any one time was invariably smaller. In information presumably taken from a missing *Examiner*, Angus Reach also reported a branch in Abbeville, France. *Morning Chronicle*, 5 February 1850. It does not appear on any extant branch list.
92 *PEEA*, vol. 9, no. 62 (8 September 1849).
93 *PEEA*, vol. 9, no. 64 (22 September 1849).
94 *PEEA*, vol. 9, no. 65 (29 September 1849).
95 *PEEA*, vol. 9, no. 64 (22 September 1849).
96 *PEEA*, vol. 9, nos. 64, 65 (22, 29 September 1849).
97 *PEEA*, vol. 9, no. 63 (15 September 1849).
98 L. Diane Barnes, 'Building Communities Out of Frontiers: The Grist Mills of Harrison County, West Virginia, 1784–1860', *Journal of Appalachian Studies* 7:2 (2001), 285.
99 *PEEA*, vol. 9, no. 66 (6 October 1849).
100 Japanning was a long-established Birmingham trade, involving the application of lacquer to tin plate, papier-mâché and other surfaces in imitation of Japanese and Chinese decoration.
101 *PEEA*, vol. 9, no. 66 (6 October 1849).
102 *PEEA*, vol, 9, no. 68 (20 October 1849).
103 *PEEA*, vol. 9, no. 66 (6 October 1849).
104 *Manchester Courier and Lancashire General Advertiser*, 25 August 1849.
105 *Preston Chronicle*, 29 September 1849. Coates's veracity was strongly called into question. See *PEEA*, vol. 9, nos. 67, 68 (13, 20 October 1849).
106 *The Lancet*, 25 August 1849. The editor suggested the 'political journals' were more appropriate.
107 The letter was originally published in the *Fifeshire Advertiser*, 21 July 1849. Papers and journals reprinting it included *Daily News* (London) and *Express* (London), 16 August 1849; *Nottingham Review and General Advertiser*, 17 August 1849; *Weekly Chronicle* (London) and *The Staffordshire Advertiser*, 18 August 1849;

Lloyds Weekly Newspaper, 19 August 1849; *Limerick and Clare Examiner*, 22 August 1849; *Bradford Observer* and *Perthshire Advertiser*, 23 August 1849; *Emigrant*, 25 August 1849; *Kings County Chronicle*, 12 September 1849; *York Herald*, 15 September 1849.
108 *The Staffordshire Advertiser*, 29 September 1849; *Fifeshire Advertiser*, 6 October 1849.
109 *PEEA*, vol. 9, no. 69 (27 October 1849).
110 *PEEA*, vol. 9, no. 73 (24 November 1849).
111 *PEEA*, vol. 9, no. 71 (10 November 1849).
112 *PEEA*, vol. 9, no. 73 (24 November 1849).
113 *PEEA*, vol. 9, no. 82 (26 January 1850). The report of the meeting comes from a letter from George Cooper.
114 *Liverpool Mail*, 1 December 1849.
115 *PEEA*, vol. 9, no. 76 (15 December 1849). See *PEEA*, vol. 9, no. 73 (24 November 1849) for Hardcastle's letter.
116 *PEEA*, vol. 9, no. 74 (1 December 1849).
117 *Staffordshire Examiner*, 15 December 1849, and reprinted in *PEEA*, vol. 9, no. 78 (29 December 1849).
118 *Wolverhampton Chronicle*, 19 December 1849; *PEEA*, vol. 9, no. 78 (29 December 1849).
119 *Ibid.*; (London) *Daily News*, 20 December 1849. A report of the Holborn meeting made its way to Australia: *Geelong Advertiser*, 22 July 1850.
120 *PEEA*, vol. 9, no. 82 (26 January 1850). Two of the winners came from Oldham, two from the Potteries (Burslem and Fenton) and one each from Edinburgh and Bingley.
121 *PEEA*, vol. 9, no. 71 (10 November 1849).

6

1850–1: Crisis and decline

Joseph Barker never made it to Pottersville. Arriving in Milwaukie from Chicago in the early morning of 3 October 1849, he wandered the streets for an hour or so before entering his lodgings, where he inquired about how to reach the emigrant settlement. As there was 'no public conveyance of any description' to take him within fifty miles, his only option was to hire a wagon, the cost of which he was unable to discover. The return journey would take up to two weeks. 'When I found how things were', he wrote in his journal, 'I gave up all thoughts of going, and resolved, after viewing the country around Milwaukie, to hasten eastward, and get home as soon as I could.' The advancing seasonal weather helped him decide: 'The days were beginning to be wet, and the nights frosty. The idea of spending nearly a fortnight travelling through the woods in an open wagon, was too much.' Before leaving for Buffalo, Barker talked to a local Potters' Emigration Society agent and others about conditions at the settlement and in Wisconsin generally. They told him that the land around Pottersville 'was good, that the Colony was likely to do well, in course of time, if its affairs were properly managed'. But there were also 'frequent disputes among the settlers, and serious difficulties with the managers'.[1]

Barker returned to England in November. He had dreamed about the United States throughout his adult life and 'long ago' determined to move there.[2] His fact-finding tour had taken him across the Midwestern states, including Ohio, where three of his brothers were living and to where he and his family would relocate in 1851.[3] For a moment his view of the Potters' Emigration Society seemed to have improved in the light of his American visit. Lecturing at the Mechanics' Institute in Manchester in the last week of November, he was asked by an audience member whether he had been to Pottersville. He replied that he had not, 'but from what he had heard, he believed the land to be good, and he had no doubt that it would prosper in a short time'. Society members present were encouraged by his comments and his promise to carefully read the auditors' report, a copy of which one of its authors, James Rowbottom, had earlier given him. They also suggested that his popular lectures on emigration could benefit the Society.[4] It was wishful thinking. Shortly afterwards a correspondent to *The People* inquired whether the potters' scheme was 'practicable or not for its members'. Barker's message was clear.

> The Potters' Emigration Society's lands I believe to be good, but they are placed in a cold climate, and in an out-way part of the world, and I have no faith in the managers of the Society. Every thing I read of W. Evans, and every thing I hear from Pottersville tends to strengthen my conviction that you would not do well to trust your money in the so-called Potters' Emigration Society.[5]

Although Barker's transatlantic sojourn had convinced him of emigration's value, as an 'extreme individualist'[6] he remained unpersuaded by the merits of associational schemes such as the potters'. In an article titled 'Emigration Societies,— *My Own* Plan', published a month after his return, he described them as 'badly managed lotteries' in which 'the managers thrive while most of the subscribers perish'. Besides, they almost invariably end in 'quarrels, lawsuits, robbery, and ruin'. He predicted the same fate would soon befall the temperance and potters' schemes. 'An Emigration Society in England, with lands in the Western States of America, can never secure full justice to itself', he insisted. He himself proposed to offer advice on all aspects of moving to America. 'If intending emigrants wish to purchase Government land ... I will engage to assist them in doing so to advantage without a farthing remuneration', he announced. 'But nine out of ten intending emigrants would act very foolishly to purchase Government lands before they spent some time in the country and got accustomed to agricultural labour. They would especially act foolishly to purchase lands in Wisconsin, the coldest of the United States.' Since Barker would provide his help free of charge, his plan stood in sharp contrast to the potters', whose total expenses of £870, extracted from the auditors' report – which he had indeed read carefully – he took relish in itemising.[7]

As Barker intensified his criticism, William Evans and Thomas Twigg embarked on the final stages of their nationwide tour. Following the New Year's Day ballot and ball in Glasgow, they addressed a public meeting on 5 January in Dundee, where the majority present 'seemed highly gratified by the flattering prospects' of the potters' scheme.[8] Two days later, in Edinburgh, they lectured to an audience of over 200 'working men' in the South Bridge Hall.[9] Heading back into England, they stopped at Newcastle-upon-Tyne and Sunderland, and on 14 January appeared at a packed meeting in Hull Town Hall, chaired by George Sheppard. Speaking first, Evans stressed the equity of the Society's rules. He said that its main object, the removal of surplus labour, had been highly successful in the pottery trade, and those emigrants who had gone to America had now sufficient means to become 'independent cultivators of their own freehold'. Next, Twigg reported on the Society's American operations. The land at Pottersville would currently realise about $4 an acre. As for the Fox River site, it 'was as good land as any he had seen in Wisconsin'. He reiterated that his main task was to raise funds for the grist mill; its construction would greatly increase the profits and convenience of corn production and enable the Society to sell its building lots, which he believed in two years would realise $200 per acre. Finally, he reassured his audience about the area's climate: 'there was no period of the year so cold, or so hot, that a man could not work out of doors'. The evening ended with a vote of thanks to Hull's mayor for permission to hold the meeting in the Town Hall. 'His Worship' replied that it should be granted at any time 'for the promotion of useful purposes'.[10]

The men's next stop was Leeds, Barker territory. Over the coming weeks Barker and Evans engaged in an unseemly bout of name-calling and recrimination ostensibly focused on a proposal, never convincingly advanced by either of them, to debate publicly the Society's record. Declining an invitation to a lecture in Manchester on 18 January, Barker called the Welshman 'faithless, lying, and malignant', a man capable 'of saying or doing anything that suits his individual purpose'. Not to be outdone, Evans named his opponent 'the foul slanderer of our society, and heartless American Land-Jobber' before issuing a 'challenge' for them to debate in Ashton-under-Lyne on 22 January, where he and Twigg were due to lecture.[11] Needless to say, Barker did not appear, claiming he had not received the notice in time; instead, he sent a man called Leach, who challenged Evans to name a day for the men to meet. Evans countered by accusing Barker of making 'false extracts' from the auditors' report, of continuing to abuse him in *The People* and of exaggerating the difficulty in reaching Pottersville. After several other questions from Leach, which, according to the *Manchester Examiner*, Evans dealt with easily, the event ended.[12] Leach's account of the exchanges told a different tale. The evening 'broke up in uproar and confusion, the Town Hall presenting such a scene of dispute and altercation as I never before witnessed', he wrote to Barker. As for Evans: 'When I presented to him your challenge, the fumes of the rum bottle met me as I approached him upon the platform so strongly, as to make me suspect that he was labouring very much under its excitement.'[13] The rancour between the two men continued, raising concerns that it was compromising the Society's business. On 13 February London members recommended that the *Examiner* abstain from further discussion with Barker or 'other opposition' and devote itself entirely to 'emigrating purposes'. Evans dutifully complied, although not before making a final gesture of 'recourse to law'.[14] Nothing came of it, naturally, and by April Barker reported that he had yet to receive any notice of legal proceedings. 'I am prepared to prove W. Evans an imposter and a swindler, either in a public meeting, or in a court of justice', he wrote.[15]

For all Barker's posturing and notoriety, it would be a mistake to underestimate his role in shaping the Society's reputation. In writings and lectures, he offered trenchant criticisms of the potters' scheme, and through *The People*, which by the end of 1849 was selling 22,000 copies in Lancashire alone,[16] facilitated the wider dissemination of anti-Society reports. One issue that resurfaced, and that would require action from the Society, concerned the legal status of the expanded organisation. A London correspondent, William Griffith, claimed that Tidd Pratt, the friendly societies' registrar, had told him that the branches opened in other areas and to other trades had no basis in law. 'There is no such thing as a Parent Society; the Potters' Society is established exclusively in Staffordshire, and beyond Staffordshire, and the Potting trade, they cannot go', Pratt is quoted as ruling.[17] In response, Evans admitted that the branches were not and never had been legalised, but argued that there was a clear distinction between 'Enrolled' and 'Branch' laws akin to that existing in other friendly organisations such as the Oddfellows, Foresters and Gardeners.[18] Barker, however, needed no more persuading. Writing to the *Leeds Times* on 23 January, he continued to insist that all branches of the Potters' Emigration Society were 'illegal'.[19]

He also poured scorn on Evans's surplus-labour claims. That the Society had either raised potters' wages or prevented their reduction he called 'a great and shameless lie'. According to his information, it had sent fewer than 100 working potters to America, a number too inconsequential to produce such an effect.[20] But Barker's most compelling charge was that Evans and the Society were defrauding workers and their families by promising something they could not deliver. On 24 and 25 January he lectured on emigration at the Temperance Hall, Bolton. With Evans and Twigg appearing at the same time in nearby Bury – where audience members raised questions about branch legality[21] – the Society had been circulating leaflets in the town, in Barker's words, falsely 'telling the people they might have a farm of forty acres, a free passage across the Atlantic, &c, &c, for £1. 2s. 6d'. Instead of obtaining a farm, 'forty-nine out of every fifty, if not ninety-nine out of every hundred' who buy tickets in the lottery 'get nothing but disappointment and misery'. Evans is 'a cheat and a swindler', he maintained, his 'mis-named Potters' Emigration Society … an imposition, and a fraud'.[22]

'About six years ago the working men of the Potteries set on foot a scheme which presented some features of novelty, and which has, so far as I can ascertain the facts, been to a degree successful.' So began the journalist Angus Reach's assessment of the Potters' Emigration Society. His article, published in the *Morning Chronicle* on 5 February 1850 as Evans and Twigg were completing their tour, was part of a series the London paper commissioned to investigate the condition of labour and the poor in England and

Wales. Unlike Barker, Reach had no axe to grind with the Society – or its general agent, of whom he made no mention. Using material drawn from the *Examiner* and other Society literature, he explained its establishment and operation, including the processes of land financing and allotment. His tone was sympathetic but open-minded. Commenting on the 'beauties and advantages of the transatlantic Paradise' glowingly set out in the Society's manifestos, he hoped that the real picture was 'as faithful as it is flattering'. However, he noted that the letters from Wisconsin settlers published in the *Examiner* were fairly selected: 'The various obstacles and hardships encountered were set down candidly enough ... and the grand chorus was "Let no one come out here who is afraid of rough living and hard work"'. Reach clarified that he had included a detailed account of the Society in his report on the Potteries 'because it was the first—and is, so far as I can learn—the only—association of working men for the avowed purpose of facilitating emigration'. Noting that the scheme modelled itself partly on the building societies' principle, he concluded that if 'association and a weekly payment can provide a man with a home in England', it was not unreasonable that the same agency 'may be employed in securing for him a freehold in the United States'.[23]

The Potters' Emigration Society stood at a crossroads in February 1850. Despite the auditors' optimistic assessment, there was no guarantee of its future. The main problem was the continuing shortfall in resources. Accounts are incomplete for much of 1849, but the surviving evidence points to revenues declining in the second half of the year, when pressure on expenditure intensified as more and more migrants headed for Wisconsin. In the final quarter (10 September–8 December) branch receipts, which comprised the majority of income, amounted to £536, down about a third from the second quarter. Receipts improved over the next period (8 December–8 March 1850) following Evans and Twigg's tour, rising to £722 before falling again in the spring and summer.[24] The totals included contributions to the grist mill fund. London and Scottish branches were particularly enterprising in their efforts to boost the fund, with the Paisley raffle in December realising an impressive £8 6s 6d.[25] To encourage branches further, the Society offered eighty bound copies of the *Examiner* 'to be raffled for the use of the Grist Mill'.[26] By the end of March the fund's total had reached £145 1s 6d – still a distance away from the sum required for the facility's construction.[27]

On 16 February the *Examiner* reported that a special delegate meeting would convene the following week in Shelton. The agenda comprised two items: 'The constitution; to the end, that the same may be *legally* enlarged in its management, so as to meet the requirements of a national federation'; and, first and foremost in the paper's view, 'The wants and financial state of the society'. It was vital, it told delegates, that they adopt a plan to increase funds 'equal to the society's emergency ... We want £2000, *and must have it*'. To press home the message, it reprinted an editorial from the previous April in which William Evans cautioned about pushing the Society 'beyond its means' and counselled restraint in the issuance of land certificates. Ten months later the situation was, if anything, more precarious. Alongside the delegate call was a letter from Peter Watkin in which he repeated Evans's warning about unlimited numbers and asked how 'the five hundred individuals, located here' would be fed if the Society did not remit all available funds.[28] Detailing his expenses since Twigg's departure in October, he reminded those at home that forty head of cattle 'are not kept for nothing'.[29] Watkin was not the only source of information on conditions at the colony. In mid-December a group of disgruntled settlers established an Emancipation Ferry committee under the chairmanship of a former lace maker, Joseph Brentnall. Addressing the central committee two days after Christmas, they described their present position as 'not bad, nor good; but what we can expect the first year in the Bush'. They too argued that the Society should grant 'as few Land Certificates as possible, until the present settlers have got their first crops in, and maintaining themselves'.[30]

Twenty-one delegates from labour communities as far afield as Dundee, Glasgow, Manchester, Birmingham, Swindon and London gathered in the Society's rooms on 25 February to address the issues of its constitution and finances. Chairing the meeting was the 29-year-old London tailor George W. Robinson, who would shortly depart for America; the secretary was John Heap from Oldham. The delegates worked hard; over three days they debated and passed a revised code of bylaws designed, as the summary put it, 'to satisfy the colonists and make the society at home a complete national confederation'. After consulting the friendly societies' registrar, they established a system of district agents and auditing to bring the organisation into proper legality. They also regularised the ballot, now to be held quarterly and rotated among the districts. The next drawing would be in June in Leeds. Following members' objections, the 1s levy for management expenses was reduced to a half-penny for every sixpence contributed. In further deference to branch feelings, delegates agreed to replace the words 'Parent Society' with 'Executive' in all future documents. They also introduced a new system of management at the colony, incorporating an estate steward, deputy estate steward, treasurer and secretary, with the positions subject to annual election at the delegate meeting. (Robinson and Peter Watkin were elected estate secretary and treasurer respectively for the first year.) Five auditors chosen from emigrants from London, Staffordshire, Birmingham, Manchester and Scotland would oversee the estate's finances. To address the problem of numbers, the delegates decided that henceforth an individual must have been a member for at least six months and paid £5 8s 6d into the

Society before drawing a land certificate. That sum, minus £1 2s 6d, would be returned on the estate in the form of equipment, building materials, food, livestock and other essentials. They further agreed that the Society should buy equipment – ploughs, drags, wagons, as well as oxen – for hiring out by the estate steward. Following a suggestion from the Hyde branch,[31] they also planned to charter a vessel for the spring crossing, provided sufficient numbers wished to travel.[32]

William Evans had often floated the idea of chartering or purchasing a ship through which the Society could expand its operations, including for use in the trading of American produce. He now made another proposal. En route to Glasgow just after Christmas, he had asked the Society's committee to consider the 'propriety of issuing a few thousands of Dollar Notes on the return of Mr. Twigg to our New Lands'. Adopting 'labour notes' could transform day-to-day transactions and simplify the estate's bookkeeping, he argued. Aside from its utility, the scheme held symbolic value, affirming the centrality of labour to the colony's progress and to humankind in general. In an echo of his former hero, Robert Owen, the best-known advocate of the idea in England, Evans wrote that the notes should represent 'the amount of labour done on the estate, and only to be issued on the *production of a given amount of bona fide wealth*'. After receiving the go-ahead, he engaged a celebrated Glasgow engraver, Joseph Swan, to design the new note, which the editor described as 'a beautiful representation of the agricultural pursuits in which we are engaged, and contains two portraits, one of Washington, and one of Franklin'.[33] Ratifying the committee's decision, the Shelton delegates specified that 'no more than 8000 dollar notes be printed at present' (see Figure 6.1).[34]

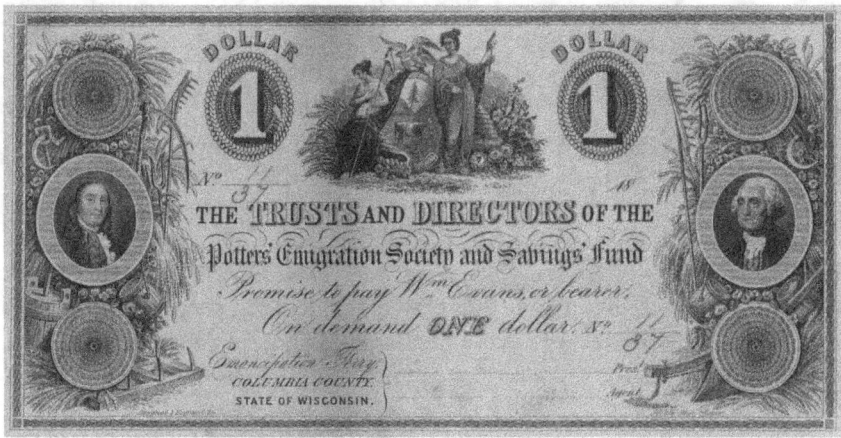

Figure 6.1 Potters' Emigration Society dollar note.

The special meeting had achieved what it set out to – up to a point. The officials expressed pride in having removed the 'many stumbling-blocks' to the Society's legality and in changes designed to make it more representative of members' interests, both at home and on the lands. But they also accepted a lack of progress in addressing the Society's financial problems. One man not completely satisfied with the delegates' efforts was William Evans. He was pleased at their adoption of his dollar note plan and ratification of another proposal for allocating 10 per cent of estate profits to the colonists' general use, but thought it was counterproductive to require emigrants to pay £5 8s 6d before receiving their land certificates. Colonists would now use funds to acquire 'implements as *private* property', thus detracting from 'the *general* available means of the society', he argued. The decision could also affect recruitment; a working man might raise £1 2s 6d for a share and £4 for a passage, but 'he cannot so easily raise £9 10s'. The delegates should instead have suspended the issuance of land certificates until the following spring.[35]

Despite his reservations, Evans believed that the meeting had helped restore the Society's confidence and standing. He was optimistic as spring approached that a 'brighter and better day is before us'. His regret was that since the meeting activists in north Lancashire had been fanning 'the coals of dissension' by withholding contributions and urging others through 'secret correspondence' to do likewise. Although the editor believed that 'the hearts of men' would prove strong enough to raise the requisite funds, he was angry about the failure of some branches to meet their obligations, while dismissing their behaviour as having no serious impact on its progress. Let London, Scotland and Manchester do their duty, 'and the society is safe', he reiterated.[36] Others shared his concerns. Writing to the *Examiner* in January, a Scottish member, Robert Blair, described 'a criminal apathy [that] reigns throughout many of the branches'.[37] Blair's 'City of Glasgow' branch was one of the largest in the country, with a reported 115 subscribers in April 1850.[38] Society accounts from September 1849 to March 1850 reveal the changing pattern of support, with some branches contributing little or nothing and others showing unprecedented returns. Confirming Evans's point, four of the ten largest contributors in December 1849 came from London and Scotland, with the 'First London' heading the list, followed by the 'City of Glasgow'; the rest were from Hanley, Oldham, Crewe, Manchester, Birmingham and Hull. Of the next ten largest contributors, two were from London and five from Scotland. Branches in Burslem, Preston and Bolton completed the list. Three months later there had been a marked shift towards the capital. Three of the leading four and five of the leading ten branches were from London. The 'First London' and 'South London' headed the list with combined quarterly receipts of £142, or almost one-fifth of the total received from the sixty-nine reporting branches. Lancashire's position had relatively declined, with none of the area's branches among the leading ten, although the amounts they contributed stayed broadly constant. Scotland was still a strong presence, the 'City of Glasgow' dropping from second to fifth place largely because of the surging receipts from London. Edinburgh, Dundee, Kirkcaldy and Airdrie were the other Scottish branches in the leading twenty that reported.[39]

What of the Potteries? The Potters' Emigration Society had retained its name but not its identity as a vehicle for the salvation of the pottery trade. Historians have dismissed the period following the demise of the potters' union in 1847–8 as a dark age, when operatives struggled to shake off their ruinous involvement in emigration: 'Terribly weak, but still alive, the potters' organisations had clambered out of the muddle into which, by their own folly and accident of circumstance, they had been thrown.'[40] Although separate trade branches survived, there was, according to this view, little appetite for reviving the industry-wide body, with the 'general mass' of potters, according to Harold Owen, 'simply disgusted' by the very name of union.[41] It is difficult to judge the validity of these conclusions, as evidence on potters' activities and attitudes is scarce. While periodic reductions in wage rates and continued employment insecurity left workers vulnerable, economic conditions had improved, potentially undermining calls for resistance. In November 1849 *The Staffordshire Advertiser* issued its most favourable report on trade in the Potteries for three years.[42] (Direct action was not abandoned; in January most Tunstall manufactories closed for several weeks after hollow-ware pressers demanded 'a slight advance in wages'.[43]) The effect of changing conditions on support for emigration is equally hard to gauge. In March 1850 there were six active branches of the Society in North Staffordshire: the 'William Evans', Hanley; the 'Pottersville', Burslem; the 'Fort Winnebago', Tunstall; the 'Emigrant's Castle', Newcastle; the 'Phoenix', Stoke; and, most recently organised, the 'New Ark', Dalehall, Burslem. (Leek's 'Liberty' branch, located just outside of the Potteries, last reported in December 1849.) Of these, Hanley and Burslem, particularly the former, far outstripped the others in contributions and membership. According to the quarterly accounts, Hanley donated nearly £43, an amount eclipsed only by the two leading London branches.

Evans clung to his belief in revived unionism and the hope that emigration could help effect it. At the end of September 1849, with the new hiring season looming, the *Examiner* announced that Burslem flat pressers would meet on 8 October to hold a ballot. The winner would receive a £10 prize which they could sell or exchange for a forty-acre farm on the Society's lands. Noting the forthcoming event, the editor revived strong memories of earlier appeals.

> Men of the Flat Branch! prepare for Martinmas! You are hourly in danger for the want of Union ... Meet together; consult together; contribute your pence together; and if you cannot remove the whole surplus hands of your branch, stand in defence of a fair price for labour ... and if you are injured on a factory, seek redemption on a farm.[44]

Eighty people attended the ballot and dinner at the Bull's Head at which Evans spoke a few words. After the meeting the flat pressers announced that eighty shares in the Potters' Emigration Society would be applied 'in the best manner possible' for the protection of the branch.[45]

The hollow-ware pressers, who retained 240 branch shares, were also determined to reassert their union and emigration credentials as Martinmas approached. Recalling their leading role in the founding of the potters' union, members of Burslem's Black Lion Lodge called for operatives in the other towns to join a reorganised branch and, through a payment of 3d a week, to recommit themselves to the removal of surplus labour through emigration. 'The Potters' Emigration Society is now solely confined to emigration purposes; and entirely disconnected from the trade's proceedings. Sorrowful to every working potter should that day be, when the severance took place', they lamented.[46] Six months later they were still insisting that emigration was the solution to the problem of underemployment. In a powerful appeal in early April, Black Lion members congratulated fellow workers on 'your recent victories'. Noting that 'the old policy of "turnouts"' was a 'hazardous and imperfect way' of resolving their situation, they insisted that removing men from the branch 'has given you the power to command a price for your labour, for which, some few years back, you did not dream'. And to avoid any doubt, it was the Potters' Emigration Society whose 'wise and practical proceedings' had given them this power. As proof, they provided a list of thirty-five Society members who had left the country for America. Heading the list were the Pottersville pioneers Hamlet Copeland and John Sawyer, but it also included labour migrants such as Enoch Bullock who had gone to work in East Liverpool in 1845. However, they admitted that the 'great mass' of operatives remained outside the surplus-labour fold. To be brought in, they would have to pay dues for eighteen months; they could then benefit from the branch shares and claim for themselves and their families 'plenteous homes, political freedom, and social independence!'[47]

The 'surplus labour executive' of the flat pressers and the turners made similar appeals a few weeks later. Unlike the hollow-ware pressers, the turners' list of 'followers' who had removed themselves to America made no specific mention of the Society. 'We have abandoned all petty dissension', they announced, 'and now work with a will for the removal of our surplus hands. Neither do we make it compulsory, as to what colony a member shall go either at home or abroad.' The turners pledged to clear the branch of all redundant workers by next Martinmas and extract from employers 'that respectful treatment and that remunerative wage, which, formerly, we all know, characterized the skilled department'.[48] Flat pressers too were proud of their contribution to the Society's founding, and especially the part played by James Hammond. Hammond had been 'a poor, struggling, hard-working Plate-maker' but now owned 100 acres of freehold land: 'Contrast this man's present position with that which he abandoned in this heavily-taxed and class-ridden country'.[49] At a meeting on 30 April in Shelton, its executive reported the enrolment of thirty new members from a single pot-bank in Tunstall. Determined to push ahead with the removal 'to Forty-Acre farms abroad', it regretted that there were now 'two distinct movements' within the trade. While wishing success to those engaged in industrial action, it urged that emigration would greatly benefit the 'turnouts', and in a spirit of conciliation agreed to devote all current contributions to removing twenty Longton strikers 'to landed independence abroad'.[50]

The *Examiner* announced at the beginning of March that Thomas Twigg would leave for New York on or about 16 March aboard the 'splendid, first-class, American-built' packet *Guy Mannering*. (On its previous departure from Liverpool in January, the ship had run aground near the outer gates of Princes Dock.[51]) Those wishing to accompany him should forward their details together with a £1 deposit to William Evans's office at the port.[52] Twigg's three-and-a-half-month visit had proved a tonic to the Society, boosting members' morale and allowing them to question him on its transatlantic plans. In gratitude, it organised a series of farewell parties, beginning on 23 February at the Swan, Burslem. There was the usual menu of songs, recitations and dancing, plus brief addresses from Twigg, Evans and another local official, Edwin Alcock. Similar events were held at Dalehall and Tunstall on 4 and 5 March, although without the star guest, owing to his 'indisposition'. In Tunstall members gave Evans a vote of confidence 'expressive of sympathy for him as regards the libels of Mr. Joseph Barker'. The evening was presided over by George W. Robinson, who had travelled to the Potteries preparatory to accompanying Twigg to Wisconsin. In his parting message to London members, Robinson proudly described his appointment as the 'General Secretary over the whole society's business in Western America'. Acknowledging the opposition that continued to bedevil its progress, he pledged 'to make our great and good institution a *practical* medium of emancipation to my poor and toiling countrymen'.[53]

The *Guy Mannering* sailed from Liverpool on 14 March, docking in New York three-and-a-half weeks later. Like many other transatlantic vessels in this period, the overwhelming majority of the Black Star packet's nearly 650 passengers were Irish. Travelling with Twigg were his wife

Hannah, their two children and Thomas's younger brother John. Aside from the Twiggs and George Robinson, the party included the families of three Staffordshire potters: John Deakin, Joseph Shaw and Philip Pointon, comprising in total six adults and sixteen children. All three families would remain in the United States. From Holborn in London came John Gunn, like Robinson a tailor, accompanied by his wife Isabella and three young children; and from Newton Heath, Manchester, Richard Tinker, who was a miller, and his wife Frances. In January Tinker wrote to the *Examiner* with expert advice on the costs of a grist mill and an offer to work free of charge on its construction.[54] Also leaving Lancashire were mill worker Joseph Shaw and his wife Elizabeth from Bury; and Bold Hilton, a 40-year-old silk weaver and long-standing Society member. His wife and daughter remained behind in Leigh. Having paid £3 4s 6d into the funds plus 15s for tools, he was looking forward to finding his 'home in the west'.[55]

Members of the party arrived at the Society's lands at the end of the third week in April. It was six months since Twigg's departure for England. What had occurred in the interim? During his visit home the agent had reported encouragingly on the colony's progress while conceding the difficulties caused by unregulated numbers and inadequate funds. In his absence Peter Watkin and his assistant, the 'book-keeper and store-keeper' John Turner,[56] had been frank about the problems they faced. Adapting to pioneer life proved a challenge for all settlers, especially those lacking in farming experience and especially in winter. Emigrant expectations were high, and varying degrees of frustration, disillusion and resentment were inevitable. Watkin and Turner bore much of the brunt. 'I am disgusted with my species', the latter complained in January.

> I always entertained the idea that there was something noble in a man, but eight months' assistance in the management of a colony, has undeceived me; and at the present moment I would rather seek companions with the screeching ravens or howling wolves, than act as some here would act, who talk loudly, and hold their heads high.[57]

The first report of discontent to reach England after Twigg's departure from the colony – Barker's hearsay aside – came from the former Estate Committee member Enoch Pickering. In a letter dated 16 November, he described how he left Pottersville the previous October 'just as I went to it, with this exception, that myself and family were naked and barefoot, with a winter to face'. He had been looking forward to Twigg and Watkin's arrival, he wrote, because he believed that the former's position as president of the Society and the latter's experience 'would have had an influence on their judgement'. Alas, it was not to be. The first stumbling block was Twigg's failure to settle the Estate Committee accounts. Pickering described the agent's story that the members had left Pottersville in order to evade their store debts as an 'unfeeling and cruel' fabrication. He had moved his own family to the Fox River settlement on land that still 'belongs to the Indians'. Much of it was of poor quality, 'nothing but sand to the surface', and he ridiculed Twigg's boast of having selected it himself. He also reported that there was 'much murmuring and dissatisfaction on the Indian Estate', and that about a third of those who had gone there had left. Although Twigg had laboured hard to get settlers land that was broken and sown, 'he has put his foot on their necks', with low wages and inflated prices for flour, pork, cheese and other staples. In what would become a common refrain, Pickering cast doubt on the Society's land tenure. American law does not allow any person 'to hold its lands but for himself: he cannot hold it for any Society', he wrote. His conclusion was fierce. Emigration societies are not ruined because they cannot work: 'They are ruined by the blindness of speculators, and men not possessed of the control of their reason; for whoever examines the whole of the actions of William Evans, can come to no other conclusion but that he is like his brother Alexander, that is—a clever madman.'[58]

The murmurings soon took organised form. On 1 December forty-four settlers attended a meeting at the Emancipation Ferry store. Although a Londoner, Joseph Twycross, had called the meeting, it was a recent arrival, James Scott from Paisley, who was directing affairs. Little is known about Scott, but he was clearly the same individual who regaled the audience on New Year's Day of 1849 in Manchester's Free Trade Hall with tales of pioneer adventures in America.[59] The Burslem settler George Cooper was highly suspicious of Scott's story of his 'great labours and travels' and professed wealth. The Scotsman had begun to find fault even before he crossed the river, Cooper wrote, 'first with the ferry, which had given satisfaction to every teamster that had crossed it; secondly, with the store; thirdly, with the land, being too sandy; and in fact with everything he met with'. Another correspondent told how Scott complained that his pigsty was too far from the house and not fit to keep pigs in; he also reportedly interfered in a transaction Watkin had made to purchase pork and coffee by telling the seller that he would not be paid.[60] But Scott had attracted some willing followers, including another Estate Committee member, Samuel Fox, and a fellow Scotsman, John Robinson. According to Watkin, it was 'the Scottites and their bosom friend Fox' who were responsible for a report of starvation. They had taken a single incident when for a week or so the colony was short of molasses and coffee and claimed 'there was famine in the settlement'. He pointed to the 'tons of flour, pork, beef, and the hundreds of bushels of potatoes' and other staples already consumed as well as the large quantities awaiting collection once the weather permitted.[61]

The advertised purpose of the 1 December meeting, according to John Turner, was to consider 'the best means of obtaining medical aid in sickness, and the establishment of a post office'. In the event, the only motion proposed was 'that a committee be formed to manage the affairs of the society'. With only twenty-four hours' notice, Turner claimed that two-thirds of the settlers were unaware the meeting was taking place.[62] The tide turned four days later when those involved again gathered at the store. Samuel Fox was the first to speak, but was asked to leave after opposition from Cooper and others. The majority present then declared the new committee 'useless and powerless'. The Lancashire engraver Martin Ellison, who had been elected chair, resigned amid angry scenes, declaring that 'he would no longer join in such a proceeding'. Most of his fellow members followed suit. In Cooper's words, the 'faction was thus broken, Messrs Scott and Robinson have no committee of management; the settlers believing that the power to elect officers and appoint auditors, rests with the Parent Society in England'. Three days later Emancipation Ferry experienced its first winter snow.[63]

The coup had failed, but the plotters soon regrouped. A week before Christmas they gathered for a third meeting at the home of a settler called George Pearson, where they formed a new committee designed to bypass existing authority and correspond directly with the Society. It was this committee that wrote to the Society's executive prior to the delegate meeting. Aside from Joseph Brentnall and Pearson, its membership included Scott and Robinson, together with Joseph Twycross, George Cocker, William Betts and, the sole representative from the Potteries, Stephen Murray. John Llewellyn of the 'Seventh London' branch served as secretary. Other supporters present included two Scotsmen, William Orr and William Gemmell. They had arrived at the colony three days earlier, having spent several months working on the construction of the Wisconsin plank road.[64] The men had encountered Scott ('the lecturer from Paisley') at Fort Winnebago and travelled with him to Emancipation Ferry. 'There seemed to be two parties', they wrote in a letter published in the *Northern Star* in February, '—the party in the store, and connected with it ... were in great favour of Twigg, and thought he would return in the spring and make every one right'; others were 'for the rights of the society, to see and make some arrangements for their general satisfaction, and for the benefit of all'.[65]

'I suppose some of the dissatisfied portion have favoured you with an address', Watkin wrote to Evans on 4 January, 'craving cash payment for their labour, and that they be furnished with tea, sugar, currants, raisins, and a few other small matters; but I can tell you Sir, they are of a class that nothing would satisfy short of all power and control both here and in England'.[66] John Turner offered a more discursive but no less damning account of the affair. He told a London colleague that the 'parties here believe, or profess to believe ... that each and all have a right to anything purchased with the society's money. My proceedings here have, I hope, taught them different.' After advising the disgruntled group that taking goods without payment was a felony, he was accused of being too young for the job and told that they would ask the Society 'to make me a servant of a committee of settlers, who, they say, ought to have the direction of affairs, as they are best acquainted with their own wants'. They had forgotten, he continued, 'that the funds necessary to supply these wants belong to the society in England', the purpose being that they will yield a profit 'to be applied to the overstocked English operative market'. Turner despised their self-importance. Those 'who cannot be content with good plain food, but sigh after tea and sugar, currant dumplings, and plum-cakes' are not fit to emigrate, he wrote.[67]

By mid-January the revolt was fizzling out. 'The malcontents ... are becoming rather more moderate, and by the time the winter has passed over, which will not be long now, I think some will be ashamed of the part they have taken', reported Watkin on 16 January. Two days later Turner informed Twigg that Scott had left the colony for Illinois: 'There is a committee in operation here, who, I believe, write occasionally to the parent society; of course we take no notice of them.' But there was no denying the challenge Scott and his allies posed to the Society's authority. Delegates at the Shelton meeting in February regarded his conduct as sufficiently egregious to warrant an instruction barring him from holding office on the estate.[68] The extent of settler discontent in this period is hard to gauge; however, if Joseph Barker's information was correct, it had been evident for some months. It was these feelings that Scott sought to exploit. His appeal was straightforward; he advised the settlers they were 'ill-used' and promised them 'every thing they could desire', wrote Watkin. Twigg, absent from the colony since October, was a prime target. Turner reported that Scott had claimed that the agent had taken a large sum of money to England and would not be returning. He also reportedly circulated a rumour that there were thousands of pounds unaccounted for at home. Fortunately, the arrival of the auditor's report undermined the charge, and Scott 'soon lost his character for veracity'.[69]

The majority who remained on the lands did not succumb to Scott's pleas; most preferred to channel their energies into work. Testimony from the winter of 1849–50 shows individuals and families buckling down impressively to the tasks of frontier settlement. Samuel Rudland from Lancashire, a late arrival, informed his wife just before Christmas that he was currently living with five Englishmen but had already built his house and begun cutting timber: 'I have 40 acres of good land, and am now labouring to make, what I trust, will prove to you a happy home.' Although he had 'plenty' of bread, beef and poultry, 'so many coming out has pressed hard on the stores, which has produced dissatisfaction amongst some of the members'.[70] 'We have ten acres of wheat on our own land; seventeen hens and a rooster; two sow pigs, and a puppy' plus 'three good cows' and a 'good dog', wrote Alfred Swetmore, who had arrived with his family the previous March. The former potter intended to build a new house in the spring and had already purchased materials for the purpose. 'I believe this to be a perfectly healthy place', he affirmed.[71] Also determined to succeed were John and Jane Scott from Stoke. 'This is the place for working men', John told his brother and sister in January. Having arrived at the colony late in the season, the Scotts thought it best to wait until Twigg's return before claiming their land. Others failed to match their patience. 'There are several started back before they had scarcely seen land, but they saw there was plenty of work and that was against their religion', John wrote.[72]

During Twigg's absence, Watkin and Turner had done their best to meet the expectations of newly arriving members. Having seen off Scott's challenge, they were optimistic that the worst of the winter's conditions had passed and that the colony would now progress. Writing to Twigg on 25 January, Watkin conceded that they had been 'a little straightened for the needful, and on that account had to pay rather high for some things', but that 'for the real necessaries of life we have been all right', notwithstanding correspondence that claimed otherwise. He was keen to emphasise the efforts made to ensure the colony's wellbeing. Provisions 'have not been procured by sitting in the store', he assured Twigg. Although Watkin was confident that he and the other officials could cope, he was anxious that his 'dear friend' return to Wisconsin as soon as possible, and suggested he cross the Atlantic by steamer rather than risk 'tossing up and down in a liner for six or seven weeks, in the early part of spring'. Among the matters Watkin felt would benefit from Twigg's presence, the 'Pottersville business' stood out. He had told those who still owed the Society money that they could only take the twenty acres next to them on the 'distinct understanding' that they were tenants 'and must work their farms on shares until they were out of debt, but the condition would be fixed when you came back'.[73]

Spring brought renewed pressure on resources. A general meeting in the Potteries on 15 April confirmed that balloted members would depart for Wisconsin between 20 May and 1 June. In William Evans's view, the decision showed that even in 'the present emergency' the Society had kept faith with its supporters, although he still believed that it should have suspended land certificates until the spring. Other developments also concerned him. The April meeting resolved that the wives of four Preston settlers, Leonard Lodge, Charles Ayrey, Thomas Beckett and James Clitheroe, should receive in passage money the balance of wages due to their husbands who had prepared homes for their arrival. Delegates in February had passed a similar resolution for the family of Oldham emigrant John Goulding. Evans regarded these decisions as 'entirely at variance with our incipient proceedings'. The rules prescribed that a member paying his own way to Wisconsin was guaranteed only a forty-acre allotment, the use of implements and twelve months' food, 'for the two latter of which, he must labour, as he receives them'. There was no provision for additional expenses. He told prospective emigrants to 'beware'; those going to Wisconsin under their own resources should take £8 or £10 in cash for house-building and farm expenses. It was not the Society's fault if they failed to do so, 'and he who expects more, deserves to be punished for his folly. At least, he may certainly calculate on disappointment.'[74]

Prominent among the disappointed was Enoch Pickering. Evans was keen to counter the effects of his letter, published by Barker in mid-February. In a blistering article he accused its author of failing to mention that he had left Pottersville with debts of upwards of £70. Instead of discharging them, he had concocted the lie that 'Twigg, Evans, and Company' had promised him twenty acres of land, a house and traveling expenses, which in two years they had *'unblushingly'* taken from him. 'The society has "taken" nothing from him, nor can they get anything from him', Evans responded.[75] Other supporters took to the public prints to defend the Society against its detractors. In March John Hull of Padiham appealed to the *Northern Star*'s 'love of fair play' for permission to counter the reports contained in Orr and Gemmell's letter. He blamed the discontent on those like Pickering who would not pay their 'just debts' and were now 'conspiring together for the purpose of upsetting the society'.[76] The following month a Londoner named Dowling, who claimed membership of the Society and the Chartist Land Company, attacked Hull's comparison of the two schemes and their leaders. His response included a characterisation of George W. Robinson as Evans's 'secretly accredited agent' in London, a man who 'carried on the smuggling trade for some years, and, when that failed, took to dog fancying, and keeping a pot-house of the lowest description'.[77] Replying, John Turner's friend E. A. Epps defended the agent against Dowling's 'preposterous' insinuations. He rebutted the charge that the Society's leaders had squandered or misappropriated money raised for the scheme. Of the £6,000 subscribed, 'Pottersville has been paid for; three stores have been erected and stocked on the new estate; a ferry-boat built; close to 1,000 members located on other lands, with farm implements necessary to cultivate it, and oxen, cows, horses, &c., &c., bought'.[78]

The *Northern Star*'s readership was declining in the spring of 1850, tempering the likely impact of these exchanges.[79] Other reports were harder to ignore. On 1 June the *Manchester Examiner & Times* published in its

'Emigrant's Column' a critical letter from an anonymous member which unfavourably compared the opportunities and rewards available at the colony with those in the surrounding area. Included was an unflattering description of Twigg's 'far-famed' store and of the house he had been allocated as a balloted member. A bricklayer by trade, he knew what he was talking about. The dwelling was in 'bad condition, the roof was not on, and the cement plaster ... is made of sludge, and thrown on with the hand without a trowel'. Impressed with the area's potential, he was unconvinced of the Society's competence and integrity.[80] Four weeks later *The Staffordshire Advertiser* printed the first of three letters from members of the *Guy Mannering* party describing their arrival in Wisconsin. Philip Pointon was a 44-year-old potter from Hanley. He travelled to America with his wife Ann and seven children. On reaching Milwaukie, they encountered two men from the Potteries – one a balloted member, James Kirkham – who told 'such deplorable tales about the land that they were not believed'. Pointon decided to go and see for himself. At the Society's store he acquired an axe, wedges and cutting rings and with others went to look for land, but could find 'no good, but what was claimed, mostly by the Yankees'. Further sorties failed to turn up anything suitable without penetrating eighteen or twenty miles into the woods, and there 'Ann would not go'. The land as a whole was 'a very bad lot', he reported. The condition of families he met also affected him. Nearly all had survived the winter on flour and water, 'but some that are in favour get a little better food than the rest'. The Society 'is a complete take-in'; Joseph Barker was right, 'and you know that I did not think so before we started'. Pointon was clear on what emigrant families needed to succeed. With members getting little for their labour and forced to pay a high price for food, they should acquire property close to a town where work was more available.[81] Determined not to waste any more time 'going to look at Twigg's sand banks', the Pointons moved to Baraboo in neighbouring Sauk County, where they purchased two lots on the river next to the home of a Potteries acquaintance, George Newson, who had arrived the previous year. 'I tell you the truth when I say it is the prettiest place we have seen since we came to America', Philip wrote.[82]

A second account of the party's arrival appeared two weeks later, penned by the Lancashire weaver Bold Hilton. Addressed to fellow branch members, it described how they received in Milwaukie the first hint 'that things were not as they ought to be at "Emancipation Ferry"'. After talking with the two men from the Potteries, Hilton and his companions set off west. At Watertown they met another balloted member, who told them 'that he would kill Twigg if he could drop across him'. Inquiring at the colony about the 50,000 acres of land they understood belonged to the Society, they received in reply 'a horse laugh'. Like Pointon, Hilton was unimpressed with the land around Emancipation Ferry, but was told that the Society had secured fourteen miles of frontage on the Fox River comprising 'a rich black loam, ranging from twelve to eighteen inches deep'. He reminded members that American law prohibited any person from squatting on more than 160 acres and that only 'the squatter himself' had a right to the land. As it had not yet been surveyed, settlers could be improving property 'they cannot possibly occupy hereafter'.

Before he set out for America, Hilton was told that he would receive food from the store in exchange for his labour 'until my land could be tilled and the crops got off'. It now transpired that only the first meal was free; the charge after that was six cents. He reported a conversation with George W. Robinson, who had examined the books 'but could make nothing at all of them'. Robinson advised him and his companions to buy a barrel of pork and other necessary items and go about twelve miles further back where they would find good land. 'I asked him how he thought I could believe that, when I had been grossly deceived in the first instance'. What did he want, retorted the agent, 'roast beef, plum pudding, pickles, &c'. No, just 'good substantial food for working for', said Hilton, which upset Robinson. The depressing litany continued: 'I saw women crying, men wandering about in a state of utter bewilderment, many with not one cent in their pockets, not knowing where to apply for work, as there was nothing to do for the society excepting chopping firewood or splitting rails.' Disputing Robinson's claim that there was plenty of work available at $1 for a day's pay, Hilton offered an alternative picture of low wages, back-breaking hours on local canal projects (which he himself failed 'to get on') and the hostility of Irish workmen, who had assaulted a fellow passenger, the Bury man Joseph Shaw. 'There are hundreds seeking employment who can find none, and, taken altogether, it is one of the most miserable places that man ever existed in', he wrote. He also reported meeting Alexander Evans, who was in a sorry condition, having suffered very bad luck, 'as a person of the name of Smith, with his family, was bringing with him some goods from England, but the steamer on which he was, got blown up on the lakes, and all perished'. He next worked on a farm 'on shares with a Yankee, who had cheated him out of every cent'. Within a few weeks Hilton had returned to his family in Leigh, his transatlantic ambitions in tatters.[83]

The damaging correspondence continued. In mid-July the *Montrose Standard* published a recent letter from Fort Winnebago by a local man, Alexander Sherret. Enthusiastic about the area, he was scornful of the Society, which 'has practised one of the most diabolical deceits ever known on their countrymen'. Much of the letter consisted of a diatribe against Thomas Twigg, beginning with his arrival the previous year. He had come and 'squatted down on the Indian Land, which as yet does not belong to

Government ... therefore it cannot be purchased until it is surveyed, and brought into market for sale'. Having 'sat down there', he had written home stating 'that he had acquired 50,000 acres of land for the society'. The land 'is of the poorest description', Sherret confirmed. Further examples of the agent's shortcomings followed, including how he left settlers to fend for themselves when he returned home, leading some to starve; and how he collected in England large sums of money for the grist mill which he was supposed to have finished this spring. Judges had examined the proposed site; it 'would scarcely move a spinning wheel, let alone a grist mill'.[84] On the same day, 19 July, another disgruntled Scotsman, 22-year-old John Oliphant, vented his feelings in a letter co-signed by eight members from Edinburgh, London, Liverpool, Birmingham and Nottingham. Oliphant was an established complainer. His letter to a Fife newspaper in March garnered a strong rebuttal from George W. Robinson, who pointed out that he was not a 'successful drawer' and so was not entitled to what he was claiming.[85] Among his latest assertions was that the proposals at the Fort Winnebago meeting included one to shoot Twigg: 'Now, I ask you to reflect on what kind of condition men, civilized men, would be reduced to, before hazarding such a thought as that.'[86]

Evans did his best to stem the rising tide of attacks. Challenging Philip Pointon's account of the Society's conduct, he described the purchase and settlement of the Pottersville estate before turning to the vexed subject of the new lands to where in two years it had sent 400 families 'comprising mechanics of all trades'. On the question of tenure, he was brief. The lands had been secured 'in pre-emption right' and 'can only be held by the *settler*, and not by the society', he explained. Evans was adamant that the Society had not deceived Pointon and his family, who had greatly benefited from its assistance and helped reduce his trade's surplus labour. Having secured crossings for his wife and children at a discounted cost, he was guided to what he himself acknowledged was ' "a fine situation on the banks of the Baraboo river" '.[87] A month later Evans returned to the fray in an article headed 'More Discouraging Letters from Three-Days Residents'. His first target was the anonymous bricklayer. Reprinting his letter, the editor showed his skill in extracting positive lessons from an unpromising source, noting that the writer spoke in 'the most flattering terms' of a working man's prospects in the region. No such redemption attached to Bold Hilton's letter, also reprinted in full. Evans made no effort to counter Hilton's criticisms of the Society; his focus was on the account of his meeting with his brother. William described at length Alexander's repeated misfortune since the family's departure from England in 1847, including the loss of their child, the tragic history of the Clark (not Smith) family while carrying goods and money and the aborted Puckaway mission. The story was in effect a

1850–1: Crisis and decline

parable; nobody was worse qualified for farming 'from the artistic nature of his original employ' than Alexander. If he could survive, anyone could, was William's message. Included was a recent letter in which Alexander asked his family to loan him $10 so that he could make improvements to his Pottersville farm. Despite modest progress, he did not regret leaving England: 'Three years' hard experience in this new and delightful country, is valuable for a poor man, no matter how poor, if he will duly strive to make his way.'[88]

In his rejoinder to the Pointons, Evans had enclosed a letter from James and Martha Hammond, dated 9 December 1849, in which James described the progress of their ninety-six-acre farm, now worth, he claimed, $1,000. The same letter resurfaced a short time later in a London weekly, the *Standard of Freedom*, paired with a highly critical account from a Londoner, James Buck, who had recently travelled to Wisconsin with his wife Mary. Buck's narrative of the couple's brief stay at the colony was an unmitigated condemnation of the emigration scheme and its officials. The points he raised were hardly new – inferior land, exploitative prices and limited employment opportunities – but he set them in a framework of repeated dishonesty and betrayal, with Twigg the principal wrongdoer but others complicit.

> You will see how the Potters' Society serves the poor man. G. W. R— and T— are feathering their nests. William E—, its founder, is privy to what is going on here. Believe no man that says it is not a swindle, and give the facts I have sent you the utmost possible circulation.

Like other correspondents, Buck questioned the legality of Twigg's land plans: 'The 40-acre allotment system cannot work … it comes into collision with the United States' pre-emption laws … [and] interferes with the individual sovereignty of the people, which sovereignty the laws of these states uphold.'[89]

Evans again had to defend the Society's reputation. Buck has been 'a London clerk', he told the *Standard*, 'and in his new position of an American Backwoods-man looks around at his difficulties; and instead of condemning his own want of energy, condemns the society and everything belonging to it'.[90] To bolster his reply, Evans published two letters whose accounts contrasted sharply with that of the Londoner's. The first was from William Mountford. The Burslem man had suffered a serious accident the previous year but was now prospering. Like James Hammond, Mountford's emphasis was on the satisfaction he and his family derived from their new life in America, 'one of the healthiest places I believe there is anywhere'. Any man 'of industrious habits' can make a good living here, he wrote. Domestic contentment fueled his optimism. His children were all thriving, and his daughter Eliza had recently wed John Peake, whose property adjoined his own. The second letter was from a Birmingham man, John Chapman. Arriving in New York the previous September on the *Aberdeen*, he spent the winter working there before joining Twigg's incoming party in the spring. Chapman's letter provides one of the more even-handed accounts of the colony's progress. The few members of Twigg's party who remained at the colony would do well, he wrote; he was less charitable about those who had left. One thing was clear: there had been 'a deal of bad management here' during the agent's absence. The shortage of funds was a 'drawback', as was the high price of flour caused by 'the great influx of emigrants of all kinds, Yankees and others'. But Twigg was doing the best he could. In words that Evans surely savoured, Chapman insisted that 'a man of determination' need not depend on the Society: 'I have not had a cent's worth of credit from them, nor do I intend it.'[91]

Introducing the Hammond and Buck correspondence, the *Standard of Freedom*'s editor highlighted the 'singular and inexplicable discrepancy' in their accounts. These sharply conflicting reports from the colony also pose problems for the historian. Twigg's record is especially hard to judge (the task made difficult by large gaps in the surviving *Examiner*).[92] There were clearly tensions following his reappearance in April. There has been 'quite a rattling among the dry bones since Twigg came back; they did not expect his return', wrote John Chapman in June. On 1 May Martin Ellison recorded a 'stormy meeting at the Ferry Store in consequence of the introduction of new rules by Twigg from England viz, stopping the store credit'.[93] Two weeks later he confirmed that the 'commotions that Twigg and the new regulations have kicked up' caused a great deal of trouble. He also rebuked him for having made the worst possible choice of officers to manage the colony during his absence.[94] Misinformation and mistrust were rife. Joseph Twycross told Ellison at the end of June that the agent had ordered 'that all members who would not sign a bond to give Twigg power over such members property must not in future have either work or food'. The report turned out to be a hoax. 'Expecting new orders', Ellison jotted.[95]

Although Ellison made no mention of it, Twigg already faced a new challenge. On 3 June a group of settlers met at Fort Winnebago with a plan to expose the Society's alleged misdeeds. They had asked Twigg to attend the meeting, but he declined to do so. In the chair was a local attorney and justice of the peace, Walter W. Kellogg (he was called away during the meeting and replaced by Alexander Sherret); a 24-year-old teacher, Luman A. Bliss, acted as secretary. The meeting revealed the continuing rift between supporters and opponents of the colony's leadership, and was provoked by the circulation of a handbill, 'The Maligners of the Potters' Emigration Society', which had greatly offended the latter. The resolutions left no doubt of the convenors' intent. It is the meeting's opinion, stated the second, that the

Potters' Emigration Society 'is a direct deception on the working classes of the British Empire'. There followed an expression of confidence in James Scott, who had been 'abused' by the officers, and a pledge to address a memorial to the radical Member of Parliament for Finsbury, Thomas Duncombe, designed to thwart further Society emigration. Before adjourning, the meeting elected a committee of five under Bliss's chairmanship to draft the document.

A reconvened meeting on 8 June unanimously accepted the 750-word memorial. The only departure was that the address had changed from Duncombe to the 'people of Great Britain'. The arguments were well-rehearsed. By its 'prospectuses, head bills, advertisements, books of rules, lectures, and by means of a weekly paper, or periodical called the "Potters Examiner"', the Potters' Emigration Society had misled the 'working and other classes' into believing its promises of a prosperous and independent life in America. Most of its statements were 'grossly false', the memorial claimed, and the promises made 'either improperly carried out or not performed at all'. Land was the first grievance. The Society's much-vaunted 50,000 acres – currently 'in the possession of the Indians' – cannot be secured by anyone until surveyed and put up for sale; all settlers are therefore 'considered as trespassers'. The land was also mainly 'sandy, or wet marsh', and 'in the opinion of many practical men very unsuitable for farming'. There followed condemnation of the 'so-called' stores and of the payment system for work which largely consisted of redeemable credit at inflated prices. The previous winter had forced members to survive on flour and water, with the result that 'some have sunk under it and met with a grave in a land far from all their relations'. As to wider employment, there was none available for miles around. The document concluded with a plea to the British people to investigate the Society's affairs, 'to prevent our fellow-countrymen from being duped as we have been, by being caused to break up their homes and quit their native land to be thrown destitute upon a strange country, without the means of extraction'.[96]

Although the memorial explicitly represented the interests of Society members, Alexander Sherret described those attending the meetings as 'inhabitants and settlers', implying wider participation. Outsider influence was clear from the start. The first chair, Walter Kellogg, was a native-born American; three of the five committee members, Bliss, James Hinman and William Ward, were New Yorkers. A fourth, Edward Shipley, while born in England, had migrated from Canada, where he had been living for well over a decade.[97] All five were newcomers – the quartermaster's ledger at Fort Winnebago shows them renting accommodation at the former barracks in 1849–50 – and unrepresentative of the Society's emigrant community at large.[98] That American settlers actively involved themselves in the Society's affairs is unsurprising given the colony's location. By the summer of 1850 the population of the Fort Winnebago/Portage area had climbed to over 2,000 and would continue to grow rapidly in the next decade.[99] Six months ago, wrote Sherret in June, there had only been three or four houses; 'now you will count 200, and as many in progress of erection. It would astonish you with what rapidity, when once a place gets a name, it springs up and fills.' Tellingly, the settlers' memorial appeared on 4 July in the first issue of the Fort Winnebago *River Times*. Established by two New Yorkers, John and James Delaney, the paper's publication was further proof of the area's emergence from its frontier stage, its title a salute to the 'great work' underway to link the Fox and Wisconsin waterways.[100]

The area was filling up fast, but not with Society members.[101] We do not know how many members left Britain for Wisconsin during the first half of 1850, but the number was considerably lower than the previous year. In March, despite the efforts of Barker and others, the Society's reputation was broadly intact. William Atkinson, a London tailor working as a hotel waiter in Peoria, Illinois, wrote to a friend that the Society was 'the best that a poor man can belong to'.[102] In the following months the reports of the colony's problems combined with a change in the Society's rules resulted in fewer members crossing the Atlantic. Among spring travellers were George Bain and his family from Midlothian, who sailed from Glasgow on 3 April (one of their six children died during the crossing). They would settle in Marquette County. From Lancashire came James Bennett, a grocer and preacher, his wife Sally and three sons, who arrived in New York two days after the Bains. Reaching Wisconsin in June, they moved in with their daughter Mary, who had emigrated the previous year with her husband John Sutcliffe. On 7 July James preached at the Ellison house to forty worshippers (his text was 1 Corinthians 3:11, 'Other foundation can no Man lay'). On 18 September Martin Ellison noted that James, Sally and their youngest son Wilson had left the colony, 'intending to go back to England'.[103] In fact, all three sons stayed and raised families in America. The Bennetts' history demonstrates emigration's often complex dynamics; six of their twelve children would ultimately move to the United States. According to family lore, the couple's equally divided offspring led them to go 'back and forth during their lives' between England and America.[104]

The largest Society contingent in 1850 left Liverpool on 4 June, reaching New York six weeks later. The *Olive Branch*'s more than 300 passengers included three balloted members: William Robbins, a blacksmith from Kent, and his wife Kate; Frederick and Charlotte Stagg and their two infant children from Lambeth, where he worked as a cabinet maker; and Enoch Barber, a 30-year-old potter from Tunstall, and his wife and young daughter. Barber was part of a group of nine potters travelling together to Wisconsin.

Four were single men, or at least men travelling without families. They included Benton Vernon from Burslem. In October 1842 he was among those acquitted of the charge of 'seditious riot' at the special assize court in Stafford held to try those arrested during the August outbreak.[105] At least two more balloted families left for New York at about the same time. Richard Ellis, a weaver from the 'Falls of Clyde' branch, journeyed with his wife Grace, five children and an older female relative on the *Marmion*, landing in the city on 12 July; with them was fellow branch member James Scoular. Nine days later Stoke potter John Hope, his wife Sarah and seven children, two of them adults, followed on board the *Universe*.[106]

If counting the numbers heading to the colony is difficult, equally so is determining how many arrived there – and how many left soon afterwards. From Martin Ellison's journal and other sources, the colony's population appears in constant flux, with families and individuals regularly arriving and departing. Many emigrants failed to leave any trace in Wisconsin, including Benton Vernon, who returned home to his wife and daughter in time for the 1851 census. More visible is the path taken by the hollow-ware presser James Kirkham, who had arrived in America on the *Aberdeen* the previous September. On 23 May Ellison recorded that the Kirkhams and another family had 'left the settlement in Magoons wagon'. Having taken his wife Esther and two children with him to Wisconsin, Kirkham had staked everything on a fresh start as a farmer. Reaching there before the onset of winter, they found conditions tough and by late March 1850 were down to their last cent. Shortly afterwards they decided to abandon the prairie experiment. Kirkham was angered by conditions at the colony, and was heard to say so loudly by Philip Pointon, who ran into him in Milwaukie.[107] Rather than go straight home to England, the family headed for East Liverpool, where by the beginning of June James was employed as a potter. At some point thereafter the Kirkhams left Ohio, and by the end of March 1851 were back in Burslem, where James had resumed work at the potbank. What prompted this final move is unclear, but non-economic considerations possibly played a role. When another Staffordshire man, James Nixon, called on the family in March 1850, he found Esther 'only a few days from her confinement'.[108] But the federal census taken on 1 June makes no mention of a child (nor do subsequent censuses), suggesting that the baby died during or shortly after birth. The Kirkhams' decision to leave America may have involved difficult domestic and emotional negotiation, therefore. Esther had been born into the Primitive Methodist Church, and the loss of extended family and religious community support – late in life Isaac Smith lamented his failure to establish a Primitive Methodist 'connection' in the area[109] – perhaps persuaded her to press for their return. Simple push-pull emigration models are inadequate in the face of such reality.

Criticism of conditions at the Wisconsin colony reached its high-water mark in the late summer of 1850. On 9 August the *Nottingham Review* printed the text of the Fort Winnebago memorial. Newspapers in Scotland, London, Staffordshire and Manchester quickly followed suit. Accompanying its publication were more reports from unhappy settlers; together, they reinforced the view of a colony and emigration scheme in crisis. Alongside it in *The People* was a letter from former potter James Thomas, who had emigrated to Pottersville two years earlier. He could not make out the 'object' of the Society, he wrote, 'except it be to send people to this country to be starved to death'.[110] With the *Glasgow Saturday Post*'s copy were two letters from a local man, identified only by his initials, who had arrived at the lands the previous autumn. After initial positive impressions, he was soon damning the Society as 'one of the greatest impositions ever practised upon the English people'.[111] A week later the *Manchester Examiner & Times* printed Martin Ellison's letter, dated 13 May, in which he denounced Twigg's management of the colony's affairs.[112] The following Saturday it published, along with the memorial, a third account of the *Guy Mannering* party's arrival in April. Richard Tinker covered much the same ground as his fellow passengers, including the meeting with Alexander Evans. He also revealed the extent of Twigg's borrowing, including him asking his travelling companions for money to purchase tools. 'I consider the society like a candle lit at both ends, and it is burning near the middle now; it will soon be at an end', Tinker wrote from Milwaukie to where he had decamped after a final unsatisfactory meeting with the agent.[113] Bold Hilton, who saw him there, described him as 'wandering about, not knowing what to do or where to go'.[114] The Tinkers would soon return to Manchester.

Another Saturday brought another exposé of the Society's failings in the 'Emigrant's Column' of the *Manchester Examiner & Times*. A friend of a Liverpool man named John Wood had submitted a letter from him as evidence 'of either the pure ignorance, or something worse, of Evans and his coadjutors'. Wood's narrative followed the usual pattern. Reaching Milwaukie, he met eight or ten families returning from the colony. They reported a desperate situation with settlers 'swearing vengeance against Twigg, Evans, and Robinson, for deluding them into a barren wilderness'. Like many of the letters published in this period, the conditions described were those pertaining to several months earlier, although readers probably failed to make the distinction. Especially eye-catching was Wood's report of a meeting with George W. Robinson, 'a talking sort of cove from London'. The Society's agent was at a loss to explain how things had come to such a pass: 'He invited me to go into the store and sit down. I went in, and found it one of the most wretched huts you can well conceive, and full of members all inquiring what was to be done, for they were starving for want of bread.'

Wood also met another Liverpool emigrant, Richard Noble, who had arrived the previous year with his family. Although successful in the ballot, he 'had been provided for just in the same manner as the rest of the unfortunate members, who could not get away from this inhospitable place'.[115]

The effect of these negative reports on members' morale in Britain was apparent before the receipt of the settlers' memorial. On 10 August the *Examiner* printed a three-page submission from the president of the Kirkcaldy branch, Thomas Ellis, based upon letters sent from the colony by members William Colville and Francis Duffy. Colville's letter described the impoverished and depressed state of settlers struggling to survive and receiving only tea, flour and salt pork for their labour. Duffy, writing two weeks later, reported being rebuffed by Twigg, who said 'he had no land to give him or any other person at the present time'. Emancipation Ferry was a misnomer; 'Desolation Ferry' was a more appropriate name for the colony's headquarters, Duffy wrote. Summing up, Ellis announced that the branch did not believe Twigg's statement about the amount of property the Society held and would withhold its contributions until it could ascertain the truth or replace the agent. He appealed to other branches to help bring about 'an investigation into these circumstances'.[116] In reply, the paper's editor conceded the privations due to lack of funds, but pointed to the period before last winter when 'the stores were well stocked, and satisfaction prevailed'. The Society expected settlers in any case to procure their own provisions. He enclosed a letter from a Londoner, Charles W. Scott, who had gone to Wisconsin the previous year. Scott was scathing about those arriving at the lands who 'made no calculation as to what sort of place they were coming to'. He advised prospective emigrants to save all they could, and to come out early in the year to make provision for the winter. Summing up, Evans again showed his frustration at the Society's inability to raise money and at the earlier failure to halt the flow of land certificates. The result was 'the confusion that now prevails at Emancipation Ferry'. He also confessed that the Society had exhausted most of its resources on meeting two bills for goods purchased from a Galena, Illinois merchant, Myers F. Truett.[117] The account, totalling £337 10s, had been paid at the end of July only with the help of loans from the Potteries' branches and the hollow-ware pressers.[118]

September brought no respite. On 4 September the *Manchester Guardian* published an extract from an undated letter by a Macclesfield member, Joseph Grimshaw, which had originally appeared in his local paper. Newspapers in Huddersfield, Dundee and Newcastle-upon-Tyne reprinted the extract over the next two weeks. Grimshaw had gone to America with the *Marmion* party in the spring of 1849. Impressed with the beauty of the Wisconsin prairie, he found Pottersville to be 'the most distressed looking place' he had seen since leaving New York. He also discovered that the lands on the Fox River, which the *Examiner* had represented as having been 'paid for', still belonged to its Native inhabitants, who were reluctant to vacate them. After four days Grimshaw returned to Milwaukie. Members who followed him brought the chilling news that one man had ventured too far into the woods and 'when the Indians called him to keep back, which he did not understand', they shot him dead. For the *Guardian*, the account confirmed its belief that any attempt – and it included O'Connor's land plan – 'to convert bodies of men, taken indiscriminately from manufacturing pursuits, into cultivators of the soil' was bound to fail. The paper hoped that the working classes who had been duped into considering emigration 'to some reported paradise in the new world' would take heed of Grimshaw's letter 'and content themselves with earning a living at home'.[119]

More negative publicity followed. On 7 September John Oliphant returned to the fray in a long communication in the *Fifeshire Advertiser*. The young Scotsman had been engaged in a protracted argument with George W. Robinson, the details of which must have tried the patience of even the most partisan. Although the paper wished to bring 'this ugly affair' to a close, it was obvious whose side it favoured. Oliphant was a talented and energetic man, whose character had been misrepresented by the Society's officials: 'As to their society being enrolled by an Act of Parliament, we need scarcely say it is a barefaced falsehood, assert it who will.'[120] The following week the Society received another blow in the form of a letter to *The Staffordshire Advertiser* from a Hanley potter, James Nixon. The Nixons' experience of emigration had proved costly; James's wife Mary and 5-year-old son had died on the sea crossing to New Orleans. Arriving at Fort Winnebago on 20 March, the rest of the party, including James' older brother Enoch and family, found conditions a long way from what they anticipated. Members they met reported the same unmitigated hardship. An 'immense number' had followed Twigg, Nixon wrote, 'but they had all gone back after they had seen the state of affairs'. Twigg advised Nixon himself to do the same. After falling out with his brother, James and his two children took lodgings with John and Jane Scott. Occasional employment, including 'whitewashing and plastering about the Fort', furnished the means to survive. So bad have things become, 'the Yankees about here' call the Society 'a regular swindle' and talk of petitioning Congress to intervene', he wrote. 'Let people come out who can get here with a little; but let them come independent of any society'.[121] The Nixons soon returned to England. By June 1851 James was living with his two children at his brother-in-law's house in New Street, Hanley and working as a 'pottery presser'.

Evans responded by insisting that nothing Nixon had written indicated that the Society had done him 'as an emigrant, the slightest wrong'. He enclosed another letter from Philip Pointon, now content in neighbouring

1850–1: Crisis and decline

Sauk County. If we are to believe Pointon's statements, he wrote, 'Mr. Nixon has been guided to one of the most prosperous and healthy quarters of the known world'. Pointon's letter was indeed hugely positive about the fast-growing community in which the family had settled. However, the more the former Hanley potter enthused about their new life, about the freedoms and opportunities it afforded them, the more apparent it was how redundant the Society had become.[122] By the late summer of 1850 few members were arriving at the colony; and those who did were invariably dissatisfied with what they found. The family are all in good health 'but not in the best of spirits', wrote Richard Ellis on 1 August. The Ellises had reached the lands several days earlier after a seven-week journey from Lanark, expecting to find '5 acres in crop, and a yoke of oxen, but there was none for me nor a balloted member that came up'. Seeking out Twigg, they discovered that he had gone to Pottersville to resolve a dispute with the settlers, 'also to get some money from England, but returned as usual, disappointed'. On his return he informed the Scotsman 'that he did not know what to do with me, that when he was in England, there was a resolution passed by the delegates, that there was to be no balloted members sent out till they sent £800, and indeed of that he had only got £18'. Over the coming days Ellis and his friend James Scoular explored the woods in search of land. Rejecting the offer of a quarter-section abandoned by a balloted member through lack of water, they came upon a claim 'with a running spring, a house, and ten acres of ground broken, which we purchased for $35'. The site was a great relief after the 'miserable place', an old store, where they had been lodging. Grace, Richard's wife, was 'bearing it well, considering the hardships she has had to endure'. As for the Society that organised their migration, he put 'no dependence' on its support. 'Were I at home I would keep my sixpences in my pocket, and I hope you will do the same', he advised branch members.[123]

On 21 September the Society's executive announced the holding of a special delegate conference in Hanley on 11 November. It had come to this decision because of 'the position in which the society is now placed, and the absolute necessity for a clear understanding as to future operations'.[124] The following week it changed its mind. The reason given was that the branches – or agencies, as they were now also known – had not been consulted (they were required to pay their own delegates' expenses). The *Examiner* also published the latest Society accounts. Covering the period 20 May to 8 September, they revealed income down by a third since March. The number of reporting branches was now sixty-two, seven fewer than six months earlier. London again dominated, with three of the top five in the contributing list; Hanley's 'William Evans' branch, in seventh place overall, led the way in the Potteries.[125]

Behind this muddle lay a wider debate about the Society's future progress and the ability of the present organisation and leadership to achieve the reforms and raise the funds necessary to secure it. Branches across the country were dismayed by reports of the colony's problems and keen to identify those responsible for causing them. At their half-yearly meeting Swindon members proposed that the estate steward establish how many colonists had settled on the land and how many had left, the results to be reported back to the Society. 'We have two members gone out this summer, and it shall not be our fault if they should want', the branch agent wrote.[126] Talk of investigations was now rife. On 12 September Paisley members petitioned the editors of the Fort Winnebago *River Times* to urge settlers to call a meeting to examine the colony's running. A 'crisis has arrived in the fate of the Society', their letter read, 'and the question now is, whether it shall exist much longer or not, and also to come to the conclusion that if the conduct of Mr. Twigg and the other officers be culpable as is reported, it is high time that they be dismissed and others appointed.'[127] Taking the lead at home were the well-organised Londoners. 'It is with deep regret that I write to you respecting the general dissatisfaction which unhappily prevails among the London members', the Pimlico agent advised Evans.[128] On 4 September the London District Committee, made up of representatives from all capital groups, initiated an investigation into the Society's affairs.[129] Two weeks later it submitted a list of thirty-five questions to George W. Robinson together with a request for all information regarding the land. These ranged from the quality of the soil, the number of arrived and departed members and the site and progress of the grist mill, to inquiries about individual transactions and debts.[130] The Committee's secretary, a 29-year-old Hackney clerk, J. A. Hay, also addressed members directly. Hay objected to the narrow legalism that threatened the Society's future, and claimed that the London members and others around the country 'would not have joined this society if they had been told at first that they must be governed by six or seven men, chosen by a handful of members residing in the Potteries'. Detailing the executive's 'vacillating and uncertain' conduct, Hay challenged members everywhere to begin the renewal by creating a truly representative body in which the will of the majority would prevail. We need 'firmer union than ever', he told them.[131]

Hay's rallying call brought a predictable response from William Evans. On 28 September the *Examiner* issued a statement outlining 'the origin and progress of the executive management of our cause'. On who should run the Society, it was unequivocal: 'In our opinion, better men could not be found than those who might be selected amongst the Staffordshire Potters.' The article acknowledged Hay's devotion to the Society, but gave short shrift to the claim that a transfer of management to London would bring the hoped-for revival: 'O! how sincerely do we wish that this desideratum could be proved! It would be giving new life to one who has made the success of the movement almost a part of his existence.'[132] The following Saturday Evans shed the flimsy mask of anonymity and addressed members personally in a letter headed 'Plain Words for a Puzzled Society'. He admitted the difficulty of making plans 'the joint operations of which may be thousands of miles apart', and recommended that the Society obtain a special charter from the state of Wisconsin giving a power of attorney to the 'legalized association'. This would solve a number of problems, including the Society's lack of legal control over the colonists. It would also create an identity of interest across the Atlantic divide. Protecting the interests of all sections of the Society was especially important regarding the new estate. In the clearest statement yet of the Society's tenuous hold on Twigg's 50,000 acres, he reaffirmed that the land 'is not purchased, nor even pre-empted. It is only "squat" upon, and has yet to be surveyed, and then brought into the market for sale and pre-emption.' Never one to duck an explanatory challenge, Evans argued that while 'principle and practice' gave squatters no legal claim over land they had improved, they did have 'a moral and customary claim, which is almost as binding as law itself'. Once the allotments had been surveyed and the day of sale advertised, colonists would proceed 'in a body' to the land office at Green Bay. Before business commenced, they would 'surround the building', guaranteeing that no one entered without a valid squatter's claim: 'This is quite a common transaction throughout the whole states, and has the full sanction and support of public opinion, which, in point of fact, is the law in that great Republic.'[133]

Evans was mistaken if he believed such reassurances would satisfy the critics. A high level of distrust now permeated the Society. In the first week of October the 'Land of Liberty' agency in Manchester demanded an inquiry into the whereabouts of the Pottersville deeds. A local balloted member named Robinson had written to his brother claiming that Thomas Twigg had mortgaged them to a Mr Stimpson of Milwaukie.[134] Calls for reform intensified. The London District Committee now formally proposed moving the administration to the capital. Members would choose a managing committee to conduct the Society's business with 'a nominal Executive' being retained in the Potteries. In response, the executive offered a compromise; it would move to London for twelve months, followed in rotation by Glasgow, Manchester and Birmingham, before returning to Staffordshire 'or elsewhere, as the Agencies may direct' in January 1855. However, the Society's printing establishment must remain in the Potteries and the *Examiner* 'printed and published as heretofore'.[135]

As the argument over the Society's future direction rumbled on, the situation in America worsened. Reporting to Evans from Fort Winnebago on

20 August, George W. Robinson laid bare the financial straits in which the colony found itself. He was not surprised 'at bad letters being sent home, or bad statements from parties who may return … Here we are now without a cent; our harvest, in consequence of adverse weather, is a comparative failure, and provisions at a famine price'. Robinson was clear that the Society had advanced too much money to men 'who have come up only to return back directly, if they come here at all, and who probably would never have left their homes but for it'. Twigg's solution, which Robinson supported, was to require cash for all future purchases and payments. Leave the letters in the newspapers alone, he told Evans, and direct all your attention 'to the restoration of the society'.[136] Two weeks later the *Examiner* published the latest report of the colony's auditors. It confirmed Robinson's account. The only glimmer of light was that the debts owed to the Society amounted to three times its liabilities. Although 'the workings of our society are deplorable enough', they concluded, with more honesty from members and 'a little rallying and patience the final success is quite possible if not certain'.[137]

Copies of the *Examiner* for the period mid-October to mid-December have not survived, so it is unclear whether Evans heeded Robinson's advice. Events in Wisconsin soon rendered the question superfluous. At the end of October Pottersville settlers called a meeting for 18 November at the Franklin House in Fort Winnebago. They were responding to the Paisley request for an investigation into the colony's management. Invited to attend were 'our suffering countrymen' at Emancipation Ferry as well as others from the area. The date and location were carefully chosen; later that day 700 acres of the Pottersville estate – 'our land, our improvements, our all' – were due to be sold at auction for payment of a debt of $2,000 incurred by Thomas Twigg on the Society's behalf. The note, to a local storeowner, Michael Keegan, had matured on 4 October; anticipating default, the previous day Keegan had filed against Twigg 'as agent of the Potters' Emigration Society' in the Columbia County Court. The settlers explained that they had retained a local law firm, Lewis & Cook, to represent them. Claiming that they were defending the interests of the Society, not just their own, they urged its leaders to 'grant such pecuniary aid, documents, and advice' as would secure to its members 'those rights in the property of the Society that have been purchased at great expense, in money and personal sacrifice, which rights the Society is in duty bound to protect and maintain'.[138]

The list of Pottersville signatories revealed familiar names from the Society's pioneer past. It included the three land officers, Hamlet Copeland, James Hammond and John Sawyer, and seven members of the original eight-man Estate Committee, among them Twigg's arch-critics Enoch Pickering and Samuel Fox.[139] Elected as the group's president was the former Tunstall flat-ware presser Henry Dooley, with Fox as agent. In an attached notice the latter made it clear that the sale of the land, which had been seized by the county sheriff, *'will be contested*, whoever may be the purchaser thereof'. Shortly afterwards the settlers obtained an injunction to halt the sale. A court of equity would now resolve the matter. Reporting the stay in a letter to members in Britain, Dooley claimed that the legal action had cost them a great deal of time, labour and expense, with much of the latter, nearly $100, borne by Samuel Fox. Defending the Society's property had taken every cent he possessed, Fox told members.[140] The meeting to discuss the crisis actually convened a week earlier than planned, on 10 November. Settlers from both estates attended; a Scotsman, Jonathan Staley, who had arrived in 1849, chaired it. He began by reading the Paisley branch letter calling for an investigation into the colony's affairs. The mood of those attending was angry, and it was clear whom they blamed most. Condemning Twigg's conduct 'as erroneous, neglectful and criminal in nature', they demanded his dismissal and the appointment of 'a more efficient' agent. A motion from Fox, supported by Dooley, proposed that the offer to sell the Pottersville estate was 'nothing more than a swindling deception effected by Twigg and others'. It passed with a unanimous vote. Fox, it will be recalled, had been a close ally of James Scott, whose continuing influence was demonstrated by the meeting awarding him its 'full confidence' and deprecating the 'false and malicious' censorship he had suffered at home.[141]

Staley described the Fort Winnebago meeting as 'numerously attended'; in fact, we have no idea how many were present. Many members on the new lands – Martin Ellison is an example – seemed unmoved by the action; there was also widespread suspicion of Fox and Scott. As their dependence on the Society weakened, settlers had less incentive to fight for its survival. It was a different matter for the Pottersville residents. The pioneers of the potters' emigration scheme, they had a strong material and emotional investment in its continuance. However, the colony's future was no longer theirs to shape. On the last day of October the Society in England received a bill for $500 from the Galena merchant M. F. Truett. If they neglected to honour it, Twigg warned the executive, 'you will deprive us of one of the best friends in the states, and the most accommodating house'. Writing to Evans, Truett explained that he had forwarded the account with the instruction that there was no need for immediate payment. He was aware of the Society's 'embarrassments' – caused, he believed, by individuals who coveted its potentially 'very valuable' lands – and would even consider payment by instalments. His consideration was to no avail; meeting on 9 December, the executive resolved that Truett's bill was 'beyond the means of, and consequently cannot be honoured by the society'.[142]

The Society was now in a parlous state. Two copies of the *Examiner* have survived for December 1850; the second, published just after Christmas, was the paper's final appearance. Most of the 14 December edition comprised a five-page article by William Evans attacking the anti-Catholic campaign of the Rev. P. B. Ellis of St Paul's, Burslem, suggesting that his priorities had already changed.[143] It also contained the latest auditors' accounts, dated 3 November, which confirmed the colony's de facto insolvency. 'We can only state that matters are in the same deplorable state as when we wrote last', they noted; 'we still have no funds, and many to whom the society are indebted, are in great distress'. The only reported grassroots activity was a notice from Sheffield members resolving 'to stand by the society, and to continue paying so long as the society will receive the money'. They wished Evans 'to make all the exertion that lays in his power to keep the society together'. There was also the last published correspondence from the colony. Letters home played a key role in the Society's history, and in recent months were largely responsible for creating the perception, true or false, of maladministration and working-class betrayal. Elizabeth Watson travelled to America in the spring of 1849 aboard the *Marmion* with her husband William and 11-year-old son. William was a shoemaker by trade. In her letter, dated 29 September, she reported favourably on life in Wisconsin. The Yorkshire family had claimed 160 acres of land. 'We have saved £40, which will pay for our land when it comes to market, so we intend been [*sic*] right in that respect', she wrote. Above all, she preached the value of self-reliance: 'I would say do not come to depend on the society for any thing – bring a friend in your pocket.' She described the different paths taken by emigrants arriving at the land and reported that local employment prospects were favourable. She could 'now do a good many sorts of work myself'. There was one caveat; this was 'a fine country; I like it very well, but we have no religion of any kind yet; this is the worst of all, but I am living in hopes there will be.'[144]

Save for a note advising London members to give 'serious consideration' to the auditors' documents, editorial comment on the reports from Wisconsin was absent from the 14 December *Examiner*. Two weeks later it became clear why. On 3 December 200 members gathered in the capital to endorse the London takeover of the Potters' Emigration Society. According to J. A. Hay's report, those attending were 'much daunted by the great accumulation of bad news' but 'firm in their purpose of trying if something could not be done with the society'. The following week the meeting reconvened at the Skinner's Arms, Bishopsgate, where members elected a new executive committee. Charles Steward, a silversmith, became the Society's new president; the tireless Hay continued to act as secretary. The hours and days to follow saw a bustle of activity as the new regime attempted to extract as much documentation as possible from the Potteries leadership. To this end, it invited William Evans to London for a meeting on the following Tuesday.

The editor responded that the notice was too short and proposed instead coming in 'about a fortnight'. It seems unlikely he complied.

The committee's first priority was the Pottersville estate; 500 acres were already sold, it reported on 11 December, and securing the remaining 940 'would be something to commence on'. Reassuring members that it would do everything it could to salvage their investment, 'so scandalously misused by our officials abroad', it pleaded for patience while the legal proceedings took their course. The secretary would write to Evans 'instructing him' to empower the Columbia County lawyers to create a deed conveying the remaining land title to the trustees of a renamed Society, if necessary forcing Twigg to sign it 'by process of law'. They would then record the deed in the land office and forward it to England for completion. The sooner this was done, the better; should the current trustees die, the estate would pass to their children, with the Society unable to touch a single acre. If protecting the Society's assets was one part of the executive's plan, devising a future settlement strategy was the other. In an unexpected move, it sought the advice of a 'Mr Thomson', whom the American Ambassador had recommended. Born in Kendal, Edward H. Thomson came to the United States aged three. Arriving in Michigan in 1837, he established a successful law practice and gained election to the state senate. In April 1849 he was appointed the state's emigration agent, and shortly thereafter produced *The Emigrant's Guide to the State of Michigan*, a forty-seven page pamphlet that included a German translation.[145] His advice to the Society's new executive was unsurprising: 'Mr. Thomson recommends Michigan State because it is considerable nearer than Wisconsin' and 'in a more forward state as regards settlement, containing now upwards of 700,000 inhabitants and the land can be bought very near markets at government price'.

By the beginning of March 1851 *The Staffordshire Advertiser* was referring to the 'late' Potters' Emigration Society. London members, it reported, had issued an address setting out the executive's 'disastrous' mismanagement of the Society's affairs. At a meeting on 8 January at the King's Head in Old Change, they endorsed the setting-up of a new society 'on a sure commercial basis'. Besides enabling members to emigrate 'in community', profits from the renamed National Emigration Society would be divided four ways: to buy in the 'scrip' of the old Society; to create a reserve fund 'for the relief of widows, orphans, and necessitous cases' in England and America; to lay out towns and villages on the land; and to provide a bonus fund for surviving shareholders. Londoners hoped to revive the spirit of the original movement, correct the errors of their predecessors and provide restitution to those who had suffered losses through incompetence and wrongdoing.[146] The only collective response to their call came from Manchester. In early January members there resolved to form themselves into the 'United

Perseverance' agency, or, if the new organisation failed, to establish a 'distinct' emigrant society. The Manchester agent, John Cowton, called on members nationwide to make 'another noble attempt to place themselves in comfortable circumstances in the free and fertile lands of America'. He pointed to a recent speech at the city's Town Hall by the American ambassador, who reported that his country's population was increasing at the rate of nearly 1 million a year.[147] Cowton admitted that economic conditions had changed and that 'a temporary gleam of sunshine rests on this tax and class ridden country', but warned members not to be deluded by 'the present fallacious appearances of prosperity'. Let the London executive 'show us a reasonable project, and depend upon it, many warm hearts and true hands, will rally round them'. The rescue failed to materialise. After several weeks' reported activity, the National Emigration Society disappears without trace from the surviving record.[148]

Notes

1 *The People*, vol. 2, no. 82, p. 233.
2 *The People*, vol. 1, no. 31, p. 247.
3 The most detailed account, aside from his own, of Barker's 1849 American visit is Brook, 'Joseph Barker and *The People*', pp. 368–74.
4 PEEA, vol. 9, no. 76 (15 December 1849).
5 *The People*, vol. 2, no. 84, p. 254.
6 Brook, 'Joseph Barker and *The People*', p. 351.
7 *The People*, vol. 2, no. 86, pp. 269–71. Barker was not alone in his opposition to long-distance projects. See *Sidney's Emigrant's Journal and Traveller's Magazine*, new series, 1:1 (1849), 12–13, which claims that no scheme with headquarters in England had 'successfully colonized an estate on the other side of the ocean ... The Potters' Emigration Society is said to be successful, but we strongly doubt it ... we have never been able to find that any of the settlers have paid back any part of their debts to the parent association.'
8 *Dundee, Perth and Cupar Advertiser*, 8 January 1850.
9 PEEA, vol. 9, no. 82 (26 January 1850).
10 *Hull Advertiser and Exchange Gazette*, 18 January 1850.
11 PEEA, vol. 9, no. 84 (9 February 1850).
12 *Manchester Examiner & Times*, 26 January 1850.
13 *The People*, vol. 2, no. 90, pp. 301–2.
14 PEEA, vol. 9, no. 87 (2 March 1850), no. 88 (9 March 1850).
15 *The People*, vol. 2, no. 101, p. 391.
16 *Northern Star and National Trades' Journal*, 10 November 1849.
17 *The People*, vol. 2, no. 89, p. 295. See also *The People*, vol. 2, no. 85, p. 263.
18 PEEA, vol. 9, no. 85 (16 February 1850).
19 *The People*, vol. 2, no. 90, p. 302.

20 *The People*, vol. 2, no. 93, p. 328.
21 *PEEA*, vol. 9, no. 85 (16 February 1850).
22 *The People*, vol. 2, no. 92, pp. 318–19. The £1 2s 6d included 1s for rules, certificate and membership card.
23 *Morning Chronicle*, 5 February 1850.
24 For second-quarter 1849 totals, see *The People*, vol. 2, no. 85, p. 263, quoting *PEEA*, vol. 9, no. 53 (7 July 1849). Final-quarter accounts are reported in *PEEA*, vol. 9, no. 78 (29 December 1849). Third-quarter accounts are missing, but Reach reported that 'branch receipts' for the period 8 June 1840 to 8 September 1849 were 'about £2871'. The '1840' is clearly a typographical error for, most likely, 1848. If so, third-quarter totals would be c.£616. Accounts for the period December 1849–March 1850 are in *PEEA*, vol. 9, no. 92 (6 April 1850).
25 *PEEA*, vol. 9, no. 78 (29 December 1849).
26 *PEEA*, vol. 9, no. 85 (16 February 1850). The bound copies comprised volumes 1–3 of the *Examiner*, together with Evans, *Art and History of the Potting Business*.
27 *PEEA*, vol. 9, no. 91 (30 March 1850).
28 Watkin wrote that he had not received a promised £60 draft; it arrived the following day.
29 *PEEA*, vol. 9, no. 85 (16 February 1850). The winter was less harsh than Watkin feared, but was 'increasing fast in severity', according to a subsequent letter. *PEEA*, vol. 9, no. 87 (2 March 1850).
30 *PEEA*, vol. 9, no. 87 (2 March 1850). Brentnall's name appears in many spellings, including Brantnell, Brintall and Brentel.
31 *PEEA*, vol. 9, no. 71 (16 November 1849).
32 *PEEA*, vol. 9, no. 88 (9 March 1850).
33 *PEEA*, vol. 9, no. 84 (9 February 1850). On Owen and labour notes, see Harrison, *Robert Owen and the Owenites in Britain and America*, pp. 202–7; and for the wider radical context, see Robert C. Hauhart, '19th-Century Labor Money Schemes, Self-Realization through Labor, and the Utopian Idea', *World Review of Political Economy* 3:2 (2012), 177–90.
34 *PEEA*, vol. 9, no. 88 (9 March 1850).
35 *PEEA*, vol. 9, no. 91 (30 March 1850).
36 *Ibid*.
37 *PEEA*, vol. 9, no. 84 (9 February 1850).
38 *Glasgow Examiner*, 13 April 1850.
39 *PEEA*, vol. 9, no. 78 (29 December 1849), no. 92 (6 April 1850).
40 Warburton, *The History of Trade Union Organisation*, p. 138.
41 Owen, *The Staffordshire Potter*, p. 105.
42 *The Staffordshire Advertiser*, 17 November 1849.
43 *The Staffordshire Advertiser*, 19 January 1850.
44 *PEEA*, vol. 9, no. 66 (6 October 1849).
45 *PEEA*, vol. 9, no. 69 (27 October 1849). The winner of the ballot was called Duncalf. It is unknown what he did with the prize.

46 *Ibid.*
47 *PEEA*, vol. 9, no. 92 (6 April 1850).
48 *PEEA*, vol. 9, no. 96 (4 May 1850).
49 *PEEA*, vol. 9, no. 95 (27 April 1850).
50 *PEEA*, vol. 9, no. 96 (4 May 1850). The flat-ware pressers' list of 'followers' is not extant.
51 *Dublin Evening Mail*, 16 January 1850. The New York-built vessel, launched the previous year, came to a tragic end on New Year's Eve of 1865 when it was wrecked off the west coast of Scotland with the loss of seventeen lives.
52 *PEEA*, vol. 9, no. 87 (2 March 1850).
53 *PEEA*, vol. 9, no. 88 (9 March 1850). Robinson's letter is dated 28 February.
54 *PEEA*, vol. 9, no. 85 (16 February 1850).
55 *Manchester Examiner & Times*, 13 July 1850.
56 *History of Northern Wisconsin*, p. 377. Turner's biography is included as a result of his subsequent career in Mauston, Wisconsin, to where he moved in 1854. His early life story should be taken with a pinch of salt; a law student in the office of Sir Richard Thornton, at 20 he 'attached himself to the Society of Chartists in Blackfriars, London and was elected to its council. He was subsequently connected with what was known as the Potters' Emigration Society.' Acting in its interest, he went to Paris, where he was caught up in the 1848 revolution, suffering 'a saber cut across the face at the hands of a careless trooper'. He returned to England on the same ship as the deposed Louis Phillippe. In London 'he found the political situation such that his blackened and disfigured face was very much to his advantage in concealing his identity. Being assured that the choice lay between transportation, and emigration, he chose the latter and made his way to the United States, being commissioned to act as book-keeper and store-keeper for the society.' The biography dates his arrival at Fort Winnebago as 4 May 1848, twelve months too early.
57 *PEEA*, vol. 9, no. 91 (30 March 1850).
58 *The People*, vol. 2, no. 89, p. 294. The letter was dated 16 November 1849.
59 See Chapter 5.
60 The writer was Charles W. Scott from London. *PEEA*, vol. 9, no. 90 (23 March 1850).
61 *Ibid.*
62 *PEEA*, vol. 9, no. 91 (30 March 1850).
63 *PEEA*, vol. 9, no. 82 (26 January 1850); Martin Ellison's diary, 30 November, 1 December 1850.
64 Construction of the fifty-eight-mile plank road from Milwaukie to Watertown commenced in 1848 and was completed in 1853.
65 *Northern Star and National Trades' Journal*, 23 February 1850.
66 *PEEA*, vol. 9, no. 87 (2 March 1850).
67 *PEEA*, vol. 9, no. 91 (30 March 1850).
68 *PEEA*, vol. 9, no. 88 (9 March 1850).
69 *PEEA*, vol. 9, no. 90 (23 March 1850).
70 *PEEA*, vol. 9, no. 92 (6 April 1850). Rudman reached Wisconsin on 3 November.
71 *PEEA*, vol. 9, no. 89 (16 March 1850).

72 *PEEA*, vol. 9, no. 91 (30 March 1850).
73 *PEEA*, vol. 9, no. 90 (23 March 1850). Iron was the item in shortest supply.
74 *PEEA*, vol. 9, no. 95 (27 April 1850). Earlier letters from Lodge and Ayrey indicate that the original plan was for the families to travel to Wisconsin with Twigg in the spring. Lodge indicated that he had worked all summer, 'and am going to work all winter, to pay back what it will cost him'. Ayrey wrote that the Oldham men would pay for the families' passage out 'in labour; there is plenty of work at the Grist Mill'. *PEEA*, vol. 9, no. 87 (2 March 1850).
75 *PEEA*, vol. 9, no. 85 (16 February 1850).
76 *Northern Star and National Trades' Journal*, 23 March 1850.
77 *Northern Star and National Trades' Journal*, 13 April 1850.
78 *Northern Star and National Trades' Journal*, 4 May 1850.
79 Chase, *Chartism: A New History*, p. 336.
80 *Manchester Examiner & Times*, 1 June 1850.
81 *The Staffordshire Advertiser*, 29 June 1850.
82 *Manchester Examiner & Times*, 29 June 1850. Newson was a stonemason. See his critical letter, dated Baraboo, 20 January 1850, in *The People*, vol. 2, no. 101, p. 391. For a contemporary portrait (May 1847) of Baraboo, see Wilbur S. Shepperson (ed.), ' "The Natives Are Grasping;" A Welshman's Letter from Wisconsin', *Wisconsin Magazine of History* 43:2 (1959–60), 129–32.
83 *Manchester Examiner & Times*, 13 July 1850.
84 *Montrose Standard and Angus & Mearns Register*, 19 July 1850. Authorship of the unsigned letter comes from internal evidence.
85 *Fifeshire Advertiser*, 2, 16 March 1850; *PEEA*, vol. 9, no. 90 (23 March 1850).
86 *Nottingham Review and General Advertiser for the Midland Counties*, 19 July 1850.
87 *The Staffordshire Advertiser*, 6 July 1850.
88 *PEEA*, vol. 10, no. 5 (3 August 1850).
89 *Standard of Freedom*, 27 July 1850. The article, including the editor's introduction, was reprinted in the *Northern Star and National Trades' Journal*, 3 August 1850. The Bucks arrived in New York aboard the *Mississippi* on 20 April.
90 *PEEA*, vol. 10, no. 7 (17 August 1850). See *Standard of Freedom*, 24 August 1850, for a reply to Evans on Buck's behalf.
91 *Ibid.*
92 The missing run covers the period 11 May–20 July 1850.
93 Martin Ellison's diary, 1 May 1850.
94 *Manchester Examiner & Times*, 17 August 1850.
95 Martin Ellison's diary, 29 June 1850.
96 *River Times* (Fort Winnebago), 4 July 1850.
97 It has not been possible to identify the origins of the fifth member, John S. Campbell.
98 See United States Army, Fort Winnebago Ledger, 1831–51. Facsimile at http://content.wisconsinhistory.org/u?/tp,54450 (last accessed 26 February 2023).
99 1850 Federal Population Census: Wisconsin. The highly transient population makes it difficult to establish firm population figures for individual localities.

100 *River Times* (Fort Winnebago), 4 July 1850. For the paper's founding, see *The History of Columbia County, Wisconsin*, pp. 531–2.
101 On settlement, immigration and mobility in the area, see Joyce McKay, *An Historical Architectural and Historical Survey of the City of Portage, Columbia County, Wisconsin* (Portage, WI: Portage Area Chamber of Commerce, 1993), pp. 71–84.
102 Thomas and Jane Atkinson to Thomas Broomfield, Peoria, Illinois, 8 March 1850, West Sussex County Record Office, Lewes.
103 Martin Ellison's diary, 23 May, 8 June, 9 July, 18 September 1850.
104 Entry for James Bennett, www.findagrave.com/memorial/137321468 (last accessed 16 May 2023).
105 *The Staffordshire Advertiser*, 22 October 1842.
106 Identification of balloted members comes from *PEEA*, vol. 10, no. 12 (21 September 1850).
107 *The Staffordshire Advertiser*, 29 June 1850.
108 *The Staffordshire Advertiser*, 14 September 1850.
109 *Wisconsin State Register*, 15 March 1884.
110 *The People*, vol. 3, no. 124, pp. 157–8.
111 *Glasgow Saturday Post and Paisley and Renfrewshire Reformer*, 10 August 1850. The letters were dated 20 May, 10 June 1850. The writer's initials were TJ or JT. The memorial also appeared in *Nottingham Review and General Advertiser for the Midland Counties*, 9 August 1850; *Glasgow Chronicle*, 14 August 1850; *Northern Star and National Trades' Journal*, 17 August 1850; *The Staffordshire Advertiser*, 17 August 1850; and *Manchester Examiner & Times*, 24 August 1850.
112 *Manchester Examiner & Times*, 17 August 1850.
113 *Manchester Examiner & Times*, 24 August 1850.
114 *Manchester Examiner & Times*, 13 July 1850.
115 *Manchester Examiner & Times*, 31 August 1850. See *The People*, vol. 3, no. 111–12, pp. 62–83 for another damning report of Wood's stay at the colony.
116 *PEEA*, vol. 10, no. 6 (10 August 1850).
117 *Ibid*.
118 *PEEA*, vol. 10, no. 4 (27 July 1850). The Truetts achieved a lasting place in history when in 1838 Myers's brother Henry was acquitted of murder. It was Abraham Lincoln's first murder case as a defence attorney.
119 *Manchester Guardian*, 4 September 1850; *Huddersfield Chronicle*, 7 September 1850; *Dundee, Perth and Cupar Advertiser*, 10 September 1850; *Newcastle Courant*, 13 September 1850.
120 *Fifeshire Advertiser*, 7 September 1850.
121 *The Staffordshire Advertiser*, 14 September 1850.
122 *The Staffordshire Advertiser*, 5 October 1850.
123 *Glasgow Saturday Post and Paisley and Renfrew Reformer*, 21 September 1850.
124 *PEEA*, vol. 10, no. 11 (14 September 1850).
125 *PEEA*, vol. 10, no. 12 (21 September 1850).

126 *PEEA*, vol. 10, no. 12 (21 September 1850). See also the report from Halifax, *PEEA*, vol. 10, no. 11 (14 September 1850).
127 *River Times* (Fort Winnebago), 14 October 1850.
128 *PEEA*, vol. 10, no. 11 (14 September 1850).
129 *PEEA*, vol. 10, no. 12 (21 September 1850).
130 *PEEA*, vol. 10, no. 16 (19 October 1850).
131 *PEEA*, vol. 10, no. 13 (28 September 1850).
132 *Ibid.*
133 *PEEA*, vol. 10, no. 14 (5 October 1850).
134 The story about the deeds no longer being in England refused to die. See Samuel Fox's claim that Peter Watkin held them at Pottersville 'to accommodate himself and Twigg in their selfish and urgent object'. *River Times* (Fort Winnebago), 19 December 1850. No evidence substantiates it.
135 *PEEA*, vol. 10, no. 16 (19 October 1850). Not all critics agreed on the way forward. 'We know that a false step has been taken in allowing Twigg to do as he has done; but shifting the seat of government, and choosing fresh officers will not undo what has been done', wrote the Halifax agent. *Ibid.*
136 *PEEA*, vol. 10, no. 14 (5 October 1850).
137 *PEEA*, vol. 10, no. 16 (19 October 1850).
138 *River Times* (Fort Winnebago), 4 November 1850.
139 The remaining member was George Summerfield. He had possibly moved to St Louis by the summer of 1850.
140 *River Times* (Fort Winnebago), 18 November 1850.
141 *River Times* (Fort Winnebago), 26 December 1850.
142 *PEEA*, vol. 10, no. 24 (14 December 1850).
143 On Ellis and local anti-Catholicism, see Catherine A. Oldham, 'Burslem: The Development of Statutory Bodies and Their Interactions with Local Institutions, 1850–1910' (MA dissertation, University of Keele, 1977), pp. 189–94.
144 *PEEA*, vol. 10, no. 24 (14 December 1850).
145 See Daniel E. Sutherland, 'Michigan Emigration Agent: Edward H. Thomson', *Michigan History* 59:1 (1975), 3–37.
146 *The Staffordshire Advertiser*, 1 March 1851.
147 On Ambassador Abbot Lawrence's visit to Manchester, see *Manchester Examiner & Times*, 18 December 1850, 1 January 1851.
148 *Potters' Press and Miners' Advocate*, 25 January 1851. The *Press* was the short-lived successor to the *Examiner*, running for eight issues.

Conclusion

In December 1850 an agent of the American Home Missionary Society arrived at Twigg's Landing on the Fox River. He was there to visit the potters' settlement which was without religious instruction following the departure in the summer of an 'English Baptist clergyman'.[1] He found a community in flux. The Potters' Emigration Society – members included 'weavers, gold beaters, coal diggers, etc.' – 'is broken up, for the present at least', he reported. Some settlers had returned home or left the area; about seventy families remained, 'trying to work along' and hoping to pay for their land when it came to market. Those he talked to were clear where the blame lay; the Society had not carried out its 'stipulations', and 'want of integrity on the part of its agent' had caused great suffering over the previous winter: 'One intelligent man, who had been a clerk for a rail road company a number of years, and has a family of seven children, said to me, "There we were put down with nothing but the acorns on the ground, and what could we do?"'[2] While these histories are hard to verify, according to a local source many families had to wait until 1852 to acquire title to property which, it will be recalled, the Society never purchased – and then only after making a ninety-mile trek on foot to the land office at Menasha.[3]

What happened to the land the Society did own, the original estate at Pottersville? The subject is mired in difficulty. A stay of execution brought the Pottersville settlers some respite after the Columbia County sheriff in October 1850 seized 700 acres, which only delayed the inevitable. Throughout 1851 and early 1852 the Fort Winnebago *River Times* published numerous notices announcing the sale by auction of various sections 'in favor' of individual creditors. Among them was the merchant (and precipitator of the Society's downfall) Michael R. Keegan.[4] In painstaking research, Roger Bentley examined the post-collapse land transactions, but the knot proved impossible to untangle. What we know is that on 10 November 1852 the Columbia County Register of Deeds recorded the transfer of the Pottersville deeds – which contrary to rumours had remained locked away in Kinnersley's Bank in Newcastle-under-Lyme – back to

Wisconsin. The surviving trustees, Charles Adams and John Johnson, were anxious to wind up the Society's affairs, and appointed Peter Watkin, James Thomas and Henry Dooley to oversee the land's divestment. In the months that followed they sold lots to individual settlers, including John Sawyer, James Hammond, Alexander Evans, Samuel Fox, George Robertshaw and Dooley himself. That was not the end of the story. In 1853 Keegan was again involved in tortuous litigation involving the estate. The following spring, in an inexplicable postscript, he refused to receive from the sheriff a certificate of sale from the Potters' Emigration Society 'on account of said land not belonging to same defendants'.[5]

Not implicated in the Pottersville litigation was Thomas Twigg, who had incurred the debts that triggered the Society's collapse. He died in early March 1851 at Twigg's Landing. His body was buried 'in the grove nearby'.[6] Only forty at the time of his death, he suffered from the lung disease common to pottery workers and had been unwell for some time. In September 1850, as criticism of his activities intensified, the colony's auditors noted the impact of the 'unjust reports' on his physical and mental state. His body is not 'a very strong one, for his complaint appears to gradually grow upon him', they confided.[7] Twigg's financial affairs proved predictably hard to settle, with notices still appearing in the local paper nearly eighteen months after his death. His widow Hannah remained at their Fox River home; a reference in January 1852 to 'Mrs. TWIGG's FERRY' points to continuing operation of the facility that played a key role in the agent's plans.[8] A few months later she remarried, her new husband Tunstall-born George Hewitt, whose own wife died shortly after their arrival in America two years earlier.[9]

Hewitt was one of many Society emigrants – up to 100 families, according to one estimate[10] – who remained in Columbia and Marquette counties. They included the three land officers and a majority of the Estate Committee party.[11] The Dooley family's contentment in the years after 1850 has already been described; notable among other persisting families was that of the former Burslem potter John Sawyer. Despite the early death of his wife Elizabeth, the Sawyers made good headway, and by 1870 John and his son Henry had accumulated real property with a combined value of $10,600. Born in 1840, John and Elizabeth's only child was the key to the family's progress. In 1862 he purchased and cleared forest land adjacent to his father, and by the turn of the century was regarded as 'one of the most successful farmers' in Columbia County. In addition to the original 120-acre holding, Henry owned a 680-acre farm in Springvale township, a portion of which he rented out. 'He has divided his attention between grain and stock', a biographical profile noted approvingly. Far from failing to make the transition from industry to agriculture, father and son successfully adapted to prairie life and work. As with many other families, marriage was an important contributor to their progress. Henry's bride was Ann Baillies from Paisley, with whom he had eight children. She came to the colony as a baby in 1849. Her large emigrant family included her grandfather John Hamilton, who lived well into his eighties. Described in the passenger manifest as a cabinet maker, he achieved local renown as a weaver of Paisley shawls. Through such widening family connections and activities, the Sawyers consolidated their status as productive and enduring members of Columbia County society.[12]

There are other examples of successful persistence and assimilation. Few Society families contributed more to the area's development and welfare than that of the former ovenman Isaac Smith. According to a local history, he was 'the first person in Columbia County to preach Methodism'.[13] As Mark Wyman notes, clergy in nineteenth-century America 'remained men of respect and influence in their communities', who in newly settled Wisconsin 'did not hold back from exercising that influence amid scenes that sometimes bordered on chaos'.[14] We have previously noted the Smiths' move to Fort Winnebago from Pottersville and Isaac's work on local bridge and canal projects; he also served as Columbia County's first coroner (the duties were not arduous; during four years in office he only investigated one death, that of the sheriff). The Smiths spent nearly a decade in the Portage area, with Isaac 'working with his hands to maintain himself and a large family on the week days, and preaching the Gospel on Sundays, as there was no other preacher in the neighbourhood at that time'.[15] In the mid-1850s the family moved across the Marquette County line to Moundville, where they acquired land originally granted to a veteran of the War of 1812. With eleven children reaching adulthood, extensive domestic resources ensured their continuing presence in the area. Isaac died in February 1884, his wife Sarah nine months later. Their homestead remained in the family, farmed by their youngest son Edwin and his descendants.[16]

Unlike the Staffordshire-born workers of industrial East Liverpool and Trenton, those who settled in Wisconsin made no effort to recreate a Potteries on the prairie. Although families doubtless spent hours recalling former lives in the company of friends and neighbours, the demands of frontier farming left little time for cultural regret. Children in particular quickly adapted to their new surroundings. Asked whether he would like to go back to England, 8-year-old William Mountford insisted he did not. His older sister, however, admitted she would return for the annual Burslem Wakes 'and then come back again'.[17] By the 1850s the area's burgeoning population was expanding the opportunities for family extension and renewal. The Smith offspring found spouses from New York and Connecticut as well as Yorkshire, Lancashire and Lincolnshire, confirming Charlotte Erickson's point about English emigrant children's 'easy absorption into American society through marriage'.[18] This widening kinship circle remained Anglo-centred; there was little intermarriage with the area's Welsh- and German-speaking communities, for example. All eight of William and Ann Scholes's children married spouses of British descent, 'either recent immigrants or old New Englanders', and not until the following generation – the couple had thirty-one grandchildren – did exogamous marriage become more common.[19]

However productive a family's marriage connections, it was economic decisions that ultimately shaped its long-term prospects. The Smiths' expanded kin included the family of the Lancashire engraver Martin Ellison; in October 1866 the Ellisons' daughter Mary married Isaac and Sarah's middle son, also Isaac. Like the Smiths, the Ellisons were of strong Christian faith; they were equally hard-working, as the father's diary fragments reveal. The entries run to the end of 1851 and demonstrate their struggles to eke out a living as farmers, including disputes with neighbours over purloined trees.[20] In 1853 Martin and his wife Alice left Wisconsin and moved to Dover, New Hampshire, where for the next two decades he worked as an engraver, returning to Marquette County, where three of the children had remained farming, for the last five years of his life. According to an obituary, through 'his artistic skill, industry and exemplary habits, he amassed a goodly portion of worldly wealth'.[21] For the Ellisons, economic progress required the freedom, flexibility and adaptability which American society could uniquely provide.[22] Martin Ellison was not the only Society emigrant to fall back on his trade, although unusual in retaining strong links to the family's original settlement. Others included the London butcher Thomas Ciscel, who moved to Milwaukie after leaving the lands; Alexander Sim, a stonemason from Scotland, who settled in Buffalo, New York; and his fellow countryman James Scoular. After two years in Columbia County, Scoular, a furnace man, spent time in Indiana working for the North West Iron Company before relocating with his growing family to Dodge County, Wisconsin, where he continued his trade.[23] Another Londoner, John Pettepher, who arrived with his family in June 1849, combined farming with carpentry before in 1856 moving 150 miles northwest to the lumber town of Eau Claire. A quarter of a century later a local history recorded the Pettephers owning 200 acres of 'mostly improved' land a few miles from the town, and John having made a valuable contribution to the construction of its buildings, including its main hotel.[24]

Although there is no evidence of pottery manufacture on the Society's lands, several potters pursued their former trade after leaving the area. Others went to East Liverpool and other emerging centres, although the prospect of returning to industrial dependency may have been a deterrent. Samuel Machin from Tunstall brought his family to Wisconsin with the

Aberdeen party in late 1849 but failed to settle.[25] He died during the 1850s, but in 1860 his widow and children were living at Alton, Illinois, where their son William, thirteen at the time of emigration, worked as a potter. It is likely that Samuel himself was drawn to the Mississippi River town by the skilled employment opportunities available there.[26] Sidney Parker from Burslem came to Wisconsin as a 9-year-old in 1848 with his parents Edward and Sarah; within two years the family had moved to Van Buren County, Iowa, where his father, a former operative, worked as a labourer. He died in 1857, and at 18 Sidney apprenticed himself to a local potter, R. M. Dickson. In 1866, with an American partner, he built and operated the Bonaparte Pottery on the Des Moines River. Selling his interest five years later, he remained a potter all his working life.[27]

Conspicuous among those who successfully utilised their pottery-making skills were the Pointons from Hanley. After their brief stop at Emancipation Ferry, the family settled in neighbouring Sauk County, where Philip, assisted by his son, also Philip, set up the Baraboo Pottery, which, according to an advertisement, sold jars, crocks, jugs, dishes, stove coolers, garden pots and other items at '75 percent below the prices usually charged for such articles'.[28] Pointon Sr died in March 1857, precipitating the manufactory's sale (in November it was destroyed by fire). Six months after his death the United States Patent Office issued the Pointons with a patent for 'certain Improvements in machines for Molding Pottery-Ware'. Modern archaeological research at the site found extensive evidence of mass-production moulding, suggesting that for these Staffordshire potters at least, mechanisation held no terrors.[29] After his father's death Philip Jr. left Wisconsin and embarked on a peripatetic career as a potter in Vermont, Quebec, New Jersey, Virginia and Baltimore. His work achieved significant recognition north of the forty-ninth parallel. In 1879, two years before his death, he was appointed manager of the important St John Stone Chinaware Company of New Brunswick.[30]

There are further examples of progress achieved by the Society's emigrants. Born in Windsor in 1812 but living and working for many years 'in the drug business' in Liverpool, Richard Noble came to Wisconsin in 1849 as a balloted member accompanied by his wife and two children. In 1855 the family moved from Portage to Gratiot in Lafayette County, where they would remain. By the time of the 1860 Census he was a fully fledged physician. Celebrated as one of Lafayette's pioneer settlers, Dr Noble died in 1900 two weeks short of his eighty-eighth birthday.[31] Two single emigrants, both Londoners, who played a significant role in the colony's history, also prospered. The Society's agent, George W. Robinson, remained in Marquette County, where four years later he married a young woman from New York, fathering six children. At the time of his death in 1871, he served as Clerk to the Marquette Circuit Court, a position he had held since 1862 – he signed Isaac Smith's naturalisation papers in 1866 – and was a substantial property owner. There is no evidence he resumed his former trade as a tailor. The ambitious young storekeeper John Turner pursued a different path, away from the Society's lands. After a few years in the Portage area, in 1854 Turner, now married, moved fifty miles west to Mauston in Juneau County, where he made his mark as an attorney, state legislator and, for over twenty years, proprietor and editor of the *Mauston Star*. Turner had a talent for reinvention, in his case as a daredevil radical fleeing from political persecution to America.[32] According to an 1889 obituary, he also claimed an advanced role in the founding of the Society's colony, where 'he endeavoured to put in practice his theories regarding the supply and demand for labour'.[33] (Typically, John's younger sister Elizabeth, who accompanied him to Wisconsin, has disappeared from view.) Another prominent figure at the colony, Twigg's deputy, Peter Watkin, remained farming in Columbia County. He and his wife Rachel died within a few months of each other in 1861.[34]

It is important to match the histories of those who made progress with those who did not. Acquiring land did not guarantee success or even survival. Many emigrants found it hard to adapt to the rigours of frontier agriculture, or at least discovered that the rewards were less than they expected – and the required labour more. Among the strugglers was Alexander Evans, whose problems his brother was always keen to reveal. Registered in the 1855 Wisconsin Census as still living in Columbia County, by 1860 Alexander and his wife Elizabeth (Betsey) had relocated to Canton, Missouri, where they boarded with their daughter Genevieve and her husband. Alexander's trade is recorded as 'painter'. With neither he nor his wife registering any real or personal property, the couple's dreams of landed independence had seemingly evaporated.[35]

There are other stories of limited progress. Samuel Cadman travelled from the Potteries to America in 1849 on the cholera-afflicted *Patrick Henry* (his wife Maria followed shortly afterwards). The Cadman's first ten years in Wisconsin proved moderately successful: in 1860, they recorded property on the 'Indian lands' valued at $450. By the end of the following decade, they were landless. In 1864 the family moved the short distance to Portage, where for the remaining seventeen years of his life Samuel worked as a depot night watchman with the Chicago, Milwaukee, St Paul and Pacific Railroad.[36] The lack of progress is also apparent in the case of Joseph Tempest. Tempest was a West Yorkshire farmer, a single man, possibly a widower, who was already in middle age when he came to the United States in 1849 under the potters' scheme. Writing to his friend Dr Joseph King of Haworth soon after reaching Wisconsin, he waxed enthusiastically and knowledgably about his agricultural prospects. Tempest reported that he had acquired a 160-acre section eight miles from Twigg's Landing, although whether he ever gained full title to the land is unclear. We do know that by 1860, now aged about 60, the Yorkshireman was firmly in the ranks of the propertyless. Ten years later the census recorded his occupation as that of 'butcher'; an unpublished childhood memoir from Marquette County adds to that bare description with a glimpse into a life that, despite its apparent setbacks, showed resilience and perhaps even a measure of contentment.

> One character who went about with horse and light wagon selling meats was an Englishman, Joe Tempest. He was about as tempestuous as a tea pot. My father would tempt him to make his standard reply to a certain complaint. Father would say, 'Mr. Tempest, this meat is a little high.' Joe would reply, ''E smells a little, but not enough to 'urt'.[37]

Other examples demonstrate the great variation in outcomes for those families and individuals who travelled to Wisconsin under the Society scheme; innumerable more are lost. Among the most elusive are those who returned to Britain. As earlier discussed, there are considerable barriers to recovering the histories of returners, with only the Lancashire weaver Bold Hilton choosing to publicise his aborted emigration in his letter alerting fellow branch members to the Society's alleged betrayal of trust.[38] Hilton's decision to leave his family behind in Lancashire suggests a conditional approach to emigration, an admission that things might not turn out as predicted or promised. Other Society emigrants, such as the Kirkhams and the Nixons from the Potteries, whose stories we have also told, had seemingly staked everything on a new beginning as farmers, making their failure to settle in America more disruptive. In addition to the Kirkhams and Nixons, Staffordshire returners included the Robinsons – John, Jane and their son Thomas – who went to Wisconsin in the summer of 1848 but like the other families returned in time for the 1851 Census and reemployment in the pottery industry;[39] and George and Charlotte Cooper and their five children from Burslem, who returned to England before 1852 in part through concerns over the health of their daughter Elizabeth.[40]

Returning migrants may have experienced difficulties in re-establishing themselves economically and domestically, although there is no evidence of any serious discontinuity in the lives of the families we can trace; those who stayed in the United States, on the other hand, faced a host of challenges in adapting to the unfamiliar environment. For some families, the most unanticipated occurred a decade after their arrival in America. Settlement required citizenship, and with it implication in local, state and national affairs. Wisconsin's liberal constitution gave newcomers unprecedented political rights; however, none of the immigrants, many of whom were tempted across the Atlantic by the prospect of freedom from industrial 'slavery', could foresee that their labour would soon be required to fight another form of servitude – that enacted by rebellious Southern planters.

The number of Society families actively involved in the war between the free-soil North and slave South that began in April 1861 was probably not large, with many of those arriving between 1847 and 1850 either too young or too old for military duty. Hannah Twigg's husband George Hewitt spent four years in the 2nd Wisconsin Cavalry after enlisting in December 1861. Returning from the war, he was 'chosen' as a Portage police officer, the appointment likely influenced by his loyal service to the Union.[41] Isaac and Sarah Smith's son-in-law Matthew Mason served in the 23rd, 34th and 35th Wisconsin Regiments after enlisting in November 1862 at the age of 37. After his final discharge in March 1866, he became an active member of the veterans' organisation the Grand Army of the Republic, under whose 'obsequies' he was buried two decades later.[42] For many immigrants, the war's onset coincided with entry to adulthood. Samuel Cadman's son-in-law Elijah Hopwood was 16 when fighting started. Joining the 1st Wisconsin Artillery in November 1864, he served until his discharge the following summer.[43] Henry Mattley had already worked for four years in a Lancashire cotton mill when he came to America with his parents as a 13-year-old in 1849. In August 1862 he enlisted in the 23rd Wisconsin. After suffering a severe wound in the arm at Vicksburg, he was taken prisoner in November 1863 before being exchanged seven months later. He and his Derbyshire-born wife Ann subsequently moved to Minnesota and Iowa, and, following the death in 1887 of their only child, to Lodi, California, where they finally put down roots.[44]

While no first-hand testimony survives from Society settlers who enlisted in the Union army, these histories suggest that their values and instincts did not significantly differ from those of their native-born neighbours or the large numbers of immigrants, including many German and Welsh, who helped sustain Wisconsin's war effort.[45] Two further examples, involving men whose age normally exempted them from military service, testify to the degree to which emigrant families had become assimilated into the fabric of national life less than a generation after their arrival. In January 1864 the former Lancashire cotton carder William Scholes enlisted in the 2nd Wisconsin Cavalry. What prompted the 49-year-old father of nine to join up is unclear – one theory suggests that the state's offer of bonuses was a factor (his two eldest daughters' husbands also enlisted in 1864).[46] However, it is equally valid to suggest that the decision reflected his belief in the Union as the best guarantor of the free-labour values that brought him and his family to the United States. (Among Society emigrants, Martin Ellison stands out for his anti-slavery convictions; his son, also Martin, served for three years in the 2nd Wisconsin Cavalry.[47]) Nine months later Scholes died from yellow fever while serving at Vicksburg, Mississippi.[48] Also dragged into the war was William Mountford's son-in-law, John Peake from Burslem, who had arrived as a single man in 1848. At the end of March 1864, now married with four children, the 44-year-old potter-turned-prairie farmer enlisted in the 37th Wisconsin Regiment. On 18 June he was wounded in the arm and hand during the federal assault on Petersburg. He died in Washington three weeks later. In a final act of assimilation, John Peake was buried at Arlington National Cemetery, many miles from his farm and family in Marquette County, and an even greater distance from the industrial community of the Staffordshire Potteries he left sixteen years earlier.

These stories, which could be infinitely pursued, uncover transatlantic emigration's complex and contingent dynamics. They also cast doubt on the accepted account of the Society's failure; many of the individuals and families who stayed in America made social and economic progress, although collectively how much is hard to assess. One qualification is in order. While we acknowledge the achievements of those who stayed on or near the Wisconsin lands, much of that progress came after exit from them. But as William Evans argued in the Pointons' case, it was the Potters' Emigration Society that facilitated these personal advances. In bringing workers and their families to America, it changed many lives for the better, irrespective of how disenchanted they were with what they found at the colony or how long they remained there. The Welshman's vision of a self-contained, self-reliant, constantly renewing community or 'town' of independent farmers mostly failed to take root, but the scheme's legacy was more fruitful than historians concede. Despite their distinctive origins, the Society's emigrants in the end did what emigrants had always done – indeed, what nineteenth-century Americans had always done: found locations and situations best designed to enhance their individual and familial prospects.

On the other hand, the scheme failed to realise Evans's ambition of transforming the pottery industry through the safety-valve of emigration. In remarks at a presentation event in Burslem in April 1854, he was cautious about claiming too much for the Society he founded, noting only that the policy of removing surplus labour had been carried out 'to a certain extent'. A week later he was more confident. In a letter to *The Staffordshire Advertiser*, he rejected the paper's description of the Society as a 'disastrous failure', arguing that it 'realized the object for which it originated, in the most complete and satisfactory manner'. The surplus hands were removed, he wrote, and the pottery industry 'through its *scarcity*, has acquired a *value* and a *power* never before known in the history of the trade'. He also rejected the picture of 'misery, starvation, and wretchedness' to describe the emigrants' experience in Wisconsin, having conceded in his earlier remarks that some families 'suffered deeply' and regretted leaving their native country. Above all, he was proud of the Society's record in sending workers to the American West, with its 'boundless prairies' of cheap and fertile land. He was also proud of what many had achieved there. Two emigrants had become magistrates, which he considered to be 'not merely a commercial but an intellectual triumph'. It showed 'that if working men were fit to sit on the judicial bench, they were capable of doing all that was required to enhance and promote their own interests'.[49] Such personal stories were vital to Evans's purpose, proof of the opportunities for renewal available to working men and their families bold enough and industrious enough to embrace them.

These claims notwithstanding, there is no evidence that the potters' emigration scheme led to higher wages or greater job security for those left behind. Writing in 1851, the Chartist Ernest Jones was scathing about the surplus-labour argument. Jones believed that most operatives who went to the land would return to their old trade, their skills enhancing the quality of American ware and ultimately causing home manufacturers' markets to close: 'Thus the emigration, which the potters thought would raise their wages, will be the very means to pull them down!'[50] Neither outcome in the event prevailed. By the second half of 1850, as the Society struggled to stay afloat, it was apparent that the scheme had exerted negligible influence on labour conditions in the pottery industry. In September disputes over wages led to strikes at several firms, but the following decade saw relations between masters and workers improve, with only a walkout by crate makers in 1853 puncturing the general calm. Favourable economic conditions and a new emphasis on conciliation and arbitration were responsible for the improvement. Although the Secession and Civil War across the Atlantic brought severe disruption to the Potteries – a reported forty manufactories were closed in November 1861, with hundreds of operatives left idle[51] – the subsequent revival in trade emboldened workers to press for an end to annual hiring, the practice that had bedevilled industrial relations at the potbank. Accommodation was finally reached in November 1866, when workers agreed not to make wage demands between Martinmas and Martinmas in return for monthly contracts and abolition of the despised yearly bond. Separate branches had negotiated the 1866 agreement. Attempts were made in the mid-1850s to revive the old union, but not until the beginning of the twentieth century did the various trades come together to form a consolidated body.[52] In the half-century after the Society's demise trade unions generally continued to involve themselves in emigration, albeit as a limited and pragmatic response to changing economic conditions.[53] There would be no return to Evans's belief in emigration as a universal working-class panacea.

The Potters' Emigration Society was not the only British emigration scheme unable to fulfil its utopian ambitions. There were other attempts in this period to establish organised settlements on the American frontier, all of which ended in failure. They included the Brazos River colony founded in January 1851 by William Bollaert, the former chemist and pupil of Michael Faraday, whose hopes of turning bank clerks, shopkeepers and other tradesmen into pioneer farmers disintegrated barely twelve months after their arrival in Texas[54]; Thomas Hunt's Owenite Equality community in Waukesha County, Wisconsin, visited by the Society's land agents in 1846; and the Hull-based Iowa Emigration Society. In the summer of 1850 its founder, the newspaperman George Sheppard, a supporter of the potters' scheme, established a colony in Clinton County, Iowa on avowedly cooperative principles derived from the teachings of the French social theorist Charles Fourier. 'Sheppardsville', however, succumbed to the familiar problems of inexperience, isolation, inadequate funding and an over-idealisation of the emigrants' prospects. Reports from disgruntled members, some of whom had returned to England, eroded trust and led to diminished interest in the colony, hastening its end. By the following autumn many settlers had relocated to towns and cities where skilled employment opportunities were readily available.[55] More resilient and, in the short term at least, more successful was the Potters' Emigration Society's Dane County neighbour, the British Temperance Emigration Society. Founded in December 1842, by 1850 it had sent out nearly 700 settlers but also suffered the same difficulties as its contemporaries, including the inability to extract rent from those it had assisted. With its final years characterised by 'chronic litigation', its end mirrored that of the potters' Society, which had borrowed its organisational model and whose history it closely paralleled.[56]

These emigrant projects formed part of a broad landscape of communal experimentation in nineteenth-century America, much of it located in the Midwestern states, including Wisconsin. In 1844 followers of Charles Fourier established a 'Phalanx' colony in Southport, 100 miles southeast of the potters' future settlement. A dominant thread throughout these initiatives, both emigrant and domestic, was the tension between communalism and individualism, between group ambitions and beliefs and personal self-interest. The Wisconsin Phalanx was actually one of the more successful endeavours in what is overall a catalogue of failure; although lasting only six years, it managed to dissolve itself with a minimum of rancour and, remarkably, with a financial profit. However, it too felt the impact of individualism; in the summer of 1849 a number of its members left the colony for the California gold fields, 'the prospect of easy money', in Carl Guarneri's words, more enticing 'than the difficult prospect of establishing communal life'.[57] Of Wisconsin colonies, only the Swiss enclave at New Glarus in the state's far south was able to retain its long-term coherence, a testimony to its strong cultural identity.[58]

Conclusion

Were the Potters' Emigration Society's colonisation efforts destined to fail like many others? The Society's genesis was rooted in the fellowship of trade unionism, whose occupational and emotional bonds were bound to weaken in a move across the Atlantic. Self-interest surfaced as soon as the Estate Committee members reached Wisconsin, with William Bradshaw determined to reserve his allotment – the only one that had been prepared – for the family's use. In 1848 the Society opened its membership to other areas and trades. Inevitably, those who travelled to America from Lancashire, London, Scotland and elsewhere had more limited investment in the Society's original mission – textile workers, for example, were much less affected than potters by the Master and Servant Acts[59] – and less incentive for subsuming their individual interests to a greater good. With their fragile contract with the Society sustaining their collective identity, it was unsurprising that many refused to tolerate its organisational and management failings and abandoned the colony for pastures new or, disillusioned, returned to Britain. The Society also suffered from its failure to attract more financial support from the Potteries, and, less documented, its failure to make progress in the out-potteries. Absent from the list of subscribing branches were the great pottery centres of Worcester, Derby and South Wales, where the revived union had made few inroads.

While there can be no doubting the industry and integrity that William Evans and his colleagues brought to the emigration project and the sincerity with which, against the odds, they attempted to carry it through, they made errors from the outset, some clearly avoidable, which affected its long-term prospects. The inability to understand the American land purchase system proved detrimental, as did ignoring the advice of George Flower and others that twenty-acre farms would not sustain a proper living – let alone repay the credit advanced to settlers by the Society. Compared to the momentum achieved by the temperance emigration scheme, the potters' progress was slow. So much of Evans's time and energy was taken up with fending off enemies, real or imagined; arguably too little involved the detailed research and planning that could have helped the Society avoid such elementary mistakes as failing to equip the land agents and Estate Committee parties with the cash resources needed to meet land acquisition and settlement expenses. The agents' trip to Washington was also of doubtful value; costly in time and money, it revealed a glaring lack of knowledge about the workings of America's 'spoils' system in which federal appointees – in this case the Land Office Commissioner – were replaced as a new political party assumed the reins of government. Errors were compounded after the scheme's expansion. The Society belatedly and inadequately explained the preemption system, leaving emigrants and other members believing it had actually purchased 50,000 acres of government land. This led to frustration and disappointment and gave ready ammunition to its many critics. Thomas Twigg's visit home in the winter of 1849–50 provided some assurance, but he struggled to reassert his authority on his return. In the end, the Society fell victim to its ambition; lacking experience, capability and resources, it was unable to overcome the inherent problems of long-distance colonisation and, by opening its doors to all and sundry, fatally lost control of the migration and settlement process.

It was the emigration scheme's achievements, not its failings, that the Society's founder returned to in the years to come. In the spring of 1851, however, he had more mundane matters to attend to, including the problem of how to make a living. He was soon enmeshed in legal wrangling over the affairs of the defunct Society, in particular the fate of its much-valued printing press.[60] Later that year he took his family back to South Wales, where he found employment as a reporter on a local newspaper. Although not well paid, the work at least allowed him, as he said, 'to keep "the wolf" from the door'. He returned to the Potteries in 1854. On 18 April, at the Swan Inn, Burslem, former colleagues presented him with a silk purse containing 'the handsome sum of £20' collected in recognition of his 'indefatigable exertions in the cause of labour', which he gladly accepted.[61] Shortly afterwards he brought his family back to Staffordshire, where he became involved in the formation of a local 'Anglo-French Free Trade Association', a project begun by pottery workers campaigning for the reduction of duties on earthenware exports. Information is sparse on his employment in this period, but in 1861 the Census registered him as an Ordnance Survey agent, with his daughters Julia and Margaret also working as map makers. Three years later he assumed the editorship of the *Potteries' Examiner*.[62] He continued to defend the rights of working potters, including testifying in 1866 to a parliamentary Select Committee on proposed amendments to Master and Servant legislation, and fighting against persisting good-from-oven practices.[63] He held the newspaper post until 1867, when he left after falling out with its owners, the hollow-ware pressers, with whom he always had a conflicted relationship.[64]

He also resumed his active involvement in emigration. In 1871 he was hired by George Sheppard, who had been recently appointed the chief European agent for the Northern Pacific Railroad, which was vigorously promoting colonisation to its western lands. Lecturing to audiences across Britain, Evans repeatedly invoked the example of the Potters' Emigration Society as evidence of colonisation's merits. In his best reported speech, at Workington on 20 February 1872, he told the story of the 1836 strike and the 'pottery riots' of 1842 before describing the Society's settlement in Wisconsin. The speech was notable for his claim that emigration would benefit workers and masters alike. 'He was present as much in the interests of capitalists as working men', the former Chartist told his audience.[65] Although Evans's employment with the Northern Pacific ended in 1874, when the corporation closed its European operation in the wake of the previous year's financial crisis,[66] his interest in emigration was undiminished and for the rest of his life he extolled the benefits of surplus labour's removal abroad. 'My experience teaches me that nothing equals foreign colonisation for the improvement of the working classes of this country', he wrote in 1879.[67] Cooperative principles were now integral to his defence of emigration. In 1877–8 he wrote a series of fourteen articles on foreign colonisation for the *Co-operative News* in which the 'large co-operative trade society' he founded thirty years ago loomed large.[68] Writing continued to take up much of his time in these years. Using the barely disguised *nom de plume* Millway Vanes, his literary output included technical articles on pottery manufacture for publications such as the *Pottery Gazette* and *Scientific American*,[69] and also fiction. An 1882 advertisement under Evans's name promised a new serial story, 'The Contrabandist' by Millway Vanes, 'the gifted and popular Author of "The Poacher", and many other tales'.[70] In his last published piece, on 'Enamel Artists', he acknowledged that great strides had been taken in the application of technology to pottery production, describing the potters' historic opposition to mechanisation as a 'great mistake'. Mechanical improvement, he now claimed, 'would have placed English pottery manufacture beyond the reach of all foreign competition'.[71]

Evans died at his home in Church near Accrington on 14 March 1887. 'Afflictions came with old age, but he bore them bravely', reported the *Pottery Gazette*. He was 71; his wife Susan, now 'smitten with blindness', survived him by seven years.[72] With his death, the Potters' Emigration Society faded from public memory, kept alive in Britain by Owen's and Warburton's studies,[73] and in America, prior to Grant Foreman's pioneering research, by local histories and the occasional obituary, although *The New York Times* did review Owen's book and noted the emigration scheme.[74] Renewed interest came in the 1960s. On a wet Monday evening in late July 1961, about fifty people, many descendants of Society immigrants, met at a site five miles north of Portage on the Fox River to dedicate a metal sign, sponsored by the Columbia County Historical Society, marking the colony's founding (see Figure C.1). While the newspaper report of the event provided a reasonable summary of the emigration scheme's origins, the sign itself made no mention of the Society's founder or of the large numbers that came from outside of the Potteries, recording only that 'here in 1849 Thomas Twiggs [sic] began a settlement of unemployed potters from Staffordshire, England' before describing the establishment of Emancipation Ferry, 'named to express the hope that here they would find freedom from the poverty of the Old World'.[75] There was no equivalent marker erected at the site of the original settlement, the formerly named Pottersville. In 1974 local interest in the scheme was

Figure C.1 Potters' Emigration Society marker, Columbia County, Wisconsin.

piqued when the British filmmaker Philip Donnellan interviewed descendants for a documentary project, *Passage West*, funded by Canada's National Film Board and the BBC. The potters' 'was the most significant industrial emigration society that ever existed, and its only memorial is in Wisconsin. There is none in England', Donnellan told a Portage newspaper.[76]

There had been a memorial attempt in the Potteries a few years earlier. A whiff of controversy accompanied it. In January 1969 Stephen Hobson, a former assistant general secretary of the National Society of Pottery Workers, wrote to the Stoke-on-Trent city housing committee suggesting that William Evans's contribution to labour history be marked by naming a street or block of flats after him as part of a Hanley urban renewal scheme. His request was supported by the Pottery Workers. Opposing the idea, Councillor Reginald Rigby claimed that Evans 'means nothing to me ... He was connected with the pottery workers' union when their standards were the lowest in history'. He added that there was nothing to be proud of in the union's history then or today. A fellow independent councillor, Percy Axon, was slightly more sympathetic; Evans, he said, was 'just another chap who had done a lot of good in the past'. The town clerk, who pointed out that all the names for the improvement scheme had been allocated, proposed instead a commemorative plaque at the site. This was adopted on condition that the Pottery Workers bore the cost.[77] Two weeks later Hobson condemned Rigby's 'discourteous remarks' in a lengthy contribution to the local paper. Under the headline 'Bands Played as They Set Off by Boat from Etruria', he gave a well-informed, sympathetic account of the emigration scheme and of Evans's life and career. 'His chapter ends having done all he humanly could for the potters in their efforts to improve themselves', Hobson wrote.[78]

The Hanley proposal was not acted upon, ensuring that the emigration scheme and its founder would continue to suffer from what E. P. Thompson termed 'the enormous condescension of posterity'.[79] Stripped of the arguments that dogged its seven-year existence and clouded its subsequent reputation, the Potters' Emigration Society stands out as a noteworthy episode in the history of nineteenth-century working-class self-help. If emigration was not the cure-all that William Evans and others claimed, the prospect of landed independence in America still gave hope to hundreds of working men and their families unwilling to tolerate conditions in industrial Britain during the troubled 1840s. Much of this history is unrecoverable; however, without *The Potters' Examiner* and its irrepressible editor, who believed that emigration was a viable, even necessary, step towards labour's rebirth, little would have been recovered at all.

Notes

1 Almost certainly James Bennett.
2 *The Home Missionary*, vol. 23, no. 11 (March 1851), pp. 258–9.
3 Bennett, 'Story of Moundville, 1849–1922', p. 1.
4 *River Times* (Fort Winnebago), 13 March 1851 and following issues.

5 Columbia County Circuit Court, 17 April 1854. Much of this paragraph is based on material supplied by Roger Bentley, to whom I am greatly indebted. He summarised his research findings in Bentley, 'The Road to "Desolation Ferry"', p. 11.
6 Turner, *The Family Tree of Columbia County, Wisconsin*, p. 73.
7 *PEEA*, vol. 10, no. 16 (19 October 1850).
8 *River Times* (Fort Winnebago), 19 January 1852.
9 *Portage Daily Democrat*, 4 January 1892.
10 Foreman, 'Settlement of English Potters in Wisconsin', pp. 395–6.
11 In 1872 William Evans noted that one of the three land agents, 'a plate-maker', had 'returned to England to end his days on the competence acquired in America'. This can only refer to James Hammond. *Whitehaven News*, 22 February 1872. However, no other sources indicate any return. A biographical profile in the *History of Columbia County*, p. 1051 describes his uninterrupted progress as a settler.
12 *Memorial and Biographical Record and Illustrated Compendium of Biography ... of ... Citizens of Columbia, Sauk and Adams Counties* (Chicago, IL: Geo. Ogle & Co., 1901), pp. 497–8.
13 *History of Columbia County, Wisconsin*, p. 627.
14 Mark Wyman, *The Wisconsin Frontier* (Bloomington: Indiana University Press, 1998), p. 212.
15 *Wisconsin State Register*, 15 March 1884.
16 Fran Sprain, *Places and Faces in Marquette County, Wis.* Volume 1 (Westfield, WI: Isabella Press, 1991), pp. 78–81.
17 *PEEA*, vol. 10, no. 7 (17 August 1850). The colony's frontier location made unlikely the development of an English associational culture, as thoroughly explored in Tania Bueltmann and Donald M. MacRaild, *The English Diaspora in America: Migration, Ethnicity and Association, 1730s–1950s* (Manchester: Manchester University Press, 2017).
18 Erickson, *Invisible Immigrants*, p. 73.
19 Henderson, 'From the First Industrial City to the Wisconsin Frontier'.
20 Martin Ellison's diary, 23 January 1851.
21 *Montello Express*, 12 January 1878. His Alice wife died in May 1882.
22 The relative ease with which English immigrants were able 'to jump back and forth between crafts and industry to agriculture' is noted by William Van Vugt, 'Relocating the English Diaspora in America', in David T. Gleeson (ed.), *English Ethnicity and Culture in North America* (Columbia: University of South Carolina Press, 2017), p. 12.
23 *History of Dodge County, Wisconsin*, p. 653.
24 *History of Northern Wisconsin*, p. 330.
25 See Alfred Swetmore's letter in *PEEA*, vol. 9, no. 89 (16 March 1850).
26 Other Society emigrants may have found employment as potters in Alton. See Wm. L. Goodwin (ed.), *Of What We Potters Are: A History of the Family of John Goodwin of Staffordshire, England, Based upon Letters from England and Other Family Letters, 1845–1898* (Galesburg, IL: privately printed, 1975), p. 131.

27 *Bonaparte Record*, 17 February 1914; *Ottumwa Daily Courier*, 17 February 1914.
28 *Sauk County Standard*, 3 December 1851 and issues following.
29 See the informative 'History of the Baraboo Pottery, Baraboo, Wisconsin', at https://madefromclay.org/wp-content/uploads/2022/04/Philip-Pointon-Pottery-2022-04-01.pdf (last accessed 26 May 2023).
30 His career is described in Jacqueline Beaudry Dion and Jean-Pierre Dion, *Philip Pointon (1831–1881): Maître-Potier, Baraboo, Cap-Rouge, Trenton, Baltimore, Saint-Jean* (Saint-Lambert: privately printed, 2013).
31 *Belmont Bee*, 1 February 1900. Noble's balloted status is noted in John Wood's letter in *Manchester Times*, 31 August 1850.
32 See Chapter 6, n. 56.
33 *Wisconsin State Journal*, 7 March 1889.
34 The Watkins' adult daughter Mary, blind since birth, lived until 1887.
35 Genevieve (also known as Jane or Jennie) and her husband William C. Pike (he called himself Robinson in 1860) achieved notoriety when in 1877 he was convicted of the murder of her alleged lover. Alexander Evans died in the late 1860s. I am grateful to Susan Schack Jensen for family information.
36 *Wisconsin State Register*, 8 January 1881. Samuel's wife died four years earlier. The couple had seven children.
37 Merlin Ennis, 'Memories 1877–1882', at www.wiroots.org/wimarquette/ennisdiary (last accessed 26 May 2013).
38 *Manchester Times*, 13 July 1850.
39 The 1851 Census records John employed as a slip maker; ten years later Jane is recorded working as a burnisher and their son Thomas as an ovenman.
40 *Staffordshire Sentinel*, 26 December 1910.
41 *Portage Daily Democrat*, 4 January 1892.
42 *Montello Express*, 7 January 1887.
43 *Portage Daily Register*, 7 April 1925.
44 *History of Franklin and Carro Gordo Counties, Iowa* (Springfield, IL: Continental History Company, 1883), p. 903.
45 For a summary of immigrant participation in the war, see Richard Nelson Current, *Wisconsin: A History* (Urbana: University of Illinois Press, 1977), pp. 48–50.
46 Henderson, 'From the First Industrial City to the Wisconsin Frontier'.
47 Information from Ellison family history on Ancestry.com.
48 His body lies in the Vicksburg National Cemetery. His eldest daughter Mary's husband, Bissell Sherwin, was killed in action in Virginia two weeks later.
49 *Staffordshire Sentinel*, 22, 29 April 1854.
50 Ernest Jones, *Notes to the People* (London: J. Pavey, 1851), pp. 262–3.
51 Pauline Booth, 'The Staffordshire Pottery Industry in the Nineteenth Century and its Markets', *Staffordshire Studies* 13 (2000), 119.
52 For the continuing story, see Burchill and Ross, *A History of the Potter's Union*.
53 Harper, 'Obstacles and Opportunities', p. 47.
54 Van Vugt, *Portrait of an English Migration*, pp. 266–7.
55 Birch, 'The Editor and the English'; Van Vugt, *Britain to America*, pp. 57–8; Shepperson, *British Emigration to North America*, pp. 102–3.

56 Vale, 'English Settlers in Early Wisconsin', p. 29 (quotation); Van Vugt, *Britain to America*, pp. 56–7.
57 Carl J. Guarneri, *The Utopian Alternative: Fourierism in Nineteenth-Century America* (Ithaca, NY: Cornell University Press, 1991), pp. 161–2, 343–4 (quotation). Also useful is Andrew E. Hunt, 'The Wisconsin Phalanx: A Forgotten Success Story', *Canadian Review of American Studies* 28:2 (1998), 119–43.
58 Wyman, *Wisconsin Frontier*, p. 193.
59 John Saville, *The Consolidation of the Capitalist State, 1800–1850* (London: Pluto Press, 1994), p. 21.
60 The matter's complexity can be gleaned from the County Court case of *Evans v. Jervis*, *The Staffordshire Advertiser*, 21 June 1851.
61 *Staffordshire Sentinel*, 22 April 1854.
62 The paper started life in 1856 as the *Potter*, part of an attempted resurrection of the potters' union.
63 On good-from-oven, see his letter to the *Bee-Hive*, 14 July 1866.
64 Burchill and Ross, *A History of the Potters' Union*, p. 94. I am greatly indebted to Mike Beckensall for sharing his research on William Evans's post-Society career.
65 *Whitehaven News*, 22 February 1872. See also *Norwood News*, 23 March 1872; *Bell's Weekly Messenger*, 29 April 1872.
66 The Northern Pacific resumed its European operation at the beginning of the 1880s. In 1882 it employed over 800 agents in Britain. See James B. Hedges, 'The Colonization Work of the Northern Pacific Railroad', *Mississippi Valley Historical Review* 8:3 (1926), 311–42; and for Sheppard's recruitment efforts in the English Northwest, Bryn Trescatheric, 'Furness Colony in England and Minnesota, 1872–1880', *Minnesota History* 47:1 (1980), 16–25.
67 *Potteries Examiner*, 13 December 1879.
68 See especially *Co-operative News*, 18 October (quotation), 8 November, 24 November, 1 December 1877. See also *Cotton Factory Times*, 23 October, 4 December 1885, in which he refers to 'The Potters' Co-operative Colonization Society'.
69 See *Pottery Gazette*, 1 March 1882, 1 October 1886, 1 March 1887; *Scientific American*, vol. 15 (2 June 1883).
70 *Publishers' Circular*, 30 December 1882, reprinted from the *Accrington Gazette*.
71 *Pottery Gazette*, 1 March 1887.
72 *Pottery Gazette*, 1 April 1887.
73 For a negative view of the Society from the inter-war period, see *Staffordshire Sentinel*, 27 June 1933.
74 *The New York Times*, 10 August 1901.
75 *Portage Daily Register*, 1 August 1961.
76 *Portage Daily Register*, 31 October 1974. For the documentary's origins, see Goodwin (ed.), *Of What We Potters Are*, appendix. Donnellan interviewed William Goodwin during his American visit.
77 *Evening Sentinel*, 10 January 1969. The plaque was never erected.

78 *Staffordshire Sentinel*, 23 January 1969. See Burchill and Ross, *A History of the Potters' Union*, pp. 245–6 for further context. In May 1982 the Victoria Theatre told the Pottersville story in a special performance, and the following decade saw a brief flurry of interest when Stoke-on-Trent tourist officials held a competition to mark the 150th anniversary of the scheme. The idea was prompted by articles written by the *Sentinel*'s columnist John Abberley. See *Evening Sentinel*, 13 March, 27 March 1995. For the follow-up, see *The Advertiser*, 17 August 1995; *Milwaukee Journal Sentinel*, 4 August 1996. BBC Radio Stoke also broadcast a half-hour documentary on 'Pottersville'.

79 E. P. Thompson, *The Making of the English Working Class* (Harmondsworth: Penguin, revised edition, 1980), p. 12.

Select bibliography

A note on primary sources

The main primary source for this study, as discussed in the text, is *The Potters' Examiner and Workman's Advocate* (later *Emigrants' Advocate*), edited by William Evans and published from December 1843 to December 1850. A small number of copies not included in the microfilm edition were consulted at the William Salt Library, Stafford. Supplementing it are local newspapers, notably *The Staffordshire Advertiser* and *Staffordshire Mercury*, and a host of other English and Scottish titles. Many of these titles were accessed via the British Library's digital archive (www.britishnewspaperarchive.co.uk); others, including the *Mercury*, were read on microfilm or in original copy. Of note is Joseph Barker's penny periodical *The People*, available at www.hathitrust.org. American titles were accessed via www.newspapers.com and www.newspaperarchive.com, supplemented by other online resources. In addition, the study made extensive use of British and American census data, transatlantic passengers lists, records of births, marriages and deaths, and other miscellaneous material, including records of Civil War participation. The principal digital gateway for this material was www.ancestry.co.uk (see below for main databases used in the study). Extensive use was also made of the compendious American local histories published in the last quarter of the nineteenth century. Extant manuscript sources relating to the Society's history are rare. Aside from those published in newspapers, no contemporaneous letters and only one diary (Martin Ellison) from Potters' Emigration Society settlers have survived. William Evans, the Society's founder and guiding spirit, left no surviving personal papers.

Primary sources

Newspapers and journals

Co-operative News
Manchester Examiner & Times
Northern Star and National Trades' Journal
Potteries Examiner
Potters' Press and Miners' Advocate
Pottery Gazette

River Times (Fort Winnebago)
Staffordshire Mercury
Staffordshire Sentinel
The People
The Potters' Examiner and Workman's Advocate (later *Emigrants' Advocate*)
The Staffordshire Advertiser
Wisconsin State Register

Local histories

The History of Columbia County, Wisconsin, Containing an Account of Its Settlement, Growth, Development and Resources ... (Chicago, IL: Western Historical Company, 1880).

History of Dane County, Wisconsin, Containing an Account of Its Settlement, Growth, Development, and Resources ... (Chicago, IL: Western Historical Company, 1880).

The History of Dodge County, Wisconsin (Chicago, IL: Western Historical Company, 1880).

History of Franklin and Carro Gordo Counties, Iowa (Springfield, IL: Continental History Company, 1883).

History of Northern Wisconsin, Containing an Account of Its Settlement, Growth, Development, and Resources ... (Chicago, IL: Western Historical Company, 1881).

Jones, J. E. (comp.), *A History of Columbia County Wisconsin: A Narrative Account of Its Historical Progress, Its People, and Its Principal Interests*, 2 vols (Chicago: Lewis Publishing Company, 1914).

Memorial and Biographical Record and Illustrated Compendium of Biography ... of ... Citizens of Columbia, Sauk and Adams Counties (Chicago, IL: Geo. Ogle & Co., 1901).

Portrait and Biographical Album of Green Lake, Marquette, and Waushara Counties, Wisconsin (Chicago, IL: Acme Publishing Company, 1890).

Portrait and Biographical Album of Morgan and Scott Counties (Chicago, IL: Chapman Brothers, 1889).

Genealogical sources

Ancestry.co.uk (last accessed 1 June 2023)

Principal databases

1841 Scotland Census
1841, 1851, 1861 England Census
1850, 1860, 1870, 1880 United States Federal Census
Birmingham, England, Church of England Baptisms, 1813–1912
England, Select Births and Christenings, 1538–1975
England, Select Marriages, 1538–1973
England and Wales, Civil Registration Marriage Index, 1837–1915
England and Wales, Criminal Registers, 1791–1892
England and Wales, Non-Conformist and Non-Parochial Registers, 1567–1970

Iowa Cemetery Records
London, England, Church of England Births and Baptisms, 1813–1920
Manchester, England, Marriages and Banns, 1754–1930
New Orleans Passenger Lists, 1820–1945
New York Passenger Lists, 1820–1957
Scotland, Select Marriages, 1561–1910
Staffordshire, England, Birth, Marriage and Death Indexes, 1837–2017
Staffordshire, England, Church of England Marriages and Banns, 1754–1900
Staffordshire, England, Extracted Parish Records
US, Burial Registers, Military Posts and National Cemeteries, 1862–1960
US, Civil War Draft Registrations Records, 1863–1865
US, Federal Census Mortality Schedules, 1850–1885
US, Find A Grave Index, 1600s–
US, Naturalization Record Indexes, 1791–1992
US City Directories, 1822–1995
West Yorkshire, England, Births and Baptisms, 1813–1910
Wisconsin, State Censuses, 1855–1905
Wisconsin, Wills and Probate Records, 1800–1987
Wisconsin Deaths, 1820–1907
Wisconsin Marriages, pre-1907

Books

Engels, Friedrich, *The Condition of the Working Class in England* (London: Penguin, 1987).

Evans, William, *Art and History of the Potting Business* (Shelton: privately printed, 1846).

Flower, George, *The Errors of Emigrants* (New York: Arno Press, 1975).

Flower, George, *History of the English Settlement in Edwards County, Illinois Founded in 1817 and 1818, by Morris Birkbeck and George Flower* (Chicago, IL: Fergus Printing Company, 1882).

Goodwin, Wm. L. (ed.), *Of What We Potters Are: A History of the Family of John Goodwin of Staffordshire, England, Based upon Letters from England and Other Family Letters, 1845–1898* (Galesburg, IL: privately printed, 1975).

Gourlay, Robert Fleming, *Emigration and Settlement on Wild Land* (Cupar: privately printed, 1849).

Hawley, T., *Sketches of Pottery Life and Character in the Forties and Fifties* (Longton: Hughes & Harber, 3rd edn, n.d.).

Newhall, John B., *The British Emigrants' 'Hand Book', and Guide to the New States of America: Particularly Illinois, Iowa, and Wisconsin ...* (London: T. Sutter, 1844).

Quaife, Milo M. (ed.), *An English Settler in Pioneer Wisconsin: The Letters of Edwin Bottomley, 1842–1850* (Madison, WI: State Historical Society of Wisconsin, 1918).

[Shaw, C.,] 'An Old Potter', *When I Was a Child* (Wakefield: SR Publishers, 1969 [1903]).

Ward, John, *The Borough of Stoke-upon-Trent* (London: W. Lewis and Son, 1843).

Article

Boyle, John, 'An Account of Strikes in the Potteries, in the Years 1834 and 1836', *Journal of the Statistical Society of London* 1:1 (May 1838), 37–45.

Website sources

Ennis, Merlin, 'Memories 1877–1882', at www.wiroots.org/wimarquette/ennisdiary (last accessed 26 May 2013).
Martin Ellison's diary, transcribed by Nathan Weber, at www.wiroots.org/wimarquette/ellisondiary.html (last accessed 4 June 2008).
United States Army, Fort Winnebago Ledger, 1831–51. Facsimile at http://content.wisconsinhistory.org/u?/tp,54450 (last accessed 26 February 2023).

Miscellaneous material

Parliamentary Papers: Children's Employment Commission. Second Report of the Commissioners. Trades and Manufactures. Part 1. Reports and Evidence from the Sub-Commissioners (London, 1842).
Rules and Regulations of the Potters' Emigration and Savings' Fund, established April 18th, 1844, National Archives, FS 1/657.
'Story of Moundville, 1849–1922', contributed by Mary Ann Miller from an original document by Mildred Jones Bennett. Copy in author's possession.
'The Last of the Potters' Society', undated, Wisconsin Historical Society, copy in Hobson Collection, PA/HOB/1, Stoke-on-Trent City Archives.

Secondary sources

The following list includes the most significant books, articles, essays and dissertations used in the preparation of this study. Details of other secondary sources are found in the endnotes.

Books

Baines, Dudley, *Migration in a Mature Economy: Emigration and Internal Migration in England and Wales, 1861–1900* (Cambridge: Cambridge University Press, 1985).
Barber, Edwin Atlee, *The Pottery and Porcelain of the United States* (New York: G. P. Putnam's Sons, 1893).
Belich, James, *Replenishing the Earth: The Settler Revolution and the Anglo-World, 1783–1939* (New York: Oxford University Press, 2009).
Berg, Maxine, *The Machinery Question and the Making of Political Economy, 1815–1848* (Cambridge: Cambridge University Press, 1980).
Berthoff, Roland Tappan, *British Immigrants in Industrial America, 1790–1850* (Cambridge, MA: Harvard University Press, 1953).

Boewe, Charles, *Prairie Albion: An English Settlement in Pioneer Illinois* (Carbondale, IL: Southern Illinois University Press, 1962).

Bronstein, Jamie, *Land Reform and Working-Class Experience in Britain and the United States, 1800–1862* (Stanford, CA: Stanford University Press, 1999).

Buley, R. Carlyle, *The Old Northwest: The Pioneer Period, 1815–1840*, 2 vols. (Bloomington, IN: Indiana University Press, 1950).

Burchill, Frank and Richard Ross, *A History of the Potters' Union* (Hanley: Ceramic and Allied Trades Union, 1977).

Burnett, John, *Idle Hands: The Experience of Unemployment, 1790–1990* (London: Routledge, 1994).

Chase, Malcolm, *Chartism: A New History* (Manchester: Manchester University Press, 2007).

Chase, Malcolm, *Early Trade Unionism: Fraternity, Skill and the Politics of Labour* (Aldershot: Ashgate, 2000).

Chase, Malcolm, *'The People's Farm': English Radical Agrarianism, 1775–1840* (Oxford: Clarendon Press, 1988).

Cohn, Raymond L., *Mass Migration Under Sail: European Immigration to the Antebellum United States* (New York: Cambridge University Press, 2009).

Cordery, Simon, *British Friendly Societies, 1750–1914* (London: Palgrave Macmillan, 2003).

Current, Richard Nelson, *Wisconsin: A History* (Urbana, IL: University of Illinois Press, 1977).

Dupree, Marguerite W., *Family Structure in the Staffordshire Potteries, 1840–1860* (Oxford: Clarendon Press, 1995).

Erickson, Charlotte, *Invisible Immigrants: The Adaptation of English and Scottish Immigrants in Nineteenth-Century America* (Ithaca, NY: Cornell University Press, 1972).

Erickson, Charlotte, *Leaving England: Essays on British Emigration in the Nineteenth Century* (Ithaca, NY: Cornell University Press, 1994).

Garnett, R. G., *Co-operation and the Owenite Socialist Communities in Britain, 1825–45* (Manchester: Manchester University Press, 1972).

Gates, William C., Jr., *The City of Hills and Kilns: Life and Work in East Liverpool, Ohio* (East Liverpool, OH: East Liverpool Historical Society, 1984).

Gerber, David A., *Authors of Their Lives: The Personal Correspondence of British Immigrants to North America in the Nineteenth Century* (New York: New York University Press, 2006).

Gosden, P. H. J. H., *The Friendly Societies in England, 1815–1875* (Manchester: Manchester University Press, 1961).

Guarneri, Carl J., *The Utopian Alternative: Fourierism in Nineteenth-Century America* (Ithaca, NY: Cornell University Press, 1991).

Harper, Marjory (ed.), *Emigrant Homecomings: The Return Movement of Emigrants, 1600–2000* (Manchester: Manchester University Press, 2005).

Harrison, J. F. C., *Robert Owen and the Owenites in Britain and America: The Quest for a New Moral World* (London: Routledge and Kegan Paul, 1969).

Hopkins, Walter Sawyer and Andrew Winkle Hopkins, *The Richard and Harriet Hopkins Family: Empire Prairie Pioneers* (Denver, CO: Big Mountain Press, 1963).

Hunt, E. H., *British Labour History, 1815–1914* (London: Weidenfeld & Nicolson, 1981).

Jaffe, James A., *Striking a Bargain: Work and Industrial Relations in England 1815–1865* (Manchester: Manchester University Press, 2000).

Johnson, Stanley C., *A History of Emigration from the United Kingdom to North America, 1763–1912* (London: Routledge and Kegan Paul, 1913).

Johnston, H. J. M., *British Emigration Policy, 1815–1830: 'Shovelling out Paupers'* (Oxford: Clarendon Press, 1972).

MacDonagh, Oliver, *A Pattern of Government Growth: The Passenger Acts and their Enforcement* (London: MacGibbon & Kee, 1961).

McKay, Joyce, *An Historical Architectural and Historical Survey of the City of Portage, Columbia County, Wisconsin* (Portage, WI: Portage Area Chamber of Commerce, 1993).

Miller, Kerby A., *Emigrants and Exiles: Ireland and the Irish Exodus to North America* (New York: Oxford University Press, 1985).

Orth, John V., *Combination and Conspiracy: A Legal History of Trade Unionism, 1721–1906* (Oxford: Clarendon Press, 1991).

Owen, Harold, *The Staffordshire Potter* (London: G. Richards, 1901).

Price, Richard, *Labour in British Society: An Interpretative History* (London: Routledge, 1990).

Prothero, Iorwerth, *Artisans and Politics in Early Nineteenth-Century London: John Gast and His Times* (London: Methuen, 1979).

Richards, Eric, *Britannia's Children: Emigration from England, Scotland, Wales and Ireland since 1600* (London: Hambledon, 2004).

Richards, Eric, *The Genesis of International Mass Migration: The British Case, 1750–1900* (Manchester: Manchester University Press, 2018).

Robbins, Roy M., *Our Landed Heritage: The Public Domain, 1776–1970* (Lincoln, NE: University of Nebraska Press, 2nd edn, 1976).

Rohrbough, Malcolm J., *The Land Office Business: The Settlement and Administration of American Public Lands, 1789–1837* (New York: Oxford University Press, 1968).

Saville, John, *1848: The British State and the Chartist Movement* (Cambridge: Cambridge University Press, 1987).

Shepperson, Wilbur S., *British Emigration to North America: Projects and Opinions in the Early Victorian Period* (Minneapolis, MI: University of Minnesota Press, 1957).

Shepperson, Wilbur S., *Emigration & Disenchantment: Portraits of Englishmen Repatriated from the United States* (Norman, OH: University of Oklahoma Press, 1965).

Smith, Alice E., *The History of Wisconsin, Volume 1, From Exploration to Statehood.* (Madison, WI: State Historical Society of Wisconsin, 1973).

Steinfeld, Robert J., *Coercion, Contract, and Free Labor in the Nineteenth Century* (Cambridge: Cambridge University Press, 2001).

Stern, Marc Jeffrey, *The Pottery Industry of Trenton: A Skilled Trade in Transition, 1850–1929* (New Brunswick, NJ: Rutgers University Press, 1994).

Thomas, Brinley, *Migration and Economic Growth: A Study of Great Britain and the Atlantic Economy* (Cambridge: Cambridge University Press, 2nd edn, 1973).

Thomas, John, *The Rise of the Staffordshire Potteries* (Bath: Adams and Dart, 1971).

Tosh, John, *Manliness and Masculinities in Nineteenth-Century Britain: Essays on Gender, Family and Empire* (Harlow: Pearson Longman, 2005).

Turner, Andrew Jackson, *The Family Tree of Columbia County, Wisconsin* (Portage, WI: Press of the Wisconsin State Register, 1904).

Van Vugt, William E., *Britain to America: Mid-Nineteenth Century Immigrants to the United States* (Urbana, IL: University of Illinois Press, 1999).

Van Vugt, William E., *British Buckeyes: The English, Scots & Welsh in Ohio, 1700–1900* (Kent, OH: Kent State University Press, 2006).
Van Vugt, William E., *Portrait of An English Migration: North Yorkshire People in North America* (Montreal: McGill–Queen's University Press, 2021).
Warburton, W. H., *The History of Trade Union Organisation in the North Staffordshire Potteries* (London: Allen & Unwin, 1931).
Webb, Sidney and Beatrice, *The History of Trade Unionism* (London: Longman, Green and Co., 1902).
Whipp, Richard, *Patterns of Labour: Work and Social Change in the Pottery Industry* (London: Routledge, 1990).
Wyman, Mark, *The Wisconsin Frontier* (Bloomington, IN: Indiana University Press, 1998).

Journal articles and book chapters

Armytage, W. H. G., 'William Evans: A Proponent of Emigration', *Dalhousie Review* 34:2 (1954), 167–72.
Bentley, Roger, 'The Road to "Desolation Ferry": The Story of the Potters' Emigration Society', *Wisconsin Magazine of History* 94:1 (2010), 2–13.
Birch, Brian B, 'The Editor and the English: George Sheppard and English Immigration to Clinton County', *The Annals of Iowa* 47:8 (1985), 622–42.
Booth, Pauline, 'The Staffordshire Pottery Industry in the Nineteenth Century and its Markets', *Staffordshire Studies* 13 (2001), 109–26.
Brook, Michael, 'Joseph Barker and *The People*, The True Emigrant's Guide', *Publications of the Thoresby Society* 46:3 (1961), 331–78.
Chase, Malcolm, '"Wholesome Object Lessons": The Chartist Land Plan in Retrospect', *English Historical Review* 118:475 (2003), 59–85.
Claeys, Gregory, 'John Adolphus Etzler, Technological Utopianism, and British Socialism: the Tropical Emigration Society's Venezuelan Mission and its Social Context, 1833–1848', *English Historical Review* 101:399 (1986), 351–75.
Claeys, Gregory, 'The Example of America a Warning to England? The Transformation of America in British Radicalism and Socialism, 1790–1850', in Malcolm Chase and Ian Dyck (eds), *Living and Learning: Essays in Honour of J. F. C. Harrison* (Aldershot: Scolar Press, 1996), pp. 66–80.
Clements, R. V., 'Trade Unions and Emigration, 1840–1880', *Population Studies* 9:2 (1955), 167–80.
Erickson, Charlotte, 'The Encouragement of Emigration by British Trade Unions, 1850–1900', *Population Studies* 3:3 (1949), 248–72.
Ewins, Neil, ' "Supplying the Present Wants of our Yankee Cousins …": Staffordshire Ceramics and the American Market 1775–1880', *Journal of Ceramic History* 15 (1997), 1–154.
Foreman, Grant, 'English Settlers in Illinois', *Journal of the Illinois State Historical Society* 34:3 (1941), 303–33.
Foreman, Grant, 'Settlement of English Potters in Wisconsin', *Wisconsin Magazine of History* 21:4 (1938), 375–96.
Frank, Christopher, ' "Let But One of Them Come before Me, and I'll Commit Them": Trade Unions, Magistrates, and the Law in Mid-Nineteenth-Century Staffordshire', *Journal of British Studies* 44:1 (2005), 64–91.

Fraser, W. Hamish, 'Robert Owen and the Workers', in John Butt (ed.), *Robert Owen: Prince of Cotton Spinners* (Newton Abbot: David & Charles, 1971), pp. 76–98.

Fyson, Robert, 'Unionism, Class and Community in the 1830s: Aspects of the National Union of Operative Potters', in John Rule (ed.), *British Trade Unionism 1750–1850: The Formative Years* (London: Longman, 1988), pp. 200–19.

Gates, Paul W., 'Frontier Land Business in Wisconsin', *Wisconsin Magazine of History*, 52:4 (1969), 306–27.

Harper, Marjory, 'Obstacles and Opportunities: Labour Emigration to the "British World" in the Nineteenth Century', *Continuity and Change* 34:1 (2019), 43–62.

Hauhart, Robert C., '19th-Century Labor Money Schemes, Self-Realization through Labor, and the Utopian Idea', *World Review of Political Economy* 3:2 (2012), 177–90.

Haynes, Michael, 'Employers and Trade Unions, 1825–1850', in John Rule (ed.), *British Trade Unionism, 1750–1850* (London: Longman, 1988), pp. 237–70.

Hoerder, Dirk, 'Labour Migrants' Views of "America"', *Renaissance and Modern Studies* 35:1 (1992), 1–17.

Howells, Gary, '"For I Was Tired of England Sir": English Pauper Emigrant Strategies, 1834–1860', *Social History* 23:2 (1998), 181–94.

Jones, Maldwyn A., 'The Background to Emigration from Great Britain in the Nineteenth Century', *Perspectives in American History* 7 (1973), 1–92.

Killick, John, 'Transatlantic Steerage Fares, British and Irish Migration, and Return Migration, 1815–60', *Economic History Review* 67:1 (2014), 170–91.

Lamb, Andrew, 'Mechanization and the Application of Steam Power in the North Staffordshire Pottery Industry, 1793–1914', *North Staffordshire Journal of Field Studies* 17 (1977), 50–64.

Lamb, Andrew, 'The Press and Labour's Response to Pottery-Making Machinery in the North Staffordshire Pottery Industry', *Journal of Ceramic History* 9 (1977), 1–8.

Lowe, R. A., 'Mutual Improvement in the Potteries', *North Staffordshire Journal of Field Studies* 12 (1972), 75–82.

MacAskill, Joy, 'The Chartist Land Plan', in Asa Briggs (ed.), *Chartist Studies* (London: Macmillan, 1960), pp. 304–41.

Malchow, Howard L., 'Trade Unions and Emigration in Late Victorian England: A National Lobby for State Aid', *Journal of British Studies* 15 (spring 1976), 92–116.

McIntosh, Montgomery Eduard, 'Cooperative Communities in Wisconsin', *Proceedings of the State Historical Society of Wisconsin* 51 (1903), 99–117.

Robbins, Roy M., 'Preemption: A Frontier Triumph', *Mississippi Valley Historical Review* 18:3 (1931), 331–49.

Rössler, Horst, 'The Dream of Independence: The "America" of England's North Staffordshire Potters', in Dirk Hoerder and Horst Rössler (eds), *Distant Magnets: Expectations and Realities in the Immigrant Experience, 1840–1930* (New York: Holmes and Meier, 1993), pp. 128–59.

Samuel, Raphael, 'Mechanization and Hand Labour in Industrializing Britain', in Lenard R. Berlanstein (ed.), *The Industrial Revolution and Work in Nineteenth-Century Europe* (London: Routledge, 1992), pp. 26–53.

Southall, Humphrey, 'British Artisan Unions in the New World', *Journal of Historical Geography* 15:2 (1989), 163–82.

Steinberg, Marc W., 'Capitalist Development, the Labor Process, and the Law', *American Journal of Sociology* 109:2 (2003), 445–95.

Sutherland, Daniel E., 'Michigan Emigration Agent: Edward H. Thomson', *Michigan History* 59:1 (1975), 3–37.

Sykes, Robert, 'Trade Unionism and Class Consciousness: the "Revolutionary" Period of General Unionism', in John Rule (ed.), *British Trade Unionism 1750–1850: The Formative Years* (London: Longman, 1988), pp. 178–99.

Thistlethwaite, Frank, 'The Atlantic Migration of the Pottery Industry', *Economic History Review* 11:2 (1958), 264–78.

Thornes, Robin, 'Change and Continuity in the Development of Co-operation, 1827–1844', in Stephen Yeo (ed.), *New Views of Co-operation* (London: Routledge, 1988), pp. 27–51.

Vale, Vivian, 'English Settlers in Early Wisconsin: The British Temperance Emigration Society', *Bulletin of the British Association for American Studies* new series, 9 (1964), 24–31.

Van Eyck, William O., 'The Story of the Propeller *Phoenix*', *Wisconsin Magazine of History* 7:3 (1924), 281–300.

Van Vugt, William E., 'Relocating the English Diaspora in America', in David T. Gleeson (ed.), *English Ethnicity and Culture in North America* (Columbia, SC: University of South Carolina Press, 2017), pp. 8–36.

Website articles

Goodby, Miranda, '"Our Home in the West": Staffordshire Potters and Their Emigration to America in the 1840s', *Ceramics in America 2003* (ed.), Robert Hunter, www.chipstone.org/article.php/75/Ceramics-in-America-2003 (last accessed 19 November 2022).

Henderson, Harold, 'From the First Industrial City to the Wisconsin Frontier: William Scholes (1814–1864), Ann Mills Scholes (1814–1875), and Their Family', *Annals of Genealogical Research* 1:2 (2005) at www.genlit.org/agr/viewarticle.php?id=5 (last accessed 26 February 2023).

Unpublished theses

Botham, Francis William, 'Working-Class Living Standards in North Staffordshire, 1750–1914' (PhD dissertation, University of London, 1982).

Fyson, Robert, 'Chartism in North Staffordshire' (PhD dissertation, University of Lancaster, 1998).

Nixon, M. I., 'The Emergence of the Factory System in the Staffordshire Pottery Industry' (PhD dissertation, University of Aston, 1976).

Unpublished paper

Boston, Ray, 'William Evans and the Potters' Emigration Society', Keele University Library, 1974.

Index

Accrington 159
Adams, Charles 116, 152, 219
Adams, William 26, 119
Adderley, Charles B. 130–1, 144
agrarianism 10, 65–6, 115
Airdrie 185
Alcock, Daniel 55, 58
Alcock, Edwin 187
Alcock, Samuel 36
allowance system 28, 29, 34, 61, 101
Alton, IL 222
American Home Missionary
 Society 218
American Pottery Company 2
Anglo-French Free Trade
 Association 230
annual hiring 25–6, 29, 227
Anti-Corn Law League 31, 57, 64
Arlington National Cemetery, VA 226
Ashton-under-Lyne 33, 135, 155,
 162, 179
Axon, Percy 233

Baker, George 131
Baraboo, WI 194
 Baraboo Pottery 222
Barker, Joseph 147–8, 177–8
 The People 147, 180
 visit to America 166, 177
Barker, Samuel 81, 99
Bennington, VT 2, 133
Bentley, Roger 218
Billingsley, William 62
Birkbeck, Morris 51
Birmingham 12, 136, 157, 158, 161,
 163, 164, 184, 196, 198
Blackburn 136

Blair, Robert 184
Blake, Dr John 93
Blake, Thomas H. 66, 90, 93
Bliss, Luman A. 198, 199
Boellaert, William 228
Bolton 19, 180, 184
Bonaparte Pottery, IA 222
Booth, John 171
Boston, Ray 8
Boyle, John 24, 25, 27
Bradford 137, 166
Brazos River colony, TX 228
Brindley, John 32
British Temperance Emigration Society
 58, 79–80, 86, 95, 137,
 150, 228
Broadhurst, James 4
Bronstein, Jamie L. 8
Buffalo, NY 221
Burchill, Frank and Richard Ross 6
Burnley 136, 168
Burslem 20, 31, 57, 68, 85, 87, 100,
 129, 138, 157, 158, 161, 184,
 185, 220, 222, 224, 226, 230
Bury 180, 188
Byrne, J. C. 134

Californian Emigration Society 145
canal, Fox–Wisconsin 155
Canton, MO 223
Cartledge, George 138
Challenor, E. & Co. 3
Chartism 9, 30–1, 32–3, 63–5, 129–30
 Chartist Land Company 58, 116,
 129, 193
 domestic land plan campaign 84–6
 Northern Star 116, 193

Chase, Malcolm 10, 115
Child, Smith 131
cholera 160
Chubb, Charles 163
Clark, Thomas 84–6
Clementson, Joseph 119
Clews, James 2
Clinton County, IA 228
Clitheroe 157
Coates, William 57, 134, 145, 153
   lectures in London 137
   tour of Yorkshire 137
Cobden, Richard 1, 57
Columbia County, WI 7, 95, 103, 161, 218, 219, 220, 231
Congleton 134
Cooke, Vincent 36
Cooper, James Fenimore's *The Pioneers* 84
Cooper, Thomas 33
Cooperative Emigration Society 80
cooperativism 55–6, 231
Copeland and Garrett 119
Cowton, John 212
Crewe 134, 138, 169, 184
Cropper, Capt. Thomas B. 91, 92

Dallas, Vice-President George M 94
Davenport, William 29
Delaney, John and James 200
Dewey, Gov. Nelson 154
Dickson, R. M. 222
Dodge County, WI 96, 103, 221
Dodge, Gov. Henry 78
Doherty, John 23
Donnellan, Philip 232
Donovan, Daniel 129
Dover, NH 221
Dowling, S. 193
Duncombe, Thomas 88, 199
Dundee 12, 17, 178, 185, 203
Dyson, Emanuel 168

East Liverpool, OH 2, 3, 62, 118, 125, 128, 133, 186, 201, 220, 221
Eau Claire, WI 221
Edinburgh 178, 185, 196
Edwards, James 119
Ellis, Rev. P. B. 210

Ellis, Thomas 203
Ellis, William 32, 34, 36
Emancipation Ferry, WI 154, 155, 169, 182, 194, 203, 231
emigrants
   Atkinson, William 200
   Ayrey, Charles 155, 192
   Baillies (Sawyer), Ann 220
   Bain, George 200
   Ball, Thomas 147, 151
   Barber, Enoch 200
   Barlow, John 125, 132
   Barnes, James 159
   Becket, Thomas 192
   Beckett, Thomas 155
   Bennett, James 200
   Bennett, Mary 200
   Betts, William 161, 190
   Boulton, David 161
   Bradshaw, Enoch 62, 125
   Bradshaw, William 113, 114, 119, 121, 229
   Brentnall, Joseph 157, 182, 190
   Bridge, David 149
   Broadbent, John H. 151, 154, 157
   Brunt, Benjamin 3
   Brunt, William 49–50
   Buck, James 197
   Bullard, John 78
   Bullock, Enoch 186
   Cadman, Maria 161, 223
   Cadman, Samuel 223, 225
   Cartlidge, Charles 91, 92
   Cartlidge, William 91
   Chapman, John 198
   Chatley, William 118
   Ciscel, Thomas 156, 221
   Clark, Joseph 122, 128, 129
   Clark, Mary 128
   Clews, Charlotte 121
   Clews, Joseph 113, 115
   Clitheroe, Charles 155
   Clitheroe, James 155, 192
   Coates, William (of Blackburn) 166
   Cocker, George 155, 190
   Colville, William 203
   Cooper, Elizabeth 224
   Cooper, George 138, 157, 189, 224
   Copeland, Ellen 94, 153

Index

Copeland, Hamlet 86, 88, 89, 92, 94, 96, 103, 104–5, 122, 152–3, 186, 208
Deakin, John 188
Denby, George 156
Dooley, Elizabeth 121
Dooley, Henry 113–15, 150, 208, 219
Dooley, Maria 150
Duffy, Francis 203
Ellis, Grace 205
Ellis, Richard 201, 205
Ellison, James 159
Ellison, Martin 154, 158–9, 190, 198, 200, 201, 202, 221, 225
Ellison, Martin (son) 225
Ellison, Mary 221
Evans, Alexander 35, 118, 119, 121, 129, 150–1, 195, 196–7, 202, 219, 223
Evans, Alexander (son) 121
Evans, Elizabeth 223
Evans, Genevieve 223
Farmer, George 158
Filcher, Thomas 50
Finney, James 133
Floyd, Elijah 90, 93, 94
Fox, Samuel 113, 114, 118, 120, 189, 190, 208–9, 219
Frankland, John 154, 155
Gemmell, William 190
Goulding, John 157, 169, 193
Greatbach, Daniel 2
Greatbach, Hamlet 133
Green, John 148
Grey, James 158
Grimshaw, Joseph 203
Gunn, John 188
Hall, Charles 133
Hamilton, John 220
Hammond, George 118, 150
Hammond, James 86, 90, 91, 97, 103, 104, 121, 122, 152–3, 187, 197, 208, 219
Hammond, John 157
Hammond, Martha 90, 105, 153, 197
Hancock, Frederick 2
Hancock, John 2–3
Hatcher, George 156
Hewitt, George 219, 225
Hilton, Bold 188, 194–5, 196, 202, 224
Hope, John 201
Hopkins, Benjamin 118
Hopwood, Elijah 225
Hopwood, William 161
Horton, William 157, 158
Howson, Bernard 3
Howson, John 3
Howson, Thomas 3
Keen, Thomas 158
Kilham, John 61
Kirkham, Esther 201
Kirkham, James 161, 194, 201
Llewellyn, John 190
Lodge, Leonard 155, 192
Lymburn, John 159
Machin, Samuel 161, 221
Machin, William 222
Maddock, Thomas 118
Maddock, William 78, 92
Mason, Matthew 132, 225
Matley, Ann 225
Matley, Henry 157, 225
Mitchell, George 156, 166
Moloneaux, Thomas 133
Mountford, Eliza 151, 197
Mountford, Robert 132
Mountford, William 134, 151, 153–4, 197
Mountford, William (son) 220
Murray, Stephen 157, 190
Newson, George 194
Nixon, Enoch 161, 204
Nixon, James 161, 201, 204
Nixon, Mary 204
Noble, Richard 203, 222
Oliphant, John 204
Orme, Frances 159
Orr, William 190
Park, Frederick 167
Parker, Edward 132, 222
Parker, Sidney 222
Parr, Thomas 159
Peake, John 133, 151, 197, 226
Pearson, George 190
Penrice, George 159
Pettepher, John 156, 221

Index

emigrants (*continued*)
- Pickering, Enoch 113, 114, 118, 150, 158, 189, 193, 208
- Pinkerton, Alexander 158
- Pointon, Ann 194
- Pointon, Philip 188, 194, 196, 201, 204, 222
- Pointon, Philip (son) 222
- Reeve, Charles 80
- Reeve, Emma 80
- Rhodes, Hannah 77–8
- Rhodes, Thomas 77–8
- Rigby, Job 49, 84
- Robbins, John 157
- Robbins, William 200
- Robertshaw, George 113, 114
- Robinson, George 138
- Robinson, George W. 164, 170, 182, 187, 193, 195, 202, 204, 206, 208, 222
- Robinson, John 189, 224
- Rudland, Samuel 191
- Sawyer, Elizabeth 89, 122, 219
- Sawyer, Henry 220
- Sawyer, John 86, 87, 89, 91, 92, 95, 97, 102, 104, 122, 152–3, 186, 208, 219
- Scholes, Ann 221
- Scholes, William 138, 157, 169, 221, 225
- Scott, Charles W. 203
- Scott, John 162, 192
- Scoular, James 201, 205, 221
- Shaw, Joseph 188
- Shaw, Joseph (of Bury) 188, 195
- Sherret, Alexander 195, 198, 199
- Sim, Alexander 156, 221
- Simpson, Thomas 133
- Skinner, George 11
- Skinner, Thomas 12
- Skinner, William 118–19
- Slater, Ainsworth 160
- Smith, Edwin 220
- Smith, Emma 132
- Smith, Isaac 13, 17, 87, 112, 113, 114, 118, 119, 120, 121, 150, 154, 201, 220, 225
- Smith, Isaac (son) 221
- Smith, Sarah 115, 120, 220
- Smith, William 132
- Stagg, Frederick 200
- Staley, Jonathan 209
- Stanton, Henry 161
- Summerfield, George 113, 114, 118
- Sutcliffe, John 200
- Sutherland, John 86
- Swetmore, Alfred 192
- Tempest, Joseph 162, 223–4
- Thomas, James 132, 202, 219
- Thompson, William 50
- Thomson, John 156
- Tinker, Richard 188, 202
- Tordoff, John 157
- Tucker, Stephen Price 84
- Turner, Elizabeth 156, 223
- Turner, John 156, 169, 188, 190–1, 192, 223
- Twigg, Hannah 188, 219
- Twigg, John 188
- Twigg, Thomas 156, 159, 161, 162, 165, 166, 190, 191, 192, 198, 205, 211
  - and Pottersville 151–2, 153
  - arrival and land acquisition 153–5
  - attacks on 194, 196, 197, 202
  - death 219
  - grist mill 164, 169, 179
  - legal action against 208
  - pleas for money 167
  - return to America 188
  - support for 169, 198
  - tour with William Evans 169–71, 178–80
  - visit home 167–9
- Twycross, Joseph 159, 189, 190, 198
- Vernon, Benton 201
- Vodrey, Jabez 2
- Walker, Samuel 62
- Watkin, Peter 50, 134, 153, 162, 165, 167, 182, 188, 189, 190, 191, 192, 219, 223
- Watkin, Rachel 223
- Watson, Elizabeth 210
- Watson, William 210
- Wells, Henry 157
- Whitmore, Richard 118
- Wilson, Charles 79, 95
- Wilson, James 157
- Winterbotham, Joshua 160–1

Winterbotham, Thomas 161
Wood, John 202
Wrigglesworth, William 80
emigration 10, 39–40, 144–5, 200
   attitudes to 46–7
   Civil War, emigrant involvement in 225–6
   Dutch 128
   early migration of potters 1–4
   economic background to 19, 127
   emigrant letters 11, 20, 49–50, 61–2, 78, 84, 181, 210
   emigrant progress, lack of 223–4
   German 225
   Irish 48, 91, 120
   marriage 220–1
   passenger trade, regulation of 46, 47, 89
   persistence and assimilation 219–23
   return migration 12, 201, 204, 224
   transatlantic emigration, growth of 47–9
   Welsh 225
Engels, Friedrich 54, 157
Epps, E. A. 193
Erickson, Charlotte 10, 11, 220
Etzler, John Adolphus 80
Evans (Miller), Susan 36
Evans, David 35, 62
Evans, Frederick William 8
Evans, George Henry 8, 98
Evans, Julia 230
Evans, Margaret 230
Evans, Susan 231
Evans, William 4–13, 17, 32, 37–40, 90, 95, 98–9, 104, 111, 117, 132, 136, 146, 153, 163, 166, 182, 184, 192–3, 202, 203, 206–7, 210, 226
   Art and History of the Potting Business 98, 100
   attacks on 146–8
   death 231
   defense of emigration scheme 226–7
   early life and activism 35–7
   emigration proposal 50–8
   explaining the emigration scheme 59–61
   and Feargus O'Connor 65–6, 83
   and Joseph Barker 178, 180
   labour or dollar notes 183
   Lancashire tour 134–6
   as land reformer 8, 98
   later life 230–1
   and mechanisation 69–71, 81, 101–2, 231
   'Millway Vanes' (nom-de-plume) 231
   national activism 88, 100
   out-potteries, tour of 100–1
   promoting the emigration scheme 115–16, 123
   religious beliefs 112–13
   reponse to American reports 196–7
   tour with Thomas Twigg 169–71, 178–80
   views of America 54–6
Ewing, William Lee D. 66–7

Faraday, Michael 228
Fenton 33, 58, 63, 69, 86
Fettes, Peter 137
Fife Advertiser 166, 204
Flower, George 51, 53, 55, 57, 67, 136
   The Errors of Emigrants 39, 51–2, 56
Foreman, Grant 7, 231
Fort Winnebago, WI 96, 149, 153–4, 158, 160, 199, 208
   River Times 200, 206, 218
   settlers' meeting and memorial 198–200
Fourier, Charles 228
Friendly Societies Act 58
Fyson, Robert 9, 117

Garner, George 62
Garrison, William Lloyd 101
Gast, John 27
Gerber, David A. 11
Glasgow 163, 171, 178, 184
Glasgow Saturday Post 202
good-from-oven 26, 27, 29, 114, 230
Gorst, Robert 79
Gourlay, Robert Fleming 145
Grand National Consolidated Trades Union (GNCTU) 24
Gratiot, WI 222
Green Bay, WI 103, 207
Greenock 156, 157
Griffith, William 180

Halifax 57, 163
Hampton, John 124
Hanley 20, 30, 31, 32, 33, 63, 64, 85, 87, 100, 116, 129, 161, 164, 169, 184, 185, 204, 205
Harnden & Company 91, 120
Harrison, J. F. C. 7–8
Hawthorn, Aaron 138
Hay, J. A. 206, 210
Haywood, W. 148
Heap, John 169, 182
Heath, Charles 147
Heath, Henry 57, 88
Henley, William Bidwell 164
Hinman, James 199
Hobson, Stephen 233
Huddersfield 57, 137, 203
Hull 145, 162, 178, 184
Hull, John 193
Hume, Joseph 137
Humphries, Edwin 100, 116
Hunt, Thomas 95, 228
Hyde 162, 183

Indiana Pottery Company 2
Ingersoll, Capt. J. B. 120
Iowa 78, 90, 95, 137
Iowa Emigration Society 145, 228

Jaeger, Prof. Benedict 52
Jeffrey, Dr J. 146
Johnson, John 152, 219
Johnson, Stanley C. 6
Jones, Ernest 227
Judd, Dr Stoddard 103

Keegan, Michael R. 208, 218–19
Kellogg, Walter W. 198
Kenosha, WI 160
Kent 200
Kinnersley, Thomas & Sons 152, 218
Kirkcaldy 12, 156, 166–7, 185, 203

Lake Michigan 77, 128, 150
Lancashire 12, 19, 135–6, 137, 200, 220, 225
Lancaster, Mark 100
land 3
   American law regarding 195, 197
   Land Act, 1820 (US) 66

land offices, Federal 80, 96, 207, 218
   Preemption Act, 1841 (US) 80, 96, 103
   Wisconsin, demand for 104
Lang, John Dunmore 145
Lawton, Charles Bourne 131
Leach, W. 179
Leeds 57, 136, 137, 157, 166, 179
Leek 134
Leigh 188
Lewis & Cook 208
Limerick 166
Lincolnshire 220
Liverpool 77, 79, 90, 119, 121, 136, 168, 187, 196, 200, 203, 222
London 57, 137, 156, 157, 159, 162, 163, 164, 166, 170–1, 188, 196, 203, 206, 207
Longton 31, 32, 33, 34, 64, 86, 100, 116, 187
Lowndes, Joseph 144

Macclesfield 134, 149, 166, 169, 203
Malthus, Thomas 46, 57
Manchester 19, 136, 137, 155, 163, 164, 169, 177, 179, 184, 188, 207, 211
Manchester Examiner & Times 193, 202
Manchester Guardian 203
Marquette County, WI 7, 12, 161, 220, 222, 224
Mart, George 32, 64, 100
Mason, C. J. 33, 39, 69
Master and Servant Act, 1823 22, 39
Mathias, Peter 10
Mauston, WI 223
Mayer, William 130
McAllister, Daniel 68
McConochie, Robert 150
McConochie, Sam 150
McGowan, Daniel 167
mechanisation 54, 222
   attitudes to 69, 71
Meigh, Charles 117
Menasha, WI 218
mesmerism 4
Michigan 211
Midlands 137
Midlothian 200

Miller, Sen. Jacob W. 93
Milwaukie, WI 79, 94, 96, 103, 121,
    158, 166, 194, 202, 204, 221
Minton & Co. 3, 19
Montrose Standard 195
Moundville, WI 220
Mountford, Enoch 148

National Association for the Protection
    of Labour (NAPL) 22–3
National Association of United Trades
    for the Protection of Labour
    (NAUT) 6, 9, 88
    campaign in the Potteries
        100, 116–17
National Emigration Society 211–12
National Society of Pottery
    Workers 233
National Union of Operative Potters
    (NUOP) 23–8
Native Americans
    encounters with 103, 150, 154
    Menominee lands 154
New Glarus, WI colony 228
New Orleans, LA 89, 148, 155–6, 161
New York, NY 77, 92, 93, 120, 121,
    156, 200
Newcastle-under-Lyme 159
Newcastle-upon-Tyne 178, 203
Newhall, John B. 78, 83, 85, 90
Nichols, Thomas 164
Northern Pacific Railroad 230
Nottingham 12, 136, 155, 157, 166, 196
Nottingham Review 202

O'Connor, Feargus 9, 31, 36, 56, 63–5,
    83, 98, 129, 204
Old Northwest 1, 78
Oldham 33, 136, 138, 148, 157–8,
    169, 171, 184, 193
Oliphant, John 196
out-potteries 23, 229
    Derby 54
    Edinburgh 101
    Glasgow 54, 63, 101
    Greenock 63, 101
    Hunslet 63
    Leeds 63, 71, 100
    Middlesbrough 63, 101, 102
    Newcastle-upon-Tyne 63, 101, 102

Rawmarsh 100
Rotherham 100
South Stockton 101, 102
Swinton 63, 71, 100
Whitehaven 63
Worcester 8, 9, 54
Owen, Harold 5–6, 69, 81, 231
Owen, Robert 8, 23, 32, 55, 137, 183
Owen, William 5
Owenism 7–8, 31–2, 55, 66
Owenite colonies 56, 85
    Equality, Spring Lake, WI 95, 228
Owens, Dr 4

Paisley 159, 181, 206, 208, 220
Parker, John Whitaker 116
Parker, William 34
Patricroft 136
Peel, William 117
Perth 166
Phoenix disaster 128–9
Polk, President James K. 94
Poor Law Amendment Act, 1834 29,
    30, 33, 47
Portage, WI 96, 151, 200, 220, 223,
    225, 231
Potteries Chamber of Commerce
    25, 26
Potteries' Examiner 230
Potteries riots of 1842 32–4, 201
Potters' Emigration Society 17,
    205, 226
    audit of accounts 164–5
    ballot 60, 123–5, 137–8, 167,
        168, 182
    branches
        London 181, 184–5, 205
        Potteries 185
        Scotland 181, 185
    calls for investigation into 203
    critical reports from
        Wisconsin 202–3
    criticism of 146, 166
    debts 208, 209
    discontent in Wisconsin 188, 192
    Emigration Clubs 125–6
    Estate Committee, arrival at
        Pottersville 121–2, 149
    Estate Committee, departure 117–18,
        119–20

Potters' Emigration Society (*continued*)
- Estate Committee, election of 105
- Estate Committee, farewell events 111–15
- Estate Committee, journey to America 120–2
- expansion 127, 131
- finances 148, 181
- first annual meeting 84
- fundraising 68, 70, 80, 82, 88, 97–8, 130–1
- grist mill campaign 164, 181
- growth of 162
- historiography 4–10
- land officers, expedition to Green Bay 103–4
- land officers, farewell dinners 86–8
- land officers, journey to America 90–2
- land officers, searching for land 94–7
- land officers, selection of 83, 84, 86
- land officers, visit to Washington 93–4
- land ownership 218–19
- London District Committee 206, 207
- London takeover of 210–12
- as model 145
- New Year's Day meeting, Manchester 137–8
- patronage of 131, 138
- popular support for 63
- proposed reorganisation 163
- public memory of 231–3
- 'Puckaway Pioneers' 132–3, 196
- registration, rules and regulations 58–9
- settler memorial 198–9, 202
- special delegate meeting 181–4

Potters' Examiner and Workman's (Emigrants') Advocate 10–11, 22, 35, 38, 63, 101, 103, 181, 198, 199, 208, 209

Potters' Friend 22

Potters' Emigration Society 229–30

Pottersville 97, 102, 104, 105, 149, 151–2, 165, 166, 169, 177, 193, 196, 203, 209, 218, 231
- deeds 152–3, 168, 207, 218
- sale of 211
- settlers' meeting 208–9

Pottery District Relief Society 127

pottery industry 20–1
- health 54
- later industrial relations 227
- trade with America 1, 21

pottery trades
- cratemakers 63, 99, 116, 227
- flat-ware pressers 21, 26, 68, 97, 125, 185–6, 187
- handlers 99
- hollow-ware pressers 21, 26, 68, 97, 99, 101, 125, 186, 203, 230
- ovenmen 68, 124–5
- packers 63, 99
- painters and gilders 68, 116
- slip-makers 99
- throwers 21, 68
- turners 21, 99, 186

Pratt, Tidd 180

Preston 135, 155, 162, 171, 184, 192

Reach, Angus 180–1
religion 113, 123, 200, 201, 218, 220
Renfrew 158
Ricardo, J. L. 31
Richards, Eric 12
Richards, John 23, 33, 36, 64
Ridgway, John 54, 69
Ridgway, William 2, 91, 119, 121
Rigby, Reginald 233
Robertshaw, George 219
Rose, Thomas Bailey 29, 33, 39, 119, 130
Rössler, Horst 9
Rowbottom, James 164, 177

Salford 161, 163
Scotland 137
Scott, Andrew 102, 115
Scott, James 138, 189–90, 191, 209
Scriven, Dr Samuel 19, 54
Seymour, Israel 2
Shaw Enoch 29
Shaw, Charles 19, 29, 33, 71, 98
Sheboygan, WI 128
Sheffield 145, 155, 210
Sheffield debt 28, 37, 81–2, 99, 145

Index

Shelton 20, 63
Sheppard, George 145, 178, 228, 230
Shepperson, Wilbur S. 6
Shipley, Edward 199
ships
   Aberdeen 160, 198, 222
   Atlantic 89
   Burlington 156
   Cataraqui 91
   Charles Chaloner 155
   Clifton 120
   Constitution 133, 147
   Cuthbert 156
   E and E Perkins 161
   Eucles 168
   Guy Mannering 187, 194, 202
   Hindostan 155
   Ivanhoe 161
   Joseph Badger 161
   Kate Hunter 158
   Marmion 133, 157, 201, 203
   New World 168
   New York 91
   Olive Branch 200
   Orezaba 119
   Patrick Henry 160, 223
   Poland 120
   Queen of the West 159
   Rappahannock 132
   Republic 132
   Silas Richards 156
   United States 77
   Universe 201
   Wenham 156
slavery 55, 94, 225
Smiles, R. W. 136
Smith, Ann 19
Smith, John 96
Sneyd, Rev. John 25
South Amboy, NJ 2
Southport, WI 77, 228
St. John Stoneware Chinaware Company 222
Stafford 170
Staffordshire 116, 155, 166
Staffordshire Advertiser 11, 64, 102, 185, 194, 211
Staffordshire Mercury 11
Stalybridge 33
Standard of Freedom 197
Stanley, Charles 58
Steward, Charles 210
Stockport 135, 146
Stoke 20, 31, 32, 33, 57, 61, 87, 100, 116, 162, 192
strikes 227
   1825 22
   1834 24–5
   1836–7 2, 26–7, 38, 81, 130
Stubbs, Henry 138
Sunderland 153, 178
surplus labour 5, 17, 53, 57, 60, 62, 180, 227
Swan, Joseph 183
Swindon 206

Thistlethwaite, Frank 2
Thomas, John 6
Thompson, E. P. 233
Thomson, Edwin H. 211
Todmorden 135
trade conditions 17–19, 28, 111, 127, 185, 227
trade unions
   anti-unionism 22–5, 30
   support for emigration 5, 57, 69, 227
Trenton, NJ 128, 220
Tropical Emigration Society 80
Troy, IN 2–3
Truett, Myers F. 203, 209
Tunstall 20, 57, 68, 86, 100, 161, 185, 187, 200, 221
Turner, George 148
Twigg's Landing, WI 155, 218, 219, 224
Tyler, President John 66

United Branches of Operative Potters (UBOP) 37–8, 56, 59, 68, 87–8, 99–100, 101, 126–7
   demise of 126–7
   reorganisation of 100, 111
United States Pottery Company 2

Vale, Rev. Benjamin 34
Van Buren County, IA 222
Van Vugt, William 7
Vernon, W. J. 4
Vicksburg, LA 225

Wakefield, Edward Gibbon 47
Wall, George 54
Warburton, W. H. 6, 19, 231
Ward, John 31
Ward, William 199
Warrington 134
Washington, DC 93–4
Webb, Sidney and Beatrice 5, 23
Wedgwood, Aaron 61, 82, 84, 122
Wedgwood, Josiah 1, 20, 21
West, John 100
Whalley, John 101
Wisconsin 78, 95, 137, 145, 154, 178, 210, 224, 226
    climate 80, 138, 147, 150, 178, 179
Wisconsin Phalanx 228
Wise, John Ayshford 131
Wishawtown 162
Wolstanton 144
Wolverhampton 170
Wood, Enoch 32
workhouse, Wolstanton and Burslem 29–30
Workington 230

Yorkshire 33, 63, 77, 151, 157, 162, 220, 223